COURTING THE ABYSS

COURTING

FREE SPEECH AND THE

THE ABYSS

LIBERAL TRADITION

John Durham Peters

THE UNIVERSITY OF CHICAGO PRESS

Chicago and London

JOHN DURHAM PETERS is F. Wendell Miller Distinguished Professor of
Communication Studies at the University of Iowa.

The University of Chicago Press, Chicago 60637
The University of Chicago Press, Ltd., London

14 13 12 11 10 09 08 07 06 05   1 2 3 4 5

ISBN: 0-226-66274-8 (cloth)

Library of Congress Cataloging-in-Publication Data

Peters, John Durham.
    Liberty and evil : the intellectual roots of free expression / John Durham Peters.
      p. cm.
    Includes index.
    ISBN 0-226-66274-8 (cloth : alk. paper)
    1. Freedom of expression—History. 2. Good and evil—History. 3. Political
science—Philosophy—History. I. Title.

    JC585.P395 2005
    323.44—dc22   2004018511

FOR MARSHA

It is necessary that offenses come; but woe to the man through whom the offense comes.
ἀνάγκη γὰρ ἐλθεῖν τὰ σκάνδαλα, πλὴν οὐαὶ τῷ ἀνθρώπῳ δι᾽ οὗ τὸ σκάνδαλον
ἔρχεται.

MATTHEW 18:7

The abyss was life itself.
Пучина зта была—сама жизнь.

TOLSTOY, *Anna Karenina*

CONTENTS

Hard-Hearted Liberalism

We boast our light; but if we look not wisely on the sun itself, it smites us into darkness.
—John Milton, *Areopagitica*

Ever since the beginnings of democratic theory and practice in ancient Athens, communication—understood as the general art of concerted living and acting in the polis through the gift of logos (speech or reason)—has been considered the lifeblood of public life. In the heart of every democrat since beats the pulse of Athens envy, a desire to put on a toga and speak swelling oratory. The early modern era adds a new item of apparel and medium of communication to the mix: friends of democracy like to fancy themselves donning powdered wigs and taking quill in hand to compose declarations and encyclopedias that will set tyrants trembling. Today voice and print media are alive and well, but being reshaped under the accumulated weight (or lightness) of the pictures, sounds, and bits that have proliferated since the late nineteenth century. Though our media environment raises questions that we are still learning how to ask, the vision of liberating—or vile—communication continues to follow and enchant every new medium, from radio to the internet. This book is about that enchantment, the ideas that shape thinking about communication's role in public and political life. More specifically, it traces the leading framework for understanding public communication in the Anglo-American world, namely, free expression, focusing especially on the notion that exposure to evil can be good for the public health.

THE INTELLECTUAL OPTIONS TODAY

From many sources we have inherited a rich broth of dreams and images about the intimate tie between democracy and communication, and many competing philosophies continue to vie for airtime in—and about—public life today.[1] On a planetary scale today, the late British anthropologist and social theorist Ernest Gellner argues, there are three basic options that vie for intellectual and moral allegiance: enlightenment doubt, cultural pluralism, and fundamentalism.[2] The first embraces modernity and its constant revolutionizing of human existence, especially the fertility of science for improving conditions. It finds the policy of rational inquiry an ennobling and energizing way to advance the common welfare and to live in the world. The second has lost faith in modernity's guarantees of progress and emancipation and points to the incommensurable swirl of moral and intellectual positions generated in human history. So abundant and conflicting are the visions of the good life that no rational or conclusive answer about the right way is possible. The third option is also nervous about modernity but in an antimodern rather than postmodern way, that is, it is alarmed rather than playful, or better, angry rather than nervous, and seeks security in sources such as revelation, scripture, and traditional authority. Unlike science, which suspends the quest for a final answer, or postmodernism, which abandons it altogether, fundamentalism prizes moral or ideological closure. The notion of the open-ended indifferent competition of ideas is itself one of the things it finds abhorrent.

Each option—modern, postmodern, and antimodern, as we might rename them—can score points against the others. Like rock, paper, scissors, none wins all the time. The modern and postmodern views call the antimodern closed-minded; the modern and antimodern views blame the postmodern for copping out on the question of truth; and the postmodern and antimodern views rebuke the modern for its destructive hubris and self-confidence. Each view also has a meta-analysis of the fact of pluralism itself and a policy about how to choose among the options. Modern science exhorts us to test all ideas empirically and has no doubt that its own practice of open inquiry will prove the most fruitful in deciding among competing

1. I have treated the competing visions of communication more systematically in "Mass Communication, Normative Frameworks," in *International Encyclopedia of the Social and Behavioral Sciences,* ed. Neil J. Smelser and Paul B. Baltes (Oxford: Pergamon, 2001), 9328–9334.

2. Ernst Gellner, *Postmodernism, Reason, and Religion* (London: Routledge, 1992). Thus Gellner updates Malinowski's triad of Magic, Science, and Religion.

doctrines; postmodern relativism denies that an ideological end game can ever be reached and has no answer about how to decide besides fate, will, taste, or preference; and antimodern fundamentalism finds claims of open-ended testing or moral undecidability little more than excuses to avoid facing the riveting call of the sacred. In terms of the globe's inhabitants today, neotraditional faith is surely chosen as often as critical rationality or cultural relativism, though less often among readers of books like this. Fundamentalism is largely antimodern rather than premodern. Its renunciation of critical self-reflection about ideological alternatives suggests a traumatic encounter with modernity, not the innocence of a tradition undisturbed. The very notion is no older than the early twentieth century. The consciousness of a medieval Christian peasant is leagues distant from a twenty-first-century believer in biblical inerrancy, for instance. Fundamentalism should not be identified with religion in general or with one religion in particular. Judaism, Christianity, and Islam alike all breed fundamentalists, as do all the great traditions (and only certain American Protestants actually call themselves "fundamentalists"). There are plenty of nonreligious fundamentalists and religious nonfundamentalists around, and the border zones are of great interest. The key is that whatever the vaguely insulting term "fundamentalism" means, it stands less for a fight between religion and secularism than for a fight between different kinds of believers.[3]

This force-field of options seems our fate at the moment; part of the aim of this book is to explore ways around the impasse. Gellner, for his part, prefers enlightenment doubt. As a rare western thinker who insisted on the global intellectual importance of Islam prior to September 11, 2001, he has a sympathetic understanding of fundamentalism's motives for rejecting unlimited inquiry and saves his choicest barbs—funny, if not entirely fair—for the postmodernists: "Sturm und Drang und Tenure," he quips, should be their motto.[4] Indeed, his stance of critical inquiry might seem the best equipped to mediate among the others and almost seems a prerequisite for even seeing the other two as options. And yet even the attempt to mediate rationally annuls both postmodernist incommensurability and fundamentalist single-mindedness, since it assumes first that evaluative criteria are possible and second that everything, even God, fire, or devotion, can be subject to inspection. From a rational point of view, cultural relativism looks like little more than a self-refutation. To say "everything is relative" fa-

3. Karen Armstrong, *The Battle for God: A History of Fundamentalism* (New York: Ballantine, 2000).

4. Gellner, *Postmodernism, Reason, and Religion*, 27.

mously implies that that statement is also relative, thus catching it in self-contradiction, just as the postmodernists' claim that there can be no more grand narratives about history presupposes a pretty comprehensive grasp of history's direction—precisely the kind of epistemological privilege that many postmodernists want to deny.[5] To a rational point of view fundamentalism looks like tenacious blindness, a refusal to be reasonable at all. The sacred is as abhorrent to modern scientists as open debate is to true believers. As far as critical rationality is concerned, its rivals amount to little more than contradictory or deficient versions of itself.

But the debate among the three is not only about the best argument; it is also about whether argument and debate are the best way to settle moral enigmas. The three options are not just reasons, but whole visions of the cosmos and of the place of reason (among other things) in it. Each is a way of being or seeing as much as a logic of argument. Their force lies as much in their performances as in their statements. Enlightenment doubt, like fundamentalism, can be a bully, and perhaps only postmodernist relativism, if understood as a positive program of aesthetic appreciation of difference and as lassitude against the aggressions of any program of final answers, is hospitable enough to entertain the full babel of alternatives. But postmodernism's price is to remove both the privilege of reason and the force of taboo, demoting them into two competitors among others on a level playing field. Science becomes one more cultural system and devotion, one more variety of human experience. For fundamentalism critical rationality is a prideful and foolish trust in the human mind, and cultural relativism is a cop-out from moral judgment. Any resting point with respect to the three options yields unease. Each moral-intellectual game has rules that say why the others miss the point.

With some translation this loose triad of options provides a map for the ideological contours of debates about freedom of expression. Those who defend complete liberty of expression are almost invariably friends of modern rationality and enlightenment, and trust in open inquiry to take care of itself. Those who employ forms of expression that risk being considered sick or offensive share with postmodernists a sense of the non-bindingness of culture and the relativity of moral norms (and are close allies with the liberals, for reasons I will explore below). Those who are sickened and offended—and they are no less essential to the social drama of free speech than the civil libertarians and the culture-busters—resemble fundamental-

---

5. Jean-François Lyotard tries to wiggle out of this performative contradiction in *The Postmodern Condition: A Report on Knowledge* (Minneapolis: University of Minnesota Press, 1984).

ists in their comparatively low threshold for disgust and their sensitivity to violation and insult. Liberal tolerance, cultural transgression, and conservative offense: such seems the repeated dynamic of free expression in our time. This triad does not map perfectly onto Gellner's triumvirate of reason, postmodernism, and religion, but there is a certain family resemblance in tone and mood.

The three actors in the social drama of free expression are not in equilibrium: the first two have a long-standing alliance against the third. Liberals generally prefer those who relativize the sacred to those who absolutize it. Since the holy remains a live option for some citizens, they take offense more readily at its desecration and are typically the odd man out in free speech debates, being treated as having the wrong kind of soul for modern liberty or as censorious voluptuaries of the dungeon and the stake. They are less prone to read acts of cultural transgression ironically, as would-be contributions to public education or debate. There is something satanic about many liberal arguments in favor of free expression—satanic not in the sense of gratuitous evil but in the Miltonic sense of confronting or even sponsoring an adversary whose opposition provides material for redemptive struggle. Defenders of free speech often like to plumb the depths of the underworld. They tread where angels do not dare and reemerge escorting scruffy, marginal, or outlaw figures, many of whom spend their time planting slaps in the face of public taste. Like well-mannered circus barkers, the friends of free expression parade their exotic friends before a gawking public. They themselves, however, remain scrupulously well dressed, coiffures unmussed by their spelunking. They profess reluctance in this dirty job. Fraternization with the outcast they consider an act of social leadership, an exhibit of the vigorous toleration all citizens must attain, a public lesson in the art of how to consort civilly with denizens of the deep. To those familiar with the sick transit of fighting faiths, they think, hell is only a passing social construction. Even if hell were dangerous, exposure to its flames would only prove the measure of one's strength. What does not kill me, they say with Nietzsche, makes me stronger. The American Civil Liberties Union's (ACLU) defense of the Nazis' right to march in Skokie is the most famous example of this kind of contrarian flexing, but such strenuous libertarianism is found more widely in the culture.

Liberals depend upon a colorful cast of characters to keep them in business. A curious crowd, real and imagined, friend and foe, populates the intellectual history of arguments for free expression. Early modern theorists made use of lurking figures eager to squelch liberty to argue in favor of openness. For Milton in the seventeenth century it was Catholics (and the

Spanish Inquisition); for "Cato" in the eighteenth it was France and Turkey (and the specter of baroque and Oriental despotism, respectively). For John Stuart Mill in the nineteenth, China and Mormon polygamy represented the dangers of intellectual compulsion, while atheism stood in need of defense. For the U.S. Supreme Court in the twentieth century, the crew of provoking subjects was even motlier, though less international: socialists, religious pamphleteers and political users of sound trucks, civil rights protestors, Klansmen, Nazis, purveyors of porn and junk mail, comedians, flag-burners, and cross-burners. While early modern adversaries were treated as villains better kept at arm's length, Mill and his many twentieth-century followers discovered the utility of the outré for constructing arguments about free speech. This cast of characters has served as the irritants that helped goad the pearls of free expression theory into being. "In freedom-of-speech cases," said Archibald Cox, "the most effective kind of client is an unpopular cause, or just some S.O.B. who has a right to be heard."[6] He had in mind his recent client—the Reverend Billy James Hargis, a 280-pound Oklahoman right-wing broadcaster and admirer of Joseph McCarthy. Similarly, a leader of the ACLU explained the codependence of the friends of liberty and the deviant: "Our fundamental civil rights often depend on defending some scuzzball you don't like."[7] There is an under-the-table transactional ethic in the free speech story, a curious coupling of straitlaced defenders of liberty and wacky or wicked pushers of limits.

The bond between liberals and transgressors points to the principle that I will call "homeopathic machismo," the daily imbibing of poisons in small doses so that large drafts will not hurt. This strategy proves to be a telling clue to the liberal temperament. The attitude of warming oneself in the fires of hell has both a long history and a wide purchase in contemporary culture, from ancient literary and religious sources through Romanticism and modernism. An understanding of these intellectual sources might help explain how some curious notions have gained widespread support—for example, that the presence of pornography or first-hand acquaintance with images and reports of mayhem is somehow good for the social order. Free speech is marvelous, and we have to pay a price for it, as we must for all marvelous things. But some friends of free expression take a positive pleasure in paying up, as if a lack of cultural transgressors on the loose would imperil

6. Quoted in Fred W. Friendly, *The Good Guys, the Bad Guys, and the First Amendment: Free Speech v. Fairness in Broadcasting* (New York: Random House, 1976), 76.

7. "A.C.L.U. Boasts Wide Portfolio of Cases, But Conservatives See Partisanship," *New York Times:* 2 Oct. 1988, 24, quoting Ira Glasser, who overlooks the possibility of a scuzzball you do like.

the public intellectual and political welfare. Just as the aged Gandhi supposedly took naked young women into his bed in order to prove his powers of
renunciation, so some liberals celebrate provocation as an opportunity to
show off the advanced state of their self-mastery. Their prayer is not to be
delivered from evil but to be led into temptation. Civil libertarians voluntarily expose themselves to trial by contraries. The free expression scholar,
and currently Columbia University president, Lee Bollinger compares the
toleration of extremist speech to spiritual asceticism: "In this secular context we derive something of the same personal meaning and satisfaction of
the religious fast, a self-initiated and extraordinary exposure to temptation
that reaffirms the possibility of self-control over generally troublesome impulses."[8] The tolerated presence and perhaps even secret collusion with the
culturally forbidden stand as a monument to civic righteousness. Liberals
are confident that any doctrine, good, bad, or ugly, should be allowed its in-
nings in the open air. Sometimes this implies a nose-holding tolerance, and
sometimes it edges into exultation at the challenge of facing down toxic
doctrine. "Let truth and falsehood grapple" say some liberals in the fashion
of a Roman emperor declaring the gladiatorial contests open.

The pairing of liberals and consorts from the abyss can be a nice arrangement for both parties. Friends of liberty get to show off their broad-
mindedness (and maybe get a secret buzz from the flirtation as well), even
though they officially profess to be repulsed by the "scuzzballs" they are
squiring, and the outrage-artists get some welcome publicity. Cultural
transgressors have a professional interest in expressive liberty and supply
the liberals with something to defend; the liberals, in turn, are often wonderfully ingenious in interpreting offensive practices as defensible contributions to public life (almost anything with the right interpreter and
enough tender loving care can have social redeeming value). Moral stunt
pilots count on masochistic audiences who enjoy the abuse of being
mocked: such enjoyment or at least sublimation of transgression is a key to
the liberal soul. Spectators of such intellectual sado-masochism are supposed, in turn, to decode it ironically—to read "diabolically," as William
Blake put it. Liberals and civil libertarians bank on the bystander's ability to
look past the apparent chumminess of liberty and evil and understand the
underlying and noble self-discipline that it takes to defend one's enemy. Indeed, the whole affair depends on the saving office of the commentator, the
critic who can interpret the irony's social value. Like all dramas, the dialogue between the principals is designed with a third party in mind.

8. Lee C. Bollinger, *The Tolerant Society* (New York: Oxford University Press, 1986), 143.

But not everyone gets the irony. The romance of liberal tolerance and cultural transgression leaves some bystanders cold. Those who do not enjoy seeing Klansmen and Nazis receiving pride of place or religious symbols painted with bodily biodegradables being defended as artistic innovation, for instance, get huffy. They fail to achieve what liberals consider the requisite inversion in their heads and the requisite frigidity in their hearts. The offended critics are, again, central to the social drama: by losing their cool they provide the friends of free speech with a counterexample of the self-suspension citizens are supposed to possess and help provide the abyss-artists, as I dub them in chapter 2, succès de scandale. The threefold drama of the liberal enabler, the convention-buster, and the outraged bystander has been repeated often enough in recent years, especially in the visual arts, to show how neatly the liberals have rigged a double bind for anyone who might want to criticize their program. Speak up against the spectacle of fraternization in liberal circles and you risk being called a bigot, prude, scaredy-cat, or friend of censorship. Critics of cultural offensiveness, or even those who want to come to terms with the tangle of a conflicted public sphere today, are left with little room to maneuver.[9]

Liberal defenders of absolute freedom of expression can be impatient and illiberal with those who criticize their commitment to life without closure. As Charles Taylor notes, "liberalism can't and shouldn't claim complete cultural neutrality. Liberalism is also a fighting creed."[10] For some, liberalism is explicitly hostile, not an open forum for the happy winnowing of competing claims. People bound by the sacred cannot embrace a doctrine advocating that everything should be out in the open. The sacred, taken as a structure of communication—or rather, noncommunication—sets apart certain things as off-limits to circulation and hems them in by prohibitions and sanctions. A policy that wants to cast light on all recesses and claims that all exploration is free of penalty can serve as a form of aggression, not just an amicable sweeping out of the closet. The sacred takes a hands-off stance to objects deemed precious or dangerous. Its obvious reference is to religion, but there are plenty of secular reasons for stopping short of complete openness of publication. Liberalism's policy of publicity is at odds with sanctity or even discretion: it never met a secret it could keep. It distrusts hermetic discourse spoken mouth to ear and is fine with almost

9. I develop the notion of an ethics of not looking in "Beauty's Veils: The Ambivalent Iconoclasm of Kierkegaard and Benjamin," in *The Image in Dispute: Visual Cultures in Modernity*, ed. Dudley Andrew (Austin: University of Texas Press, 1997), 9–32.

10. Charles Taylor, "The Politics of Recognition," in *Multiculturalism: Examining the Politics of Recognition*, ed. Amy Gutmann (Princeton, N.J.: Princeton University Press, 1994), 62.

everything being spoken from the rooftops. "Uninhibited" is usually a term of praise for liberals; others prefer awe or circumspection. Where liberals see little besides the healthy ventilation of attics and crypts, others see a vaporization of the power they seek to preserve, whether it belongs to love, friendship, art, or religion, all of which flourish in the penumbra, not in the direct sunlight of reflection. "In nature, as in law," Melville wrote, "it may be libelous to speak some truths."[11]

Most people who have thought about the trio of liberal defenders, habitués of transgression, and offended bystanders consider the first the least worry. People on the Right generally think the problem is the abyss artists who want to tickle every taboo and unhallow everything holy. People on the Left generally think the problem is the offended bystander, both freelance and state-sponsored, who would muzzle edgy experimentation and social progress. The Right attacks liberalism for not recognizing the potential for evil or moral erosion; the Left attacks it for not acknowledging social structure or concentrated power. Both are correct. The middle ground seems the most fruitful soil to till, if you can stand the cross fire. In this book I hope to offer something new, or rather something old, by taking liberalism itself as the chief problem. The liberal defense of free speech, as it is often told today, has a certain nihilist deposit. Defending the speech we hate does not mean we need to learn to love it or think it is really good stuff. Refusing to make laws prohibiting speech and expression does not mean that speech and expression are necessarily free of ill effects. One can oppose censorship while maintaining a capacity for judgments about the value and quality of cultural forms. The communicative conditions of our times offer unprecedented access to representations of things that were culturally contained through most of human history, and a commitment to abstract rights should not keep us from thinking intelligently about those conditions. Many liberals today have a profound respect for autonomy and liberty and a shallow understanding of human nature, social order, and mass media. The intellectual tradition, however, fortunately provides strong medicine against such recent flattening of vision.

LIBERALS, CIVIL LIBERTARIANS, AND LIBERALISM

My loose use of the term "liberal" thus far needs attention. Coined in Spain in the 1820s, "liberalism" is one of the most slippery of all modern political

---

11. Herman Melville, "The Encantadas or Enchanted Isles," in *Billy Budd and Other Stories* (New York: Penguin, 1986), 115. The law has since changed; whether nature has is unclear.

terms, and anyone who sets out to analyze it, as I do, has to take responsibility for the inevitable semantic variety of a concept whose dominion has grown so large. Already by 1877 its expansion of meaning was lamented: "It is unfortunate that the term 'Liberal' is also wanted for other purposes, social and theological, and it is perhaps to be regretted that we cannot go back to 'Whig' as the purely party definition."[12] Since the late nineteenth century, the term has had a split inheritance. In European and Australian politics "liberal" tends to mean conservative, that is, the advocacy of free markets; in the United States "liberal" tends to mean social democrat, that is, support for the state's role in sustaining social welfare, together with a respect for the unmanageable diversity of human choices. For Mill, who in many ways is the headwater of both streams, free trade and free expression were two sides of the same coin, the sovereignty of the individual to act as he or she pleased (within limits of social harm). This combustible mixture has yielded various and incompatible elements ever since: "liberal" can mean latitudinarian, socially tolerant, open-minded, fuzzy-minded, deregulationist, pro-state intervention, optimistic, and countless other things. Today the chief rifts in the term refer to free markets (neoliberal), free expression (civil libertarian), and an attitude of tragic acceptance of the plurality of human ends. That the term can encompass figures as diverse as the free-market economist Milton Friedman, the ACLU's Nadine Strossen, and the political philosopher Isaiah Berlin (who each represents these strands respectively) is part of its fuzziness and thus also of its usefulness. I will try to keep its usage within reasonable bounds, but I have no illusions that I can master this (or any other) signifier.

"Civil libertarian" refers to a slightly different constellation of meanings. Civil libertarians typically believe in strong laws (and such strength can include laws precisely *against* the mixing of church and state or laws *against* censorship) but often distrust the state. Though many liberals are also civil libertarians, these are not overlapping sets. Oliver Wendell Holmes Jr. was a civil libertarian but hardly a liberal: he had a Social Darwinist's vision of progress and a cynic's view of human nature. Anti-statist libertarians, anarchists, and even an occasional maverick Republican—none of whom we normally consider liberal—can be civil libertarians.[13] Not everyone who believes in freedom of expression necessarily signs on for the accompany-

12. Editor's note in George Cornewall Lewis, *Remarks on the Use and Abuse of Some Political Terms*, ed. Roland Knyvet Wilson (Oxford: Thornton, 1877), 188.

13. Consider Sheila Suess Kennedy's provocative book title, *What's a Nice Republican Girl Like Me Doing in the ACLU?* (Amherst, NY: Prometheus Books, 1997).

ing ideological package of faith in progress and hope for human nature that tend to mark liberal thinkers, though a majority probably does. Civil libertarians tend toward the colder and harder end of the emotional spectrum, and liberals tend toward the warmer and softer end. In what follows, the terms "liberal" and "civil libertarian" sometimes blur when I use liberal as the more encompassing term for the political-philosophical tradition of fighting for liberty. Cataloguing the full animal kingdom of liberal kinds awaits another day, though chapter 2 does focus on some of the leading figures of the drama of free expression.

The concept of "liberal" also creates some retroactive mischief, being applied to theorists who never heard of the term. The concept gathers diverse thinkers in its net—Milton, Thomas Hobbes, Benedictus de Spinoza, John Locke, Immanuel Kant, Mill, Oliver Wendell Holmes Jr., John Dewey, Jürgen Habermas, and John Rawls, among many others. Every concept, as the Argentine writer Jorge Luis Borges would say, invents its ancestors. In this case a lot of the inventing was done by twentieth-century civil libertarians eager to secure themselves a noble intellectual ancestry. As a rule historians dislike the term's crumbliness, and a common game in intellectual history involves showing why canonic "liberal" figures are the victims of post-hoc political readings. Milton, for instance, is better thought a Puritan radical or republican, many argue; others argue for Locke as a victim of retroactive myth-making, Mill as a radical, a Romantic, a utilitarian, or even a republican, Holmes as a pragmatist or nihilist, and Dewey as a radical democrat.[14] Such revisionism is quite legitimate, since a hatred of paternalist meddling by state, church, or neighbors can go together with wildly diverse moral, political, epistemological, and aesthetic commitments. There should be something suspicious about a single category that nets the atheist Hobbes and the devout Milton, the empiricist Locke and the rationalist Spinoza, the deontologist Kant and the utilitarian Mill, the tender-minded Dewey and the tough-minded Holmes. Even so, thinkers can share an attitude without sharing everything else; a common element among many does not necessarily make a family, but *can* make a team. By "liberal" I mean a cluster of existential-political stances, such as insistence on religious and

14. For two examples, see J. G. A. Pocock, "The Myth of John Locke and the Obsession with Liberalism," in *John Locke: Papers Read at a Clark Library Seminar, 10 December 1977* (Los Angeles, 1980), 3–24; Robert Westbrook, *John Dewey and American Democracy* (Ithaca, N.Y.: Cornell University Press, 1991). For Mill as a crypto- or ambivalent Miltonian republican, see Stewart Justman, *The Hidden Text of Mill's Liberty* (Savage, Md.: Rowman & Littlefield, 1991), especially chap. 2, an argument that works better for Mill's social thought in general than for *On Liberty* specifically.

other forms of ideological diversity, rejection of conscious design as the ultimate source of social order, respect for due process and for guarantees of equal protection against the tyranny of the majority, and appreciation for eccentric behavior. Liberals equally hate the sleep of reason and the frenzy of passion. That said, it will still be hard to keep such diverse thinkers safely herded into a single fold; at least all liberals abhor censorship.

Though clichéd, the liberal hall of fame gives us an ample array of resources, many of which can be used against the latter-day thinness of its heirs. By focusing on the lineage later invented by civil libertarians, "I consciously work within the framework I am trying to debunk (or enlarge)."[15] It is a productive cliché that these thinkers all belong to a single marketplace-of-ideas tradition since each one offers something that undermines that cliché and opens new vistas of thought. Milton, after all, was one of history's great painters of hell in *Paradise Lost*, and the risky benefits of exploring its pits are central to his earlier call for unlicensed printing in *Areopagitica*. Blistering political radical and devout Puritan, Milton defies the divisions of the contemporary intellectual landscape. Adam Smith places sympathy, and its inevitable failure, at the heart of social life in a way that both highlights the default Stoicism prescribed for the public subject and moves beyond it for an ethics of listening and openness. Mill's understanding of free discussion is shaped by both Romantic eccentricity and Stoic self-mastery, and his arguments are both symptomatic of and diagnostic for the muddled thinking that follows in his wake. Holmes sponsors a harsh and martial nihilism as the philosophical basis of free expression, something that his less sternly thoughtful heirs have smiled and hoped away. These figures would have all understood, with various qualifications, the point of Adam Michnik's dictum that the best society has weak laws and a strong church.[16] Classic theorists of liberty—Milton, Smith, and Mill— knew how to make evil part of the equation. Twentieth-century libertarians as a rule have been less circumspect, some from optimism (such as Zechariah Chafee, the leading American scholar of free expression in the first half of the twentieth century), others from nihilism (such as Clarence Darrow, the self-described "attorney for the damned"). Discovering how to sustain deep respect for liberty and evil at the same time is a chief task of this book.

Contemporary intellectual defenses of freedom of speech are often hostile to theological frameworks that warn against the potential harm or even

15. Stephen Jay Gould, *Time's Arrow, Time's Cycle* (Cambridge, Mass.: Harvard University Press, 1987), 4.

16. John Keane, personal communication, March 2000.

evil of certain speech acts. Many civil libertarians trace their lineage to the radical enlightenment of Spinoza, Voltaire, Thomas Paine, and others who generally (Spinoza is more complicated) saw in traditional religion little more than a dungeon thick with spider webs. A related story also inspires agitation for free speech, the battle against the Inquisition, which tells of a contest between a conveniently villainous church and conveniently heroic rebels.[17] The battle of truth against power is a seductive narrative told for centuries by Protestant reformers, *philosophes,* and progressive crusaders: who could possibly sign on with power, given that choice? But other things can be smuggled below the radar of the anticensorship crusader's upright conscience—a philosophy of history as progress, religion as neurosis, reason as panacea. Liberals can be fond of history as a graduation narrative: we have outgrown the old world and entered into a new one without angels or demons. Such a simple vision of progress often leaves liberals ill-equipped to deal with either the sublimity or the vehemence of doctrines that have doubts about publicity or the unending glare of critical reason, and silences people who protest the liberal philosophy of history, culture, or moral life. In the twentieth century such libertarian heirs of the radical enlightenment as Holmes, Bertrand Russell, I. F. Stone, even Noam Chomsky, relish their autonomy from theological sources. All are admirable at least for their courage and energy (and I often agree with their practical politics). But if these are the best liberal thought can offer, we have lost touch with important sources and shrunken in moral and intellectual vision. The project of liberty can no longer act as if religion is either a cardboard enemy or on the verge of withering away.

Liberalism both denies and depends on religion in public life. Much of what is best in liberalism derives from Greco-Roman and Judeo-Christian roots, and I would hesitate longer about both of those contentious elisions if they were not so apt for a certain Paul of Tarsus, the surprising hero, one of them at least, of this book. Paul believes in liberty, actively entertains the other side in his discourse, and has a robust account of cultural sensitivity. What is so suggestive about him is the way elements in his writings sustain—and also thus transcend—the rationalist, relativist, and fundamentalist options. Figures such as Paul and Milton combine a radical theory of liberty with a moral program of wary respect for the potential harms of crime and noxious doctrine. Paul is a libertarian who is also civil (Milton, in contrast, can only be called an uncivil libertarian). The philosophy of free

17. See Edward Peters's brilliant book *Inquisition* (Berkeley: University of California Press, 1988) for a critical analysis of these narratives.

expression does not fully make sense without its fertile theological roots, and it cannot flourish in the ideological competition of the contemporary world without a greater sympathy for those who object to its intolerance of arguments derived from the sacred. Enlightenment has many paths, and they all have something to do with liberty. Liberalism would foster a more genuine pluralism by forfeiting its monopoly claim on the proper management of pluralism.

Free speech theory, at base, is an antinomian heresy: Congress shall make no law. Antinomians believe that the law is suspended, and faith alone can save. Liberal defenses of open debate unerringly return to the night journey, salvation by passing through the flame of contraries, while long having abandoned an understanding of self or cosmos that would make a descent into hell even intelligible as a good thing for a person to seek. There is a long tradition, running from Greek and Hebrew antiquity to Christianity to Romanticism and modernism, that finds in evil lessons for the good and relishes the clash of the two; the dilution or hardening of this tradition makes moral and political deep-sea diving today less secure. Arguments defending freedom of expression are often twisted in their celebration of what they oppose. The First Amendment has become a chief latter-day site for the old heresy of redemption through sin. How did a high dose of negativity become institutionalized in the core doctrines of free speech? How did the ironic mode—the liberal *via negativa*, of sponsoring study-abroad sojourns in the land of fire and brimstone—become a favored option among people who believe in progress and reason? Whence came the policy that the best way to defend liberty is to defend its enemies? Liberal citizens are supposed to run the gauntlet of what disgusts them and to find a little poison gas in the air a good immunization against bigger woes. Citizens grow in wisdom by passing through folly, and dalliance with demons adds up to the greater education of all. Rancid discourse has become what early Christianity called the *felix culpa*, the happy sin. Our souls are supposed to be able to take publicly what we hate privately. This book is an attempt to understand this strange argument.

THE FREE SPEECH STORY

What is the current narrative and how did we get there? The heroic version of the liberal story about free speech continues to define much popular and academic thinking about the relation of democracy and communication (although the story's dominant form is a product of the middle of the twentieth century). The story tells of courageous revolutionists and stout-hearted printers who risked life, limb, and profit by defying the censorship of crown or church (this, again, is a variant on the story of the fight against the Inquisition). By ignoring the inhibitions and edicts of the censors, these heroes (so the story goes) formed a "marketplace of ideas" where any notion, good, bad, or ugly, could be evaluated on its own merits and whose price would be set by nothing but free and open competition. This marketplace is supposed to be the motor of democratic life and the place where the public blossoming of the logos so central to democracy can occur. In Protestant nations the printing press attained near mythological status as a world-historical agency of enlightenment and emancipation and as the central enabling institution of popular sovereignty. The press had a privileged role in disseminating news and views; every citizen had the potential power to speak the word of truth. The intellectual hall of fame in this story includes such figures as Milton, Locke, the authors of *Cato's Letters,* Adam Smith, Thomas Jefferson, Mill, Holmes, and Louis Brandeis, among many others. More recently investigative journalists, members of the American Civil Liberties Union, librarians, radical reformers, and renegade lawyers are often (self) nominated for inclusion as well.

Most of the themes of the free speech story are well rooted in seventeenth- and eighteenth-century thought, though confidence in truth's ultimate triumph over error was a distinctive feature of both the biblical and the philosophic tradition. As Spinoza put it, "truth reveals itself," a characteristic belief, as Karl Popper argues, of liberal thought.[18] Spinoza's confidence reflects the rationalism of the radical Enlightenment, as well as the Jewish tradition's deep confidence that speaking the right words can be a way to divide the light from the darkness. Locke's version follows Paul's conviction that a law is written in the hearts and conscience of Jew and Gentile alike (Rom. 2:15). Though the world is full of parties eager "to cram their Tenets down all Men's Throats," Locke says, using an idiom still favored by liberals annoyed at ideological pressure, yet "the Candle of the Lord [is] set up by Himself in Men's minds, which it is impossible by the Breath or Power of Man wholly to extinguish."[19] How he squares the "Candle of the Lord" with his professed empiricism is a debated point in Locke studies, but he thereby expresses his confidence in the independent powers of mind that is so characteristic of free expression arguments. In a passage Jefferson would echo in his *Notes on the State of Virginia,* Locke writes: "the truth would cer-

18. Karl Popper, "On the Sources of Knowledge and Ignorance," in *Conjectures and Refutations* (New York: Harper & Row, 1963), 3–30.

19. John Locke, *An Essay Concerning Human Understanding,* IV.iii:20.

tainly do well enough if she were once left to shift for herself. . . . Errors, indeed, prevail by the assistance of foreign and borrowed succors. But if Truth makes not her way into the understanding by her own light, she will be but the weaker for any borrowed force violence can add to her."[20] Locke and Spinoza are two of the leading seventeenth-century representatives of the confidence that truth alone is persuasive.

Two decades after Locke's *Letter on Toleration* (1693), John Trenchard and Thomas Gordon, writing under the characteristically Roman Stoic pen name "Cato" on the benefits of a free press, asserted: "Only the wicked governors of men dread what is said of them. . . . Guilt only dreads liberty of speech, which drags it out of its lurking holes, and exposes its horror and deformity to day-light."[21] Such words still inspire advocates of liberty, as well as those who do not care so much about liberty but like making money under its ideological protection (such as, indeed, Rupert Murdoch).[22] "Cato" mobilizes all the righteousness on the side of publication, for only those who are "at enmity with the truth" fear free speech. "Misrepresentation of publick measures is easily overthrown, by representing publick measures truly." There is a certain smugness in their certainty of the automatic victory of truth: "Truth has so many advantages above error, that she wants only to be shewn, to gain admiration and esteem."[23] A later American analogue can be found in Tunis Wortman's *Treatise Concerning Political Enquiry, and the Liberty of the Press* (1800), which Leonard Levy says is "the book that Jefferson did not write but should have."[24] Wortman calls for a society in which everybody would "be permitted to communicate their ideas with the energy and ingenuousness of truth. In such a state of intellectual freedom and activity, the progress of mind would infallibly become accelerated . . . Exposed to the incessant attack of Argument, the existence of Error would be fleeting and transitory; while Truth would be seated upon a basis of adamant, and receive a perpetual accession to the number of her votaries."[25] In a comment on the *Times* of London, Ralph Waldo Emerson

20. John Locke, *Letter on Toleration*, 3–4, 8, 15.

21. John Trenchard and Thomas Gordon, *Cato's Letters: Essays on Liberty, Civil and Religious, and Other Important Subjects*, ed. Ronald Hamowy. 2 vols. (Indianapolis: Liberty Fund, 1995), 1: 111, 114.

22. James Curran, *Media and Power* (London: Routledge, 2002); John Keane, *The Media and Democracy* (London: Polity Press, 1991).

23. Trenchard and Gordon, *Cato's Letters*, 717.

24. Leonard Levy, *Emergence of a Free Press* (New York: Oxford University Press, 1985), 328.

25. Tunis Wortman, *A Treatise Concerning Political Enquiry, and the Liberty of the Press* (1800), ed. Leonard W. Levy (New York: DaCapo Press, 1970), 121.

did not quite scale the heights of bluster that Wortman did, but he did state the secret dream of every investigative journalist since: "There is no corner and no night. A relentless inquisition drags every secret to the day, turns the glare of this solar microscope on every malfaisance, so as to make the public a more terrible spy than any foreigner; and no weakness can be taken advantage of by an enemy, since the whole people are already forewarned."[26] This dream of universal surveillance, of panoptic light penetrating every nook and cranny, is still with us, for good and evil.

Alleles from such arguments persist in the intellectual gene pool. A faith in the power of the airing of ideas to reveal truth over the din of public relations and the dullness of public ignorance still pops up often and in the strangest places. "I believe in the right of people to judge the truth for themselves in the court of public opinion," said Mick Hume, editor of *LM* [*Living Marxism*] *Magazine,* in an important British libel trial on 14 March 2000, whose harsh penalty for libel many interpreted as a symptom of the urgent need for a British equivalent to *Times v. Sullivan,* the 1964 case that raised the bar significantly for defamation suits against the press. Hume invoked all the key terms: the people, enthroned as a judge, autonomously sifting evidence, public opinion as a court. It does not matter that Hume is a Marxist; in a pinch, all the old liberal safety nets still come to the rescue. Liberal rhetoric is a standard default position for people who find their liberty threatened.

Another amusing example of the confidence that the public takes care of itself is a BBC television program that scored no viewers in the ratings system; it did not even attract the 2,500 pairs of eyeballs necessary to register at all. Was the program in danger of being cancelled? Not at all, said a BBC spokesman: "This is public service broadcasting and we're not in a ratings war." Mailing videotapes to the actual viewers, said an insider wit, would have been cheaper than broadcasting it.[27] The BBC's official line is that broadcasting is a duty and benefit regardless of the audience, and that some sort of service is rendered even if there is no one there to receive it. The ethic of abandonment and hope that lurks in such arguments for dissemination is deeply rooted in the intellectual tradition. That arguments about the self-righting public are still somehow persuasive after decades of debate about the public and its problems shows something about the immunity of the free speech story to theory or fact. The undeserved moral favor this story confers upon market economics does not seem to hurt its popularity either.

26. Ralph Waldo Emerson, *English Traits,* in *The Selected Writings of Ralph Waldo Emerson,* ed. Brooks Atkinson (New York: Modern Library, 1992), 592.

27. Simon De Bruxelles, "BBC Show in Wales Attracts 'No Viewers,'" *The Times:* 7 Mar. 2000, 2.

Despite the waning of pure laissez-faire thinking in economics (even the most fervid free-marketers have had to make their peace with national and global regulatory bodies) and a myriad of intellectual and historical dents in the Enlightenment credo of reason and progress, the free speech story is alive and kicking. The free speech story is as much a cultural commonplace as an explicit doctrine; it can be heard on daytime television, in undergraduate classes, in junior high social studies courses, in the voices that crowd one's head. It is a flattering tale for people who read and write for a living, and reporters, civil libertarians, civics teachers, among others, tell it often. They like to imagine themselves as *philosophes* fighting against clerics, dungeons, popes, and inquisitions to establish liberty of speech and the press.[28] The *Des Moines Register*, for instance, ran a rather smarmy ad picturing five of its editors in 2001. The accompanying text read, in part: "The Des Moines Register is dedicated to bringing readers the complete news, every day. But sometimes elected officials or government agencies don't want the whole story told. That's when Register editors go to battle, with the First Amendment in hand, protecting your right to know."[29] The First Amendment here props up the privileged professional position of journalists as crusaders against the scheming state—itself a story as old as the eighteenth century, though Watergate gave it new life, at least in the United States.[30] Though I have no wish to disrespect excellent journalism, this bit of advertising flotsam mobilizes the First Amendment for private advantage and secures the forces of the good totally on one side (that of the newspaper). Such are common habits of talk among journalists and journalism educators.

Michael Moore's preface to the British edition of his bestseller *Stupid White Men* (2002) is another example of the dubious moral bonus that tellers of the free speech story can enjoy. He tells of a villainous publisher owned by the über-demon of media monopoly, Rupert Murdoch. The publisher wants Moore not only (horrors!) to rewrite his book—in order to better fit the new sensibilities of a post–September 11 world in which the appetite for irreverent criticism of America might be dampened—but also to pay for the cost of a new printing. Moore, outraged but stymied, discusses his stalled book project on his cross-country lecture circuit. The hero of the piece is a librarian who attends one of his lectures and mobilizes an internet crusade against the "censorship" of the book (and librarians are perhaps the

28. As in the case of Milton and "Cato," the anti-Catholicism of this tradition is explicit, which also fits the Inquisition narrative.

29. *The Des Moines Register:* 1 Aug. 2001, 3C.

30. On eighteenth-century struggles over publicity, see Jürgen Habermas, *Structural Transformation of the Public Sphere* (1962) (Cambridge: MIT Press, 1989), secs. 4, 9, 12, 13.

most passionate believers in the free speech story in the United States, together with the ACLU). Before the collective wrath of the nation's librarians, the publisher wilts into submission, and the book is published. Hooray for free speech! Moore gets to be a martyr in a noble cause and sell a lot of books at the same time. By attacking censorship he secures for himself an impregnable position—who, after all, could argue against someone who argues against something so obviously wicked as censorship?[31] Noble ideals lend themselves to hijacking. Crusading against censorship can be a moral cloaking device. Moore writes well, raises important points, is often funny (even if he consigns a monopoly of stupidity to a class that already controls too many of the planet's other resources), offers wild and imaginative solutions to social problems, supplies a global demand for reasons to mock the United States, and above all, never takes himself out of the picture. He exemplifies the sin of pride that infests the free speech story.

To take a final and (let us hope) passing example, the George W. Bush administration's Patriot Act is a piece of legislation greeted as a sensible defense of homeland security by political conservatives and condemned by others as the entering wedge of Big Brotherism, the worst threat to human liberty since the invention of the Czarist police or the Brown Shirts. The one side claims the act is a reasonable measure in dark times, and the other sees it as a sinister effort to "roll back" (the verb of choice in this rhetoric) constitutional rights. Forced to choose, I would find the latter position easy to prefer, but I wish it were a more interesting choice. The twin bogeymen of government censors poring over my library check-out records and terrorists abusing the liberties of an open society scarcely seem adequate images of the danger and evil that are so obviously loose in the world today (or yesterday). These demons make evil something conveniently alien to our own lives and practices. The political scene seems destined to keep hosting fights between self-satisfied conservatives and shrill liberals. In the process we are often left to choose between a tepid theory of liberty and a tepid theory of evil.

These current American and British examples of the free speech story are not meant to be exhaustive, merely to point us to some of its central claims. Censorship is wicked; the truth will out; the public is best left to its own devices; even (or especially) vile people and doctrines deserve to be heard; the free market and the free press go hand in hand; and defenders of liberty can justifiably fraternize with extremists. Even if such views are sometimes implausible, the free speech story is remarkably resilient.

---

31. The morally and politically extortionist quality of the historical narrative of the battle against censorship is noted by Curran, *Media and Power*, especially 4–7, 79ff, 127ff, 227ff.

Though it can sound hackneyed, "a legacy of old saws," it refuses to go away, despite calls for a decent funeral.[32] The newspaper, said Walter Lippmann, who more than anyone both destabilized and reinforced the dream of the press as a beacon of truth in a foggy social sea, "is in all literalness the bible of democracy, the book out of which a people determines its conduct."[33] In the face of ample opportunity for disillusionment—the checkered history of journalism, the manifest apathy and ignorance of much of the citizenry, the persuasive power of the market and the state, or the catastrophes of the last century—ideals of a free speech, free press, and autonomous public have hardly been scratched. The content of news seems to have little to do with its self-image. "Rome had her gladiators; Spain her bull-fighters; England her bear-baiting; and America her newspapers," Henry Ward Beecher wrote in 1879.[34] The free speech story is largely impervious to evidence, being a creature of collective identity and hence of collective wishful thinking. Talk of free speech often serves genuflection more than reflection and dooms most discussion of democracy and communication to oscillate between great expectations and great horrors. (Discourses of perfection have this polarizing effect.) Inspiring quotes about the glorious role of the press from some Founding Father will show up about as often as indignant complaints about the latest degradation of the media. The stubborn utopia of free speech will not go away.

One reason for its hold on the imagination has been mentioned already: the free speech story has an uncanny ability to secure itself a monopoly of righteousness. The defense of free expression can be an all but foolproof method of claiming the moral high ground. A favored pastime of the friends of liberty is to lather themselves into a righteous fury against censorship; bystanders eager to not be associated with the powers of darkness find themselves cheering on the spectacle of fearless souls speaking truth to power. Ironically, all the lather against censorship can end up creating a moral monopoly at exactly the same moment it is claiming to burst one. Making counterarguments against certain views is so ticklish that the opposition often chooses to remain silent.[35] During his administration, for in-

32. James Curran, "Mass Media and Democracy Revisited," in *Mass Media and Society,* ed. James Curran and Michael Gurevitch. 2nd ed. (London: Arnold, 1996), 81.

33. Walter Lippmann, *Liberty and the News* (1920) (New Brunswick, N.J.: Transaction, 1995), 44.

34. Quoted in Kenneth Cmiel, *Democratic Eloquence* (New York: Morrow, 1990), 135.

35. Paul F. Lazarsfeld and Robert K. Merton, "Mass Communication, Popular Taste, and Organized Social Action," in *The Communication of Ideas,* ed. Lyman Bryson (New York: Cooper Square, 1948), 95–118.

stance, Ronald Reagan declared "war" on such enemies as drugs, terrorism, and kidnapping. All were failsafe politically because critics of his policies would risk being seen as fans of drugs, terror, or child abuse. In the same way no one wants to look like a fan of censorship. To their credit some liberals have the courage of just this sort of perversity: "let the Nazis march" (sometimes followed quickly by the qualification, "so that we all can see how sick they are"). Ferocious anticensorship rhetoric can make those who have doubts about a lights-on-all-the-time policy into the bad guys. Some civil libertarians have a hard time imagining how anyone could possibly resist their vision of freedom of speech, thus shutting down the people who, according to the liberal love of contraries, they should be most eager to listen to (their critics). Anticensorship crusaders thus procure the spot of unquestionable truth that their own theory should deny them.[36] Fortunately, there is more space for life and thought than the simple choice between censorship and openness would suggest.

Liberal openness may have had its moment of supremacy as an official doctrine in the United States around the two middle quarters of the twentieth century, but it is now falling on hard times (as the Patriot Act suggests). In court decisions, legal theory, political will, and cultural mood, the faith in open-ended debate is losing ground as a mainstream consensus or is being kidnapped by the neoliberal narrative about the glories of free markets. Liberal *glasnost* and strenuous toleration of the extremist are no longer the lukewarm sea in which the common culture floats but rather a beleaguered, even minority position. Worldwide, relatively few nations prize freedom of expression as a leading value; it is found chiefly in historically Protestant zones. The global viability of liberalism requires a historic turn away from its antireligious past. Its drift from cultural eminence may owe something to its self-righteousness and its forgetfulness of its intellectual roots. Its critics are legion, and confidence in free expression as a political panacea has eroded, even though its tropes remain indispensable for anyone caught in a pinch. I join the chorus of critics in the past couple of decades, but with counter-cyclical aspirations: hoping to salvage the dangerous, unacknowledged, and sometimes valuable heart—the attitude toward pain and evil—that has often seemed the most objectionable part of liberal thought. In my view the liberal story needs spring cleaning. What has often been a robust vision has degenerated into platitudes and dogmas. We have irreconcilable stances: the strong nihilists of free speech who call for stoic cool in the face of offense, the saccharine defenders of truth's automatic victory who think

36. A danger clearly noted by Bollinger, *Tolerant Society,* especially 215.

everything's copacetic in the public realm without further trouble, and the critics of both who think, quite rightly, that the former are harsh, and the latter foolish. My aim is to defend liberal ideals in a fresh way: with a tragic philosophy of history (instead of optimism or meliorism), a social basis of solidarity or compassion (instead of veils of ignorance, norms of deliberation, or other equalizing expedients), and a communicative norm of receptivity (instead of interactivity or dialogue). Liberalism is in part a story about overcoming suffering (enduring offensive speech), and pain turns out to be a secret key to the puzzle of how the public life of democratic solidarity might work. In particular this book examines the prohibition of personal feeling in public life, an old bittersweet story. It is a meditation on Nietzsche's question, what is the meaning of ascetic ideals? One answer to "compassionate conservatism" might be hardhearted liberalism.

SELF-ABSTRACTION AND STOICISM

The Stoic tradition teaches a hard heart as the price of public life. Free speech is, to use the New Testament term, a *skandalon,* an offense designed to bring about some greater end. In the face of offense citizens are supposed to be able to "take it," to see clearly rather than seeing red. The notion that the ability to suspend personal interests and sentiments is a prerequisite for public communication has been described in several overlapping vocabularies, notably, philosophical aloofness, cynical dissidence, Stoic indifference, epicurean moderation, Christian virtue, Gnostic escapism, gentlemanly honor, military discipline, Romantic transcendence, and most recently, professional objectivity. These deposits blur and blend in Anglo-American political culture, and this book examines several varieties of ethical suspension. (Something similar arose in the Confucian cultural zone of China, Japan, and Korea.) Sorting out the lineages is less important here than a more basic point about the afterlife of antiquity, whose fossil fuels have long inspired theorists of liberty. The Anglo-American tradition of free speech arose in the shadow of self-abstracted statesmen like Pericles, Cato, and Marcus Aurelius and, to a lesser degree, self-destructive mourners like Achilles, Antigone, and again Cato. With the waning of Greco-Roman antiquity as a moral and political model in Anglo-American education and culture, or more explicitly, of the genteel version of *Romanitas,* the notion of self-abstraction has become detached from its intellectual moorings and has sometimes drifted into hard-boiled masculinity or just-doing-my-job professionalism. Legitimations of Stoic public character since the late nineteenth century have often lacked the cultural and literary context to sustain them. The engine of professional objectivity, like that of civic self-denial, runs on nonrenewable moral resources; once they are used up, the defense of free speech can become arid and absolutist. One question taken up in this book is whether the gist of these doctrines can be saved without the brutality and machismo that long followed them.

The long history of disinterestedness dates probably to something primal in human history, the ecstatic emptying of the self before the sacred. For the ancient Greeks theoretical contemplation (*theōria*) meant transcending one's particularity. As Socrates says in the *Phaedo*, philosophy means learning how to die. Before the sublime vastness of the universe we sense our mortal puniness. *Theōria* is related to "theater," both of which come from the Greek verb *theaō*, meaning to look. (This link is also preserved in the Latinate tie of "speculation" and "spectacle.") To look upon the universe in its beauty and order (we get the word cosmetic from *kosmos*) was to abandon oneself to something greater, and *theōria* may originally have suggested out-of-body experiences practiced in the mystery cults that sought to glimpse the place beyond the heavens Plato mentioned in the *Phaedrus*. Such abandonment of body and soul had both cognitive and moral aspects, since order was not only seen but helped impregnate the soul with new truth. To view the cosmos, the self had to be purged. Part of this vision persists in the idea that science is an activity to which partisan interests are indifferent (i.e., objectivity). But the moral or aesthetic notion— that theory reveals the good and the beautiful as well as the true—has gone underground today.[37] Cognitive self-abandonment still is supposed to have a direct moral and political benefit.

Stoic and other ancient potions shape the free speech story not only in the vision of the moral life of the citizen, but also in the vision of the shape of public space.[38] Stoics praised the order of nature as the model for human life and rationality. Seen under the aspect of eternity, all people are kin, all countries are one's homeland, and no personal pain or worry is of any consequence. Cosmopolitanism—being a citizen (*politēs*) of the world (*kosmos*)—is a concept of Stoic origin. Indifference to one's own pain is in many ways the ethical analogue to the political act of toleration. The big picture vanquishes potential upset and offense. Stoicism gives a vision of public space as both ordered and beyond the control of any individual, and

---

37. Here I summarize Jürgen Habermas, "Knowledge and Human Interests" (1965), appendix to *Knowledge and Human Interests,* trans. Jeremy J. Shapiro (Boston: Beacon, 1971), 301–17.

38. For lucid and witty guidance in theorizing public space, see Michael Warner, *Publics and Counterpublics* (New York: Zone, 2002).

like many ancient teachings, exhorts us to love our fate (*amor fati*). In his claim that uncoordinated private enterprise adds up to public order, Adam Smith sits squarely in the neo-Stoic tradition, something that is even clearer in his moral theory. When Mill claims that censorship is a claim to infallibility, he echoes the old Stoic criticism of the hubris of forgetting that one is mortal. In the Stoics and their latter-day liberal followers, public openness licenses the ignoring of consequences. *Fiat libertas, pereat mundus.* Let there be freedom, though the world perish. The liberal public is a machine that will go of itself. Much that is good and bad in liberal thought owes to Stoic sources.

I know of no clearer example of how classic (generally) and Stoic (specifically) notions inform the notions of public and private than the statement of Sir George Cornewall Lewis in 1832:

> *Public,* as opposed to *private,* is that which has no immediate relation to any specified person or persons, but may directly concern any member or members of the community, without distinction. Thus the acts of a magistrate, or a member of a legislative assembly, done by them in those capacities, are called public; the acts done by the same persons towards their family or friends, or in their dealings with strangers for their own peculiar purposes, are called private. So a theatre, or a place of amusement, is said to be public not because it is actually visited by every member of the community, but because it is open to all indifferently; and any person may, if he desire, enter it. The same remark applies to public-houses, public inns, public meetings, &c. The publication of a book is the exposing of it to sale in such a manner that it may be procured by any person who desires to purchase it; it would be equally published, if not a single copy was sold. In the language of our law, public appear to be distinguished from private acts of parliament, on the ground that the one class directly affects the whole community, the other some definite person or persons.[39]

Though Cornewall Lewis does not explicitly talk of classical virtue or enlightened self-suspension, the key Stoic themes are all here: impersonality, indifference, universality, publication as open exposure. The public involves official "capacities"; the private concerns "peculiar purposes" or "definite persons." The public, like a statue, remains invariant regardless of audience or response. Availability, not reception, is the criterion of publicity (the BBC defended its unwatched program on precisely these grounds). The actual audience does not affect the public nature of the act. Public places are open to all indifferently.[40] Private places, in contrast, may limit membership without censure. A book would be equally published whether

39. Cornewall Lewis, *Remarks on the Use and Abuse of Some Political Terms,* 163–64.

40. Cornewall Lewis's definition is also classic in the sense that only men can be "any person," given that women found it hard to enter public inns and meetings "indifferently."

it sold any copies or not. Individual persons are irrelevant to an act of parliament.[41] The public is a place of indifference, an open empty space where personality does not matter. This conviction resonates through most twentieth-century thinking about mass communication. The ethic of the public, in a curious way, is not activity but passivity. Nowhere is there such a memorial to the virtue of passivity as the liberal hope that citizens can refrain from lashing out against the speech they hate. Perhaps this is the best way to save the long, deep ethic of Stoic withdrawal from its masochistically macho pleasure in pain.

THE METHOD OF PERVERSITY

Some may find the mission of this book too precious. Why in a world of increasingly concentrated corporate and state power in communications should one trouble oneself with the philosophical program of free speech or the foundations of democratic communication theory? Why in a world where poverty is a huge problem should one criticize humanitarianism's pity, condescension, or imperialism (as I do in chap. 6)? Why in a world filled with countries where censorship is still a major problem should one complain about the moral capital that people can accrue by waging war on censorship? Why, in short, pick at the foibles of the well-intended when there is so much more obvious evil from the ill-intended or the oblivious? No doubt fighting injustice and securing a deep respect for free speech, publication, worship, assembly, and creativity in all their infinite variety are crucial. Yet the irreducible pluralism of the world prevents any program— even the liberal one—from predominating without question. This book attempts to treat the problem of liberalism's illiberal tendencies. Though it opposes liberal high dudgeon, my argument is not censorious. It wants to perform surgical debridement on the illiberal argument culture around core liberal beliefs. "The doctrine of hatred must be preached as the counteraction of the doctrine of love when that pulses and whines," said Emerson.[42] Sometimes one must part a path through the guano.

Without feeding on its opposite, liberal thought withers. Its preying on transgression deserves to be more explicit. Conscious perversity is usually

---

41. S. I. Benn and G. F. Gaus, *Public and Private in Social Life* (New York: St. Martin's, 1983), 31, call Cornewall Lewis's definition the best statement of the liberal vision of the public, but he is drawing on his classical education and interest in philology and is in fact quite critical of liberals such as Jeremy Bentham.

42. Ralph Waldo Emerson, "Self-Reliance," in *Selected Writings of Emerson,* ed. Donald McQuade (New York: Modern Library, 1981), 133.

practiced more often by liberalism's foes. Mocking bourgeois propriety, Marx indulged in a bit of black humor by praising the enormous productivity of the criminal, who, much more than the proprietor, exemplifies the logic of capitalism: the criminal sustains not only police and jailors, but also novelists and social workers, and so on.[43] Nietzsche, sick of a pulsing and whining doctrine of love, argued that pity (*Mitleid*), sometimes thought to be an unmixed moral good, was the tool of an aggressive and subtle *Schadenfreude,* a delight in other people's suffering. In *Discipline and Punish* Foucault opens with a terrifyingly vivid description of a 1757 public execution: his point was not to indulge in a bout of nostalgia for the good old days of torture, as it might at first seem, but rather to show what is lost by the humanitarian horror of physical pain. The dean of contemporary cultural studies, Stuart Hall, with his colleagues, suggested that "mugging" in 1970s Britain created a moral panic that was more dangerous than the risk of being mugged: one is a street crime, the other is an oppressive social system resulting from a history of colonialism, collusion between the news media, "common sense," and the state.[44] The muggers are mugged by racism, as it were, but the authors take pains to neither praise violence nor treat it as an open-and-shut moral issue. Stuart Hall and colleagues risk perversity—suspending moral condemnation—to read crime as cultural and racial politics; they practice what Søren Kierkegaard called a "teleological suspension of the ethical."[45] All these theorists mine the dark side of moral oppositions—as Paul and Milton did before them.

Pointing out the crime of the culturally favored and the strength of the rejected portion is a frequent gesture in recent critical theory. Derrida repeatedly shows how the supposed effect turns out to be a cause. The art of deconstruction reveals how the accursed part that the social order has sacrificially singled out as exceptional and blameworthy actually represents the symptomatic truth of the whole order. The very fact of its exceptionalism reveals the processes of self-justification (rejective pure-making) that depend on exclusion. (Deconstruction is the technical name for the act of selective perversity.) William Blake's "proverb" suggests the method nicely and lays bare the alliance of liberty and transgression: "Prisons are built with stones of Law, Brothels with bricks of Religion." Public institutions

43. On the productivity of crime, see Ernest Mandel, *Delightful Murder: A Social History of the Crime Story* (London: Pluto Press, 1984).

44. Stuart Hall, Chas Critcher, Tony Jefferson, John Clarke, and Brian Roberts, *Policing the Crisis: Mugging, the State, and Law and Order* (New York: Holmes & Meier, 1978).

45. Søren Kierkegaard, *Fear and Trembling: A Dialectical Lyric* by Johannes de Silentio (1843), trans. Alastair Hannay (New York: Penguin, 1985), 83ff.

charged with uprightness might be secretly in league with the things they denounce. Blake, Marx, Nietzsche, Foucault, Derrida, and Hall all fit in the long post-Miltonic tradition of sympathy for the devil and redemption of criminal vitality. They sometimes like to flirt with hellish naughtiness, but their responsible critical purpose is to rescue the use from the abuse, to show that the part is not the whole. They show us how the ironic circular method of performance by liberals might be practiced more rigorously. And yet, because prisons feed off of law does not make all laws corrupt, as our sophomore deconstructionists might fancy. Just because mugging is a culturally constructed crime does not free the person who whacked me on the head and stole my wallet from the consequences of the law. Offenses must come, but woe unto him through whom they come (Matt. 18:7). The tragedy of transgression is that though it bears larger fruit, the transgressor must still pay the penalty.

Following free speech theory upstream to its headwaters brings us to a much larger question: when may we break the law? When is it good to be bad? Despite the stridently secular stance of civil libertarians, many of whom are still busy fighting off the Inquisition, the free speech story's central tenet that transgression can be redeemed for the benefit of the social whole has deep roots in the theological idea of the fortunate fall, the *felix culpa,* the notion that servitude in Egypt made the people of Israel better. This book probes, ultimately, the mystery of iniquity: how to deal with the harsh moral fact that evil seems in some way necessary and even at times beneficial.

This book is an exercise in anamnesis—unforgetting—that attempts to sound, banish, and rebuild the liberal tradition. It is an immanent critique and reconstruction of the default philosophy governing the relation of communication and democracy in the United States, England, and many other places. Its central method is to inventory intellectual resources, that is, to reread major texts by canonical figures to illuminate the choices and dilemmas that bother us in public and private life today. This is not to offer a botanical history of ideas but to attempt to understand current problems in the firelight of past arguments. Just because you cannot find a distinguished and articulate mouthpiece for a particular intellectual position (though you usually can) does not mean that it is not viable or influential. Philosophical texts can stand in as more articulate versions of the grammars and legacies that persist in ordinary thought. In this book I try to practice intellectual history as cultural criticism. The book reads canonic texts—Paul's epistles, Milton's *Areopagitica,* Smith's *Theory of Moral Sentiments,* Mill's *On Liberty,* key decisions of the U.S. Supreme Court—as comments on larger moral and political problems. There may well be better ways to illuminate media and public life today; so much thinking and research remain to be done about the abundance of media content and channels, the alteration of modes of interaction, the respacing of communication, the political economy of global media industries, legal and policy transformations in a neoliberal era, and the tectonic shifts induced by digital technologies.[46] There are many laborers in the vineyard; this book aims to clarify the intellectual stakes and sources of current debates. It ponders media as if moral philosophy mattered and moral philosophy as if media mattered. I trace arguments to the source not only because the water is purer, but because the arguments are often balder and bolder; not because Mill and Holmes, say, made my students speak a certain way, but because they offer the strongest possible version of the argument to grapple with.

The book, like Gaul, is essentially divided into three parts. Chapters 1–2 treat the productivity of crime, and seek to enrich free expression theory by showing its long flirtation with transgression and sin. Chapters 3–5 show the unacknowledged centrality of suffering in liberal visions of public life. They examine varieties of moral suspension, ranging from self-control before pain, tolerance of offensive speech, and sublimating one's personal preference to the rigors of data. Such suspension is an unacknowledged deposit from the ancients within the principles and practice of public life in the Anglo-American world. John Stuart Mill and his legacy preside over all three chapters. Chapters 6–7 explore democratic communication theory and practice today, focusing especially on what it means to be a witness. The book's structure is at the same time chiastic: chapters 1 and 7 ponder the advantages of impersonality; chapters 2 and 6 explore the abyss; chapters 3 and 5 address cognitive abstemiousness; and the First Amendment sits at the center in chapter 4. In a previous book I examined the history of the idea of communication, focusing especially on communication between two people in private settings. This book takes up questions of mass communication and the public sphere. *Speaking into the Air*'s subtext was eros; this book's subtext is democracy. Since the Greek notions of eros and democracy have always gone together (minimally, eros is the mediated absence of two bodies, and democracy the mediated presence of many bodies), there is a deep kinship between the two books. Both aim to contribute to the project of understanding the meaning of communication in the modern world.

46. I have attempted an overview of the key issues confronting us today in "Media and Communications," in *Blackwell Companion to Sociology*, ed. Judith M. Blau (Oxford: Basil Blackwell, 2001), 16–29.

CHAPTER ONE

Saint Paul's Shudder

Sin is behovely.
—T. S. Eliot, *Little Gidding*

THE PUZZLE OF PAUL

Paul of Tarsus is one of those figures about whom too much has been written and said; his name is invoked for good and evil throughout the world. He is often associated with some of the most troubled sides of Christianity: the institutional church and its oppression of women, sexual minorities, and Jews.[1] Holy man or empire-builder, proud Roman citizen or defier of earthly powers, theological codifier or religious ecstatic, arch-patriarch or voice for equality of the sexes, joyous proclaimer that the law is dead or life-hating foe of the flesh: there is not much consensus about who he was. We hardly know what to call him. Saint Paul? Saul? Paul of Tarsus? This intense man stood, perhaps more than any other figure in history, at the railroad switch between Hebrew, Greek, Roman, and Christian civilizations. Whether he distilled or destroyed Jesus's message is still an open question. His legacies, real and imagined, are diverse: sources for universalism, racism, Protestantism, Romanticism, Marxism, liberalism, even psychoanalysis, can be found in him. Augustine saw in Paul a forerunner fighting the battle of the flesh and the spirit; Luther read him as foreshadowing his own religious agony; Renan, speaking for much of the nineteenth century,

---

1. Alain Badiou, *Saint Paul: La fondation de l'universalisme* (Paris: Presses universitaires de France, 1997), 1–3.

took him as the founder of institutional Christianity and thus, to a large extent, the perverter of the religion of Jesus. For Nietzsche, Paul epitomized
what he most hated—in what must rank as one of the most magnificently
willful receptions of another's views in the history of thought, considering
the remarkable structural similarities in their main ideas. More recently
Paul has been resurrected as an interlocutor in cultural theory and philosophy by atheists and Catholics, Jews and Protestants, and the odd Lacanian:
Giorgio Agamben, Alain Badiou, Stanislas Breton, Daniel Boyarin, and
Slavoj Žižek.[2] Paul anticipates modern philosophical terms such as Hegel's
dialectic, Marx's *class,* Nietzsche's *anti-Christ,* and Weber's *calling.*[3] "Paul
and the reactions to Paul are thus a major source for a historicization of our
cultural predicament."[4]

One can study Paul only, to use his phrase, with "fear and trembling"
(Phil. 2:12). One central difficulty is the sheer militancy of his doctrine, his
pressure to force a commitment on the part of the reader. To appropriate his
thought for purposes other than the direct preaching of the cross is seemingly to violate his omnipresent purpose. His boastfulness, self-referential-
ity, apparent inconsistency, defensiveness, and tirades have long constituted
a high barrier for some readers. His extraordinarily evocative eloquence, his
knack for parallelism, and his excursions into hymn and poetry, on the
other hand, have made him deeply beloved of others. How many weddings
have been graced by his chapter on love, 1 Corinthians 13? Augustine called
Paul "our great orator."[5] Paul can erupt into great geysers of eloquence. He
is the master of the denunciation, the preemptive self-clarification, the
pithy nugget, or a swoop into the valley of mortality. The occasional fury
and violence of his language sometimes seem at odds with the attitudes he
counsels. As Matthew Arnold noted, "Never surely did such a controversial-
ist, such a master of sarcasm and invective, commend, with such manifest
sincerity and such persuasive emotion, the qualities of meekness and gen-
tleness!"[6]

John Locke, one of many readers of Paul in the liberal tradition and one

2. Giorgio Agamben, *Le temps qui reste: Un commentaire de l'Epitre aux Romains,* trans. Judith Revel (Paris: Éditions Payot et Rivages, 2000); Badiou, *Saint Paul;* Daniel Boyarin, *A Radical
Jew: Paul and the Politics of Identity* (Berkeley: University of California Press, 1994); Stanislas Breton, *Saint Paul* (Paris: Presses universitaires de France, 1988); Slavoj Žižek, *The Ticklish Subject:
The Absent Center of Political Ontology* (London: Verso, 1999), chap. 3.

3. Agamben, *Le temps qui reste.*

4. Boyarin, *A Radical Jew,* 9.

5. Augustine, *De doctrina christiana,* IV.7.

6. Matthew Arnold, *St. Paul and Protestantism* ([1869]; New York: Macmillan, 1897), 32.

of the few who explicitly admitted it, tried to account for the peculiar plasticity of his texts, which, Locke noted, abound in meaning for ordinary readers but puzzle the learned. He attributed the diverse reception of Paul to several factors: (1) the nature of epistolary writing, in which much may be tacitly understood between writer and recipient; (2) the odd character of New Testament Greek generally, which is heavily influenced by Hebrew and Aramaic; (3) Paul's loose use of personal pronouns (such as his frequent floating "we"); and (4) the posthumous division of his writings into chapters and verses so "that not only the common people take the verses usually for distinct aphorisms."[7] Though he did not add another, more recently noted factor, (5) the dense interleaving of first-century rabbinical and Hellenistic culture, Locke fingers some of the key problems. Lost shared references, a moody style, an alien world, and fragmentary format: all these things make Paul one of the great inkblots for nearly two millennia of opinion. Paul's letters are a script from which both friends and foes since have taken speaking parts.

To read Paul as a theorist of communication, as I do here, is also to enter into communication difficulties with a figure who perhaps best exemplifies the principle that authorship is a slippery matter of authority more than of who really put pen to paper. All we have of Paul are communications at a distance, composed in conditions of absence, to specific people and situations of which we have often only the vaguest notion. All of his writings are occasional, oriented to a specific situation of specific people. We have no general treatise from him, though the epistle to the Romans has often been read this way. We still know his letters by their intended audiences (Romans, Corinthians, etc.), in contrast to the general New Testament letters known by their ascribed authors—James, Peter, John, and Jude. Paul's epistles were not theoretical treatises sent to whom it may concern, but traces of interactions, and we have access to only his half of the conversation. We are cryptographers eavesdropping on messages not intended for us. We belated readers of Paul are in a situation similar to that of his first readers: deciphering texts sent from afar. Discourse liberated from an immediate situation, the rhetorical brilliance of his letters creates and implies new situations, and writes itself into many others. Since the first century people have been writing in his name, and just what Paul wrote has been a puzzle that modern scholarship has tried to untangle (seven of the letters

7. "Preface: An Essay for the Understanding of St. Paul's Epistles, by consulting St. Paul himself," in *A Paraphrase and Notes on the Epistles of Saint Paul: The Works of John Locke* ([London: Thomas Tegg, 1823]; reprint, Aalen, Germany: Scientia Verlag, 1963), 8: 3–23.

attributed to him in the New Testament canon have escaped serious doubts about Pauline authorship among modern scholars, the so-called undisputed letters: Romans; 1 and 2 Corinthians; Galatians; 1 Thessalonians; Philippians; and Philemon, all of which were written between 50 CE and 58 CE). After his death Paul grew into texts he did not author in the same way that his audiences, once the members of tiny Christian communities throughout the Hellenized Mediterranean, subsequently grew into hundreds of millions. (Modern scholarship calls Ephesians, 2 Thessalonians, and Colossians "deutero-Pauline," and 1 and 2 Timothy and Titus "pseudo-Pauline.") Paul's literary remnants are a giant switchboard for connecting senders and receivers in a communication network distended over space and time. As with Homer and other founders of traditions, mysterious authorship is often as enabling as it is debilitating.[8] That Paul's name was an attractive authority for early Christian writers suggests what W. H. Auden said of Freud: "to us he is no more a person / now but a whole climate of opinion."[9] Reading Paul's letters has constituted perhaps the central hermeneutical enterprise in the European tradition.

The discourse-network of Paul's time informs his reflections on communication, specifically, about the difference between speaking by letter and speaking in person, presence and absence.[10] Paul effectively adapts the letter as a genre of preaching and intervention in Christian culture. Paul's letters were dictated to an assistant (except for Galatians where Paul admits, not perhaps without a pride in classy sloppiness like the handwriting of doctors today, to have written the letter with his own hand; Gal. 6:11). His scribe for the epistle to the Romans was appropriately named Tertius ("third party" or "witness" in Latin), who takes the liberty of adding his own greeting to Paul's long list of personal greetings to the saints at Rome (Rom. 16:22). His letters began and ended as voiced speech and were designed to be read and heard aloud in the assembly (see 1 Thes. 5:27), not as private silent reading, which was relatively rare in antiquity anyway. Few people in Paul's time would ever even face a written document.[11] The intimate letter, sent from one person to another for their eyes only, is historically recent. There were no envelopes or mailboxes in the Roman Empire. "The transmission

8. James Porter, "Homer—The Very Idea," *Arion*, 10.2 (2002): 57–86.

9. W. H. Auden, "In Memory of Sigmund Freud," ll. 67–68.

10. The notion of discourse-network I take from Friedrich A. Kittler, *Aufschreibesysteme, 1800/1900*. 3rd ed. (Munich: Fink, 1995).

11. Richard Wallace and Wynne Williams, *The Three Worlds of Paul of Tarsus* (London: Routledge, 1998), 58–59. See also Jesper Svenbro, *Phrasikleia: Anthropologie de la lecture en grèce ancienne* (Paris: Éditions la Découverte, 1988).

of letters was entirely a matter of private arrangements between individuals. Although there was an imperial post, it was exclusively for the use of the emperor's staff, and it was not available to the general public. To send a letter to another city, it was necessary to find someone who was going there and would be willing to take it."[12] (Phoebe the *diakonos* delivered Paul's letter to the Romans, for instance.) Paul's use of the epistle certainly had cultural precedents: the *epistula* was a literary genre in Roman culture, and Cicero's or Seneca's letters were intended as generalizable ethical counsel, not private advice, just as Acts, like the Gospel of Luke, was addressed to Theophilus ("friend of God"), a name with perhaps both a generic and a specific reference (as Luke-Acts was probably intended for publication on the Roman literary market). Addresses, like authors, are usually approximations.

All letters are apologies for absence, but Paul's letters also seek to explain Christ's absence, the delay of the *parousia* (presence, i.e., his return). The proximate cause of his first letter (that we know of), 1 Thessalonians, is the concern that Christ's return, which Paul had announced, was taking longer than expected. (Deutero-Pauline 2 Thessalonians tries to clarify 1 Thessalonians.) We might read Paul as an apologist for absence, and communication theorists are always more interesting when they start with absence rather than presence. Paul is absent from his friends; Christ is absent from the church; the church is absent from itself, being spread across diverse cities. Paul's epistolary practice, as Peter Simonson argues, figures the church as a community dispersed in space, not unlike the social configurations later enabled by print culture and broadcasting. Paul's vision of a collective that is united ritually at a distance is a central source for the western tradition of theorizing mass communication and anticipates print culture's national readerships and electronic media's simultaneous but dispersed audiences.[13] The salutation that opens 1 Corinthians, for instance, is addressed to "the church of God which is in Corinth . . . together with all those who are calling upon the name of our Lord Jesus Christ in whatever place [*en panti topō*], both theirs and ours" (1 Cor. 1:2). Here is the imagined "horizontal comradeship" among a geographically dispersed population that Benedict Anderson regards as the origin of the modern nation.[14] The

12. Wallace and Williams, *The Three Worlds of Paul*, 16

13. Peter Simonson, "Assembly, Rhetoric, and Widespread Community: Mass Communication in Paul of Tarsus," *Journal of Media and Religion* 2 (2003): 165–82.

14. Benedict Anderson, *Imagined Communities: Reflections on the Origin and Spread of Nationalism.* 2nd ed. (London: Verso, 1991). Paul's collection for the Jerusalem church is a kind of diasporic space-bridging and may serve as a founding moment of distant humanitarianism. See

phrase "theirs and ours" is grammatically ambiguous, suggesting both "their Lord and ours" or "their place and ours." Either reading gives us a far-flung assembly—Paul's term for church, *ekklēsia*, classically signified a political assembly—united by forms of communication that bind people together across various places, an assembly that, as the subsequent history of his letters suggests, can stretch across hemispheres and millennia. Paul calls on the church; the church, in turn, calls upon Christ. He calls a body that is calling. His letter serves as the first step in a two-step relay, the communicative means of constituting the assembly, which then, in step two, unites in calling yet another source. Paul joins the two key types of mass communication—broadcasting (one calling to many) and acclamation (many calling to one). Paul and Christ take similar structural positions in the circuit of communication: twin termini, the mouth (Paul) or ear (Christ) of the calling. Apostle/epistle: agents that are sent to extend presence across distance and absence.

In a sense the problem of how to read Paul was alive from the beginnings of the New Testament canon. This is a chief topic of many of the letters directly from Paul, as well as the letters that purport to be from him (e.g., Ephesians or 1–2 Timothy) or clearly respond to him (2 Peter, Jude).[15] Acts, written decades after Paul's death, weighs in on his identity as well, portraying him as a heroic missionary to the Gentiles, performing miracles, surviving shipwrecks, defending his doctrine before magistrates, judges, philosophers, and priests, on a triumphant journey through the eastern Mediterranean world that culminates geographically and symbolically in Rome. The Paul of the letters is an equally cantankerous but different fellow from the Paul of Acts. Paul in Acts is a courageous crusader, a brilliant master of the standard genres of Hellenistic eloquence, an unstoppable force; in the epistles he is a more gnarled and tender figure, all too human compared with the resourceful hero of Acts, by turns apologetic, furious, browbeating, and rhapsodic, gifted with an original theological and moral imagination of the very first order. Acts also makes Paul a student of Gamaliel (Acts 22:3), the respected rabbi who defends the young Christian movement in a strikingly libertarian way. Noting an earlier messianic movement that came to a bad ending (the short life of so many past "fighting faiths"), Gamaliel exhorts the Sanhedrin: "Let them alone: for if this council or this work be of humans, it will be destroyed; but if it is of God, you will not be able to

---

Günther Bornkamm, *Paul: Paulus*, trans. D. M. G. Stalker (New York: Harper & Row, 1971), 40–42, 58.

15. Thanks to Christopher Mount for this and many other helpful suggestions.

destroy it" (Acts 5:38–39). Either way toleration is the best policy, leaving truth or error to fend for itself. Gamaliel the Elder—and the rabbinic tradition—are thus one source for what we think of as liberal tolerance, as I suggest below.

My aim is to read Paul as a theorist of communication and of public space, including as a source of ideas about liberty of expression. Paul offers a variety of resources toward understanding communication and public life today. Fortunately this approach requires little straining, since liberty and communication are among the most prominent themes in his letters. It exceeds my competence to explore the details of Paul's situation in first-century culture or discuss important but technical debates about exegesis. Paul has been given new life in recent decades by the so-called new perspective on Paul, which saves him from being the sole interpretive property of theologians (especially the Lutheran tradition, which long read him as a rebel against Judaism) and makes him available to cultural history as one of the most interesting and influential thinkers in world history.[16] Recognizing Paul's Jewishness is not only intellectually important, but also morally and politically important, since it allows for fresh recognitions of affinity and ancestry. The founders of Christianity were Jews: this obvious fact has rarely been grappled with fully (it is a variant of the foreign-founders script).[17] Despite the placement of Paul's letters in the New Testament after the four Gospels and Acts, they deserve a special status not only as the earliest surviving canonical documents of early Christianity but also as an unparalleled glimpse into the spiritual autobiography of a first-century Jew.[18]

To use his own term, Paul is a figure (*typos*) of things to come (Rom. 5:14). Nineteen and a half centuries later, brief passages call for attention as the embryos of entire cultural problems we face today in public communication. Single phrases in Paul's writings now resound with meaning for our contemporary condition. This is the principle of retroactive enrichment: the accumulation of intellectual residues makes texts richer in maturity than they were in youth.[19] Paul is a rich quarry for the variety of options

16. Discussed by N. T. Wright, "A Fresh Perspective on Paul?" *Bulletin of the John Rylands Library* 83 (2001): 21–39; and Boyarin, *A Radical Jew*. Key figures in this movement are E. P. Sanders and W. D. Davies.

17. Bonnie Honig, *Democracy and the Foreigner* (Princeton, N.J.: Princeton University Press, 2001), chap. 2.

18. Boyarin, *A Radical Jew*.

19. John Durham Peters, "Retroactive Enrichment: Raymond Williams's *Culture and Society*," in *Canonic Texts in Media Research: Are There Any? Should There Be? How About These?*, ed. Elihu Katz et al. (Cambridge: Polity Press, 2003), 217–30. For a richer account, see Ralph Waldo

that confront us for thinking about public space: the notion, shared by liberals and civil libertarians, that everything is permitted; the tactic, shared by "abyss-redeemers" such as John Milton and his many legatees, of edging as close as possible to the crest of the abyss without falling in; the antinomian or Romantic faith that strength of conscience has the power to define right and wrong; the pragmatist sense that collisions of interest must inevitably compromise world-making ambitions; and the insistence that knowledge is not necessarily the best way to cope with evil. I will focus on a repertoire of attitudes in Paul's writings: the advantages of absence; the priority of the onlooker; the (uneasy) demarcation of zones of religious neutrality; the benefits of impersonality; the willingness to play host to dangerous doctrine; and the hope that crime can be redeemed. This family of gestures makes an important intervention in contemporary debates about social theory generally and free expression in particular. My point is not that the historical Paul necessarily thought all these things, but that his texts authorize such thoughts. Paul gives us almost everything that recent civil libertarians do—respect for autonomy and appreciation for liberty—without the nihilism or moral thinness. As a religious theorist of liberty who encourages critical analysis of self and society, Paul is suggestively situated beyond (or before) the impasse of critical rationality, cultural relativism, and fundamentalism.

THE CASE OF MEAT AT CORINTH

Paul's thinking on liberty and publicity is nowhere clearer than in his arbitration of what the saints in Corinth could eat. What he said exactly is disputed, since it is hard always to tell what should be taken as his own voice, as a quotation, or even as ventriloquism or parody of the other's supposed viewpoint. My interest here is not so much what he said as the bundle of problems that he takes up in thinking about liberty in the face of an offended conscience, the central problem of modern free expression theory since Milton.

As in the courts, so in religion: mundanely intricate fact situations can lead to profound doctrinal rulings. Corinth in the first century was a prosperous town with an overland passage between an eastern and a western harbor, making it a strategic location for trade in the eastern Mediterranean. The infant Christian community there included both the poor and,

---

Emerson, "Plato," in *Representative Men: Seven Lectures,* ed. Andrew Delblanco (Cambridge, Mass.: Harvard University Press, 1996).

it seems, the eminent.[20] Corinth was also a leading producer of mirrors, a medium of self-construction that Paul famously invoked ("through a glass darkly") in 1 Corinthians 13.[21] Converts to the new movement came from both Jewish and pagan backgrounds. A pressing problem was what to do with the public sacrifices. In both Hebrew and Greek religion, eating animals was a religiously tinged act; in Hebrew, as in Arabic, the same word means to butcher and to sacrifice. "In pagan religion, a sacrifice was a meal shared between the god and the worshippers."[22] Further, in ancient Greece meat was rare in the diet, especially for the lower classes, whose chance to eat it would be confined to polis-sponsored banquets or festivals dedicated to the gods of the city. The question was: should followers of Christ join in feasting with the pagan gods; shun even the thought of doing so; or, denying that the gods exist, pragmatically take advantage of the opportunity to partake of a nice meal?

Some of the members in Corinth took the third option. Claiming to possess knowledge (*gnōsis*) that freed them from cultural-religious worry, they apparently argued that since there was only one true god, and the pagan gods were nullities, they could eat freely (1 Cor. 8:4). Why let scruples left over from a dead religion interfere with a tasty roast? Paul agreed with the so-called Gnostics in theory, but not in practice. Those with *gnōsis* risked harming their less intrepid brothers and sisters. "Since some have been so accustomed to idols until now, they still think of the food they eat as food offered to an idol; and their conscience, being weak, is defiled" (1 Cor. 8:7). Those who possess higher knowledge should take responsibility for the effects that the spectacle of their choices might have on the weak. "But take care that this liberty of yours does not somehow become a stumbling block to the weak. For if others see you, who possess knowledge, eating in the temple of an idol, might they not, since their conscience is weak, be encouraged to the point of eating food sacrificed to idols?" (1 Cor. 8:9–10). Those with a strong conscience may eat freely, knowing that the gods are nothings, until their actions pass within the range of spectators possessing less robust consciences. The eyes of others alter private liberty: this is a strange and delicate moral standard. The culinary situation is subject to radical redefinition by the gaze of the other. If you go into the markets, Paul

20. Gerd Theissen, *The Social Setting of Pauline Christianity: Essays on Corinth* (Philadelphia: Fortress Press), chap. 2.

21. Eugen Netoliczka, "Katoptron," in *Pauly's Real-Encyclopädie der classischen Altertumswissenschaft*, rev. ed. (Stuttgart: J. B. Metzler, 1922), 11: 36. Thanks to Robert Hariman for this lead and suggestions including the notion of "Pauline pragmatism."

22. Wallace and Williams, *The Three Worlds of Paul*, 120.

exhorts, buy and eat whatever you want without worry about religious scruples (1 Cor. 10:25). If you are invited to dine at the house of a nonbeliever, "eat whatever is set before you without raising any question on the ground of conscience" (1 Cor. 10:27). You may munch happily away—unless others are present with more highly tuned scruples: "if someone says to you, 'This has been offered in sacrifice,' then do not eat it, out of consideration for the one who informed you and for the sake of conscience—conscience, I say, not your own, but that of the other" (1 Cor. 10:28–29). A feast is suddenly transmuted by a speech act performing someone else's religious worry. The other's conscience pollutes my meat. For Paul the limit of my liberty is the other's conscience—harder doctrine than the liberal notion that the private conscience is impregnable to regulation from without.[23] Paul is a libertarian absolutist in theory but a friend of social responsibility in practice.

Paul walks a tightrope between complete libertarianism and conscientious civility. "All things are lawful unto me, but all things are not expedient; all things are lawful for me, but all things edify not" (1 Cor. 10:23). What a gap lies between the first and second parts of each of those phrases. "All things are lawful" suggests a wild radicalism that two millennia of antinomian interpreters have taken in various directions, heretical and otherwise; the book of Jude, for instance, seems written to refute licentious readings of Paul. "All things edify not" suggests an acute sense of social decency or perhaps even a repressive policy of preemptively regulating speech and conduct. Paul's strange mixture of radicalism and neighborliness, of bold endorsement that anything goes and cautious worry about the smallest offense, and of scruple-free action and scrupulous monitoring of effects on others makes him an inkblot for free expression theory. We can read in him the full intellectual genome of current controversies. He offends liberals with his voluntary self-suppression of liberty to soothe the scandalized other; he offends fundamentalists with his notion that all things are lawful; and he offends relativists with his conviction that nothing matters but the crucified Messiah. Paul was a testy character, and he has lost none of his power to annoy after all these years.

Whether Paul considered food a zone of religious indifference is unclear, but what is interesting here is his displacement from the object to the subject, from the meat itself to the conscience of the eater. Though the historical Paul seems to have thought food a crossroads haunted by diverse spiri-

23. Compare the Talmudic notion of *marit ayin,* the sin of committing an apparent sin in the eyes of somebody else.

tual powers (a relevant notion today, when food and dieting constitute the central spiritual drama for many people in the planet's rich nations), his style of argument anticipates modern understandings of toleration: nothing we take in is unholy in itself, though our attitudes may make it so. If it is eaten with an unhindered conscience, great. (Paul's solution might seem to favor the wealthy, who can afford to eat their meat behind closed doors and out of the eyeshot of the offendable.) If it is eaten in defiance of the tender conscience of an observer, then this is sin, an offense against a brother.

Paul's attitude about other religious positivities is similar. Take the Sabbath day. "Some judge one day to be better than another, while others judge all days to be alike. Let all be fully convinced in their own minds" (Rom. 14:5). We could celebrate the Sabbath on any day of the week if we are only firm enough in our conviction. Circumcision, a continuing sore point in his mediation among Jews, Christians, and Jewish Christians, did not matter in the foreskin but in the heart. Paul seems to deny the religious importance of key Jewish religious practices—kosher laws, Sabbath observance, male circumcision. Dogmatic sacredness drains away from religious objects and rituals: it is all up to the purity of the will. Hegel's point about Christianity as the religion of inwardness rests upon such a reading of Paul, though one might pare away Hegel's echo of Luther's view that Paul was the critical rejecter of Jewish religion as stolidly concrete and legalistically outward. What Milton does with books, Paul does with food: he leaves purity up to the eye of the beholder. Paul's hint of object-neutrality is distant from the view expressed in Deuteronomy that when the false gods of other peoples are destroyed, not even the gold may be salvaged; for the Torah nothing touched by foreign gods can be considered neutral matter. Though Paul shared the fundamental Jewish distrust of idolatry and was alarmed at the effects of demon-infested food on the weak, he did not categorically regard meat sacrificed to the Hellenistic deities as unclean. He placed profanation in the far more unstable environment of the private conscience, with fateful historical consequences.

His own summary captures his well-knotted thinking: "nothing is unclean in itself; but it is unclean for anyone who thinks it unclean" (Rom. 14:14). Romans chapter 14 is one of the trickiest texts ever. If the conscience of the other prevails, it can be read as a defense of civility. If private conviction is to triumph, then it is a brief for bold nonconformity, public opinion be damned: "do not let your good be spoken of as evil" (Rom. 14:16). What kind of redeemed mind is it that wilts when it sees another's raised eyebrow? In another key verse in the same chapter, Paul writes: "The faith that you have, have as your own conviction before God. Blessed are those who have no reason to condemn themselves because of what they approve" (Rom. 14:22). Translation difficulties loom in this rendering by the New Revised Standard Version (NRSV, a title consisting of four qualifications in a row). There is no "conviction" in the Greek; the first sentence might be rendered, "let the faith that you have according to yourself be the faith that you have before God"—that is, dare to let your private conviction shape your dealings with God. Paul might seem to be endorsing a moral co-legislation between self and God. The second phrase of verse 22 also lends itself to a more radical translation. The NRSV's "blessed are those who have no reason to condemn themselves" suggests that there might well be good reasons to condemn yourself, as if there were objectively better and worse things to believe. The Greek text says "blessed is he who does not judge himself in that which he approves." Reading daringly, something Paul often encourages if only for brief moments (as I argue below), one could take this as saying something quite different from the NRSV's rendition, such as "blessed is whatever you do without pangs of conscience." "All that is not of faith is sin" says the next verse (Rom. 14:23). Whatever Paul meant, a long antinomian tradition says: blessed are those whose conscience is not afflicted with self-doubts, who are strong enough to defy their own inhibitions. That impurity or sanctity depends on the input of the beholder is an option Paul opens up to later thinkers. With a strong enough conviction (Paul's term *pistis* might be better rendered "conviction" than "faith"), perhaps Adam and Eve could have eaten the fruit of the tree of knowledge without sanction. Emancipation from inhibition is a central theme in Milton's *Areopagitica* that also resounds in later thinking about freedom of expression, with its love of strong-minded assertion without self-consciousness. Samuel Johnson's couplet captures one possible reading of Paul's sense:[24]

> Thy mind, which voluntary doubts molest,
> Asks but its own permission to be blest.

Paul makes the conscience the battlefield of liberty. He seems to authorize a contradictory range of policies from anything-goes absolutism to protectionist decency aimed to shelter the weak. He admires both the boldness of a conscience free from doubt and the brittle conscience sensitive to the slightest perturbation of the other's gaze. Paul gives us a double whammy: bits of his texts both praise a consciousness free of nagging doubts and endorse self-reflection about one's commitments and influences. This is one of his greatest and most difficult legacies; he at once

---

24. "Lines in Hawkesworth's *The Rival*," in *Samuel Johnson*, ed. Donald Greene (Oxford: Oxford University Press, 1984), 32.

praises liberation from inhibition and makes us acutely self-conscious of the complex sources of inhibition. (In the double formula of emancipation from and intense scrutiny of inhibition, Paul is a forerunner of psychoanalysis.) The law, as he famously argues in Romans, brings about sin and a guilty conscience; Christ brings about new life and relief from the works of death. Paul's inward analysis of sin in Romans curiously parallels his social analysis of diet in 1 Corinthians: both sin and scruple emerge from external sources of inhibition. Hegel lampooned this double way of being as the "unhappy consciousness" and found it in Paul, the Stoics, Descartes, and Kant alike.[25] You learn that you were innocent only after you have lost your innocence. That is, knowledge of lost innocence is both the sign of the loss and the loss itself. By making us acutely conscious of our duty to weaker minds and hearts, does Paul tie loopholes to his promise of emancipation? What do you do once you know that it might be better to be free of knowledge? How are we supposed to be firm in our own conviction that the Sabbath should be Friday, Saturday, or Sunday when there are millions of others whose consciences tell them differently? The instability of Paul's *pistis*—both firm enough to mold the cosmos and brittle enough to give way before another's protest—will resonate in later theorists of liberty, such as J. S. Mill (chap. 3).

Though the historical Paul would surely resist the antinomian heresies he seems to hatch, some of his words seem to suggest that strong enough heads can handle anything. If you doubt, you deserve our fallen world. If you do not doubt, you can claim God's blessing for what you are doing, a striking anticipation, both for good and bad, of the post-Kantian idealist and Romantic doctrine of the all-creating subject. Our minds, and other minds, go around staining the world. Or purifying it. Being held responsible for the mood of the entire universe was a major burden for the German and British Romantics, who were certainly late inheritors of Paul's problem of the role of consciousness shaping the universe. "One wandering thought," said Shelley, "pollutes the day."[26] The edifice topples when faith flags. The burning joyful clarity of a free conscience is delicate. Paul's warning against those who still get circumcised after being released from the demands of the law seems partly a rebuke for letting ancient compunctions cloud their newfound liberty (Gal. 5:3). In for a penny, in for a pound: the

25. *Phänomenologie des Geistes*, paras. 207–30. The *Phenomenology* is famously free of proper names, but it is easy to read between the lines.

26. Percy Bysshe Shelley, "Mutability," l. 10, in *The Norton Anthology of English Literature*. 4th ed. (New York: Norton, 1979), 2: 664.

whole law comes crashing in on you once you assent to be circumcised. Minute acts can tilt the cosmos awry. Paul introduces the blight of self-consciousness by celebrating our liberation from it.

The tar baby of self-consciousness also arises in the Sermon on the Mount. As in the discussion of food in 1 Corinthians, Jesus praises a psychic state free from the self-consciousness of being watched. Here it is not only the eyes of others but your own that you need to avoid performing for: let not your right hand know what your left hand is doing (Matt. 6:3). This vivid metaphor suggests a kind of action that is not self-intelligible, a deed not plain to self-consciousness. The Sermon on the Mount notes a species of virtues that grows only on the margins of self-consciousness. The act of giving is susceptible to moral corruption if it turns into theater—even theater with an audience of one, the self. Care for others, like mushrooms and eros, grows best in the dark, away from the sunlight of self-regard. If given self-consciously, gifts threaten to be self-exaltation rather than a benefit to others. Just so, Ben Franklin noticed that his efforts to become humble made him proud of his humility. "I like sincerity. I lack sincerity," wrote the grunge rocker Kurt Cobain.[27] Good deeds must be done indifferently to spectatorship.

In the Christian economy moral goodness is unknown to its possessor, a major departure from the classical conviction represented by Socrates that virtue and knowledge were one. Jesus worries that observation may corrupt the purity of motives; Paul worries that it might stain the happy consciousness of the eater. In both cases the eye of the other (or the self) ruins uninhibited authenticity. Matthew 6 tells us to act without self-observation (though Matthew 5 says to let your light shine). Hannah Arendt, like Hegel, sees Christianity as sealing Plato's retreat from the public realm: the beauty of the polis and its all-consuming citizenship is replaced by membership in an invisible and eternal kingdom.[28] For the ancient Athenians truth shone. The good was glorious and unashamed. It wanted to catch every eye. The idea that you've got to hide your love away would make no sense. There is a massive shift with the conviction that the good lies in dark places. For the classical Greeks there was no salvation in spelunking. But for the Christians (as well as for many other movements in late antiquity), the way of knowledge is hard, and not necessarily conducive to happiness. (This conviction today is a sign of our distance from Socrates, as Hegel, Nietzsche, and Fou-

27. Kurt Cobain, *Journals* (New York: Riverhead Books, 2002).

28. Hannah Arendt, *The Human Condition* (Chicago: University of Chicago Press, 1958). For a similar narrative, see G. W. F. Hegel, "The Positivity of the Christian Religion" (1800), in *Early Theological Writings* (Philadelphia: University of Pennsylvania Press, 1988), 151–64.

cault all noted.) Christianity names what it causes and seeks to escape from: self-consciousness about goodness. For Christianity publicity corrupts— so different from the classical sense that the public realm is both the field and the record of brave action. Do good in the closet, says the Sermon on the Mount; let no one see but God. How are you supposed to act once you are conscious that it is better to act without self-consciousness? The switch between the forgetful bliss of liberty and a guilty conscience is so easily thrown. Nothing shows the inner kinship of Christianity and Romanticism more clearly than the strange psychic oscillation between the joys of unconsciousness and the inhibitions of self-reflection they share.

The German and British Romantics often spun on this merry-go-round. They sought to hold self-consciousness at bay when the inspiration was flowing, for nothing is more brittle than inspiration; all it takes, in Coleridge's famous story about his poem "Kubla Khan," is a knock on the door by the man from Porlock to dispel the beautiful vision. As the American poet William Stafford says, "Poetry is the kind of thing you have to see from the corner of your eye. You can be too well prepared for poetry. A conscientious interest in it is worse than no interest at all, as I believe Frost used to say. It's like a very faint star. If you look straight at it you can't see it, but if you look a little to one side it is there."[29] The tricky art of not watching is something liberals, Stoics, Romantic geniuses, and public officials all must do: turn away from their audiences (whether internal or external). How to elude the blight of self-consciousness—this Romantic concern is the same as Paul's concern about how to escape the corrupting command of the law (or the gaze of the other). The splendors of nature, said Emerson, "if too eagerly hunted, become shows merely, and mock us with their unreality. Go out of the house to see the moon, and 'tis mere tinsel; it will not please as when its light shines upon your necessary journey."[30] (Stafford's star is a distant echo of Emerson's moon.) Accidental beauty coincident to necessity is always more wondrous than delectation directly sought. Schelling put the delicate balance in creative consciousness well if archly in his High Romantic treatise: "Thus it can only be the contradiction between conscious and unconscious in the free act which sets the artistic urge in motion."[31] Like his onetime co-conspirator Hegel, Schelling was trained in an elite theological

29. William Stafford, *Writing the Australian Crawl: Views on the Writer's Vocation* (Ann Arbor: University of Michigan Press, 1978), 3.

30. Ralph Waldo Emerson, *Nature,* in *Selected Writings of Emerson,* ed. Donald McQuade (New York: Modern Library, 1981), 11.

31. F. W. J. Schelling, *System of Transcendental Idealism* (1800), trans. Peter Heath (Charlottesville: University of Virginia Press, 1978), 222.

seminary, and his phrase "the contradiction between conscious and unconscious in the free act" nicely states one part of Paul's legacy.

The Romantics were also famously prone to dejection, and this may stem from rooting the welfare of the world in the fickle stuff of consciousness. It was after all Milton's Satan and not God who said:

> The mind is its own place, and of itself
> Can make a heav'n of hell or a hell of heav'n. (*Paradise Lost*, 1.254–55)

The problem is that the mind does not always cooperate. There is something blessed, Wordsworth thought, in the state of natural piety, of immediate union with the cosmos without interruption or reflection. But it can also be loathsome and bleak. A distemper in the self can make the universe go blank. The self thus has a supreme task—the constant sustenance of everything that appears. But does it have stamina to match? Should the self waver, the universe starts to flicker, dejection sets in, and the enchantment vanishes. A lapse of soul blights the countryside more quickly than any industrial revolution. A bad mood can put the galaxy out of sorts. The imagination is fickle. Strange fits of passion doom the Romantic program—and ensure its longevity. Only a superhuman or a child can bear the burden of keeping the world's body and soul together. That Romanticism is psychically unstable is not news; my interest is how it copes with the awareness that it is more blessed to live without awareness, a path that Paul sends us down. Once you are conscious about the blessings of not being self-conscious, you can swirl into the maelstroms of reflection that brilliant parodists of liberal rationality like Kierkegaard, Kafka, and Woody Allen have made famous. Paul is one source for the torture that stalks introspective souls: If you have no doubts, you are free, but the fact that you are worried suggests that you *should* be worried. Drugs, madness, infatuation, faith, and art above all are paths Romantics have trod in quest of divine self-forgetfulness. (As chap. 5 shows, social science is another approach to the burdens of observation.)

This discussion of the instabilities of the private conscience may seem a digression from Paul, but it sets up a key theme for this book as a whole. Liberals believe in a program of self-consciousness. Their preferred kind of soul is not single-minded but buffeted by contraries of reflection. Kierkegaard's saying that "purity of heart is to will one thing" seems like monomania to them. Die-hard believers—who share with the Romantics a critique of modernity that can lead in nostalgic and nationalist-conservative directions, even though historically many leading Romantics such as Blake, Shelley, and Byron were political radicals—are much more likely to take some kind of purity or authenticity seriously, and hence find themselves constantly provoked by the liberals' call for everyone to line up to have their conscience pricked. Liberals like to break the illusion and to spoil the innocence of unreflectiveness. Liberalism is a fighting creed, as Charles Taylor says. Their preferred model would be the Gnostics who eat whatever they please without concern for what others think. Paul's argument sets up the cast of characters in the debate about public exposure to the forbidden (a core issue in modern theories of free expression), but he suggests a more patient response to the unenlightened. Paul's response to the social dynamics of taboo is to ask those in the know to bend to the ignorant rather than requiring the ignorant to come into the know. He respects those who do not know or choose not to know, something the liberal tradition has rarely excelled at. Paul makes space for those who opt out of his theory and thus offers one antidote to illiberal tendencies in liberalism.

In even briefly entertaining the notion of religious neutrality, Paul provides a foothold for secularization and moral differentiation. Christian thought has long incubated secularism, the possibility of a world of matter divorced from divine nature or guidance. The notion of secularization is of Christian origin: *secula* as the age of the world opposed to the age of God. You render to Caesar and to God. Even the idea that you can make a strategic or provisional distinction between the sacred and the secular, as Paul does, is for some believers a dangerous reduction of God's holiness; refusing this distinction might be one of the features common to the variety of convictions united by the sloppy term fundamentalism. A distinction of sacred and secular is of course essential to liberalism, though it is more often cast as a contrast between private conviction and public toleration. But that too is a Pauline pattern. Paul, like most religious innovators, is a critic of religion. The notion that we may be freed from all worry about food, days, or anything else—"all things are pure"—leaves matters of religious observance open for debate, requires tolerance, and pushes the sacred back into convention, preference, or better, *pistis*. In opening the question of the sacred for continued puzzlement, Paul establishes the terms for the fundamental debate about censorship—is anything scandalous in itself or only in the eye of the beholder? Paul anticipates later liberalism by establishing breathing room for varieties of conviction, but goes it one better by also allowing for those who would resist that leveling move.

THE PRIVILEGE OF THE OTHER

A more obvious place for exploring Paul's understanding of public communication is the discussion of speaking in tongues in 1 Corinthians 14. In

Corinth, it seems, ecstatics performed their linguistic hodgepodges before the assemblies as a kind of virtuoso spirituality. Such charismatic scat-singing was not widely understood, and Paul gave his opinion on the issue. (Anyone who does not understand why people might want to address others in languages they cannot understand has not attended enough poetry readings or academic conferences. Martin Buber, once asked if he could speak Hebrew, replied: well enough to be understood, but not well enough to not be understood. As a German philosopher, he ruled with unique authority on the uses of obscurity.) Paul delivers a communicative imperative for the assembly. He has no objection to ecstatic or difficult language as such—his own prose reaches summits of each. He is no tyrant of clarity; many are the uses of unintelligibility. He regarded tongue-speakers as revealers of spiritual mysteries (1 Cor. 14:2) rather than, as modern linguists do, as practiced recombiners of minimal phonetic bits of natural languages.[32] Yet the core of his *Diskursethik* is to subordinate private liberty voluntarily for the edification of others. Here again, in public one is called to sacrifice for the other. The public realm has a smaller bandwidth of communicative style than the private does. This is one of his core principles of public communication. Paul is Habermasian, or rather, Habermas is Pauline.

Paul values speech oriented to collective understanding—"prophecy" —over speech for private edification. The ecstatic prays to God or him- or herself, not to humans and to the church. Paul rates prophecy—which here seems to mean public speaking—above tongues, not only because of its other-oriented nature, but also because of its appeal to a fuller range of human capacities: "I shall sing praises with my spirit, and I shall also sing praises with my mind" (1 Cor. 14:15). Both spirit and mind, *pneuma* and *nous,* need nourishment; though unintelligible vocalizations may thrill the spirit, they leave the mind barren. Prophecy makes sense to the stranger (*idiōtēs,* "private person") who may be listening in. As with food and conscience, Paul lets the lowest common denominator set the communicative level. "If, therefore, the whole church comes together and all speak in tongues, and outsiders or unbelievers enter, won't they say that you are raving [*mainesthe*]?" (1 Cor. 14:23). If people speak in tongues in the church, the meaning should be explained. Language play is fine, and Paul boasts that he can outdo anyone in speaking in tongues (pity the fool who would chal-

---

32. As it happens, Ferdinand de Saussure was one of the first to explain glossolalia thus. See Wolfgang Hagen, *Radio Schreber: Der 'moderne Spiritismus' und die Sprache der Medien* (Weimar, 2001), 99–106.

lenge him!), but in the church assembly understanding overrules amazement. If there is no interpreter, the ecstatics should keep silent or speak to themselves. Paul has no problem with tongues, only with time, place, and audience. In the *ekklēsia* "the coefficient of intelligibility," to use Malinowski's terms for two aspects of language use, trumps "the coefficient of weirdness."[33]

Whether diet or discourse in the church, the chief principle of communication in 1 Corinthians is the priority of the other. The insider should see with the eyes and hear with the ears of the stranger. In an overly literal translation, Paul exhorts the church to consider how things look to those who "occupy the place of the idiot" (1 Cor. 14:16; *idiōtēs* = noninitiate, newcomer here). Believers must practice self-reflexivity and consider not only the value of expression for the speaker but its social force. We should be strangers to ourselves—for the sake of others. Paul's notion of communication stresses the privilege of the receiver and, like many liberals later, he refuses the pleasurable security of the subjective point of view. Perhaps our single-mindedness is thus broken, but self-division (a liberal mantra) is the beginning of wisdom. Here is another anti-Romantic moment in Paul: the strong poetry of tongues is tamed for community usage and benefit. Paul wants discourse tinged by self-consciousness. No doubt his requirement that odd speech must serve social value will make most civil libertarians deny Paul membership in their club. He has altogether too fragile a picture of feelings and sensitivities for their taste.

Does Paul's focus on the priority of the audience make him guilty of pandering or manipulation? Is Paul a Machiavellian, a skilled rhetorician who crafts appearances to supersede content? Some suggest that Paul's familiarity with ancient rhetorical theory includes all the resources of the "Socratic tradition."[34] Paul openly engages in "passing" and orchestrates appearances. He is acutely conscious not only of how others regard him but also of how he affects others. "Give no offence to Jews or to Greeks or to the church of God" (1 Cor. 10:32). Whereas Jesus taught a form of speech or action indifferent to all response, an immobility so deep as to be thing-like ("turn the other cheek"), Paul would have us be so responsive that we subordinate even our diet to the sensitivities of observers. Paul freely varies his self-presentation depending upon his audience. "Though I be free from all

33. Bronislaw Malinowski, *Coral Gardens and Their Magic* (1935). 2 vols. (New York: Dover, 1978).

34. Hans Dieter Betz, *Der Apostel Paulus und die sokratische Tradition* (Tübingen: Mohr, 1972).

men, yet have I made myself servant unto all, that I might gain the more" (1 Cor. 9:19). To the Jews he was a Jew; to those without the Jewish law, that is, pagans, he was as a pagan; to the weak he became weak. "I have become all things to all people, that I might by all means save some" (1 Cor. 9:22). Paul is not above using means, even when he does not believe in them as ends. He acts so that his audience may understand. Whether this is image politics, opportunism, sleaziness, kindness, or civility is a difficult question. Is there a legitimate chameleonism? An other-oriented Machiavellianism? What keeps Paul's performative stance and communication ethics from being a fancy form of pandering? Is his policy on sacrificed meat a benevolent fraudulence, a bolstering of audience prejudices without integrity of belief? (Nietzsche accused Paul of teaching people to love lies.) Keeping up appearances is enjoined in the Sermon on the Mount: the almsgiver must conceal good works, and the one who fasts must appear as if in robust good comfort. This injunction, as Kierkegaard notes, is the fount of Christian irony. Christianity always distrusted public space as a space of appearance, and Paul is happy to play the game, he thinks, to a higher end. Here begins the long history of Christian communications, ambivalently trafficking with the medium for the sake of the message.

Paul's advice about lingual performance might be read as a subtle exercise in excluding alternate voices—not only those with something different to say, but those with a different way to say it. Codes of decorum and public communication, as some critics have argued, are not neutral, but are designed to fit some kinds of people better than others—men, the educated, the propertied, the white.[35] Damning for any interpretation of Paul as an egalitarian would seem verses 34–35 in 1 Corinthians 14 that command women to be silent in church. Is Paul's discussion of tongues the founding moment of the patriarchal suppression of l'écriture féminine, women's language, rather than a call for civil and intelligible public discourse? Is Paul a source for a theory of communication whose requirements excludes women? Any account sensitive to Paul's received images would be incomplete without Paul the authoritarian misogynist. Even so, historicity helps. The text in verses 34–35 has likely been subject to post-Pauline tampering in an effort to secure Paul's blessing on an issue he did not endorse; the

35. Nancy Fraser, "Rethinking the Public Sphere: A Contribution to the Critique of Actually Existing Democracy," in *Habermas and the Public Sphere*, ed. Craig Calhoun (Cambridge: MIT Press, 1992), 109–42.

manuscript evidence for such tampering is persuasive to this nonexpert at least.[36] Paul elsewhere acknowledged that women played key roles in the church in Corinth such as praying, prophesying, and speaking (1 Cor. 11:5), so why would he forbid them here? Textually and logically, the *Frauenverbot* makes no sense.[37] Paul clearly worked closely with women, whose central role in early Christianity is beyond dispute.

Paul called for the transcendence of gender, not its hardening. Many of the more objectionable gender norms attributed to Paul occur in letters whose authorship by him is dubious. Instead, his strategy is to affirm the standard classical norm (of male dominance), and then apply it to both parties. "The wife has no power over her own body, but her husband does": the first clause states the standard patriarchal order. The second clause flips that order: "just as the husband has no power over his own body, but his wife does" (1 Cor. 7:4). Paul establishes universality by the inversion of inegalitarian rules.[38] His brinkmanship is even more extreme in chapter 11 of 1 Corinthians. "For the man is not from the woman but the woman is from the man: for the man was not created for the woman, but the woman for the man" (vv. 8–9). Thus Eve was taken from Adam's rib and made his partner.. So far, the skeptical reader says, so good: Paul is a patriarch of the most traditional sort. Yet verse 11 calls for a kind of gender incompleteness, a denial of masculine or feminine autarchy: "neither is the woman without the man nor the man without the woman in the Lord." The crossover dribble comes in verse 12: "For as the woman comes from the man, so also comes the man by means of the woman: but everything comes from God." Eve came from Adam, as every male comes from his mother. Thus any claims of ontological or historical priority of one sex over the other are cancelled.[39] A bit of close reading and higher criticism allows for a picture of Paul free of old patriarchal stains.

36. Gordon F. Fee, *The First Epistle to the Corinthians* (Grand Rapids, Mich.: Eerdmans, 1987), 699–708, argues that 14:34–35 is inauthentic, an interpolation by a Jewish Christian author.

37. For a useful discussion, see Tracy P. Thorpe, "To Let the Oppressed Go Free: A Feminist Reading of the New Testament" (Senior thesis, UCLA, 1995), 72–77.

38. Badiou, *Saint Paul*, 111–13.

39. I have skipped over verse 10, which recommends head coverings for women in the *ekklēsia*—and thus serves as a proof-text for the same sort of debates within feminist circles about whether veiling represents oppression or empowerment—but I rest with those interpreters who say Paul is praising the power of women, not imposing an added burden on them. As he has just said in verse 5, women may pray, prophesy, and speak in the church. See Tracy Thorpe, "To Let the Oppressed Go Free," on the notion of *kephalē*.

IN PRAISE OF IMPERSONALITY

Paul both celebrates the impersonality of the universal and respects the un-deniably personal claims of the particular. His notion that identity is im-possible gives us an alternative to either liberal blindness or multicultural particularism, Stoic self-abstraction or socialist revolution, though parts of his thought resemble all of these incompatibles. That he can hold them all is in part what is unique. Central is his notion that the self is made of imper-sonal stuff. "There is neither Jew nor Greek, there is neither slave nor free, there is no male and female: for you all are one in Christ Jesus" (Gal. 3:28). Thus he dispatches all the leading markers of social distinction in his time and place. There is no *diastolē* ("distinction") between Jew and Greek, male and female, no difference between foods or days; all are alike unto God. "God is no respecter of persons," says the King James Version in Galatians 2:6; "God shows no partiality," says the modern translation (compare Rom. 2:11). More literally, Paul says that God does not receive the human face: prosōpon theos anthrōpou ou lambanei. *Prosōpon* in Greek, like *persona* in Latin, means both "face" and "person," and here Paul celebrates the divine effacement of all people before the gaze or grace of God, the bliss of all pos-itivities being erased: whether one is circumcised or not, male or female, bond or free, does not matter. In the church at least (in its claim to offer a form of sociability different from all others), all human differences are given a sabbatical. If you seek for a textual anchor for the strange and won-drous Christian doctrine of the universal equality of all people in the sight of God, look no further. If you say that this doctrine has not been tried yet in practice, you would be right, but that does not make it any less important or wondrous.

Paul's point is subtle: he says not simply that all humans—including slaves and women—are persons (an important step for sure, but no differ-ent from liberal universalism), but that persons are indifferent. Paul estab-lishes universal equality not by granting everyone concrete personhood, but by stripping them of positivities, reducing them to the one thing that unites them all, their impossible relation to the universal. We humans uni-versally fall short of the should. On the puzzling question of what a person is, Paul emphasizes the importance of abstraction. Durkheim, drawing on Leibniz and Kant, usefully explains that personality has both an abstract and a concrete face. Membership in a human society makes you a person *a priori;* your status as a person derives from the impersonal powers of the collective. You do nothing to merit this status; it is ascribed to you simply by birth. Moreover, there is no such thing as a single person; personality is an iterative principle. To be a person there must be other persons. People are persons in what they share with others (for Durkheim, the key shared feature is access to the common symbolic universe of the social order), not in what makes them unique. Contrary to common usage, "personal" and "individual" in many ways are opposites. And yet each person is also by definition unique and unlike everyone else. No person can fully share a body, life history, or self-consciousness with anyone else (the relations between mothers and fetuses and Siamese twins raise other problems). Our words *everyone* and *everybody* underscore the singularity of being a person. Each person is thus both abstract and individuated.[40] The things that everyone shares as a person (a will, a body, a face, rights) are also things that nobody shares (unique consciousness and body). We all share the trait of being selves. It is common to all people that no one fits the norm.

As persons, Paul seems to say, we are singular in our universality and universal in our singularity. We die alone and sin alone, and yet the Messiah, the *khristos,* somehow raises us out of that predicament. Grace is the mediator between the lost enclosure of individuality and the beneficial impersonality of love. Paul is more interesting as an exposer of the impossibility of all identity than as the forger of a new meta-identity (that of "Christian").[41] As Kierkegaard said, all the true Christian could ever say is "I am not (yet) a Christian." To say "I am a Christian" as a positive identity is to betray one of Paul's central claims, the inadequacy of the human emulation of the good, the sense that the time of perfection is both always nigh and always postponed. That "Christian" became one among a welter of other competing partial identities is a sign of its apostasy from the messianic world of suspended commitments, its all too rapid descent into one more party among the contestants of Mammon.[42]

Paul's argument immediately sends up two red flags. The radical social critic complains: it is all jolly well if God treats people alike if people do not treat each other alike. What good is abstract equality as long as domination continues to depend on/stigmatize/fabricate human difference? Paul's foreshadowing of the favorite saying of economists, ceteris paribus ("all things being equal"), might be answered by Ralph Ellison's wry parenthetical: "All other things having been equal (or unequal)."[43] The liberal individualist,

40. Émile Durkheim, *Les formes élémentaires de la vie religieuse* (1912) (Paris: Presses universitaires de France, 1985), 386–90.

41. Though Agamben, *Le temps qui reste,* 87–89, attacks Badiou on this point, I take both as saying that Paul discovers the impossibility of identity, not that he creates a new meta-identity.

42. My debt to Badiou, *Saint Paul,* chap. 5, and Agamben, *Le temps qui reste,* is obvious here.

43. Ralph Ellison, *Invisible Man* (1952) (New York: Vintage, 1980), 15.

in turn, objects to Paul's delight in negating personal differences. How could effacement of personality be a good thing? Facelessness is standard issue in the quiver of complaints among modern social critics. Paul's church might look like a total institution, with him a kind of Lenin, and so we must, says this voice, defend the uniqueness of each individual against the violent vacancy of the universal. The radical voice is wary of utopian mystifications, and the liberal celebrates personality as a source of authentic experience, but I do not believe that Paul's stress on the impersonality of personality, our impossible relation to ourselves and the universal, leads to either social complacency or totalitarian fusion. Paul is acutely aware of the concrete ways that social and individual differences work in the world. In practice Paul does not treat people as Procrusteanly equal—as in the old joke about how the law treats rich and poor equally by prohibiting everyone alike from sleeping under bridges. Paul recognizes real differences in his discussion of the church as one body with many members (this is an old and profound pun, organizational members as bodily organs). "If the foot were to say, 'Because I am not a hand, I do not belong to the body,' that would not make it any less a part of the body" (1 Cor. 12:15). He attacks absurdly self-isolating speech, and the confusion in which a part envies another part. As Theodor W. Adorno said of feminism, the task should not be to make women more like men in their damaged state; it should be to make both more like humans. The foot's jealousy of the hand misses their mutual dependence on the whole. The hand may have more privileges, but it is nothing without the rest. All the parts are equally partial, even though they are not equal. The relative privilege of one part should not cancel their common dependence on the whole. No identity is complete.

If this were all that Paul said on this topic, it would seem one more conservative deployment of the body metaphor to justify social hierarchy and inequality. Yet Paul calls for extra care for the less-privileged. "On the contrary, the members of the body that seem to be weaker are indispensable, and those members of the body that we think less honorable we clothe with greater honor, and our less respectable members are treated with greater respect; whereas our more respectable members do not need this" (1 Cor. 12: 22–24). In a complicated metaphor Paul uses dress customs to stress compensation for inequalities: just as our clothes cover the less glamorous parts—the feet, the torso, the genitals—but leave the face and hands unadorned, so the weak have fair claim on extra care. The less-honored deserve greater attention. Paul at once appreciates difference, calls for almost social-democratic adjustments for the disadvantaged, and squelches particularistic jealousy. His point is to foster differences without justifying inequality. All the parts are distinct, but all are alike in their dependence on the whole. Paul calls for abstraction in the micro and concreteness in the macro—to use ugly but useful sociological parlance. In other words Paul both celebrates the effacement of personal particulars and appreciates the injuries of social inequality. Paul finds both glory and degradation in the suspension of personality as a moral and political principle. Paul's stance resembles that of (to use Ross Posnock's term) "anti-race race men and women" like W. E. B. Du Bois, who both thought race a philosophically empty category and did everything to fight racial oppression.[44] On the other side of a celebration of effacement lies a respect for the specific injuries of difference. When you put together *kharis* ("divine favor," "grace") and *agapē* ("universal love"), you get preferential treatment for all.

Personality is intractable. We do not know how to cope morally and politically with the traits that human beings are born into. Persons have parts. Friends and kin love and like each for who they are. But what makes people who they are? Am I my toes? My house? My dear ones? My thoughts? My unrealized dreams? My experiences? My face? My right hand? My books? William James's famous description of the self had us spilling in all kinds of directions, into our bodies, works, property, social relations, even bank accounts.[45] The shapes a bright container can contain! Obviously we are in some ways all of these things: personhood is mobile and plural in its extensions. And yet we can lose those extensions without losing our personhood. We are not different people if we lose our eyes, or hearing, or hands, or legs. (Paul constantly discusses the indifference of body parts, especially the foreskin.) There are persons without eyes, ears, noses, faces, arms, legs, hands, genitals, hearts, vertebrae, thyroid glands, even brains. It is the animal minimals that are common to all people—the liver, respiration, integuments. Friends are not friends who care only about our parts, but friends are also not friends if they do not care about our parts. Like gravity and death, the universality of indifferences is both glorious and awful.

Impersonality is not necessarily dehumanizing. Kant compares two husbands. One says: "I love and appreciate my wife because she is beautiful, affectionate, and clever." The other says: "I shall treat this person lovingly and

44. Ross Posnock, *Color and Culture: Black Writers and the Making of the Modern Intellectual* (Cambridge, Mass.: Harvard University Press, 1998), 5ff.

45. William James, *The Principles of Psychology* (1890), 2 vols. (New York: Dover, 1950), 1:292–96. James's mention of "bank account" has made him a target for Marxists and feminists. All generalizations are insufficient.

with respect, for she is my wife."[46] The former's love, says Kant, is subject to the fragility of external things—age, beauty, and health. The latter's is immovable, *a priori*, not subject to the whims of time and change. No question which Kant, his Stoic colors flying, prefers. Fidelity and care for family and friends can mean precisely *not* looking too closely at personal traits and features. You do not love your children any less when they are in jail or drunk. Too much objectivity about loved ones is a bad sign. Friends and family can be blindly silly in their commitments to each other. Abstraction can be part of the inalterability of love, an essential part of the most intimate relationships.

Paul's ethic of suspension owes something to the Jewish messianic tradition. The coming of the Messiah, according to the mainstream of the Jewish tradition, does not mean an apocalyptic rapture, a single divinely catastrophic event, as it does for many Christians, but rather a transformation of life on earth to a state of justice.[47] The reign of the Messiah is the Sabbath in the seven eras of creation. This is clear in one of Paul's most stunning dicta, the announcement of the great *Aufhebung* of everything existing: "that things which are not might make inert things which are" (1 Cor. 1:28). What are these things that are not? We know things that are: sin, crime, hate, idolatry, oppression. Things that are not might include grace, love, faith, hope, even God in some sense. Paul is no onto-theologian (since the negative has priority over being); he is a proclaimer of the news that the Messiah has come (i.e., he is an apostle). Just how do these things that are not make inert things that are? He does not mean destruction. The word translated as "make inert" is *katargeō*, one of Paul's favorite words. It combines the preposition *kata* ("down") with a verbal form of the adjective *argos*—formed from the privative *a* plus *ergos* ("work"). *Argos* ("late," "unemployed" in modern Greek) meant "inactive" or "nonfunctional" in ancient Greek, in which sense it supplies the chemical name for the inert element argon. Prior to Paul, it was relatively rare in Greek usage. The Septuagint used it for the suspension of activity on the Sabbath. Paul, who quotes the Hebrew Bible in its Septuagint (Greek) translation, surely knew this usage. Things that are not bring things that are into a state of sabbatical cessation and pause. Such a notion clarifies his view of the law: the need for good works or obedience continues, but the law takes a sabbatical. Moreover, as Agamben further points out, when Martin Luther translated *katargeō* into

46. Immanuel Kant, *Beobachtungen über das Gefühl des Schönen und Erhabenen, Werke in Sechs Bände* (1764), ed. Wilhelm Weischedel (Wiesbaden: Insel, 1960), 825–84, 839.

47. See Gershom Scholem, *The Messianic Idea in Judaism* (New York: Schocken, 1971).

German, he chose *aufheben*, a term that Hegel would later make central to dialectical thinking. The characteristic move in Hegel's thought—negating while also raising—has a central debt to the Pauline theology of both suspending and transfiguring the law.[48] The verb *katargeō* catches precisely Paul's conception of hang-time and foreshadows the idea that sabbatical passivity (inertness) can be worthy. In this dialectical knot of language influences, we find Paul anticipating much in modern thought, especially the modes of ethical suspension that this book explores.

Some interpreters read "things that are not shall furlough things that are" sociologically: the poor, the unlettered, the despised (things that are not) shall win over the rich, the learned, and the glamorous, a reading that fits the social context of 1 Corinthians in any case.[49] The political value of Paul's narrative of a "new creation" (Gal. 6:15) continues to resonate. Christ, he says, made the old world evaporate: tradition, inhibition, custom, difference, gender, religion, class, race, hierarchy. Sin and its law are vanquished once and for all. In his willingness to cast aside everything, Paul, as has often been remarked, is an archetype of a radical. He knows nothing but "Christ and him crucified" (1 Cor. 2:2). Paul's discovery of messianic suspension is refracted in Nietzsche's discovery of the exhilaration of having transcended the law, Kierkegaard's discovery of the dizziness of having done so, and Milton's discovery of, the good and ill that can follow from transgression. In many ways Nietzsche is Paul's rival, not his adversary. As Badiou convincingly shows, Nietzsche's key themes—the self-legislating moral actor, the escape from slavery, the catastrophic rupture of history into past and future by the overpowering "now," the vanquishing of death in the name of an affirmation of life—are also Paul's. Rather than being a *dysangelist* (a bringer of bad news, as opposed to an evangelist), as Nietzsche called him, Paul proclaimed the death of death, not the death of life.[50] The law vanishes, leaving us with nothing but the strong justification of faith, which as we have seen in the case of Romantic oscillation, can open up the poles of Nietzschean Übermenschen on the one hand and dejected melancholics on the other. Kierkegaard noted that Abraham, who suspended "the ethical" (universal moral laws) in favor of the absolute (the command of the living God) and bound his son Isaac for a human sacrifice, leaves us with the difficulty of

48. Agamben, *Le temps qui reste*, 152–64, gives much of this detail and more.

49. Theissen, *The Social Setting of Pauline Christianity*, 70–72, marshals convincing evidence that "things that are not" has a social sense (i.e., those who have nothing in worldly standing).

50. Badiou, *Saint Paul*, 64–78. For the view that Nietzsche was parodying Paul, see Agamben, *Le temps qui reste*, 176.

distinguishing the father of the faith from a murderer.[51] There can be a spooky resemblance between seers and psychopaths, saints and criminals —figures who transcend the law. Jesus was executed as a common thief and tried as a blasphemer. Whatsoever is not of faith is sin: so is whatever is of faith no sin? Faith divides the clean from the unclean, the law from the crime. Liberation from conscience's pangs: in this the criminal and the believer are one. In both Paul and the liberal story of free expression, the heroes and the transgressors are so hard to tell apart.

HOSTING DANGEROUS DISCOURSE

Paul's arguments about sin anticipate the liberal notion that we should maintain space for poisonous opinions if they disagree with our own. In his theology of redemption, crime—the transgression of Adam and Eve— plays a saving role. In this he foreshadows subsequent accounts of the grace that jarring speech brings forth, of the higher political value of transgression. In Romans 3:5–6 he asks: "And if our injustice serves to confirm the righteousness of God, what shall we say? That God is unjust to inflict wrath? I speak as a man [lit., "according to the human," *kata anthrōpon*]. Let it not be! For then how could God judge the world?" Paul starts out asking how we should respond to the odd fact that our sinfulness is requisite for God's justice to be manifest. Dare we accuse God of injustice? Paul flirts with danger: disputing the justice of God. In this he is squarely in the mainstream of the Jewish prophetic tradition of talking back to God, calling him to task for injustice, haggling over the legalities of the contract he has made with Israel: Abraham, Moses, Job, Jeremiah. Israel = he who struggles with God. But the precedents do not make Paul's gesture any less radical; nor does the possibility that he is simply speaking in (or quoting) the voice of an opponent. Paul allows for a space of speech in which contrary, unholy, perilous things can be said, even if they are quickly swallowed up in a gesture of denial or self-conscious qualification of his own speech act ("I speak as a man"). Whatever the vehemence of his retraction—"let it not be!"—the fact remains that Paul, writing as an apostle, did, at least for a moment, call into question the reasons for and fairness of God's wrath. He not only permits but actively gives voice to speech, in one of his preferred phrases, *kata anthrōpon*, according to the human. He does not banish doubts about

51. See Søren Kierkegaard, *Fear and Trembling: A Dialectical Lyric* by Johannes de Silentio (1843), trans. Alastair Hannay (New York: Penguin, 1985).

God's justice as they appear to mortal questioners; rather, he sponsors sentences "of venturous edge" (Milton) in his own discourse.

Paul's flirtation with daring doctrine is even more evident in the famous treatment of law and sin in Romans where he poses risky rhetorical questions that are immediately followed by the subjunctive, *mē genoito* (lit., "let it not be," i.e., "by no means"). "What then shall we say? Should we continue in sin, so that grace may abound? Let it not be!" (Rom. 6:1–2). In chapter 5 Paul explains how Christ's grace overpowers and overcompensates for Adam's transgression. The transgression of one brought about grace for many. "And law came in so that the trespass might abound; and where sin abounded, grace overflowed" (Rom. 5:20). Because sin and grace might seem to be in a symmetrical relationship—the greater the sin, the greater the grace, since it is unprovoked and undeserved to an even greater degree—does that mean we should bring out more grace by sinning all the more vigorously? The theological insight about general principles is at odds with the ethical one about particular behaviors. He has invited an alien voice into his reasoning, that of an outsider who might draw the conclusion that sinning is a good thing since it provokes God's grace. The practice of giving the other side a voice in your discourse is of course as old as the *dissoi logoi* ("antagonistic arguments") of the Sophists; what is important here is the envelopment of hell and inversion within the discourse of salvation. The idea of the devil's advocate, after all, is a Christian invention, though it doubtless owes something to the contrarian attitudes of the Hebrew prophets.

Paul gives full voice to the opposition within his discourse—the radical doctrines that the law is sin, that sinning encourages commensurate free gifts of grace, that leading a life of sin is a path to obtain grace. Yet Paul denies anyone the license to sin. "What then? Shall we sin since we are not under the law but under grace? Let it not be!" (Rom. 6:15). Quite practically he reminds the Romans that consequences still matter; every act proves whose servants we are (Rom. 6:16). We reap what we sow. "What therefore shall we say? Is the law sin? Let it not be!" (Rom. 7:7). The law brought about sin. Without its intrusion, we might have remained in an undifferentiated state of namelessness. But the law is not the cause of sin, only its necessary condition; sin comes from human will and choice. Law is perhaps like a catalyst, necessary for the chemical reaction but not part of it; it sears conscience and stamps reflective worry on our doings. Perhaps the law instilled a capacity to disobey by alerting us to other options; every commandment suggests its violation. Why else would the tree of knowledge of good and evil have been so provocatively forbidden unless God had wanted Adam and Eve to eat its fruit? In this scenario even God cannot state his will publicly.

Paul's treatment of sin betrays an attitude, as it were, of willing reluctance. The fall of Adam and Eve was ultimately fortunate; crime can be productive.[52] Paul's backhanded recognition of the fruits of evil marks a certain kind of double-speak—not unlike the civil libertarians who consort with outlaws in order to show the higher law. Paul's addressee is exhorted to shun sin, with the insight that the others will inevitably produce enough sin to give the world its grit and anguish. The message implies an unstated message: "do not sin" does not mean it would be good if there had never been any sin in the world. Since Paul's circle of addressees will exceed that small circle who will understand the implications of his doctrine, he must take care to give the right public impression. Paul grants the opposition with one hand and officially bans it with the other—like the Romantic poet not wanting to look directly at the star or moonlight. He entertains a doctrine he does not agree with. Is sin good? No. Should we sin more so that more mercy may abound? Heaven forbid. Does the law corrupt innocence? Yes. What would our prospects be without the historic sin of Adam and Eve? Barren and void. We can rejoice that sin called forth redemption, but not indulge ourselves in taunting God to provide fresh rainfalls of grace. Paul argues by way of brinkmanship: he moves to the edge of the theological abyss where Christ is accursed and sinning brings about grace and then calls, No Way! He peers in, shudders, and says, not at all. He likes to look. Skokie meets Tarsus; like latter-day liberalism, Paul's moral position requires a brief dalliance with darkness. He speaks the heresy between the lines for those who have ears to hear, but designs an official statement that will not mislead unprepared audiences. (People already have reasons enough to sin without theology adding to the list.) Deprived of his retractions, Paul would not be far from Nietzsche. Paul allows privately (that sin is fertile) what he denies publicly (that it is good to sin), a communicative maneuver reminiscent of the question of meat sacrificed to the pagan gods: we avoid doing publicly what we condone privately. Paul was not kidding in his famous line: "For that which I do I allow not; for what I would, that do I not" (Rom. 7:15). We should read this statement not simply as an autobiographical confession of a contorted soul, but as a description of a particular sort of

---

52. Paul (and thus Christianity) raises the fall to central theological importance. The Jewish tradition reads the Genesis tale of the fruit and the serpent in a more satirical light. See Samuel Sandmel, *The Enjoyment of Scripture: The Law, the Prophets, and the Writings* (London: Oxford University Press, 1972), 74–75.

selfhood and moral stance, one that later liberals and civil libertarians would cultivate. The gesture of allowing the crime because of the greater good it enables or represents but denouncing it for its particular evil is precisely that of liberal Nazi-defenders. Paul has a kind of statistical sensibility in his ability to think distinctly about individual actions and aggregate patterns. Sin is good only at a macro level of analysis; at the micro level it should never be encouraged. Yet if that teaching against sin had always been obeyed perfectly, the whole point of redemption would be moot. Someone has to sin, somewhere, sometime, to activate the gift of redeeming grace, but Paul leaves that event to happen outside the scope of his official exhortation, like some kind of statistical perturbation that falls all around the central tendency. His doctrine requires a sub-rosa supplement, a secret codicil that is apart from the account but essential to its working. Paul needs transgression, but does not preach it; civil libertarians need Nazis, but do not sanction them. This backhanded blessing on the devil is clearest in J. S. Mill (chap. 3). Paul quickly recovers from his daring ideas.

My point is not to perform deconstructionist surgery on Paul, which is suspiciously easy. He openly invites it, leaving readers of such a bent to get stuck in the quicksand of their own vainglory. With Paul deconstruction is a trap instead of an illumination. He does not force a papier-mâché totality for the critic to take apart, but openly admits the gaping holes, claming the superiority of folly to wisdom. A reading of Paul that sought to outsmart him—which is what, too often, garden-variety deconstruction amounts to—would ipso facto reveal the reader's failure to grasp Paul's central point about human indebtedness.[53] Paul is an original handler of the problem of universality in normative theory. He knows the world is plural, that the doctrine he preaches is not the only one and in some way needs other doctrines. He leaves a gap between his theory and the world for surprises to break through. "But knowledge is not in all people" (1 Cor. 8:7): he has a healthy sense of the limits of his doctrine's hold on others. *Should* is not the same as *is*. Paul knows that the world has its madness and its weather still. He is a normative theorist who lets the heterogeneous play of the actual have its due. He threads a needle through the loopholes of the norm, at once proclaiming it and implicitly recognizing its inadequacy. Paul knows that the world is not as it should be, as any honest considerer does. He also knows that good things can happen when shoulds fail. (Sin educates; law multi-

53. The master knows better: "the enterprise of deconstruction always in some ways falls prey to its own work." Jacques Derrida, *Of Grammatology* (1967), trans. Gayatri Chakravorty Spivak (Baltimore: Johns Hopkins University Press, 1974), 24.

plies sin; crime is a catalyst.) So the task of normative theory is limited from the start, since a world in which only norms were obeyed would lack much of our most precious experiences. Paul cannot fully account for the world without admitting (or more dangerously for him, legitimizing) the insufficiency of his norms, their weakness in gripping things. He proclaims things that are not. Normative theory is an exercise in what is legitimate to be said about the world, not in saying what the world is. The dynamics of the argument's public effects are as important as their truth. Perhaps this is what Nietzsche meant when he said Paul was in the business of lying. For him Paul lacked the courage to see the world as it is.[54] Perhaps. But perhaps also Paul saw quite clearly how the world was but chose not to state it openly out of responsible concern for how dissidents to his gospel would take it. Perhaps he did not want to corrupt their faith with self-consciousness—with the looming awareness of the other's conscience. Openness has its corruptions as much as the closet, a term coined by the King James translators of the Sermon on the Mount (Matt. 6:6). Paul anticipates the policy advanced by John Rawls: one may privately hold a comprehensive theory of the good and regard it as ultimately binding on all people, but also believe it politically wrong to enforce it on other people.[55]

Paul answers the implied counterquery all normative theorists face: what happens when you apply it to your own situation? He cannot press his norms too hard, however true he believes them to be, since he allows for the coexistence of others who do not believe his gospel and perhaps even find it offensive or dangerous. "For one believes that he may eat all things; another, who is weak, eats vegetables. He who eats should not judge him who does not, and he who does not eat should not judge him who eats, for God has received him" (Rom. 14:2–3). Those who are most emancipated from their inhibitions should be the most patient with people who do not share their enlightenment. And just who might the liberated be? As Karl Barth answered, they are those who have been convinced by Paul's arguments.[56] Paul's social theory has a self-limiting clause, an account of the good that refuses to let its adherents think they are among them. Though believers are persuaded, they must not forget that others are not. Paul's key difference from other revolutionaries is that the radical bows to the conservative. Those possessing higher knowledge have a duty to live with a double-consciousness that

---

54. See Nietzsche, *The Anti-Christ*, secs. 47, 52, 58.

55. John Rawls, *Political Liberalism* (New York: Columbia University Press, 1996), 138.

56. Karl Barth, *The Epistle to the Romans*, trans. Edwyn C. Hoskins. 6th ed. (Oxford: Oxford University Press, 1933), 502–7.

includes those without it. Double-consciousness is a privilege and responsibility, not only a curse (as Du Bois, a famous user of this notion for race theory, clearly recognized).[57] In all this Paul is a model of the liberal consciousness of opposing views and a willingness to play host to them, the sense that one's discourse is always haunted by a different conscience.

Paul gives no ground for a fundamentalist conviction of one's rectitude. "In one condemnation of folly stand the whole universe of men."[58] In a way structural hypocrisy—in the sense of honoring ideals we cannot fully obey—is inevitable in the Pauline universe, since we cannot be human without aping the law, and cannot do so without falling short. Ideals corrupt, compelling us to sinful mimesis, which then consigns us to be debtors to grace. Paul recognizes the performative impossibility of his position. Ideals—impossible in deed but honored in word and imagination—corrupt us. The need for the ideal and the limitations of our ability to live up to it is a tragic, not disillusioning, fact. Faith, hope, and love outfit us for the interim. Compromise is the political correlate of uncoordinated selfhood. Our humanity is not wrecked when we fail to achieve ideals; it would be wrecked if we did (we would be gods—or robots). This is not to encourage double-dealing or lying, but to avoid both the disappointment that attends those who keep their ideals too shiny and the mud that clots the treads of those who do not have any.

Extraordinary gestures: sneaking heresy into one's doctrine only to retract it swiftly, and preaching a universal norm that lacks universally binding force. These are maneuvers fit for all-too-human creatures. Paul's swerve into the human mode is not a mere lapse. Just as in the history of salvation no grace would have been made manifest without sin, so in the act of his discourse no summit of religious truth would have been reached without deviant questions. His argument accommodates a small moment of delay and lingering in doubt. He writes not as an angel to whom all mysteries are revealed and all puzzles solved, but as a mortal arguing to fellow mortals for whom God's justice is a real enigma. What Milton said of himself counts for Paul: both sing "with mortal voice" (*Paradise Lost*, 7.24). Meeting people where they are, even in error and confusion, is permitted: "I speak in human terms [*anthrōpinon legō*] because of the weakness of your flesh" (Rom. 6:19). In asking a single question such as, Is God unjust?, even phrased so as to expect a negative answer, Paul pokes a brief hole in the whole sanctified

57. W. E. B. Du Bois, *The Souls of Black Folk* (1903) (New York: Penguin, 1995), chap. 1. The term double-consciousness was used by Emerson, but is a staple of German idealism.

58. Ralph Waldo Emerson, "Friendship," in *Selected Writings*, 212.

fabric of the universe to ravel a habitat for literature and philosophy, practices that consist quintessentially of discourse *kata anthrōpon,* textual tapestries woven within the mortal point of view. Even if human puzzlements are way stations on the path to a more perfect understanding, "face to face" (1 Cor. 13:12), Paul does not banish them. Indeed what Paul does in argument mimics in miniature what Christ's redemption performed in magnitude, the pitching of one's tabernacle in a mortal realm. The rhetorical practice reflects the theology: the sojourn amid sin and death was needed to discover grace and salvation.

As Spinoza pointed out with explicit reference to Paul, apostles speak differently than prophets. The prophet declares in the name of God and burns with the surety of a divine commission. An apostle can step back to offer a private opinion, as Paul frequently does, and play host to an opposing viewpoint. The apostle's discourse is qualified and open to cross-examination. In 1 Corinthians 7, Paul gives advice about marriage not by mandate, but by opinion. Prophets speak directly as God's mouthpiece; apostles reason, speak in their own name, and admit uncertainty or the possibility of rival opinions.[59] The apostle enjoys split subjectivity; the prophet is all holiness and does not countenance the opposition. Paul can even insert an ironic self-commentary mid-sentence: "I am talking like a madman" (2 Cor. 11:23).[60] The prophets Isaiah and Ezekiel never interrupted themselves for a self-consciousness pit stop. They *always* talked like madmen, but never realized it. Apostles orchestrate many voices, yet can step back from them; the prophetic voice of thunder—or the still small voice—obliterates any subjectivity. Apostles speak with the self-consciousness of a church to run, but prophets speak without the burden of self-consciousness. Imagine Isaiah telling us of his tears or travels or of giving any hint of the prophet's two bodies: he is just a blaze of light and a torrent of words, so confident that the word "confident" does not even apply.

Agamben offers another contrast of the two offices: a prophet speaks in the future of the coming of the Messiah; an apostle speaks in the present of the Messiah who has already come.[61] Agamben's interpretation of Paul reveals his membership in the tribe of Walter Benjamin, more specifically, Paul's decisive interest in messianic time, which we have already seen. Insisting, with indubitable philological correctness, that *khristos* be translated as

59. Spinoza, *Tractatus Theologico-politicus,* chap. 11. See also Breton, *Saint Paul,* 13–15.

60. The comment can be also read as a commentary on the genre—foolish speech—that Paul is employing in his self-defense: Hans Dieter Betz, *Paul's Apology, 2 Corinthians 10–13, and the Socratic Tradition* (Berkeley, Calif.: Center for Hermeneutical Studies, 1975).

61. Agamben, *Le temps qui reste,* 103.

Messiah rather than as the proper name of Jesus of Nazareth, Agamben shows Paul's deep affinities with conceptions of time associated with Benjamin and his lifelong friend, the great scholar of Jewish mysticism Gershom Scholem.[62] Paul's "the present moment," *ho nun kairos,* is the precise equivalent of Benjamin's *Jetztzeit* or the medieval *nunc stans,* the "time of the now" into which all history is contracted or recapitulated.[63] Paul sees history doubling on itself via secret arrangements or *typoi* (*figurae,* as Jerome called them), and the evidence Agamben supplies for Paul's influence on Benjamin's philosophy of history is quite compelling.[64] In his most famous example, Paul wrests the Exodus story from its historical continuum to treat it as "*typikōs,*" that is, as a precursor or figure of the present moment. And this present is not just a cross section of the rope of linear time: the Exodus story "was written as a warning to us, unto whom the extremities of time have met" (eis ous ta telē tōn aiōniōn katēnteken; 1 Cor. 10:11). Messianic time brings past and present simultaneously together in a leap across the *a-b-c-d-e* of chronological history. The past is not interred in a sealed vault but can be summoned forth. Paul's gospel is centrally news about the nature of time: the suspension of its irreversibility. His trio of virtues, faith, hope, and love, are not emotional states, but modes of dwelling in time, ways to cope with the fact that the Messiah has come but our work is not yet done.[65] Death and sin, even if they have already taken place, are no more eternally inscribed than anything past is. Though the redemption has already occurred (via the resurrection), this is not a frozen historical event that occurred some time in the fourth decade of the first century, but rather a dormancy awaiting to explode at any moment. History is always in waiting. The present is catastrophic: anything can happen in it. The past is solid, and the future is gas, but the present is liquid. Any event must be threaded through the needle's eye of the present. Messianic power lies in freeing the past from its sentence of irrevocability. (This is the point of precise convergence of Paul and Walter Benjamin.) The slightest split second can be a portal through which the Messiah can come, and one's past crimes can dissolve into nothing more than admonishments to be remembered (as in Augustine's *Confessions*). For both thinkers the present moment is an open door for any fresh departure. Paul's position here is thoroughly undecidable between Jewish and Christian sources, as it should be. His is a voice from a historical moment when some

62. Walter Benjamin, "Theses on the Philosophy of History" (1940), in *Illuminations* (New York: Schocken, 1968); Scholem, *The Messianic Idea in Judaism.*

63. Paul uses the phrase *ho nun kairos* in Rom. 3:26, 8:18, 11:5; and 2 Cor. 6:2, 8:14.

64. Agamben, *Le temps qui reste,* 215–27.

65. Agamben, *Le temps qui reste,* 121–24, 127–28.

Jews were Christians and many Christians were Jews, and points to possibilities of gathering and reconciliation.

The standard narrative of the intellectual history of free expression theory focuses on a succession of English-speaking Protestants named John— Milton, Locke, Mill, Dewey, Rawls—together with assorted other figures, who all try to imagine the lineaments of a soul fit for modern public life. In chapter 3 this book both follows and complicates this story, arguing that much of what is best of this tradition stems from Stoic moral philosophy, particularly from such doctrines as *apatheia* and *magnanimity*. The Stoic influence, as I will show, is clear on Locke, Adam Smith, Kant, Mill, and Holmes. The depth of Paul's familiarity with Stoic thought is debated, but he lists Stoic virtues and vices, quotes Stoic maxims, and appropriates Stoic ideas. Resemblances between Paul and Seneca, the Stoic moralist and dramatist, were noted already in antiquity. Born within a couple years of each other, and both dying directly or indirectly from Nero's orders, Paul and Seneca would be among the most influential moral thinkers for the next two millennia. Though apocryphal epistolary exchanges between the two were later fabricated, we do know that Paul met Seneca's older brother Gallio. When Gallio was serving as proconsul of Achaia, Paul got dragged before the tribunal (*bēma*) by some members of the local Jewish community (Acts 18:12–17). Gallio, distinguishing between church and state, declared the case not a public question of crime but a private one of religious belief, and refused to rule. Specifically, he judged that the early Christian movement fell under the Roman policy of treating Judaism.[66] The episode concludes with Gallio ignoring the beating of Sosthenes, the leader of the synagogue and Paul's accuser (it seems), in the Stoic gesture par excellence: looking away from pain (Acts 18:17). Taking Paul as a Protestant is not hard to do, because a long but increasingly troubled interpretive tradition since Luther has taught us to do so; but taking him as resonant with Stoicism and its liberal offshoots makes eminent sense.

A second source for the deep history of free expression is ancient Greece. Socrates has often been baptized as a liberal *avant la lettre*, and his *Apology* read as the first great defense of freedom of thought and speech. More specifically the rhetorical tradition produces many notions that either still

---

66. Paul's encounter with Gallio is a temporal anchor for dating the external history of Acts. See Joseph Fitzmyer, *The Acts of the Apostles* (New York: Doubleday, 1998), 620–23, 628.

fund or were reinvented in modern thinking about free expression. The romance of flamboyant public debates, the Sophistic contests (*agōnes,* the
same word used in modern Greece for the Olympic games) of *dissoi logoi*
were public entertainments of the first order in fifth-century Athens. The
thesis and antithesis form of argument and discovery, used both by the
Sophists and their chief critic Plato, continues to supply the format fit for
the liberal hope that nasty talk will call forth countervailing words of equal
force and greater wisdom. Indeed, for many Plato's dialogue format is still
the epitome of how contraries can clash to reveal some higher truth. His dialogues also show, at their best, just how surprising the turns of inquiry can
be. You never know, as in the *Symposium,* when a drunken Alcibiades will
crash the party late and offer a speech that tops one you never thought
could be topped. The tightness of the historical tie of the Socratic and
rhetorical traditions to Paul is disputed, but it is at least plausible that a man
who was educated in a cultural crossroads such as Tarsus, traveled throughout the first-century Mediterranean world, and wrote so skillfully if idio-
syncratically in the lingua franca of *koinē* Greek would have some familiarity with rhetorical ideas and practices.

Paul's tie to the Jewish tradition, however, is indisputable. It is clear that
he regarded himself as a Jew, and not as a rejecter of Judaism, but rather as
its reformer or even fulfiller. (Paul probably invented the term Judaism—
loudaismos; see Gal. 1:13.) Here we find perhaps the richest of all deep
sources for the philosophy of free expression. The brief appearance of
Gamaliel the Elder in the book of Acts, as we saw, suggests the long Hebrew
lineage for modern notions of antagonistic public debate. In the rabbinical
traditionTorah study is radically agonistic, and the preferred mode of study
to this day is oral argument between two face-to-face opponents. The tradition appreciates argument to the point that opposite opinions can both be
regarded as God's word. If one wants a picture of the marketplace of ideas,
jousting and colliding interpretations in public spaces, one could do no better than to consult a page of Talmudic text and commentary, opinions
crowding out the text and each other edgewise. Such study is ever dialectical, both in oral cross fire and on the palimpsestual page itself, and no argument is ruled out of bounds. No religious tradition in the history of the
world has allowed and even promoted such diverse self-criticism as Judaism (Christianity is its most successful heresy). Jewish courts could apparently not legally pass a death sentence with a unanimous vote, the assumption being that only collusion could produce consensus in something
so serious. (Disagreement is the default position.)

Though this book's focus on Paul and Milton might seem to tilt toward

Christian sources of free expression, both are deeply Hebraic thinkers (Milton may well have known Hebrew as well as Paul did), and most of their key themes are already found in Jewish thought. The Roman Catholics have their *advocatus diaboli,* and the Reformation (and the printing press) loosed a thousand dissenting tongues, leaving scriptural interpretation up to the Holy Spirit and the private conscience, but the Jews have older ways of prizing the divergent voice. The prophets were contrarian social critics who dared to rebuke king (Nathan, Elijah) and people (Isaiah, Ezekiel, Amos) alike; they could violate public morality when it seemed right (Hosea married a prostitute, and Ezekiel went around naked in two key allegorical performances of sinning for a higher cause); and they sometimes even took God to task for his apparent crimes (Job, Jeremiah, the Psalms).[67] King David even models the stance of nonretaliation against public attacks. Fleeing an army led by his rebel son Absalom, his entourage runs into Shimei, who, as a member of Saul's family, had long nursed a grudge against David. Shimei throws stones at David and his servants, insults them, cursing all the while. David's lieutenant Abishai is enraged that the king should be thus reproached and asks permission to kill Shimei. David in turn is enraged at Abishai and teaches the whole company a lesson: "Let him alone, and let him curse, for the LORD has bidden him. It may be that the LORD will look upon my distress, and the LORD will repay me with good for the cursing of this day" (2 Sam. 16:11–12; NRSV). David's faith in the Lord's eventual compensation allows him the cool objectivity of preserving the life and voice of one who is violently cursing him. He is strong enough to let the insults go on (he stoically notes that if his son can revolt against him, why can't someone else rage against him?). Here we have the archetypal triad of the offender (Shimei), the offended (Abishai), and the protector of the offender (David).[68] Like the ACLU defending the Nazis in Skokie, David defends the rights of his enemy to curse his life.

The sense that history has an ironic way of working out is one of the greatest and most influential of the great and influential ideas the world owes to the Jews, and that idea is key to modern notions of the good results that can come from ill communication. Paul continues in the ironic view of history perhaps discovered by the Yahwist textual layer of the Pentateuch, whose imputed author is traditionally called "J": Joseph, sold by his broth-

---

67. J. S. Mill praised the Hebrew prophets as a "precious unorganised institution" that provided a progressive "antagonism of influences," and compared their social function to the modern free press. *Considerations on Representative Government* (1861), in *Great Books of the Western World,* ed. Robert Maynard Hutchins (Chicago: Encyclopedia Britannica, 1952), 43:341.

68. On his deathbed, however, David gave Solomon orders to kill Shimei. 1 Kings 2:8–9.

ers into slavery in Egypt, becomes the agent who saves his brothers' lives. Rejection and spite are the path to reconciliation and exaltation. Consider the wry comment on how Pharaoh's abuses affected the people of Israel: "But the more they were oppressed, the more they multiplied and spread" (Exod. 1:12). Or the terrible story of a God who could ask his faithful servant Abraham to offer the miraculous son that God promised him as a human sacrifice, only to withdraw the request at the last second (Gen. 22). The sense of the value of irony and the sanctity of argument echo through latter-day theorists of open public debate, in a Jewish lineage that runs from Spinoza to Moses Mendelssohn to Louis Brandeis, a tradition that runs alongside, and mixes with, that of Locke to Kant to Oliver Wendell Holmes, Jr. Jews have swelled the ranks of twentieth-century civil libertarianism, and there are some deep affinities that chapter 4 explores.

In the diversity of ideas that he can sustain, Paul is himself a forum of open communication. The network of texts and audiences held together by that name sustains an astonishing variety of readings, most of which I have barely touched on. For my part I find Paul amazing and sublime, and yet in the end I find a similar interpretive quandary in reading figures such as Hegel, Freud, and Dewey. They are all apostles of liberty who, after the liberation is done, want to plug us back into some sort of system. Hegel discovers a careening, dynamic way of thinking that threatens to unravel the western library, and then tells us that history has come to an end and the absolute is encompassed in his philosophical system. Freud emancipates us from the spell of neurosis and then subjects us (in any sense of that verb) to his regime of psychoanalysis with its fifty-minute sessions and scientistic vocabulary. Dewey discovers the bliss of aesthetics and the thrill of democratic solidarity, only to remind us that he is really talking about the American experience with all its flaws. After the sublime revelation, the apparatus returns in all its official weight. The shoulds come out again. Paul offers both the experience of messianic redemption and membership in an assembly, a church. Readers after two millennia of official Christianity may distrust his swing from liberty to obedience, though the *ekklēsia* for him consisted of small groups of people who cared for one another. The sublime is unstable in its representations; it turns banal so quickly. These figures leave one seeking a way to rescue the radical moment from the system in which it is embedded or to use the radical moment within and against the institution. It is easy to resent thinkers who deny us the prize of Romantic purity, but their pragmatism may be the thing that makes them fruitful. Prophets can be irresponsible to things that are, but apostles never can be. The stain of compromise forever blesses their labors.

CHAPTER TWO

"Evil Be Thou My Good": Milton and Abyss-Redemption

Reflect on the price you pay for the scope of your mind, and you will appreciate how much I spare my idiots.
—Erasmus, *The Praise of Folly*

'AREOPAGITICA,' A MISPLACED CLASSIC

John Milton, the fierce Puritan radical and one of the greatest English poets, is a more conventional nominee in the intellectual tradition of free expression than Paul of Tarsus. His *Areopagitica*, "a speech for the liberty of unlicenc'd printing" addressed to Parliament in 1644, is often hailed as a landmark in the English tradition of liberty.[1] It has recently been called "the foundational essay of the free speech tradition."[2] *Areopagitica*'s elevation to this status was late in coming, just as the notion of free speech and a tradition extolling it are themselves twentieth-century inventions (and the tract was just one of many arguments for toleration in early-seventeenth-century Europe). As late as 1890 the New England poet James Russell Lowell could exaggerate: "It cannot be said that the prose works of Milton have ever been in any sense popular or read by any public much more numerous

---

1. "Areopagitica: A Speech for the Liberty of Unlicenced Printing, to the Parliament of England" (1644), in *John Milton: Complete Poems and Major Prose*, ed. Merritt Y. Hughes (New York: Odyssey Press, 1957), 717–49. Page citations hereinafter are given parenthetically in the text. Multiple passages from the same page are given after the last passage.

2. Vincent Blasi, *Milton's 'Areopagitica' and the Modern First Amendment* (New Haven, Conn.: Yale Law School Occasional Papers, 2nd series, no. 1, n.d.), 1.

than the proofreader."[3] Because of its posthumous status, *Areopagitica* is often read as a contemporary partner to the arguments of Mill and Holmes and the Warren Court.

In this chapter I examine *Areopagitica* and Milton as the inspiration for a more general analysis of the cast of characters that continues to act out the dramas of free speech. Milton's central place in the liberal pantheon is, in many respects, a misunderstanding, but it is a fortunate one. *Areopagitica* does argue richly for unlicensed publication, but it is no unambiguously happy text about liberty. Its key place in the intellectual tradition is deserved not because it offers a crystal-clear defense of openness in communication, but rather because it offers a more robust account of the harms and benefits of rude speech than modern liberals can muster. In historical interpretation, the ways that texts surprise us are usually more important than the ways they confirm standing prejudices. *Areopagitica* is a source for the notion of untrammeled liberty, but also for the praise of robust strength facing evil that would prove so important for both artistic expression and professional culture later. The essay far exceeds its famous excerpt about the wrestling match of truth and error: "Let her [Truth] and Falshood grapple; who ever knew Truth put to the worse, in a free and open encounter" (746). It is a tract for the chosen status of the English nation; a defense of the Protestant Reformation; and, most importantly for our purposes, a theological and artistic justification of a brokered coexistence of good and evil. Its political, theological, and aesthetic arguments give an expansive context for thinking about unlicensed acts of expression. It calls for strong poetry, not weak stenography. More generally, Milton's work brings us directly into confrontation with questions about freedom of expression that are often left to languish in implicitness: how to cope with hell; when is sinning justified; the wiles of innocence; and the philosophy of history, that is, the question of how evil can be explained with a happy ending.

Areopagitica is regularly handcuffed by friendly anachronism. Perhaps the worst of the intellectual frameworks commonly foisted on the essay is that of the so-called marketplace of ideas, a notion that did not come into widespread circulation until the 1950s.[4] Milton's pamphlet against licensed printing is a difficult masterpiece—though he dismissed his political prose

---

3. James Russell Lowell, introduction to *Areopagitica* (New York: Grolier Club, 1890), xxxix.

4. I have analyzed this notion more fully in "The Marketplace of Ideas: History of a Concept," in *Toward a Political Economy of Culture: Capitalism and Communication in the Twenty-First Century*, ed. Andrew Calabrese and Colin Sparks (Boulder, Colo.: Rowman & Littlefield, 2004), 65–82.

of the 1640s as "writings for the left-hand"—and is usually remembered as either the proclamation that truth, in a "free and open encounter" with falsehood, will triumph or as a savage attack on Catholicism, as if to expose Milton's hypocrisy. In writings about free expression, fragments often weigh more than whole texts, and the chief retailers of Milton as a market theorist are lawyers and journalists. The legal scholar Thomas Tedford, for instance, states: "Milton demonstrated his belief in what some have called a 'marketplace theory' of free speech—a viewpoint suggesting that ideas 'grapple' in the field (or marketplace) open to merchants of all shades of opinion, and that after due consideration thoughtful consumers 'buy' the product that to them represents truth."[5] Tedford wisely attributes this reading to an unnamed "some," since nothing in *Areopagitica* sustains such a reading. Among the some we *can* name is the journalism historian Jeffery A. Smith, who imputes the notion to a wide range of figures—including Milton, Shaftesbury, Thomas Paine, Jefferson, and Thomas Erskine. According to Smith, "The marketplace of ideas concept—the proposition that truth naturally overcomes falsehood when they are allowed to compete—was used continually during the eighteenth century as a justification for freedom of expression."[6] Though notions of tolerance, truth triumphant, and press freedom circulated widely in the eighteenth century, there was no such notion as the marketplace of ideas at that time.

Another historian of journalism, Herbert Altschull, offers a richer textual analysis of *Areopagitica* than Tedford or Smith, but his emphasis on "the self-righting principle" misses the mark: Milton simply has no notion of a counterbalancing system, economic or otherwise.[7] Self-righting can be read into a variety of eighteenth-century notions—the deist's solar system, the political theorist's checks and balances, or the political economist's order emerging from the disjunctive activities of many buyers and sellers— but Milton is a century too early. The closest Milton gets is his call to build a house of truth from the diverse labors of individuals: "nay rather the perfection consists in this, that out of many moderate varieties and brotherly dissimilitudes that are not vastly disproportional arises the goodly and graceful symmetry that commends the whole pile and structure. Let us therefore be more considerate builders, more wise in spiritual architecture,

5. Thomas Tedford, *Freedom of Speech in the United States.* 3rd ed. (New York: Random House, 1997), 371.

6. Jeffery A. Smith, *Printers and Press Freedom: The Ideology of Early American Journalism* (New York: Oxford University Press, 1988), 31.

7. J. Herbert Altschull, "John Milton and the Self-Righting Principle," in *From Milton to McLuhan: The Ideas Behind American Journalism* (New York: Longman, 1990).

when great reformation is expected" (744). The notion that independent acts cumulatively can form a single "pile and structure" may resemble Adam Smith's economics or twentieth-century pluralism, but Milton calls for conscious collaboration instead of Smith's unorchestrated private enterprise. Richard Schwarzlose rightly notes Milton's theological vision and the absence of clear market language, but then proceeds to treat Milton's notion of gathering truth as if it were a market anyway.[8] Refreshingly, John Nerone grasps Milton's spirit with acuity: "Clearly, Milton did not conceive of public discourse as a marketplace. Rather, he seems to have conceived it as a church; it is easy to imagine him chasing the money changers out of it."[9]

To what extent does Milton use market talk in *Areopagitica*? Two passages employ economic metaphors. In a negative comparison of truth to goods, he states: "Truth and understanding are not such wares as to be monopolized and traded in by tickets, and statues, and standards. We must not think to make a staple commodity of all the knowledge in the land; to mark and license it like our broadcloth and our woolpacks" (736–37). Though he seems to be rejecting economic models for mental life here, he is ever the opportunist where a metaphor is concerned: "More than if some enemy at sea should stop up all our havens and ports and creeks, it [a blockade] hinders and retards the importation of our richest merchandise, truth" (741). These two passages—one denying that truth can be traded like wool, one affirming truth as England's richest merchandise—are the closest Milton gets to the "marketplace of ideas." The question turns on what we mean by a market. If we mean that Milton argues that reading and writing should take place in an unrestricted, open-ended, and voluntary space, fair enough. But if we mean that laissez-faire economics is the best way to operate broadcasting and news media, that regulation should be scrapped and the realm of ideas allowed to operate like that of commodities, then Milton can end up buying lunch for the media industries. Milton is not Adam Smith, not John Stuart Mill, not Oliver Wendell Holmes Jr.[10] He is no neoclassical econo-

8. Richard A. Schwarzlose, "The Marketplace of Ideas: A Measure of Free Expression," *Journalism Monographs* 118 (1989): 4–7.

9. John C. Nerone, "The Invention of a Marketplace of Ideas," in *Last Rights: Revisiting 'Four Theories of the Press,'* ed. Nerone (Urbana: University of Illinois Press, 1995), 46. The best reading of *Areopagitica* by a scholar of free expression is Vincent Blasi, "Free Speech and Good Character: From Milton to Brandeis to the Present," in *Eternally Vigilant: Free Speech in the Modern Era,* ed. Lee C. Bollinger and Geoffrey R. Stone (Chicago: University of Chicago Press, 2002), 63–95.

10. Lee C. Bollinger, *The Tolerant Society* (New York: Oxford University Press, 1986), 59, manages to conflate Milton, Adam Smith's invisible hand, and Holmes's *Abrams* decision on one page.

mist.[11] Forgive my pedantry: in interpreting Milton what is at stake is the specification of what is honorable and dangerous about markets as normative frameworks of communication. Call him radical, call him Puritan, call him republican, but do not call Milton (neo-)liberal.

Milton's defense of liberty is moved by the conviction that God's forces will win in the end but that, in the meanwhile, passage through a fallen world is needed for our moral and mortal tempering. For him, art is a chief means of such tempering, since it allows trial by contraries that could not safely be attempted in life. Certain aspects of the essay do legitimately vibrate to a liberal ear. One is Milton's pluralism, the assumption that many minds are needed to build a house of truth. He also despises compulsion. Truth is not Proteus, says Milton, who only speaks truly when bound: "Yet it is not impossible that she may have more shapes than one." Truth's strength is surpassed only by the Almighty; "she needs no policies, nor stratagems, nor licensings to make her victorious, those are the shifts and the defences that error uses against her power" (747). His equation of censorship with murder in one of the more cited passages of the essay also wins him points: "who kills a Man kills a reasonable creature, God's Image; but he who destroys a good book, kills reason itself, kills the Image of God, as it were in the eye. Many a man lives a burden to the Earth; but a good book is the precious life-blood of a master spirit, embalmed and treasured up on purpose to a life beyond life." This extraordinary passage was written by a man who would be totally blind eight years later. Books are extracts of spirits, the "living labors of public men." Censoring a book is not "the slaying of an elemental life, but strikes at that ethereal and fifth essence, the breath of reason itself, slays an immortality rather than a life" (720). Books as bottled souls, spiritual extracts, embalmed souls, "the orphan remainders of worthiest men after death" (736): this is a way of thinking more creepy—and interesting—than free expression commentators usually manage.

But it is also puzzling fare from a man whose central intellectual mission was to combat idolatry: the imputing of human or divine traits to inanimate objects. God prefers "Before all Temples th'upright heart and pure" (*Paradise Lost*, 1.18). Does Milton think books are fetishes, living beings, objects worthy of special protection normally reserved for spiritual beings? Stanley Fish alerts us to the performative dialectics of *Areopagitica*. If the essay is to successfully treat the problem of how to discern between good

---

11. For the (not altogether persuasive) argument that these passages endorse the commodity-form in emergent British capitalism, see Christopher Kendrick, *Milton: A Study in Ideology and Form* (New York: Methuen, 1986), 31, 40–42.

texts and bad, it cannot give a definitive answer without assuming the authority to rule on matters that no text, including itself, has the authority to rule on. A text advocating radical freedom for all texts would land itself in the contradiction of claiming the authority its own theory says it cannot have. *Areopagitica*'s "self-effacing office" and "tonal instabilities" thus stand in a loyal performative relation to its argument. "In short, if the *Areopagitica* is to be faithful to the lesson it teaches, it cannot teach that lesson directly; rather, it must offer itself as the occasion for the trial and exercise that are necessary to the constituting of human virtue." (Here is one source for liberal indirection.) The reader of the piece passes through a trial of sorting the wheat from the chaff, rather than being the passive recipient of a ready-made doctrine ex cathedra: "by continually defaulting on its promise—the promise of separating the true from the false—the *Areopagitica* offers itself as a means by which its readers can realize that promise in their very activities. In this way, the tract becomes at once an emblem and a casualty of the lesson it teaches: the lesson that truth is not the property of any external form, even of a form that proclaims that very truth."[12]

Though Milton hates licensing, he has no problem with punishment for bad books. Milton, unlike most of his "marketplace of ideas" interpreters, does not suffer from an underdeveloped sense of wickedness; as the author of *Paradise Lost* and hence of one of the most compelling characters in world literature, Satan, he is one of the great experts on the subject. He reserves his concern for "good books"; "scandalous, seditious, and libellous books" can happily rot as far as he is concerned: "it is of greatest concernment in the Church and Commonwealth, to have a vigilant eye how books demean themselves, as well as men; and thereafter to confine, imprison, and do sharpest justice on them as malefactors" (720). Tolerant waiting does not mean "tolerated Popery, and open superstition, which as it extirpates all religious and civil supremacies, so itself should be extirpate," provided that all charitable means to reclaim the misled are attempted (747). We may "suppress the suppressors" (e.g., Dominicans). He would require the publisher's name on every publication: "Those which otherwise come forth, if they be found mischievous and libellous, the fire and the executioner will be the timeliest and the most effectual remedy, that man's prevention can use" (749).

Milton's intolerance is something later interpreters often get wrong, treating him, in a debunking fashion, as a hypocrite for his censure of Ro-

12. Stanley Fish, *How Milton Works* (Cambridge, Mass.: Harvard University Press, 2001), 196, 203, 205.

man Catholic doctrines, with the obligatory discussion of his later employ-ment as Cromwell's secretary of foreign languages.[13] The attack on Catholi-cism is perhaps the second-best-known passage from *Areopagitica*. Milton was an anti-Catholic fiend, no doubt. But the passage is usually cited by those delighted to be playing "gotcha" and thus revealing the putative intol-erance lurking among the supposedly open-minded. The zeal of citation owes first to a misreading of Milton as Mill, as if there should be a scandal in a libertarian saying this; only people dim to Milton as a Puritan radical should be shocked. Second, the luscious lingering by Miltonic censorious-ness suggests a guilty conscience, the sense that liberty is predatory and that its fine doctrines are at best poorly rehabilitated wrecks with new paint jobs. Milton takes his liberty without guilt. Third, what is most depressing about many criticisms of Milton's rage is the failure of his program to have an ef-fect on his readers: the willingness to make a journey to hell, to the heart of the other's doctrine at its most objectionable, and try to encompass it. Un-derstanding Milton's intolerance does not corrupt the mind. It reveals the fury of his vision—in which conviction and truth matter deeply. He has no time for the prissy defense of the other's right to speak while utterly ignor-ing what they say. The citing of Milton's intolerance attests to the failure to have learned what he taught: "Assuredly we bring not innocence into the world, we bring impurity much rather: that which purifies us is trial, and trial is by what is contrary" (728).

PROVOKING OBJECTS

Milton was never a happy liberal who thought that evil was really good in disguise, and that if we would only tolerate it, it would alchemically turn into good by either giving truth a dark background against which to shine more brilliantly or teaching us toughness and tolerance. Rather refresh-ingly, Milton thinks evil is evil and does not like it. Though one may differ profoundly with him on what evil is, there is still something useful in the sheer vigor of his position. Like Paul, he recognizes that evil is inevitable and sometimes performs beneficial service. A general policy of tolerance does not deprive us of the right of personal abhorrence. There is nothing in-consistent in Milton being worried about dangerous books; anyone with-out an adequate sense of wickedness has no business speculating on politi-cal themes. Even if he generally defaults, as Fish shows, on the promise to

---

13. Smith, *Printers and Press Freedom*, clarifies Milton's duties as "censor," clearing him of the worst charges.

tell us what is good and bad to read, Milton does clearly differentiate among some texts at least, perhaps too subtle a move for sunnier temperaments. And the key point: "thereafter" is the time for punishment. He is not calling for prior restraint. But neither does he say that speech is always harmless; he thinks it has power, sometimes dangerous power that can need a strong response.

A better way to understand Milton is as the founder of a long line of English-speaking friends of liberty up to Karl Popper in the twentieth century who are angry at Plato's call for controlled communication in the *Republic*. Milton's critique of censorship is not just opportunistic (since he could not get a license for his earlier essay on divorce): he makes noble stuff from the nasty contingencies of private fact (thus showing how good can come from evil). Censorship is fruitless, he argues. Vice has a thousand other ways to spring up besides books; outlawing something makes it alluring, a fact he analyzes in the Garden of Eden sections of *Paradise Lost;* the censor would shoulder a terrible burden of having to read endless boring books; and besides, licensing is an insult to the natural wits of England. Milton notes that Plato sought to regulate not only printing but also dance, music, poetry—all the mimetic arts. But the task is unmanageable: we would need at least twenty licensers just to inspect the lutes, violins, and guitars. "And who shall silence all the airs and madrigals, that whisper softness in chambers?" (732). Milton, in his reductio ad absurdum, already has a sense for the impossible diffuseness of the media of communication, the panspermic spilling of public media into private life, an insight we should note that Plato also had in the *Phaedrus* (though he did not approve) and one that remains central to what is good in liberal thinking of public discussion as an open forum. Milton's critique of Plato is a classic Protestant attack on utopias. In a highly Protestant phrase, which Martin Heidegger exploited for similar purposes at a later moment, we are always "in the world." Withdrawal is impossible because we take our fallen natures with us wherever we go. A change in object does not mean a change in subject: "To sequester out of the world into Atlantic and Utopian polities, which never can be drawn into use, will not mend our condition" (732–33), a double-barreled attack on Bacon and Plato—and Catholic monasticism.

For Milton the human task is to dwell amid vice and virtue and choose virtue freely. You cannot remove sin without removing virtue (a point resonant with Madison's arguments in *Federalist* no. 10): As Milton put it, "They are not skillful considerers of human things, who imagine to remove sin by removing the matter of sin." It was not divine providence that made Adam transgress. Adam would have been merely an artificial Adam, a being of motions without conscience (a golem). It was his free choice: "God therefore left him free, set before him a provoking object." Here is Milton's theology of freedom: God did not will Adam to fall, but let him make the choice, God having a plan to clean up the mess. Freedom's fruit is perversity and rebellion—and also, Milton hopes, love and obedience. Offenses must come, but woe unto him who commits them! Adam and Eve ate the fruit in an act, to put it precisely, of civil disobedience, breaking a law and accepting the penalty, so that a greater drama might be advanced. Milton theorizes desire here, "provoking object" and all. (He, in a sense, is Lacan's grandfather via Freud.) God has given us "minds that can wander beyond all limit and satiety." Though a covetous man may lose all his treasure, one small gem left over is enough to keep that vice alive; neither can you foster virtue among youth by cloistering them. "Suppose we could expel sin by this means; look how much we thus expel of sin, so much we expel of virtue: for the matter of them both is the same; remove that, and ye remove them both alike." We need dissonance, opposition, the negative, "both to the trial of virtue, and the exercise of truth" (733).

Milton, like Paul and the book of Acts, takes food as a spiritual issue: "To the pure all things are pure, not only meats and drinks, but all kind of knowledge whether of good or evil; the knowledge cannot defile, nor consequently the books, if the will and conscience be not defiled. For books are as meats and viands are; some of good, some of evil substance; and yet God in that unapocryphal vision, said without exception, Rise, Peter, kill, and eat, leaving the choice to each man[']s direction." In the choice of books, God leaves us on our own, lest "law and compulsion should grow so fast upon those things which heretofore were governed only by exhortation" (727). The contrast of compulsion and exhortation is Pauline, the kind of distinction that, according to Spinoza, an apostle, but not a prophet, can make. Defilement comes from the inside out. With books, as with foods, the only constraint is private conscience. But the analogy of books and food, Milton notes, breaks down: bad food will not nourish even the healthiest constitution, yet "all opinions, yea errors, known, read, and collated, are of mean service and assistance toward the speedy attainment of what is truest" (727). Even bad books provide "mean service" to learning truth, if only as whetstones to sharpen the intellect. Truly Milton could say with Nietzsche: what does not kill me makes me stronger. Or with Paul: whatever I take with a robust conscience can bring no harm.

Liberty in printing follows directly from Milton's understanding of the human estate as betwixt and between. "It was from out of the rind of one apple tasted, that the knowledge of good and evil as two twins cleaving together leapt forth into the World" (728). "Good and evil we know in the field of this World grow up together almost inseparably." Here he alludes to the parable of the wheat and the tares (darnel grass), wheat seed having been sown in a field and an enemy by night having sown tares, which are hard to distinguish from wheat until they reach maturity (Matt. 13:24–30). The servants of the master are eager to weed the tares, but the master asks them to wait, lest they uproot the good sprouts with the bad. The parable teaches waiting, suspension, *in medias res*, and in this foreshadows the liberal virtue of patiently tolerating annoyance instead of reacting rashly. We mortals are hung in the meanwhile—another line of plot always waits. The meaning of any utterance or act lies in the future, and the future is labyrinthine and multiple. The wheat and tares are an apt parable for media of communication: the means and the message intertwine, inseparably. Purity of consumption is not in our grasp (though purity of conscience may be). Knowledge of good and evil grow together, and we cannot rush the harvest in which they will ultimately be separated. Pluralism, tolerance, suspended judgment are the logical consequences of this analysis of the human estate. The cross purchased the liberty "which Paul so often boasts of. His doctrine is, that he who eats or eats not, regards a day, or regards it not, may do either to the Lord." We have no business judging others: "it is not possible for man to sever the wheat from the tares, the good fish from the other fry: that must be the Angels['] Ministry at the end of mortal things" (747). Friends of liberty love to quote Milton's line, "Give me liberty to know, to utter, and to argue freely according to conscience, above all liberties" (746), but they often miss the Pauline overtones in his proviso "according to conscience."

The gathering of truth he likens not only to constructing a building but also to gathering the limbs of a corpse. It is a complex conceit: "Truth indeed came once into the world with her divine Master, and was a perfect shape most glorious to look on." But soon "a wicked race of deceivers" rose up and "took the virgin Truth, hewed her lovely form into a thousand pieces, and scattered them to the four winds. From that time ever since, the sad friends of Truth, such as durst appear, imitating the careful search that Isis made for the mangled body of Osiris, went up and down gathering up limb by limb still as they could find them. We have not yet found them all, Lords and Commons, nor ever shall do, till her Master's second coming. He shall bring together every joint and member, and shall mold them into an immortal feature of loveliness and perfection" (741–42). The whole passage is bizarre to current ears. Why should a mangled woman's body represent truth? Milton works on many layers: rage at Catholic apostasy; the biblical trope of the church as the bride of Christ; and a baroque interest in the corpse. Milton's rhetoric of embalmings, rent limbs, and the body in pieces is not unusual by seventeenth-century standards.[14] As with his discussion of an Adamic golem, the living labors of men preserved in book form, his notion of the fragmentary exile of truth through the world may owe something to the Kabbalah, the tradition of Jewish mysticism. Milton was a painter of the abyss and one of the great thinkers about the morality and aesthetics of facing violence.

One can hardly read *Areopagitica*'s defense of the mingling of wheat and tares without thinking of Milton's larger theological and literary practice. For Milton poets are not only seducers, as Plato thought, but crafters of vicarious experiences that can educate us to the consequences of sin without the sting thereof. Thus Spenser passes through "the bower of earthly bliss that he might see and know, and yet abstain" (729). Literature is a safe flight simulator for life: "Since therefore, the knowledge and survey of vice is in this world necessary to the constituting of human virtue, and the scanning of error to the confirmation of truth, how can we more safely, and with less danger scout into the regions of sin and falsity than by reading all manner of tractates, and hearing all manner of reason? And this is the benefit which may be had of books promiscuously read" (729). Without contraries, there is no knowledge; without knowledge, there is no virtue. In this Milton offers a beautifully clear justification for liberty of publication: diverse writings and arguments teach us good and evil—or good via evil. When Satan tempts Eve with the forbidden fruit—"if what is evil/Be real, why not known, since easier shunn'd?" (*Paradise Lost*, 9.698–99)—it sounds as if he has been reading *Areopagitica*. As John Carey notes, "if Milton had been in Adam's place, he would have picked the apple at once and written a pamphlet justifying it."[15]

SCOUTING INTO THE REGIONS OF SIN

If readers have leave to scout regions otherwise forbidden, what of writers? Milton is a chief exhibit of the early modern confidence that playing host to evil is an ultimately redeemable practice. Francis Bacon, in his role as spokesman for modern science, put it well: "the sun enters the sewer no less than the palace, yet takes no pollution."[16] Milton thought it no shame for a

14. Jonathan Sawday, *The Emblazoned Body: Dissection and the Human Body in Renaissance Culture* (London: Routledge, 1995).

15. John Carey, *Milton* (New York: Arco, 1970), 68.

16. Francis Bacon, *Novum Organum*, aphorism cxx, in *The English Philosophers from Bacon to Mill*, ed. Edwin A. Burtt (New York: Random House, 1967), 79. Bacon's original Latin word for sewer is *cloaca*.

believing poet to make Satan's arguments eloquent and persuasive, just as Johann Sebastian Bach did not shrink from giving beautiful music to Pilate, the bloodthirsty mob, and Judas in his *Saint Matthew Passion.* Leibniz thought some evils could not be prevented without inhibiting greater goods. Artemisia Gentileschi had no scruple about painting decapitation scenes as voluptuous studies of the victory of right over wrong. Milton, Leibniz, Bach, Artemisia, all great baroque masters (if we can blur the historical boundaries of the baroque), admitted and even performed evil—sometimes with slightly suspect zeal—in the parts, but found a patterned theodicy in the whole. These figures all had reasons to contemplate corpses and play host to wickedness. Like their later liberal descendants, they favor the triumph of the good; unlike them they envision, to varying degrees, real risk in the struggle.

Milton argued a lofty precedent for the practice of objectionable expression. In his *Apology Against a Pamphlet* (1642), he notes that the biblical prophets did not shy away from harsh language, and Christ, though "himselfe the fountaine of meeknesse[,] found acrimony anough to be galling and vexing" to the Pharisees. That "there may be a sanctifi'd bitternesse against the enemies of truth" he must have found relevant for his own practice as a polemicist. But Milton goes on to scout even more deeply. The spirit of God, which is "purity it selfe," sometimes fails to abstain "from some words not civill at other times to be spok'n." He seems to have in mind several biblical passages where God warns the rebellious people of Israel, "in a terme immodest to be utter'd in coole blood, that their wives shall be defil'd openly."[17] Milton is annoyed at those who would deny God the right to use vulgarities. His target seems the rabbinical practice of distinguishing between what is read with the eyes (*ktiv*) and what is spoken with the mouth (*kri*). "God himselfe uses the phrase; *I will cut off from Iereboam him that pisseth against the wall.*" The rule that "obscene" words in scripture should be replaced with "civill" ones might render the phrase more gently, but Milton thinks God knew what he was doing: "God who is the author both of purity and eloquence, chose this phrase as fittest in that vehement character in which he spoke. Otherwise that plaine word might have easily bin forborne." God is no more limited in language than anything else and finds no fault with using means to reach audiences who might otherwise ignore him. "Fools who would teach men to read more decently then God thought good to write." Milton steadfastly refuses to water down deity or divine language.

---

17. Deut. 28:30, for instance, has the Hebrew equivalent for "fuck"—not read aloud. Thanks to Elihu Katz.

The theological lesson—that God may use obscenities when it suits his purposes—gives us "leave and autority oft times to utter such words and phrases as in common talke were not so mannerly to use." Occasion and purpose may call forth objectionable speech. The full range of expression cannot be set in advance: "all words and whatsoever may be spoken shall at some time in an unwonted manner wait upon her [virtue's] purposes."[18] In this daring speculation into a central riddle raised by both readers of the Bible and by that text itself—why does God sometimes act in ways that seem wicked? May the author of the law suspend the law?—Milton provides a deep justification for tolerating offensive speech. God himself becomes the great fount and origin of mixed civility and obscenity in public discourse.

For Milton nothing is off limits to the imagination since it is not exposure to evil but the choice to act on it that corrupts. The Holy Spirit fears neither height nor depth—"Heav'n hides nothing from thy view/ Nor the deep Tract of Hell" (*Paradise Lost*, 1.26–27)—and such inspection serves as an aesthetic mandate of sorts as well, especially for one who wrote deep tracts that often burned with brimstone. Milton partook of the Puritan fearlessness of exploration—or exploitation—of the cosmos.[19] While his fellow scientists felt calm in dissecting cadavers, he explained the creation and fall from God's point of view. Something of this ruthless audacity is found in a letter Henry Oldenburg wrote to John Winthrop on 13 October 1667, the year *Paradise Lost* was first published, inviting him to participate in the Royal Society's invisible college: "Sir, you will please to remember, that we have taken to taske the whole Universe, and that we were obliged to doe so by the nature of our dessein."[20] Thus the Secretary of the Royal Society— the founding institution of modern science created in 1660—wrote the Puritan governor of Connecticut. Within pious hearts the potions of modern science and art were brewed, so different from almost all previous doctrines in the confidence that it was healthy, even necessary, to transgress limits. The modern civil libertarian's love of "uninhibited" speech, as Justice Brennan famously put it in *Times v. Sullivan* (1964), echoes arguments in early modern thought about fearless self-assertion in scientific or theological inquiry.

18. John Milton, *An Apology Against a Pamphlet* (1642), in *Complete Prose Works of John Milton* (New Haven, Conn.: Yale University Press, 1953), 1: 900–903. Emphasis in the original.

19. Charles Taylor, *Sources of the Self* (Cambridge, Mass.: Harvard University Press, 1989), pt. 3.

20. *The Correspondence of Henry Oldenburg*, ed. and trans. A. Rupert Hall and Marie Boas Hall (Madison: University of Wisconsin Press, 1966), 3 (*1666–67*): 525. The letter was not received until June 1668.

Most recent commentators interested in Milton as a theorist of free expression fail to appreciate his other relevant works besides *Areopagitica*, though his writing has long been read as contributing to the tradition of British radicalism.[21] Milton's greatest work, and the greatest epic in English, *Paradise Lost,* is after all an extended wrestling match between "Truth and Falsehood." Even the existence of a work of literature on divine themes announces the conviction that it is morally justified to tarry among the wheat and tares, to give extended attention to the arguments and opinions of demons, and to paint the fires of hell as well as the ethers of heaven. Look no further if you seek an origin for the cultivated contrarianism of later thinking about free speech. *Paradise Lost* not only calls for a fight of Truth and Falsehood; it performs it, magnificently and perhaps unstably. Milton gives Satan marvelous blank verse just as Bach, another devout Christian (Lutheran instead of Puritan), gives the bad guys marvelous music. Milton and Bach paint the foes of their official religious convictions with all the grace of their craft.

The question is just how much they enjoyed the flirtation with Mammon, whether their ultimate loyalties were with God or Art. *Paradise Lost*'s most compelling character is clearly Satan, and it has long been said that Milton gave him the best lines. Milton claimed *Paradise Lost* was supposed to justify the ways of God to men, but he does not do much to rescue heaven from the charge of being dull; his God the Father, it has often been remarked, behaves rather like a Stuart king, while his Satan bubbles with appetitive vitality. Opinion has long been split on Milton's sympathy with the devil. Writing in the eighteenth century, Samuel Johnson found Milton's Satan fairly banal, but it was the Romantics, led by William Blake and Percy Bysshe Shelley, who found in Milton an uninhibited spelunker of the abyss. As interpreters of Milton, they are about as trustworthy as Augustine and Luther are as readers of Paul: that is, they conjure the spirits of the dead to channel their own strong thoughts. In Blake's famous line, "The reason Milton wrote in fetters when he wrote of Angels & God, and at liberty when of Devils & Hell, is because he was a true Poet and of the Devil's party without knowing it."[22] (Blake, as a printer and practitioner of the art of ironic encoding and decoding, ought to get his fair place in the British pantheon of free speech theorists.) Shelley in turn thought Milton's Satan morally supe-

---

21. See Christopher Hill, *Milton and the English Revolution* (New York: Viking, 1977), for a leading example of a scholarly treatment of Milton as a radical.

22. William Blake, "The Marriage of Heaven and Hell," plate 6, in *The Oxford Anthology of English Literature: Major Authors Edition* (New York: Oxford University Press, 1975), 2: 34–44.

rior to his God. Milton's God was "one who in the cold security of un-
doubted triumph inflicts the most horrible revenge upon his enemy, not
from any mistaken notion of inducing him to repent of a perseverance in
enmity, but with the alleged design of exasperating him to deserve new torments." Whereas Shelley dislikes such chilly calculated punitiveness, "nothing can exceed the energy and magnificence of the character of Satan as expressed in *Paradise Lost.*" In High Romantic style, Shelley concludes: "this
bold neglect of a direct moral purpose is the most decisive proof of the supremacy of Milton's genius."[23] Shelley endorses what Kierkegaard would
later call a "teleological suspension of the ethical."[24] Audacity of artistic
imagination means the holding at bay of moral compunctions. As John
Keats wrote Shelley in 1820, "*an artist* must serve Mammon."[25] The strong
poet works free from the scruple of the other's gaze, another resonance
from Paul. Milton's baroque theological boldness serves here as a warrant
for Romantic aesthetic boldness.

Milton was a key inspiration for the Romantics, both British and German, both poets and painters, just as the Romantic reading of Milton was an
inspiration for radical literary theorists in the 1960s and 1970s who rejoiced
in Satan as the archetype of Promethean creativity, Harold Bloom most notably. (First having read *Paradise Lost* in high school in 1974, I am still wean-
ing myself of this filter.) Scholarship since then has nuanced our understanding, but Bloom and the Romantics are at least always interesting.
Stanley Fish has long acted as the peacemaker in the pitched battle between
the Satanists and the anti-Satanists among Milton scholars. In his famous
analysis in *Surprised by Sin* (1967), Fish argues that Milton uses the full power
of his art to tempt the reader to succumb to its spell—and thus to be provoked into self-correcting strength. In the act of reading, the drama of temptation and transgression is freshly recreated by exposure to forbidden fruit
such as poetic beauty, seduction, and self-assertion. Readers find themselves
seduced by Satan's rhetoric and thus mentally reenacting the drama of the
fall without incurring the guilt of actual sinning. The reader's response to
Paradise Lost offers precisely the sort of arm's-length experimental simula-
tion that *Areopagitica* calls for in reading generally.[26] It also offers a forerun-

23. Percy Bysshe Shelley, *A Defense of Poetry* (Boston: Ginn, 1891), 30–31.

24. Søren Kierkegaard, *Fear and Trembling: A Dialectical Lyric* by Johannes de Silentio (1843),
trans. Alastair Hannay (New York: Penguin, 1985), 83ff.

25. Keats to Shelley, 16 Aug. 1820, in *The Oxford Anthology of English Literature,* 2: 617. Emphasis in the original.

26. Stanley Fish, *Surprised by Sin: The Reader in Paradise Lost* (New York: St. Martin's Press,
1967).

ner of the civil libertarian practice of being at once a safe collaborator with and a spectator of wickedness, of participating at a distance.

More recently, Fish has updated his position to give us a religiously single-minded, aesthetically flirtatious Milton, dedicated to making friends with the intellectual and artistic Mammon of unrighteousness while relentlessly using that friendship to bear witness to the one true God: "the surface energies in his work are almost always attached to the perspective and forces he would have us repudiate."[27] Fish's tour de force is responsible both to the historical integrity of Milton's beliefs and to the colorful effects his words still have on readers' imaginations. Milton is no crypto-Satanist or proto-Romantic in Fish's reading, but a militant witness to God's supremacy—in values, life, art, politics, everything. The truth lies in the heart—Paul's statement in Romans 14:14 could describe Milton's frighteningly exigent reading protocol: "nothing is unclean in itself; but it is unclean for anyone who thinks it unclean." Such inwardness allows trafficking in the things of this world, including poetic fancy, with a certain impunity. (Making the heart's assent the measure of virtue opens up a raft of antinomian heresies.) In reading Milton nothing less than the reader's moral temper, the orientation to the universe is on trial. Fish's Milton repeatedly asks the Augustinian question, "whom do you love?"[28] Do you consent to be dazzled by the pyrotechnic temptations the poetry offers or do you *use* them solely, remembering that only God is to be *enjoyed*? Fish argues that the Romantic reading of Satan as the strong poet par excellence is a trap Milton laid for unsuspecting readers, among other temptations that line the text. Rather like another great performance of tarrying with the negative, Hegel's *Phenomenology of Spirit, Paradise Lost* is full of partial understandings that clamor to be taken as full truth. The task for the reader is to avoid the temptation to tarry before each beautiful part as the whole. Like Paul, Milton asks daring questions—Is the law sin? Is God unjust? Is Satan sympathetic?—but does his best to prevent readers from going off the deep end. Blake and Shelley are to Milton as the early antinomians were to Paul, people who took the bait of the daring without its orthodox recuperation.

DRAMATIS PERSONAE

My aim in the rest of the chapter is not to settle on the proper reading of Milton but rather to explore the attitudes he authorizes, or at least the

27. Fish, *How Milton Works*, 138.
28. Fish, *How Milton Works*, 543.

moral stances toward liberty of communication that can be discovered in his tangled texts. (The method of reading is thus very similar to that of chap. 1). Every political or moral theory presupposes a cast of characters—often both mutually dependent and mutually oblivious.[29] Satan represents a key figure in the dramatis personae of free expression, the troublemaker who nonetheless brings about, by the very force of his negativity, good in the end. I will call such figures "abyss-artists," or borrowing a term from cinematic special effects, "inferno-artists." Their sins are catalysts. They operate by inversion, that is, by irony. "Evil be thou my good," perhaps Satan's most famous line (*Paradise Lost*, 4.110), can stand as their motto. The key gesture of inferno-artistry is perversity: to prize what "normally" is rejected. Transgression is creative, degradation divine. They gather grapes from thorns and figs from thistles. Abyss-artists are the archetype of the productive criminal. They learn to luxuriate in hell's warm sulfurousness, enjoy their own naughtiness, and take pleasure in the musky stench of sin. As a rule abyss-artists are not what William James called "healthy-minded." They enjoy prodding the repressed with a sly knowingness of the shock it will bring to innocent bystanders. These figures find in corruption delights not known in the celestial spheres: "the enjoyments of Genius," said William Blake, "to Angels look like torment and insanity."[30] (Blake's angels look like modern liberals: those whose monopoly of good intention corrupts them.)

In *Paradise Lost* a clear statement of this strategy comes from Mammon, one of Satan's partners in crime, who exhorts the assembled hosts at Pandemonium (a word Milton coined) not to submit to heaven's "splendid vassalage," but to

> . . . rather seek
> Our own good from our selves, and from our own
> Live to our selves, though in this vast recess,
> Free, and to none accountable, preferring
> Hard liberty before the easie yoke
> Of servile pomp. (*Paradise Lost*, 2.253–57)

Mammon's gesture certainly resonates for a host of moderns. Bertrand Russell, who never tired of playing up his reputation for wickedness, flattering himself with the deliciously tormenting thought that he was Satan in the suburbs, was never less original than when, in his essay "A Free Man's

---

29. Alasdair MacIntyre, *After Virtue: A Study in Moral Theory.* 2nd ed. (Notre Dame: University of Notre Dame Press, 1984), 27–31.

30. Blake, *The Marriage of Heaven and Hell*, plates 5, 6.

Worship," he deployed the old tactic of inversion to build his faith on the foundation of despair.[31] That vigorous self-creation beats blissfully obedient submission is a theme with almost endless variations repeated by sundry modern figures: romantics riding the demonic, modernists exploring the juxtaposition of the organs of generation and excretion, avant-gardists. Such figures often confound profanity and profundity, and consider themselves the beacons of liberty and free play, pushing the envelope "to none accountable." Thus "hard liberty" (or hard bondage) is the cuisine of choice for a line of sexual heresiarchs—the Marquis de Sade, Charles Baudelaire, Georges Bataille, Luis Buñuel, Jean Genêt, Michel Foucault— all French or Francophiles, a culture known for producing fine things from putrefaction (cheese, wine, poetry). Perhaps the finest soil for abyss-artists is Russian culture, with authors such as Dostoevsky, Turgenev, and Bulgakov. "Plonger au fond du gouffre, / Enfer ou Ciel, qu'importe?" asked Baudelaire.[32] Part of Baudelaire's point, of course, was to make the choice of heaven and hell indifferent. Rimbaud's *Une saison en enfer* (1873), a notebook of a damned soul, gives us a textbook sojourn in hell. "Le malheur a été mon dieu. Je me suis allongé dans la boue. Je me suis séché à l'air du crime. Et j'ai joué de bons tours à la folie."[33] Rock stars picked up his mantle (Jim Morrison, most explicitly). The Canadian folk-rocker Neil Young said of his 1972 megahit, "Heart of Gold": it "put me in the middle of the road. Traveling there soon became a bore so I headed for the ditch."[34] Rap musicians, too, like to see themselves as the latest in a long line of *poètes maudits*. The repertoire of abyss-artistry shows up in punk rock lyrics, performances, album art, and hairstyles (often based on stuff they learned in art school). The life and writings of William S. Burroughs inspired Lou Reed, Nirvana, and other musical connoisseurs of the ditch.

Voluntarily heading for the ditch is far from a modern theme. The book of Ecclesiastes, which like free speech theory is influenced by Stoicism, gives us a notebook, not quite of the damned, but at least of one who desires to sound the range of "all things that are done under heaven": "And I gave my heart to know wisdom, and to know madness and folly" (Ecc. 1:13, 17). To know madness and folly is the business of abyss-artistry, whose modern

---

31. Bertrand Russell, "A Free Man's Worship," *The Independent Review* 1 (1903): 415–24.

32. "To plunge to the depth of the abyss / hell or heaven, whatever." Charles Baudelaire, *Le Voyage*, VIII. See also his "Hymne à la beauté," ll.21–22.

33. "Unhappiness was my god. I have stretched myself out in the mud. I have dried myself in the air of crime. And I have played some good tricks on folly." Arthur Rimbaud, *Une saison en enfer, Oeuvres* (Paris: Classiques Garnier, 2000), 207.

34. Liner notes to *Decade* (1977), CD release 1986, recording no. 2257–2.

form enjoys the added aura of Promethean rebellion or Faustian striving. The "black writers of the bourgeoisie," as Max Horkheimer and Theodor Adorno called Machiavelli, Sade, Nietzsche, and the like, were all engaged in teaching an *amor intellectualis diaboli* as the counterpart to (and hidden truth of) Enlightenment reason.[35] The films of Luis Buñuel and David Cronenberg, the writings of Cathy Acker and J. G. Ballard, the art of Paul Thek, Damien Hirst, and Adriana Varejão, all put animal and human guts on display. Implied in most abyss-artistry is a kind of moral strenuosity, the implication that the wild side is more rigorous than the boredom of bourgeois morality. In this, abyss-artistry has a hidden affinity with the Stoic stance of the professional, especially the medical doctor, who shies away from nothing and has the strength of character to resist the voices of conscience and inhibition (chap. 5).

It goes well beyond the scope of this book to catalog varieties of inferno-artists, but the essential gesture should be clear. Consider a second actor, the abyss-redeemer. Abyss-artists and -redeemers have a symbiotic relationship. In the language of pop psychology, redeemers are "enablers," people who provide material or emotional support for other people's vices, yet often keep themselves aloof from such behaviors. Milan Kundera's novel *Immortality* provides an even better label: "the willing ally of [their] own gravediggers."[36] Kundera mocks liberals for their habit of giving airtime to people whose projects would destroy their own. Liberals like to look, as long as someone else is doing the dirty work. Some things may not be good to do, but may be good to watch. Offenses must come, but not by me, thank you! The reasonable pick up the tab for the revolutionaries, whose surfeit of appetite they both admire and feel guilty about. Milton describes the modus operandi: Satan, setting out to tempt Eve in the getup of a serpent, goes "with tract oblique[;] . . . side-long he works his way" (*Paradise Lost,* 9.510, 512). Enablers dress up in the satanic tract oblique, sure that the indirection of their defense will add up to greater truth in the end. The drama enacted by the Nazis and the ACLU is just one version of a much larger modern theme: the co-dependence of abyss-artists and abyss-redeemers. The latter recognize the peril of the fiery deluge but believe that (vicariously) fathoming hell's lessons justifies the risk of the descent and trust that enlightenment will follow their forays into darkness visible.

35. Max Horkheimer and Theodor W. Adorno, *Dialektik der Aufklärung: Philosophische Fragmente* (1944), in Adorno, *Gesammelte Schriften* (Frankfurt: Suhrkamp, 1981), 3: 139, 114. Their phrase "Intellectual love of the devil" inverts Spinoza's *amor intellectualis dei,* the intellectual love of God.

36. Milan Kundera, *Immortality,* trans. Peter Kussi (New York: Grove Weidenfeld, 1991), 122.

Kundera is a wonderful mocker, and his lesson of lightness is one that liberals richly deserve. And yet, as we will see in the cases of J. S. Mill and the U. S. Supreme Court in the following two chapters, there is more than standoffish voyeurism, Pollyanna hope, or strenuous masochism in the defense of speech one hates. The mark of abyss-redeemers is to enter hell for the sake of the lesson and get out again quickly (if they can find the way out). *Facilis descensus averni,* as Virgil warned: the way into hell is easy. Milton is an abyss-redeemer; Satan is an abyss-artist. One tolerates hell within a larger discourse of redemption; the other burrows into hell with perverse relish. Classic abyss-redeemers know the serious risks involved, so different from many latter-day liberals and civil libertarians, so certain of their theodicy that "the marketplace of ideas" will somehow take care of itself. Paul swoops into brief moments of heresy—Is God a liar? Should we sin so that grace may abound?—only to reemerge on the other end with a shudder at the thought he has just entertained. Let it not be, he exhorts. The warning label, the clarifying caption, the moral commentary that tries to salvage and justify the excursion into the abyss (of atheism, rebellion, sin, violence, the self) is the mark of the abyss-redeemer. Milton tells us he wrote *Paradise Lost* to justify the ways of God to men. Though suspicious critics can always find reasons to distrust such avowals and discover ulterior motives in the work of abyss-redeemers (such as the flirtation with danger or rebellion), the willingness at least to supply an explanation of moral purpose does genuinely distinguish abyss-artists from abyss-redeemers—and binds them together.

Take Michel Foucault's brilliantly gory opening to his very influential book *Discipline and Punish* (1975). With loving detail he describes the execution of Robert Francis Damiens in 1757, who had attempted to murder Louis XV.[37] It is hard to say which is more shocking, the excruciatingly documented description of the quartering and burning of the regicide's body or Foucault's studied silence on the experience of the victim and the refusal to probe the sufferer's soul.[38] He rigorously refuses to contain the spectacle

---

37. Edmund Burke mentioned the torture and execution of Damiens in his *Philosophical Enquiry into the Origin of our Ideas of the Sublime and Beautiful* (1757). The execution may also inform two key works from 1759 on the problem of suffering, Adam Smith's *Theory of Moral Sentiments* and Voltaire's *Candide.*

38. Foucault's interest in the spectacle of the damned has roots in the Christian tradition, as he recognized. See Jeremy R. Carrette, "Prologue to a Confession of the Flesh," in *Religion and Culture by Michel Foucault* (Manchester: Manchester University Press, 1999), 1–50. Carrette takes pains to correct what he regards as James Miller's over-interpretation of Foucault's erotic mysticism.

of the broken body in any way. He rides the ticklish edge of moral abstemiousness where you can never quite tell whether he is celebrating cruelty or implying a larger critical purpose. The public execution, the reader is
left to infer, reveals a species of pain free of the modern humanitarian over-
lay, in something of its old awful truth. Like Nietzsche, Foucault sees older
forms of punishment—what he calls an "art of unbearable sensations"—as
less vicious than the new "economy of suspended rights," with its surveillance and disciplines; claims of humanist compassion are, for Foucault, in
league with what he calls the "carceral" order itself. [39] His account of the
écartèlement of Damiens is scrupulously without affect, and the target of his
wrath seems not the flamboyant brutality of corporal punishment but the
supposedly humanitarian practices of pity, which Foucault believes spiritu-
alize cruelty into an icier and more vicious form. Taking cruelty seriously
allows one to "think otherwise," uses the past as an alternative to the present, and criticizes an insidious regime of power that probes our bodies and
makes subjectivity the great locale of truth. The disciplinary agents who
peer into our souls and orifices profess to be moved by compassion. For
Foucault, as fierce an antinomian as Milton, such inspection is always illegitimate.

Foucault stages a theater of cruelty, leaving the reader with the unpalat-
able option of assuming that he is taking a sadistic glee in the torture and
inviting the reader to enjoy the show. In my experience of teaching *Discipline and Punish*, at least, many students read Foucault's account of the torture as an ironically mute exposé of cruelty and suffering. They read him—
incorrectly, I think—as a modern humanitarian outraged at suffering instead of the great critic of modern humanitarianism's smugness. To exult
in or at least describe without flinching the torn limbs of a fellow human
being undercuts knee-jerk squeamishness and avoids the historically recent
piety that suffering is evil; Foucault unfurls a world in which the systematic
infliction of maximal pain was a conscious policy. He wants his readers to
undergo the discomfort of recognizing how their very resistance to the
spectacle of the damned is a precise symptom of the historical processes
that have shifted punishment from body to soul, from pain to discipline.
The conflict in the reader's heart in the face of Damiens's execution drives
home the point of the book: that the horror of physical suffering is a recent
and largely hypocritical effort to maintain our delicacy in pity without admitting our pleasure in mayhem. *Discipline and Punish* thus practices the

---

39. Michel Foucault, *Discipline and Punish: The Birth of the Prison* (1975), trans. Alan Sheridan (New York: Vintage, 1979), 11.

"dialogue of provocation" invented by the ancient Cynics that Foucault later analyzed as central to the western tradition of truth-telling: participants in such dialogues are supposed to be convicted by their own consciences as they discover how easily their anxiety or repulsion can be taunted into being.[40]

Notice how I have managed to construct a critical purpose out of Foucault's coolly delirious lingering by Damiens's miserable body. Foucault, in contrast, never turns around and explains that he told the tale of torture for higher purposes. I have just played abyss-redeemer to his abyss-artist. Foucault jettisons any interest in looking squeaky clean, in justifying his interest in torture. Paul of Tarsus does not want to risk leading anyone astray, but Foucault wants us to abide in the aporia. Foucault reads—and writes—diabolically. He does not provide captions for his pictures. In this he is an odd cousin to the ACLU. Both give airtime to realms of culture marked as forbidden or morally sick (torture and genocide). Both run the risk of public attack for consorting with demons. Both often leave their larger purpose unexplained, in part because these are performances, not statements, though there is usually someone willing to come to the rescue to explain their contrarian tactics. Both act out a drama of self-control, of abstinence from standard morality. Just as the ACLU's defense of Nazis requires people who get it, Foucault's complicated gesture of withholding sympathetic commentary (pity) requires interpreters who can identify a moral purpose (much recent Foucault criticism wants to save him from James Miller's reading—one that Foucault left open—as a sado-masochist who rather enjoyed the stuff). Violence can offer aesthetic lessons in strangeness and perspective, in toying with ethical suspensions and unpracticed combinations of feelings. Foucault induces a Pauline shudder: I am glad that criminals are not quartered in public any more, but am constrained to grant the terrifying daring of his art of unbearable sensations. Perhaps pity is often corrupt rather than blessed. In life, rather than art, there is a crucial difference between sublimation and mayhem, between the gaze and the gallows. Foucault knows this; his epigones sometimes do not. You may blame me for thus domesticating his radicalism, but this is the office of the abyss-redeemer. To admit that such shows are art, imagination, or metaphor, and not incitement, jeopardizes their power. Abyss-artists both need and dislike those who explain their performances.

We find a similar example of the interdependence of abyss-artists and

40. Michel Foucault, *Fearless Speech* (1983), ed. Joseph Pearson (New York: Semiotexte, 2001), 115–33.

abyss-redeemers in a recent essay by the cultural theorists Lauren Berlant and Michael Warner. Their central argument is that the public-private divide is neither neutral nor natural but saturated with "heteronormativity." They tell of adventures in the sexual underworld of New York City, specifically their witnessing of a performance of "erotic vomiting" during a special night in a leather bar. A young man wearing a dog collar interacts with a male partner, who pours food and milk down his throat and body in an undulating choreography of disgust and eros that culminates in an orgasmic spew of vomit. This episode of climactic barfing is lovingly told, as if it were the latest installment in a long line of transgressive grossness—which it may well be, for all I know.[41] Warner, the author of this section, treats the performance as a Blakean "enjoyment of genius" in a virtuoso interpretation quite like Foucault's account of the torture of Damiens. Foucault portrays violence, and Warner sex (if indeed we should call it that) without any moral intervention. As Foucault will not stoop to sympathize, so Warner refuses to pathologize what is clearly a Richter scale–busting bit of mutual degradation. Both want to make the normal abnormal—queer, as Warner would put it—and do so via the performative Pauline tactic of a strategic *skandalon.* Neither prefaces his story with: watch how high I can fly this thought experiment, how long I can manage to keep going without succumbing to pity or disgust. If the audience is shocked by the events or their narrations, that reaction only serves as evidence of how deep its complicities go—whether with Foucault's jailor's regime or Berlant and Warner's heteronormativity—and of the degree to which apparently spontaneous feelings such as pity or disgust are already facts of power. Warner can bank on an academic audience thinking it is bad form to look uptight in public; "prude" is nearly as bad a thing in culturally liberal spheres as "Nazi" or "racist," since it implies not only a moral deficiency but weakness in taste. The first person caught holding his or her nose loses. If you feel grossed out, then perhaps you ought to reflect on whether your compunctions are complicit with oppression. Guilt makes liberals enablers. Abyss-artists practice a leading kind of moral suspension: refusing to pass judgment and operating, perhaps, like Warner's performers, just "at the threshold of gagging."[42]

This tale of performative reflux is another classic "dialogue of provocation." Abyss-artists and their friends like giving high-minded people the fidgets, knowing they have an audience that enjoys being abused. As Hume

41. Lauren Berlant and Michael Warner, "Sex in Public," in Warner, *Publics and Counterpublics* (New York: Zone Books, 2002), 206–8.

42. Berlant and Warner, "Sex in Public," 207.

said of spectators at tragic plays, "they are pleased in proportion as they are afflicted."[43] Morally or politically motivated abyss-artists bank on an unspoken collusion with audiences. The ACLU banks on an audience able to discern how defending the rights of the Ku Klux Klan serves the public good. Warner presupposes a liberal audience.[44] Only those with advanced training in self-doubt and stoic self-control would reinterpret their own prissy reaction to a tale of disgust as a symptom of insufficient thoughtfulness, rather than as a justified response to a provocation. The right audience for abyss-artists knows both how to supply the critical caption to the performance and why the performer cannot do so. Some kinds of art consist in the refusal to say, This is Art! Skill at keeping a straight face is central to performance art. To admit an ultimate cathartic purpose too early is to lose the ballgame. If Jonathan Swift had called his satire "A Modest Proposal"— which suggested that Ireland's population explosion be handled by eating its excess children—"An Ironic Proposal," the whole joke would have been spoiled. Explicitness kills irony. The unstated makes possible the duet of two voices, the straight and the arch, upon which irony depends. The interpretive tension evoked in the listener—is this sick or genius?—is designed to be part of the effect, hovering, as it does, along the troubling question of our pleasure in taboo or mayhem. This, again, is the cynical practice (in the ancient cheerful not modern bitter sense of cynicism) of engaging audiences in performative games in which the rules are so constructed that every move, including hesitation, is a soul-exposing moral choice. As William Blake noted, "The wisest of the Ancients considerd what is not too Explicit as the fittest for Instruction because it rouzes the faculties to act."[45]

The relation between performers and commentators, artists and redeemers, involves a curious division of communicative labor. In *On Liberty* (examined in depth in the next chapter), Mill wanted speakers to proclaim their passionate convictions without scruple, and listeners to consider with the coolest of reflective reason. The irrational speaker aids the mental and moral exercise of the rational listener. The speaker's outrageousness is supposed to stimulate the listener's reasonableness. If the moderation of the listener were to infect the speaker or the certainty of the speaker were to infect the listener, the check-and-balance system would be upset. Liberal theory

43. David Hume, "Of Tragedy," in *Essays: Moral, Political, and Literary.* Rev. ed. (Indianapolis: Liberty Fund, 1987), 217.

44. Charles Taylor made this point in a discussion of Berlant and Warner's original paper presented at a conference on Citizenship Under Duress, Northwestern University, 12 April 1997.

45. William Blake to Dr. John Trusler, 23 Aug. 1799, in *The Norton Anthology of English Literature* (New York: Norton, 1979), 2: 83.

locates irony in the communication system, rather than in the individual role. Abyss-artists alone would just stir everything up; abyss-redeemers alone would run out of things to explain. In spite of what both its friends and foes typically say, the liberal public is not solely rational or discursive. It depends, instead, on what we can precisely call a separation of powers between performance and criticism, action and commentary, drama and critique. To understand it we need what George Herbert Mead called a "philosophy of the act."[46] No one, including the actor, ever quite knows the full meaning of an act. Art and action are subject to vagueness, as C. S. Peirce put it.[47] Action, performance, gesture, and art all defy complete reduction to verbal reason. (And even language is subject to open-ended significance.) Each medium has its own laws. Canons of public reasonableness apply to discourse sooner than to performances. Theorists such as Habermas who make critique the ruling value of the public sphere risk choking off breathing space and scare off the duplicitous demons—or ambiguous angels—of the implicit. Abyss-artists depend on third parties to decipher their dumpster-diving.[48] The whole strategy of liberal public space, from Mill through the ACLU, depends on a collaboration between offensive social dramas and explanation by reasonable bystanders of their higher purpose, the translation of act into word.

Even though abyss-artists (Mill's outrageous speakers) like to postpone the public admission that they are serving an ultimate cathartic purpose, they are parasitic on abyss-redeemers for funds, forums, and legal protection. They like to loll in the danger of transgression and work hard to keep the old redeeming-hell narrative from taming their work with a happy ending. But as soon as they face charges of slumming for the sport alone, they can claim socially redeeming values. In a pinch friends of the cultural-transgressors—serving in the office of spectator-critic—will invoke the "critical purpose" or "art" argument when those less used to the homeopathic regime of small doses of poison start howling debauchery, indecency, or criminality. Abyss-artists otherwise resist warning labels. They prefer not to provide resources for interpretation but to leave the audience to get it on their own. Critics can read the twentieth-century Francis Bacon's paintings as a critique of western metaphysical terror, of our oppres-

---

46. George Herbert Mead, *The Philosophy of the Act* (Chicago: University of Chicago Press, 1938).

47. Charles Sanders Peirce, "Critical Common-Sensism," in *Philosophical Writings of Peirce,* ed. Justus Buchler (New York: Dover, 1955), 294–96.

48. The importance of performance and action in democracy is further developed below, especially in chap. 7.

sively prissy reaction to flesh.[49] They can read Sam Peckinpah's blood ballets as cinematic criticism of the violence-laden culture of the United States in the Vietnam era. Barbara Kruger says that her advertising-based graphic art is a critique-by-exaggeration of capitalist rhetoric. In each case the work abstains from telling you to read it ironically. (Art that tells you how to read it is usually not art.) Innocent onlookers might be forgiven for thinking that Bacon and Peckinpah rather enjoy the splattered flesh-and-blood or that Kruger glamorizes the commercial sensibility at the same time she criticizes it. If these artists are at war with violence or capitalism, they certainly do not seem to mind fraternizing with the enemy. Creating a dizzy uncertainty of purpose is part of their point. Audiences are expected to bring their own minds to the critical picnic, and the liberals' refusal to teach plainly what they regard as right and wrong has always irritated those who find clarity of doctrine superior to irony and indirection. Liberals respect the autonomy of reason too much for that. "Some assembly required" and "batteries not included" might be the twin mottos of the liberal public sphere.

The categories of abyss-artist and abyss-redeemer do not exhaust the options. Probably the great majority of people alive would not hear tales of erotic vomiting or gruesome torture as calls to repent from their oppressive ways. It is too obvious a point that the world has lots of types besides self-reflective liberals in it. (The world also has lots of people—probably about six billion—who cannot hear certain things without wanting to hit somebody.) Abyss-avoidance is a third option. Many cultures do not train souls for the ironic contortionism that liberal subjectivity calls for. Comparative modernization studies suggest that cultures with strong support for free expression are clustered in the Protestant cultural zone of northern Europe and America, plus Australia and New Zealand, and even there it does not have uniform support.[50] For Africa, Latin America, southern and eastern Europe, and Asia, absolutist tolerance of offense is rarely the majority public opinion (though such publics can also be less sensitive to outrage and scandal than their high-strung, richer neighbors to the north). And even among elite opinion worldwide there are important differences. In debates after World War II in the United Nations on freedom of the press, delegates from diverse countries had very different ideas about the social responsibility of the press, the right of reply, and the legitimacy of indecent speech;

49. Robert Newman, "(Re)Imaging the Postmodern Grotesque," in *The Image in Dispute,* ed. Dudley Andrew (Austin: University of Texas Press, 1997), 205–22.

50. Ronald Inglehart and Wayne E. Baker, "Modernization, Cultural Change, and the Persistence of Traditional Values," *American Sociological Review* 65 (2000): 19–51, interprets results from a series of fascinating empirical studies.

only the United States, Britain, the Netherlands, and Australia consistently supported robust press freedoms.[51] The notion that transgressions are the symptoms of liberty is rather exotic on a planetary scale. Cultures that have gone through the Protestant Reformation, legal-bureaucratic rationalization, and what the sociologist Norbert Elias called "the civilizing process" might know what to do with erotic vomiting and the slain body, but most of the world chooses not to stretch itself in the mud voluntarily.[52]

Liberals sometimes find themselves shocked at the outrage of some, the bafflement of others, who cannot make sense of their eager fraternization with demons. Curiously, they fail to reflect on the ways their own program is offensive—or perhaps they are so used to the notion that offenses are the entering wedges of progress that they do not care. (The more rigorous civil libertarians sometimes take pride in their offensive defense of the offensive as a necessary lesson for an intolerant society.) Disdain for the experience of people who do not obey its rules of rationality is one of liberalism's worst sins. In the free speech story, toleration of diverse opinions helped bring about a world-historical graduation from bad tempers. Those who cannot tell sticks and stones from names are stuck, in this view, in a previous era. People who think that correct words and ideas matter mortally need to get a grip. Good modern citizens in this story know how to set aside firm conviction and enter into congress with any doctrine, at least enough to engage in a civil exchange of wits with it. Lee Bollinger suggests that one of free speech's roles is to teach minds to be disobedient.[53] Moses, Confucius, Socrates, Buddha, Jesus, and Muhammad would all be puzzled by a high value placed on disobedience. Irreverence is prized only in some cultural systems. Liberals risk mistaking conviction as blindness, and solidarity as stubbornness, and rarely understand why someone would willingly reject self-reflection as a model of mind and heart. Knowledge does not necessarily bring happiness. For comfort and "quality of life," there is no beating the prosperous regions of the modern world, but no one claims that this world has solved the age-old riddles any better than the older wisdoms (with all their follies). Lacking limits to inquiry accounts for much of what is great and terrible about the modern world. Milton authorizes an attitude of

---

51. Kenneth Cmiel, "Human Rights, Freedom of Information, and the Origins of Third World Solidarity," in *Truth Claims: Representation and Human Rights,* ed. Mark Philip Bradley and Patrice Petro (New Brunswick, N.J.: Rutgers University Press, 2002), 107–30.

52. Norbert Elias, *Über den Prozess der Zivilisation: Soziogenetische und psychogenetische Untersuchungen* (1939). 2 vols. (Frankfurt: Suhrkamp, 1997). Translated into English as *The Civilizing Process.* 2 vols. (New York: Pantheon, 1982).

53. Bollinger, *The Tolerant Society,* 247.

avoidance. "Be lowly wise:/Think only what concerns thee and thy being;/ Dream not of other worlds," Raphael advises Adam (*Paradise Lost,* 8.173– 75). Neither abyss-artists nor abyss-redeemers have much time for lowly wisdom. Those who choose to avoid the produce of the deep are regularly tarred as pusillanimous by righteous transgressors of all stripes, and yet avoidance (or at least circumspection) is very much a live option for that part of the world's population too busy for snorkeling. Early morning sunshine tells me all I need to know. Paul thought you only needed to know one thing.

Liberal tell-all-ism, with its insistence that everyone be exposed to antigens, gives no civic shelter against the storms of steel, no protection against a hardened heart, and continues modern thought's contempt for the virtues of softness. You cannot, it says, avoid the abyss. Abyss-redeemers think you have to whiff the civet to be able to enjoy the perfume; some more recent, less thoughtful liberals do not think there is even really an abyss to worry about. For latter-day Stoic professionals, only weaklings and fools refuse to pass through the purifying flames of hell (as later chapters show). Satan, trying to persuade Eve to eat the forbidden fruit, explains the invigorating effects that will follow its consumption:

Thenceforth to Speculations high or deep
I turn'd my thoughts, and with capacious mind
Consider'd all things visible in Heav'n,
Or Earth, or Middle. (*Paradise Lost,* 9.602–5)

Such claims, in their unexceptionable virtue, are also a potential form of arrogance and tyranny. Contrast the Spartan boast recorded (or invented) by Thucydides: "And we are wise because we are not so highly educated as to look down on our laws and our customs, and are too rigorously trained in self-control to disobey them."[54] Know-nothings and survivalists agree that it is better to bypass the swamp. So does a host of decent people in the modern world of science, pluralism, and conflict. The great majority of human beings now or ever alive does not enjoy the luxury or disease of doubting everything. Some people have no inclination to expose themselves to the dark or have reasons why they might want to outfit their souls otherwise. They find tarrying with the negative too expensive. I am not romanticizing such people—they are creatures with bowels and nostrils like the rest of us, doing what they need to do. A "capacious mind" is not always the best way to live. Holy fools may miss something important—the pleasure of the con-

54. Thucydides, *History of the Peloponnesian War,* 1.84.

trast effect—but they also may retain a less bloody furniture of mind. A decent respect for the corruptibility of the heart might enjoin caution in making general policies about exposure. Compare the ancient notion of *theōria:* true knowledge gives not just a picture of the universe to admire, but a model of order for the soul to emulate. The ancients did not deny that the heart is full of corruptions. They were no spokesmen of a positive mental attitude, staying too perky to notice the darkness. But neither were they guilty (ah, there's the rub) of repression. To be alert and modern is to know rapine, nuclear catastrophe, death camps, Nazi medical experimentation, ad infinitum. The thresholds of disgust are set extremely high. Satan was not kidding when he told Eve about "Speculations high or deep." Does the capaciousness of our minds have no limits?

Liberal openness, since it recognizes no zones of sanctity, endorses a form of consciousness full of compassings of abstract ill. The civilized take pride in their ability to entertain abominations. The world is too much with us. Pigheaded ignorance is stupid, but it is something very different from a conscious decision not to subject certain parts of life to the inspections of reason. (Note how I have already lapsed into a liberal vocabulary with the mention of "conscious decision." There is no neutral standpoint.) Must civic consciousness be mixed with detailed knowledge of evil? Consider the exhortation of *The New Republic* to watch the video of the American journalist Daniel Pearl being decapitated by his kidnappers, which in June 2002 was, inevitably, put on the internet. "The images are, to put it mildly, tasteless; but surely there are times when truth is more important than taste," opined *The New Republic*. Surely? Anyone got a counterargument handy that taste is more important than truth? (Where is Oscar Wilde when you need him?) The editors have already won a monopoly on rectitude. Those who would prevent the video's distribution, the editorial continues, are motivated by "a more generalized squeamishness about the reality of the universe that the video shows: the facticity of evil. This fear must be fiercely resisted, if we are to have clarity about the struggle in which we now find ourselves. For this reason, a viewing of this hideous video is as instructive an experience as it is a shattering one."[55] Anyone with reasons to resist watching a murder—scruples about the feelings of Pearl's family, the certain self-knowledge that one would not be able to watch without grossly riveted fascination or some hardening of the heart—is treated as a scaredy-cat not

55. "Notebook," *The New Republic*, 24 June 2002: 8. For another interpretation of this video, see Susan Sontag, *Regarding the Pain of Others* (New York: Farrar, Straus, Giroux, 2003), 69–70.

ready to confront the abyss of how vile terrorism is. For the *New Republic* the only legitimate post-Holocaust consciousness is one that is constantly being seared afresh by knowledge of genocidal crimes against humanity. One understands this stance to images of mayhem as a reflection of the journal's politics of defending the state of Israel at all costs, but it does not work as a general moral recipe. The writers find in abyss-avoidance a kind of head-in-the-sand irresponsibility. Such arguments make me tired. There are perhaps better resources for convincing us of the facticity of evil than watching a pirate video. We might start with a mirror, invite some reflection on the dark night of the soul, and end with a study of history up to the present moment. In this sense we never avoid the abyss; we just choose the forms we take it in.

THE MORALITY OF TRANSGRESSION

This cast of characters—abyss-artists, -redeemers, and -avoiders—enacts much of our contemporary scene of free expression. They are a more detailed portrait of the trio mentioned in the introduction. Each is a caricature that only loosely describes specific people—except perhaps for the multitudes many of us contain. There are also varieties within each caricature such as the stoic professional that I will treat in chapter 5. Where do my sympathies lie with this quarrelsome bunch? I am writing this book to find out. It is already clear that liberal righteousness is a chief target. Yet an unmistakable sign that something of the liberal temper informs my argument is its penchant to criticize potential allies and ignore—or indulge—obvious enemies, to find something amusing or instructive in the foes of critical inquiry.

Milton, at least, is an abyss-redeemer, and his theme of transgression in the name of a greater good is an old script. Both the Jewish historians and the Christian theologians developed this vision. God, like humans, could break the law for reasons that subsequent history might or might not disclose. The Hebrew Bible is full of sublime and ridiculous ironies. The most basic story of Christianity, in turn, about a god despised and crucified as a common criminal who saves the world, likewise shows an ironic sensibility and a narrative sense for inversion. Paul excelled in both of these. The first shall be the last and the last shall be the first, as Jesus said. Even modern critics of Christianity find themselves occupying positions that had already been staked out and recuperated in advance. Nietzsche's pronouncement that God is dead reproduces a line found in a seventeenth-century Lutheran hymn, though with a very different thrust.[56] Everything can be assimilated by an ironic mode of interpreting history that pulls good out of evil and finds wisdom in the bitter fruit. As Adam says near the end of *Paradise Lost:*

O goodness infinite, goodness immense!
That all this good of evil shall produce,
And evil turn to good. (12.469–71)

Such irony, in a watered-down form, informs the liberal faith that no heresy is too frightening to be banned. Something of this tract oblique persists in the defense of extremist speech, so eager to digest all that is contrary. The free speech story in the twentieth century does without both God (except for its faith that all ideas will somehow add up to a useful social soup in the end) and radical evil (the worst sins it knows are censorship and close-mindedness). Like many other twentieth-century intellectual currents, it owes much to early modern thought and classical and biblical culture, especially in its ironic mode, its faith in inversion, and its rigorous openness to whatever happens. We should not place Milton in the pantheon of free speech theory because he said a few edifying and quotable things about truth vanquishing error, but rather because he taught us how to give Satan a chance to ply his eloquence and to learn from the encounter. He saw the human estate as the task of making choices in the field of good and evil, and held a philosophy of history that could discover a certain morality in transgression. Much more than a simple foe of censorship, Milton helped to write the twisted theology of redemption that, in diluted form, echoes unacknowledged through liberal defenses of liberty of communication. This theology helps fund the modern view of transgression as creation, the sense that moral justice comes in by crossing over to the dark side, from scouting the regions of sin and consorting with the friends of darkness. Peirce thought the following sentence from Henry James, Sr. solved the problem of evil: "It is no doubt very tolerable finite or creaturely love to love one's own in another, to love another for his conformity to one's self: but nothing can be in more flagrant contrast with the creative Love, all whose tenderness *ex vi termini* must be reserved only for what intrinsically is most bitterly hostile and negative to itself."[57] Love would be insipid if it only loved its like. An open contest between good and evil is the condition of real choice, and real care. This force-field houses at once human freedom and human condem-

56. G. W. F. Hegel, *Lectures on the Philosophy of Religion: The Lectures of 1827*, ed. Peter C. Hodgson, trans. R. F. Brown et al. (Berkeley: University of California Press, 1988), 468. Thus Hegel anticipates Nietzsche. See also his *Phänomenologie des Geistes*, paras. 752, 785.

57. Peirce, "Evolutionary Love" (1893), in *Philosophical Writings of Peirce*, 362.

nation. Humans find themselves in the field of wheat and tares, deciding how to respond to all the provoking objects. Whether the need for opposition in all things solves the problem of evil, it certainly gives us a rich set of reasons why offensive or difficult or dangerous speech might be permitted. Without transgression, grace would have remained inert. No one understood this better than he who explained the topsy-turvy human estate to the believers in Rome and left traces on Milton and you and me: "For God shut them all up in disobedience so that he might have mercy on them all" (Rom. 11:32).

CHAPTER THREE

Publicity and Pain

*. . . among the ancients, that celebrated Delphic inscription, Recognise Yourself . . . was
as much to say, divide yourself, or be two.*
—The 3rd Earl of Shaftesbury, *Characteristics*

English philosophers have a long-standing reputation for marvelous, superficial ideas. C. S. Peirce compared their philosophical approach to building entire houses of papier mâché.[1] The idea of liberty is one of the world's
greatest, and yet for at least two hundred years the liberal tradition has been
attacked in fairly predictable patterns, almost all of them having to do with
its conception of the self.

The critiques are largely of three types. One of the most persistent is that
liberalism is spiritually enervating. Since at least the Romantics, Locke and
his heirs have been charged with a deadening dullness. The program of liberty carried a flat account of the psyche and an empty account of society.
Tolerance is a form of arrogance, said August Schlegel; it passes over ultimate things as merely of private interest. Tolerance clips the wings of the
imagination. As an official policy it forces the admission that religious, political, or imaginative claims lack universality. It makes metaphors into sim-
iles: one's beliefs are at best "like" reality, not reality. The insult of the "as-if"
clings to every act of the imagination in Locke's universe. Of all the Romantics William Blake hated Locke worst, and Blake's disciple Yeats's lines long
sealed Locke's reputation as a soulless agent of a new mechanized universe:

---

1. Charles S. Peirce, "The Architecture of Theories" (1891), in *Philosophical Writings of Peirce*,
ed. Justus Buchler (New York: Dover, 1950), 315.

"Locke sank into a swoon;/ The Garden died;/ God took the spinning jenny/ Out of his side."[2] Whether the charge of heartless rationalism is fair of Locke is debatable, but it is certainly fair of James Mill, the utilitarian father of John Stuart Mill, who gave him one of history's most extraordinary educations. J. S. Mill eventually found himself in a spiritual crisis recounted in his *Autobiography* and sought to infuse his father's philosophical and political rational progressivism with the emotional and imaginative sustenance of poetry. His task was to combine Coleridge (the conservative Romantic poet) and Bentham (the radical utilitarian reformer). Mill's own critique of the liberal tradition from within has been repeated against him and his intellectual heirs in turn: liberal thought always seems to require a supplement, some art or vision, some fresh blood to fend off the anemia. This critique can come from the political left, center, or right, and usually is fundamentally aesthetic in its attack: liberalism gives us an ugly universe and a violated vision of the self.

Another long-standing critique is that liberalism has an atomistic sense of social relations. For Hegel, liberal politics denied solidarity, the rich ethical ties of *Sittlichkeit* ("ethical life"). He wanted a richer conception of human sociability that combined both individual self-realization and community-flourishing. Tocqueville and Dewey made similar points about the way individualism erodes public spirit and called for voluntary associations and enriched forms of community participation. Their lead has been followed by a burst of communitarian thinkers since the 1980s.[3] The requirement that civic selves be purged of personal commitments, these critics contend, dries the wellspring of political action—real human interests as worked out historically within communities. Calling for a self that is supposed to conjure up a devil's advocate for every argument and search every strange notion for shards of possible truth, as liberals enjoin, undermines grounds for firm political conviction and endorses a notion of disembedded rationality that is both foolish (since it does not exist in fact) and dangerous (since it legitimizes, and thus helps in part to realize, such fictions). Thus communitarians attack the core liberal doctrine of self-abstraction, which they think leads to nihilism, moral indecisiveness, and tabling questions that require urgent action or at least warrant public deliberation.

The third chief historical attack on liberalism targets its social exclusion, its failure to adequately account for power. Marx, of course, saw talk of

2. William Butler Yeats, "Fragments," *The Tower* (New York: Macmillan, 1928).
3. Such as Robert Bellah, Alasdair MacIntyre, Michael Sandel, Charles Taylor, and Robert Westbrook.

rights as a cover for class interest, and the coexistence of slavery, patriarchy, and class oppression with liberal philosophies as a badge of shame. The communitarian critique generally comes from the political right or center, and this one comes from the left. Liberal claims of abstraction and due process and impartiality serve as covers for more subtle kinds of discrimination. Recent multicultural critics have found liberalism to be racist and sexist. Self-abstraction, diverse thinkers argue, is not a universally available option but is culturally coded to harmonize with the historic experience of white propertied males. The deck of citizenship, they charge, is stacked in terms of gender, class, race, sexuality, and (dis)ability, as well as age, region, and religion. Not all selves are equally able to check their bodies at the door of the public sphere, and the requirement that they do so is at best a difficult barrier to participation and at worst a form of cruelty, a refusal to recognize a diversity of styles of embodied experience. The promise of universal inclusion, by virtue of its perpetual postponement, has proved itself a lie. Liberalism is blind to social structures and historical traumas, insists wrongheadedly on blind principles—such as "free speech"—in the face of obvious and rampant inequality, and ignores the ways that the very idea of a "public" sphere shunts aside much of foremost political importance as "the private" (gender, sex, family, property, the workplace, etc.). The liberal public thus is held to foster rather than transcend domination; its idyll of equal and open participation comforts those already nestled in the unmarked networks of power while abusing historically oppressed others. The call for public toughness can be a psychically damaging regime encouraging self-loathing in those whose bodies are marked in ways that make such distance impossible. This picture, rather exaggerated here, can be found in some feminist, poststructuralist, and postcolonial and critical race theory, and has diverse roots in social movements and in social thought.[4] Liberalism, long used to thinking of itself as the champion of universality and the enemy of cruelty, finds itself attacked as partial and cruel.

All three of these critiques place the liberal vision of self-transcendence front and center. For one it impedes an embodied experience of lived vital-

---

4. See, for example, Nancy Fraser, "Rethinking the Public Sphere: A Contribution to the Critique of Actually Existing Democracy," and Michael Warner, "The Mass Public and the Mass Subject," in Habermas and the Public Sphere, ed. Craig Calhoun (Cambridge: MIT Press, 1992), 109–42 and 377–401, respectively; Catherine MacKinnon, Only Words (Cambridge, Mass.: Harvard University Press, 1993); Mari J. Matsuda et al., Words That Wound: Critical Race Theory, Assaultive Speech, and the First Amendment (Boulder, Colo.: Westview, 1993); and David S. Allen and Robert Jensen, eds., Freeing the First Amendment: Critical Perspectives on Freedom of Expression (New York: New York University Press, 1995).

ity, for the next it blocks a collective vision of the good, and for the third it obscures social privilege. The liberal public looks either like a dull morass, a resounding failure, or a violent distortion. In this chapter I will suggest that one key bone of contention is the strenuous attitude toward suffering, the lingering traces of a martial masculinity that inform the liberal ideal of self-abstraction. In political and moral theory today it is not the Cartesian cogito, as Slavoj Žižek claims, but rather its cousin, the Stoic self impervious to pain, against which the hosts are arrayed in battle.[5] Those who attack the liberal tradition for its atomism, egotism, or idealism—common post-Hegelian critiques—make telling but glancing blows. The deep dissatisfaction lies in the self-suspension of the liberal subject, the long legacy of traumatophilia. As Michael Warner said over a decade ago, "The political meaning of the public subject's self-alienation is one of the most important sites of struggle in contemporary culture."[6] Locke, Smith, and Mill give us one glimpse into the "hearts of men," at least of a certain class, race, and nation, at least as those hearts are imagined in theory (which may, in turn, be part of what is wrong with those hearts).

THE PUBLIC REALM AS SUBLIMATION

When we unearth the Stoic substratum in liberal ethical and political thought, we discover that classic liberals were not spinning ahistorical rationalist formulas. On the contrary, they were intensely interested in ancient moral theory. Foundational thinkers of liberty revved their engines on the high octane stuff of intense suffering and its overcoming. While Locke is certainly a polemical individualist, he does not give us a go-it-alone cowboy selfhood, but has a deep sense of human fallibility and frailty. Locke, in my reading, sees the self less as a utility-maximizer than a fallen godling. Adam Smith, in a much profounder way than Locke, sees humans as deeply social animals, and in this he is in the mainstream of the Scottish Enlightenment. The complication is this: our judgment and regard for each other are radically public, but our feelings of sorrow or delight are bounded by the limited circumference of sympathy. Pain, for Smith, can make no special claim on public attention. His suppression of pain is not an indifferent withdrawal from human fellowship or a callous endorsement of toughness, but a call to live together without overtaxing the limited wells of public care and

5. Slavoj Žižek, *The Ticklish Subject: The Absent Centre of Political Ontology* (London: Verso, 1999), 1–2.

6. Warner, "The Mass Public," 387.

thereby to find emotionally sustainable political regimes. Smith's half-praise of self-love is partly a critique of the wastefully violent ethic of male honor and valor that preceded him.[7] John Stuart Mill, in turn, whose call for asceticism in the realm of opinion still resounds in certain cultural zones and institutions, mixes a Romantic notion of self-expression with a strenuously rational self-suspension. Locke, Smith, and Mill all advocate, sometimes in ways that are shockingly graphic to our comparatively tender tastes, a stance of insensibility to the entreaties of pain, whether from within or without. To give suffering a privileged voice in public debate, they believe, is to let the show-stopper of egocentric privilege onto the stage: all of us, being mortal, necessarily know suffering, but all of us, being human, think our own pain more special than anyone else's.

Pain, more than anything else, defies intersubjectivity. At its worst the liberal tradition of public toughness can degenerate into a wanton celebration of truth's power to take the punishment. At its best it provides a check on egoism, a public-spiritedness, and a receptivity to other people. In the most generous reading, by freeing public actors from the insistent demands of the body, liberal thinkers hope to teach the preeminently political art of imagination, the ability to appreciate the viewpoints of others.[8] This is the reading for which I cast my vote: self-abstraction not as macho asceticism but as other-oriented listening.

Liberals are not alone in their conviction that self-transcendence is the prerequisite for public life. This is a core Stoic notion, and one that has shaped thinking about public life since antiquity. There is often something harsh in the public. Defining exactly what is public and private is a difficult task, but one key is the sublimation of the body. Bodies are baptized, punished, married, and buried in public. You are put on the spot, frozen and pinned down before the eyes and ears of strangers. Private parts and private interests are not allowed to be published. In public you don fig leaves; you discover the third person—Satan in both Genesis and *Paradise Lost* is a third party who teaches Adam and Eve shame. Benvolio in *Romeo and Juliet* states a classic view of the public realm:

> We talk here in the public haunt of men:
> Either withdraw unto some private place,
> Or reason coldly of your grievances,
> Or else depart; here all eyes gaze on us. (III.i)

7. Stephen Holmes, *Passions and Constraint: On the Theory of Liberal Democracy* (Chicago: University of Chicago Press, 1995), chap. 2.

8. Hannah Arendt, *Lectures on Kant's Political Philosophy,* ed. Ronald Beiner (Chicago: University of Chicago Press, 1982).

The public is the regime of witnesses and third parties. Since antiquity the distinctive feature of the public realm has been its liability to the gaze and hearing of strangers. Public words and deeds are "on record." The law of the public is accountability. Public words and deeds are subject to accountants and notaries; "public" is that which is entered into the record. The public realm is like a press conference, a recording studio, a film set: a site in which every move is potentially observed and noted. Publicity fixes what people say and do without mercy before (potentially) everyone. The Greeks had the word *kleos,* or acoustic fame, as the prize or curse of anyone caught in a public act. Hannah Arendt and Milan Kundera have both treated "immortality," a fame or reputation that never dies (for good and ill), as the mark of the public realm. The public realm countenances no purely dyadic relations. Every public act or utterance engages third parties, whether as eavesdroppers, spectators, inspectors, police, judges, enemies, or friends. This definition was shared by thinkers as disparate as John Dewey and Jean-Paul Sartre.[9] In ancient Greece the theater was coeval with democracy and its key mass medium of communication, and both theater and democracy involve dialogue whose actual audience is not the interlocutors, but those who listen in.[10] This communicative constellation—dialogues between two or three people staged for a third party—is symbolic of public settings generally.

The impersonality of the public—its communications deflected to third parties—is a close fit with Stoic norms of public speaking to whom it may concern and without self-regard. Public affairs are staffed by officers and officiators, figures whose personal identity is irrelevant. Common carriers— postal workers, telephone operators, railway conductors—may pass no judgment on the specifics of what is carried; as persons they are indistinct. Messengers are ideally uninformed about the message they carry, in the mode of the classically discreet English butler who hears nothing but understands everything. The simplest and perhaps oldest definition of an office (*officium* in Latin, "duty") is something that you do not personally profit from. Using an office for private gain is the definition of corruption. The official is ideally immune to the temptations attendant to the job: why the doctor is considered a hero of professional control. Self-interest is banished in public. The Roman vision of the official continues in the modern

9. John Dewey, *The Public and Its Problems* (New York: Henry Holt, 1927), chap. 1; Jean-Paul Sartre, *Critique of Dialectical Reason* (1960), trans. Alan Sheridan-Smith (London: NLB, 1967), 1: 253–69.

10. See Paul Cartledge, "'Deep Plays': Theater as a Process in Greek Civic Life," in *The Cambridge Companion to Greek Tragedy,* ed. P. E. Easterling (Cambridge: Cambridge University Press, 1997), 3–35.

world in Prussian bureaucracy, the British civil service, and the American social sciences. The captain goes down with the ship. Flight attendants read the safety instructions even though nobody is listening. Buses follow their routes even if there are no passengers. Extras in films and plays do not break character even when they are peripheral to the scene. Radio and TV stations broadcast a signal even if they do not know whether anyone is listening or watching. Many scientists ignore the end-use of their work. All these familiar gestures model the ethic of passive invariance that is supposed to define the duty of public service. J. V. Cunningham's "Motto for a Sundial" catches this ethic beautifully: "I who by day am a function of the light/Am constant and invariant at night."[11] Somewhat like Indo-European notions of the sacred, the meaning of "public" has both a cursed and a blessed aspect.[12] The public is the site in which personal standing is sacrificed to the whole, in glory or infamy. "Public" comes from the Latin *poplicus,* an early form of *populus* ("people"), and was influenced by the related word *pubes,* meaning the adult male population that could be mobilized for war.[13] Curiously, the immobility and abstraction of public things refers to something we regard as quintessentially private. "Public," as the persistent typos tell us, is etymologically related to "pubic."[14] The original meaning of *pubes* may have been "pubic hair," a prerequisite in Rome for serving both as a soldier and as a witness (*testis*). "Privates"—in the sense of lacking rank or honor—applies equally to soldiers and the genitals, as in Guildenstern's bawdy pun about Dame Fortune in *Hamlet:* "Faith, her privates we."[15] Similar imagery shows up in various senses of the Latin verb *publicare* across a significant range of registers: "a. To make public property, place at the disposal of the community. b. to exhibit publicly. c. to prostitute."[16] Indeed, the term prostitute comes from the Latin meaning "to stand in public" (i.e., before the temple—*pro-fanum*—in profane space). What concerns the people as a collective requires public exhibition, which carries the duality of shame and honor. The first sense of *publicare,* after all, means to confiscate private

11. J. V. Cunningham, "Motto for a Sundial," in *Literature: An Introduction to Fiction, Poetry, and Drama,* ed. X. J. Kennedy (Boston: Little, Brown, 1976), 517.

12. Émile Benveniste, *Indo-European Language and Society,* trans. Elizabeth Palmer (Coral Gables, Fla.: University of Miami Press, 1973), 452ff. See Josh. 6:18–19 for a Hebrew juxtaposition of consecration and curses.

13. Lucian Hölscher, *Öffentlichkeit und Geheimnis: Eine begriffsgeschichtliche Untersuchung zur Entstehung der Öffentlichkeit in der frühen Neuzeit* (Stuttgart: Klett-Cotta, 1979), 37, 41.

14. J. N. Adams, *The Latin Sexual Vocabulary* (London: Duckworth, 1982), 76, 68.

15. *Hamlet,* II.ii.231.

16. P. G. W. Glare, *Oxford Latin Dictionary* (Oxford: Clarendon Press, 1982), 1512.

property for the common purse. (Communitarian dreams of a civic-spirited public boil down at least to paying taxes.)

"Public" partly means unbounded potential access, authorization to enter without invitation.[17] The public is ruled by exposure, in every sense of that word: exposure to the elements (danger), photographic exposure (documenting), indecent exposure (body revelation), uncovering of the hidden (exposé).[18] Persons, places, and things are more freely inspectable in public places. Soundproof rooms or walls are one mark of the private.[19] Public objects of state veneration, like flags, national memorials, and state capitals, are well-lit at night, while private things, if not entirely dark, appear in chiaroscuro. In both the post office and the university library in Iowa City—the one a federal space, the other a state of Iowa space—there are posted warnings that any concealed package may be inspected, and that anyone suspected of theft or a weapons violation may be subject to a strip search by a member of the same sex.[20] We all waltz through the potential Panopticon. In public spaces the power to reveal everything hidden, down to the body in its nakedness, is constantly, if subtly, reaffirmed. According to J. S. Mill, "All places of public resort require the restraint of a police."[21] Without the possibility for sanction, there is no public. A musical work in the public domain means that no individual claims copyright; it may be performed promiscuously. The Greek notion of *parrhēsia*, often translated as "freedom of speech," means more precisely the courage to hold nothing back, to tell all.[22] The public is potentially a place of nakedness.

The double-edged ideal of impersonality is perhaps most explicit in the gender associations: a public man was, until recently, a civil servant, while a public woman was a prostitute. Both were assumed to offer their services indifferently to any comer. The loose coupling of public life was a matter of honor to men and of shame to women, as reflected in this lingering semantic asymmetry.[23] Statuary, which captures public figures in a single gesture,

17. Vitruvius, *Ten Books on Architecture* (De architectura libri decem), trans. Ingrid D. Rowland (Cambridge: Cambridge University Press, 1999), 6.5.1.

18. Page duBois, *Torture and Truth* (London: Routledge, 1991).

19. Erving Goffman, *Behavior in Public Places: Notes on the Social Organization of Gatherings* (New York: Free Press, 1963), 8.

20. One more little bit of heteronormativity to add to the list: Lauren Berlant and Michael Warner, "Sex in Public," *Publics and Counterpublics* (New York: Zone, 2002), 195.

21. J. S. Mill, *Considerations on Representative Government* (1861), in *Great Books of the Western World,* ed. Robert Maynard Hutchins (Chicago: Encyclopedia Britannica, 1952), 4: 315.

22. Michel Foucault, *Fearless Speech* (1983) (Los Angeles: Semiotexte, 2001).

23. According to Ulpian's *Digest,* i.16, 195, "feminae ab omnibus oficiis civilibus vel publicis

but deprived of flesh and blood, is likewise differentiated along gender lines, in England at least, where it splits into specific men and generic women. Statues of men are historic figures (Horatio Nelson), and those of women are of abstractions (Truth).[24] Both roles probably originate in the temple complex: the public man as priest whose individuality is only a cipher as he officiates for the whole in sacrificing and slaughtering the animal, and the public woman as temple prostitute. Priests concern themselves (discreetly) with the disposal of the burnt carcass, the cleaning of the blood off the altar. They have leave to desecrate the sacred in the line of duty. This is the attitude of doctors, soldiers, reporters, judges, and social scientists. Female professionals, in this old bad narrative, at least have the option of compassion and feeling, but the special privilege of suspending one's normal feelings of disgust or outrage or compassion has a long history.

Stoicism plays a strong role in these notions of public immobility and impassivity. The public figure puts private interest on hold, is the empty vessel of the community, speaks to whom it may concern, and vents no sign of emotion. Like sundials or statues, public figures will not budge from their appointed role. They reason coldly of their grievances. Stoic philosophy—which was massively influential on Anglo-American moral and political thought and culture, especially via Cicero (whose philosophy is eclectic rather than Stoic)—regarded abstraction from one's emotions and interests as a portal to the natural order. The capacity for such abstraction revealed the universal relatedness of human beings as rational creatures. Cicero's *De Officiis* (On the Duties) "is the most widely read text in moral philosophy in the western tradition, period."[25] In the New Stoicism of Cicero's time, which emphasized moral and political concerns over the cosmological and physical themes that had occupied earlier Stoics, the good could appear only when viewed without partiality. *Apatheia*—a Greek term that is the forerunner of our word apathy but is better rendered as indifference, equanimity, or tranquility—is a key virtue for Cicero. To see life under the aspect of eternity demands obliviousness to one's own private welfare.

remotae sunt" (Women are free from—or removed from—all civil or rather public duties). Quoted in *Encyclopedia Britannica*. 11th ed. (1911), 28: 782.

24. Marina Warner, *Monuments and Maidens: The Allegory of the Female Form* (London: Weidenfeld & Nicholson, 1985).

25. Quentin Skinner, "The English Revolution as a War of National Liberation." Lecture at the Center for the Study of Democracy, University of Westminster, London, 9 May 2000. See also Martha C. Nussbaum, *The Therapy of Desire: Theory and Practice in Hellenistic Ethics* (Princeton, N.J.: Princeton University Press, 1994), 512.

("Sullen apathy," said Hume, preferring the sociable virtues.[26]) Cicero argues that a vision of cosmic order can help found an analogous order in the state and the soul. "Again, we must keep ourselves free from every disturbing emotion, not only from desire and fear, but also from excessive pain and pleasure, and from anger, so that we may enjoy that calm of soul and freedom from care which bring both moral stability and dignity of character." Freedom from passion is especially valuable for public servants: "Statesmen, too, no less than philosophers—perhaps even more so—should carry with them that greatness of spirit and indifference to human things to which I so often refer, together with calm of soul and freedom from care."[27] Cicero is perhaps recalling Plato's requirement that philosopher-kings be reluctant to rule. Like cowboy heroes, they must be coaxed into service; eagerness for power is ipso facto a disqualification. Stoic notions of a transcendent rational order and world citizenship were influential on such figures as Huig de Groot (Grotius), the inventor of international law, and Immanuel Kant, who, among other, better-known accomplishments, envisioned a worldwide body dedicated to the pursuit of eternal peace, a sort of proto–United Nations. Kant had little interest in compassion and considered apathy a virtue.[28] In the neoclassical eighteenth century, Stoic notions infused revolutionary fervor in both the United States and France. The heroic regimen of self-abstraction enabled both moral virtue (solidarity with one's fellows) and cognitive virtue (openness to truth greater than the self).

In today's common parlance, "stoic" refers to an attitude of self-denial advantageous for dieters and joggers, rather than to a long philosophical tradition. As "one of the permanent moral possibilities within the cultures of the West," however, Stoicism continues to inform, often in dangerously diluted forms, notions of public life, including of public expression and communication.[29] My aim is not to trace its manifold branches and influ-

26. David Hume, "The Stoic," in *Selected Essays,* ed. Stephen Copley and Andrew Edgar (New York: Oxford University Press, 1998), 88.

27. Cicero, *De Officiis,* trans. Walter Miller (Cambridge, Mass.: Harvard University Press, 1938), I.xx, para. 69, I.xxi, para. 73.

28. Max Horkheimer and Theodor W. Adorno, *Dialektik der Aufklärung: Philosophische Fragmente* (1944), in Adorno, *Gesammelte Schriften* (Frankfurt: Suhrkamp, 1981), 3: 115.

29. Alasdair MacIntyre, *After Virtue: A Study in Moral Theory.* 2nd ed. (Notre Dame: Notre Dame University Press), 170. A leading interpreter of the continuing relevance of Stoicism is Martha C. Nussbaum. See, in addition to her *Therapy of Desire, Upheavals of Thought* (New York: Cambridge University Press, 2001).

ences but rather to explore the understanding of public character as tempered by the fire of suffering. Stoicism was long the favored philosophy of the warrior class, and it is a tradition that praises in equal measure the virtues of discipline, military valor, courage, and even suicide when duty demands. Some Roman Stoics met gruesome deaths: Cicero had his tongue and hands nailed over the rostrum, Cato killed himself, and Seneca slit his wrists in obedience to Emperor Nero's (his former student) implied command. Marcus Aurelius wrote his *Meditations* in his leisure time during border skirmishes with Germanic tribes, as dramatized in the film *Gladiator* (2000). The tranquility and self-abstraction taught by Stoics often went together with killing. Stoicism is in part a doctrine of toughness that teaches those who kill to be indifferent to death, their own or that of others.[30] This makes it both an edifying and a dangerous doctrine, a moral educator that teaches us to deal with our own mortality and an amoral bane that can teach us to harden our hearts to pity for the deaths of others. Stoicism echoes in the free speech story via the notion that the civic heart should be able to withstand the assault of any doctrine, and has robust exponents in Locke, Smith, Mill, and Holmes, as we will see.

LOCKE'S PROJECT OF SELF-DISCIPLINE

Cicero's influence on John Locke is readily visible in his *Some Thoughts Concerning Education* (1693), which, with Cicero's *On the Duties,* is one of the most influential educational treatises in European history. In the *Thoughts* Locke recommends "Tully's *Offices*" for "the Principles and Precepts of Virtue for the Conduct of his Life" and for "the true Idea of Eloquence" (Tully = Marcus Tullius Cicero). Locke considers hardening the body and mind to be the chief tasks of education. Children should avoid fruits, cold drinks, and wine, expose their heads and feet to cold, eat nothing but bread for breakfast, and sleep on hard beds to toughen their bodies, and they must also develop mental fortitude. "As the strength of the Body lies chiefly in being able to endure Hardships, so also does that of the Mind. And the great Principle and Foundation of all Virtue and Worth is plac'd in this: That a Man is able to deny himself his own Desires, cross his own Inclinations, and purely follow what Reason directs as best, tho' the Appetite lean the other Way." Such discipline belongs to a particular class, gender, and race: "A Gentleman in any Age ought to be so bred, as to be fitted to bear Arms, and be a Soldier." Locke was essentially writing a recipe for English

---

30. Horkheimer and Adorno, *Dialektik der Aufklärung,* 3: 116.

public school education. Pain is a key part of the curriculum for gentleman-soldiers: "inuring Children gently to suffer some Degrees of Pain without shrinking, is a way to gain Firmness to their Minds, and lay a Foundation for Courage and Resolution in the future Part of their lives."[31] Let us be clear. Locke is no celebrant of pagan brutality or Christian asceticism; he is a champion of moderation. Since pain is inevitable, fostering an ability to cope with it is one of education's chief tasks. That Locke is not afraid of a certain moral hardness is clear in his definition of power elsewhere: "Political power I take to be a right of making laws with penalties of death."[32] A gentle man and a gentleman, Locke calls for the purgatorial trials of self-discipline as training for citizenship. Such doctrine funds modern visions of free expression: as we sleep on hard beds, so we should hear harsh words. Locke's ideas about firmness of mind and courage are clearly located in the cultural matrix (patrix?) of British gentility. Is there a way to foster these virtues without dragging along that baggage? Is the notion of virtue itself (a word deriving from the Latin *vir*, "man") corrupted by its long historical tie to manliness and virility?

In his historical context Locke is a moderate, part of the entering wedge of latitudinarian mellowness, and quite distant from the fiery hells painted by Puritan piety (outstandingly by Milton). His distinction between persuasion and coercion, like that between public and private, both of which are central to his *Letter Concerning Toleration* (1693), is aimed to allow peaceable zones of humane intercourse free of terror or compulsion. "The care of souls" is no business of any public authority, whose only concern can be the "civil interests" of "life, liberty, health, and indolency of body," a plumper version of Jefferson's more famous triad. In good Protestant style Locke places responsibility for salvation on each individual alone.[33] "Nobody is obliged . . . to yield obedience unto the admonitions or injunctions of another, further than he is himself persuaded. Every man has in that the supreme and absolute authority of judging for himself. And the reason is because nobody else is concerned in it, nor can receive any prejudice from his conduct therefrom." Since everyone is fallible, no one should wax dogmatic. The magistrate may punish people to enforce laws, but never to en-

31. John Locke, *Some Thoughts Concerning Education* (1693) (Cambridge: Cambridge University Press, 1902), 160, 162, 21, 12, 99.

32. John Locke, *Two Treatises of Government* (1689), ed. Peter Laslett (Cambridge: Cambridge University Press, 1991), 268.

33. It is difficult to capture the full complexity of Locke's philosophy of religion with the baggy label of Protestant. For one suggestive treatment, see W. M. Spellman, *John Locke and the Problem of Depravity* (Oxford: Clarendon Press, 1988).

force religious faith: "It is only light and evidence that can work a change in men's opinions; which light can in no manner proceed from corporal sufferings, or any other outward penalties." Fire and sword neither convict error nor teach truth. The individual has an inviolable liberty that no being, even God, can infringe. "God Himself will not save men against their wills." Because "everyone is orthodox to himself," the temptation to persecute others whose beliefs differ is almost overwhelming. The tendency to justify ourselves, to play favorites with our own beliefs, Locke argues, needs constraint. True Christianity consists not in interreligious strife or missionary zeal but in self-mastery: "Whosoever will list himself under the banner of Christ, must, in the first place and above all things, make war upon his own lusts and vices."[34] A similar discipline is required in our opinions. Our efforts to make the world more rational should start with training the self to abstract itself from what it thinks most assured.

The "sovereignty of the individual" (to use a phrase from Mill) can be secured, in part, because it is socially inconsequential. Locke drives matters of ultimate concern into the lair of conscience: "If any man err from the right way, it is his own misfortune, no injury to thee." Clashing convictions about ultimate things need not disturb the peace. "If a Roman Catholic believe that to be really the body of Christ which another man calls bread, he does no injury thereby to his neighbor."[35] The seemingly cavalier indifference finds another famous echo in Jefferson's declaration that it does not pick his pocket if his neighbor believes in one god or twenty. By privatizing controversy Locke and friends hope to keep the public realm clear of combustible materials. Locke's price of public peace is the sequestering of the most contentious matters to the private or personal realm. Locke provides the basic ingredients of the liberal theory of public space: the guiding contrast between coercion and persuasion, the inviolable liberty of individual conscience, the social productivity of public conflict, the hiding of intractable kinds of contention in private life, and the hope that truth will work its way to the fore. But he was clearly no Mill or Holmes who would defend the right of almost anyone to say almost anything. Like Milton's, his tolerance had limits. His umbrella would extend no protection to atheists, and he believed the Holy Ghost would ultimately settle the most difficult disputes.

In both the *Education* and the *Letter Concerning Toleration*, Locke made war on what the ancients called *philautia* ("self-love") and the moderns

---

34. John Locke, *A Letter Concerning Toleration*, in *Great Books of the Western World* (Chicago, Encyclopedia Britannica, 1952), 35: passim.

35. Locke, *A Letter*, 35: 6, 15.

would call amour propre or egotism. In his most famous work, *An Essay Concerning Human Understanding* (1690), Locke worked out a mode of human knowing that was in part built to teach people self-discipline in cognitions. Thomas Hobbes spoke for the whole conflicted tradition of English philosophy when he noted that most people are "vehemently in love with their own new opinions . . . and obstinately bent to maintain them."[36] Locke seeks to moderate such vehemence. Taking up a theme as old as Plato—the delirium of *doxa*—Locke notes our natural preference for our own opinions even when they are unfounded. "May we not find a great number (not to say the greatest part) of Men, that think they have formed right Judgments of several matters; and that for no other reason, but because they never thought otherwise? That imagine themselves to have judged right, only because they never questioned, never examined their own Opinions?" Locke is not condemning his fellow humans; he is assessing our cognitive equipment. Certainty is correlated with lack of reflection: "And yet these of all Men hold their Opinions with the greatest stiffness; those being generally the most fierce and firm in their Tenets, who have least examined them." Such firmness, stiffness, and fierceness in holding opinions is, Locke notes, a potential source of civil strife. Yet none of us, practically speaking, can ever examine all our beliefs or find sure proofs of them, and even the most thoughtful of us cannot reconstruct all the reasons for holding them. Nor would it be fair or wise to expect people to change their beliefs every time they found themselves unable to answer counterarguments (Locke's mental discipline, as we will see, is less exigent than Mill's). So "to maintain Peace, and the common Offices of Humanity, and Friendship," he proposes mutual toleration of opinions. The practice of examining opinions in order to make them rest as much as possible on reason rather than tradition or inertia makes us better neighbors and citizens. "The necessity of believing, without Knowledge, nay, often upon very slight grounds, in this fleeting state of Action and Blindness we are in, should make us more busy and careful to inform our selves, than constrain others."[37]

A beautiful example of Locke's ethic of cognitive abstemiousness occurs in his essay on Paul. Ordinary readers, he complains, not being aware of the multiple ways that Paul's letters are mediated (by editing, history, language, etc.), unwittingly take them as a mirror of their own minds. "Sober inquisitive readers had a mind to see nothing in St. Paul's epistles but just what he meant; whereas those others, of a quicker and gayer sight, could see in them

---

36. Thomas Hobbes, *Leviathan* (1651) (Cambridge: Cambridge University Press, 1996), 48.

37. Locke, *An Essay Concerning Human Understanding*, IV.xvi: 3, 4.

what they pleased. Nothing is more acceptable to fancy than pliant terms, and expressions that are not obstinate; in such it can find its account with delight, and with them be illuminated, orthodox, infallible at pleasure, and in its own way." The mischief of reading in this way is bringing one's orthodoxies "to the sacred Scripture, not for trial, but confirmation." Locke worries here about interpretive narcissism. "This is to explain the apostles' meaning by what they never thought of whilst they were writing; which is not the way to find their sense, in what they delivered, but our own, and to take up, from their writings, not what they left there for us, but what we bring along with us in ourselves." Instead, we should read the epistles as wholes with an internal shape, remembering Paul's skill as a speaker and allowing the text its historicity. Never was there a clearer call for transparent historical reading: "until we, from his words, paint his very ideas and thoughts in our minds, we do not understand him."[38] The reader is to be a passive medium, a screen for projecting authorial meaning alone. "I have, for my own information, sought the true meaning, as far as my poor abilities would reach. And I have unbiassedly embraced what, upon a fair inquiry, appeared so to me. . . . If I must believe for myself, it is unavoidable that I must understand for myself." Such scruples, he claims, "exempt me from all suspicion of imposing my interpretation on others." Locke warns his readers not to rely on his interpretation alone, or that of anyone else: "We are all men, liable to errors, and infected with them."[39] Locke's advice on how to read Paul provides a resonant set of gestures: fidelity to the authorial meaning, a Protestant respect for each individual as a reader, and the scruple, so relevant in enlightened climes today, of not imposing interpretations on others. Here he offers a linked understanding of communication, historical investigation, civility, and the morality of knowing. In all his works, whether on education, tolerance, knowledge, or scripture, Locke's project was centrally to create selves capable of self-separation and -mastery, whether bodily, moral, political, or cognitive.

ADAM SMITH AND THE FORTUNATE IMPOSSIBILITY OF SYMPATHY

Adam Smith, a key figure in the Scottish Enlightenment, sits at the center of a major reorientation in attitudes toward pain in the mid-eighteenth cen-

---

38. Thus Locke foreshadows positivist historiography 130 years before Ranke.

39. John Locke, "Preface: An Essay for the Understanding of St. Paul's Epistles, by consulting St. Paul himself" (1823), in *The Works of John Locke* (Aalen, Germany: Scientia Verlag, 1963), 8: 3–23 passim.

tury, the rise of the modern humanitarian sensibility.[40] Like Locke, Smith owes much of his ethical thought to Cicero and the Stoics. Both were philosophical eclectics heavily influenced by Stoicism, and Smith is in some sense a latter-day Cicero. Smith's *Theory of Moral Sentiments* (1759) offers a vision of selfhood that blends tenderness and harshness.[41] Eighteenth-century Scottish thought insisted, against Hobbes, Locke, and the main lines of seventeenth-century political thought, that human society resulted from natural gregariousness, rather than being an artificial body composed of contracts. At the heart of the Scottish Enlightenment were soft virtues: sensibility, sympathy, communication.[42] In the eighteenth century gentlemen wore tights, silks, and wigs, bore names such as Anne and Maria, and explored a new range of sentimental expression. For David Hume sympathy was instantaneous, an almost physical transfer. For his disciple and executor, Adam Smith, in contrast, the only access to another's thoughts or feelings was through the imagination or reason. Hume thought humans have a quick faculty of analogical inference or receptive empathy that allows them to divine the thoughts and feelings of others. The "minds of men," he wrote, "are mirrors to one another." "No quality of human nature is more remarkable than that propensity we have to sympathize with others, and to receive by communication their inclinations and sentiments, however different from or even contrary to, our own." [43] Communication for Hume is a sharing more primal than words, an almost animal intimacy between people. Hume may have thought he was describing nature, but his vision of the mutual tenderness to human feelings is part of an important shift in opinion, a historically new moral tenderness and emotional sensitivity. In Hume and Smith's era, codes of masculine behavior were shifting from the prickly violence of an honor ethic to compassion with others' torment;

40. See Karen Halttunen, "Humanitarianism and the Pornography of Pain in Anglo-American Culture," *American Historical Review,* April 1995: 303–34; and Thomas L. Haskell, "Capitalism and the Origins of the Humanitarian Sensibility, parts 1 and 2" (1985), in Haskell, *Objectivity Is Not Neutrality: Explanatory Schemes in History* (Baltimore: Johns Hopkins University Press, 1998), 235–79.

41. On Smith and Stoicism, see A. L. Macfie, *The Individual in Society* (London: Allen & Unwin, 1967); John Dwyer, *Virtuous Discourse* (Edinburgh: John Donald, 1987); and M. A. Stewart, "The Stoic Legacy in the Early Scottish Enlightenment," in *Atoms, Pneuma, and Tranquility: Epicurean and Stoic Themes in European Thought,* ed. Margaret J. Osler (Cambridge: Cambridge University Press, 1991), 273–96.

42. Gladys Bryson, *Man and Society: The Scottish Inquiry of the Eighteenth Century* (Princeton, N.J.: Princeton University Press, 1945).

43. David Hume, *A Treatise of Human Nature* (New York: Oxford University Press, 1978), 365, 316.

Smith's "spectatorial notion of sympathy" is one of its fullest expressions. As Karen Halttunen argues, the humanitarian impulse—the instinctive sense that suffering is an evil that deserves aid and relief—is less a natural capacity than a historical and cultural development.[44] Before anesthetics, pain was both an unavoidable and perhaps even courted experience: we shiver at the strenuousness of the gauntlet and the monastery today. Christianity had long seen pain as a means to engage in the *imitatio Christi* or purge the demons of the flesh. In the eighteenth century pain starts to become a source of moral motivation and reform.

Smith's *Theory of Moral Sentiments* is, says Julie Ellison, "part of the core curriculum of liberal emotion."[45] The book starts with a standard Stoic scenario: the spectacle of torture. "Though our brother is on the rack, as long as we are at our ease, our senses will never inform us of what he suffers. They never did and never can carry us beyond our own persons, and it is by the imagination only that we can form any conception of what are his sensations."[46] Yet we cannot remain dispassionate bystanders. "By the imagination we place ourselves in his situation, we conceive ourselves enduring all the same torments, we enter as it were into his body and become in some measure him, and thence form some idea of his sensations, and even feel something which, though weaker in degree, is not altogether unlike them" (TMS, 9). Even though Smith suggests a metaphoric sort of spirit-travel— "we enter as it were into his body"—our access to the pains of the other can only be a faint cognitive replica. His notion of sympathy is not a symmetrical affair nor a mutual sharing of feelings. The living, for example, commiserate with the dead, not because the dead have miserable feelings to impart—they have none, says Smith—but because the living would feel miserable if they, being alive, were moldering in the ground.[47] In one of several ghoulish expressions, Smith writes that we lodge "our own living souls in their inanimated bodies, and thence conceiv[e] what would be our emotions in that case" (TMS, 13; compare 71). Seeing a madman singing and laughing can make an onlooker feel miserable, not because the madman feels that way—indeed he seems rather jolly—but because we would feel

44. Halttunen, "Humanitarianism."

45. Julie Ellison, *Cato's Tears and the Making of Anglo-American Emotion* (Chicago: University of Chicago Press, 1999), 10.

46. Adam Smith, *The Theory of Moral Sentiments* (1759), ed. D. D. Rafael and A. L. Macfie (Oxford: Clarendon Press, 1976), 9. Hereafter cited in the text as TMS.

47. Esther Schor, *Bearing the Dead: The British Culture of Mourning from the Enlightenment to Victoria* (Princeton, N.J.: Princeton University Press, 1994), notes that Smith's views of the dead differ from later Victorian ideas of mourning, which allow for contact with departed spirits.

wretched if we, being sane, were mad. Sympathy, then, is not a secret tunnel between two people's inner feelings, but a judgment made by a spectator, an act of interpretation that never transcends the subjective point of view. Unlike the nineteenth-century Romantics, Smith holds no hope for communion with the inward recesses of another soul. All we can attain is our own conjecture of what we would feel in another's place. I never feel how you feel; I can only feel how (I imagine) I would I feel if I were you.

The Theory of Moral Sentiments repeatedly offers up scenes of torment with an almost Foucauldian relish: we are not supposed to burst into tears of pity but to recognize the limits of sympathy. To care for others is not always to match their pain: a good doctor will skip sympathizing with the patient and tend to the wound directly; a parent may ignore the squalls of an infant receiving a bath or fresh diaper. (So much for communication and care understood as shared thought or feeling.) Smith gives multiple examples of the virtue of "self-command": moderating the expression of passion so as not to strain the sympathy of onlookers. The man who vents no groan when undergoing severest torture "commands our highest admiration. His firmness enables him to keep time with our indifference and insensibility" (TMS, 30–31).[48] Warfare likewise provides an occasion for emotional heroics: a "man who has lost his leg by a cannon shot, and who, the moment after, speaks and acts with his usual coolness and tranquility" (TMS, 147) deserves our approval. War is the "great school both for acquiring and exercising this species of magnanimity" (TMS, 239). Smith even foreshadows the cinematic stereotype of the unflappable British officer: "His behavior is genteel and agreeable who can maintain his cheerfulness in the midst of a number of frivolous disasters" (TMS, 47).[49] Gentility means equipoise in the midst of calamity. Smith's Theory of Moral Sentiments, like Locke's Thoughts, is a self-help manual for gentlemen, a genre that in some ways stretches back to Aristotle's Nicomachean Ethics: "people of a manly nature guard against making their friends grieve with them, and, unless he be especially insensible to pain, such a man cannot stand the pain that ensues for his friends, and in general does not admit fellow-mourners because he himself is not given to mourning; but women and womanly men enjoy sympa-

48. Since ancient Greece, silence under torture has been a sign of aristocratic bearing: P. DuBois, Torture and Truth. See Euripides, Iphigeneia in Aulis, 11. 446–53, on why noblemen don't cry.

49. J. B. S. Haldane, A. R. P. (London: Victor Gollancz, 1938), 57, writing of his experiences in the Spanish Civil War, noted that responses to air raids were diverse. "Some people talk volubly, others are silent. . . . Personally I generally think that I shall be killed, and say to myself, 'Well, well, so this is the end of me. How curious.'" Another unflappable Brit.

thisers in their grief, and love them as friends and companions in sorrow."[50] Aristotle's gendering of the division of sentimental labor is more extreme even than Adam Smith's. There is no doubt that Smith thinks men are more exposed to pain than women, and therefore more constrained to sublimate their agonies, but his argument goes in a rather gender-blending direction, praising the virtues of both sympathetic care and Stoic self-command.

Self-command is not the exclusive province of British gentlemen. One passage gives an extended fantasy about the "absolute self-command" of the "savages in North America." "They often bear, in the sight of all their countrymen, with injuries, reproach, and the grossest insults, with the appearance of the greatest insensibility, and without expressing the smallest resentment." When a prisoner of war is taken by an enemy tribe, he will receive his sentence of death without any sign of emotion, and "afterwards submits to the most dreadful torments, without ever bemoaning himself, or discovering any other passion but contempt of his enemies." These torments can include slow roasting over an open fire, and while he hangs there by his shoulders, "he derides his tormentors, and tells them with how much more ingenuity he himself had tormented such of their countrymen as had fallen into his hands." If the tormentors relieve the victim from the flames for a spell, the victim will continue to be "indifferent about nothing but his own situation." Savages prepare themselves their entire lives, says Smith, for bravery in the face of death. "The same contempt of death and torture prevails among all the other savage nations." Is Smith's interest in savage stoicism a subtle justification of the enslavement of non-European peoples on the grounds that pain does not mean the same thing for them? (The central tenet of modern humanitarianism is that all are equal in the ability to suffer.) Clearly not. He laments that such noble people are made the chattel of men of lesser virtue: "Fortune never exerted more cruelly her empire over mankind than when she subjected those nations of heroes to the refuse of the gaols of Europe" (TMS, 206). He is much closer to his sometime acquaintance Rousseau in praising savages for their superior virtue.

Smith's is an explicitly theatrical ethics: compassion comes by seeing the sorrow of another. The "amiable virtues" of humanity, sympathy, and pity concern the ability of a spectator to sympathize with an actor. Their foremost example, "humanity," is a readiness to be moved by the sorrows of others. The "respectable virtues" of self-command, magnanimity, and public spirit, in contrast, concern an actor's power to moderate the expression of passion so as not to strain an onlooker's capacity for feeling for him or

50. *Nicomachean Ethics*, ed. W. D. Ross (Oxford: Oxford University Press, 1980), IX:xi (1171b).

her. Its chief exhibit is "self-command."[51] Humanity has to do with our ability to sympathize with other people; self-command with our ability to turn down the volume of our own feelings. We sympathize with other people's limited ability to sympathize with us. Humanity is an audience virtue; self-command is an actor's virtue. The amiable virtues are motivated by care for others, just as the respectable virtues are animated by the desire to lessen the demands our feelings make on a jury of real or imagined peers. Smith recommends two moral options: increasing our sensitivity to other people's feelings and decreasing our sensitivity to our own. "As to love our neighbor as we love ourselves is the great law of Christianity, so it is the great precept of nature to love ourselves only as we love our neighbor, or what comes to the same thing, as our neighbor is capable of loving us" (TMS, 25). Smith here delivers a pithy synthesis of Christian and Stoic ethics ("nature" is an old code word for Stoicism). Christianity says treat the other like a self; Stoicism says treat the self like an other.

In its basic social theory, much of *The Theory of Moral Sentiments* seems a gloss on a line from Augustine's *Confessions:* "Thou [God] hast appointed that man should from others guess much as to himself."[52] The simultaneous selfish and sociable nature of humankind is the seat and origin of morals. Our partiality to ourselves makes it difficult to see ourselves with the coolness, impartiality, and candor that others do: "this fatal weakness of mankind, is the source of half the disorders of human life. If we saw ourselves in the light in which others see us, or in which they would see us if they knew all, a reformation would generally be unavoidable. We could not otherwise endure the sight" (TMS, 158–59).[53] The "impartial spectator," perhaps the most famous idea in the work, sees to this constant reformation. The impartial spectator is described variously by Smith and his interpreters as the conscience, an inmate of the breast, a superego, the man within, and the higher tribunal of human conduct, and at times it sounds like Kant's categorical imperative or G. H. Mead's "generalized other." Smith believes in the morally beneficial effects of surveillance by self and other. As has been often noted, the impartial spectator resembles Kant's principle of publicity. One will "regard himself, not so much according to the light in which [others] actually regard him, as according to that in which they would regard him if they were

---

51. Smith devotes pt. 4, sec. 3, of *The Theory of Moral Sentiments* to a lengthy exposition of self-command.

52. Augustine, *Confessions,* book 1, sec. 10.

53. Smith's fellow Scot Robert Burns was born the year *The Theory of Moral Sentiments* was first published, 1759. His 1784 poem, "To a Louse," has the lines: "O wad some Power the giftie gie us / To see oursels as ithers see us!"

better informed" (TMS, 116). The impartial spectator imagines a spectatorial public purged of informational defects; it is the dream of publicity idealized, omniscient, and omnipresent. In this way it anticipates the idea of panoptical inspection in Bentham and exposure in James Mill. For Smith at least, the notion that the public is a mechanism of sanction does not disclose something corrupt at liberalism's heart (its complicity with cruelty, as Foucault in *Discipline and Punish* would have it) but rather discloses an ordinary fact about the social origins of and checks on human motives.

In a stunning passage added in the second edition of *The Theory of Moral Sentiments* (1761), Smith creates a test case for his theatrical ethics, a scene of disaster to end all disasters: a hypothetical earthquake that swallowed up the whole of China. (The text went through six editions in his lifetime, the sixth and last in the year of his death, 1790.) What would "a man of humanity in Europe, who had no sort of connexion with that part of the world" do upon hearing the news? Smith imagines that he might feel sad for the loss, think weighty thoughts about the vanity of life, and even ponder the economic aftereffects of the disaster on world trade. But once "all this fine philosophy was over," the European would resume his affairs as if nothing had ever happened. "If he was to lose his little finger tomorrow, he would not sleep tonight; but, provided he never saw them, he will snore with the most profound security over the ruin of a hundred millions of his brethren." (TMS, 136). Smith's point is not to snore about the death of millions, but to refute the notion (current in the Scottish Enlightenment) that natural benevolence would prevent people from rating the loss of their pinkie over the destruction of China. Benevolence, like the subatomic strong force, works only at short distance. Despite Smith's sense of human self-absorption, he clearly finds it shameful that anyone could prefer a little finger to a nation. Hence the need for the correcting force of the impartial spectator: "the natural misrepresentations of self-love can be corrected only by the eye of this impartial spectator" (TMS, 137). Being weak and magnetized to the ego, the passions need the steering of reason. Greater is the love that is less attached to particular objects.

Smith's ethics of sympathy is also an ethics of not sympathizing. He gives us both a bleeding heart and a way to stop the hemorrhage: "Provided he never saw them." Television and photojournalism have banished Smith's qualification. Smith's historical universe can contain the pathos of suffering at a distance in way that ours cannot.[54] In much of eighteenth-century Eu-

---

54. Luc Boltanski, *La souffrance à distance: Morale humanitaire, médias, et politique* (Paris: Éditions Métailié, 1993).

rope, medical students read Galen, strategists read Caesar, and architects read Vitruvius. They traveled on Roman roads; physical effort in most cases set the bounds of the possible.[55] Smith sits on the historical cusp of ancient and modern. His "man of humanity in Europe" acts in an emerging world economy with an ancient moral compass, both contemplating the meaning of the disaster in China for "the trade and business of the world in general" and yet possessing "no connexion with that part of the world." Smith does not imagine China as anything but an abstraction for Europeans. Revolutions in transportation (the steamship and railway) and communications (post and telegraph) by the mid-nineteenth century would leave Smith's man of humanity quaintly marooned. A lifetime can barely make a few friends, but every life requires the unseen help of vast multitudes.[56] Smith is an original analyst of the unanticipated consequences of action at a distance but, as an ethical theorist, he draws borders to the circumference of sympathy much like the ancient Stoic demarcation of family, city, world.[57] Though we may be citizens of the world in trade, for Smith our sympathetic virtues have a lease on the face-to-face setting.

Smith's readiness to take a moral holiday from cosmic worry takes a position in a very old debate. In Jewish and Christian ethics, the fortunate always had the duty to keep the poor in remembrance.[58] Some might espy a link between *The Theory of Moral Sentiments* and *The Wealth of Nations*: Smith teaches the beneficiaries of capitalism to harden themselves to the burdens of conscience. The *Theory*'s tie to the *Wealth* has been debated as ferociously as the tie of the young to the later Marx, especially because of the apparent clash between the *Theory*'s ethics of sympathy and the *Wealth*'s blessing on self-interest. The contrast is most dramatic, however, if you do not read either book. The one recognizes the insuperability of self-love, and the other never quite celebrates simple selfishness. The surprise that ethics and economics might be profoundly linked reflects more our poverty than Smith's strangeness. There is more of Stoic substance in the *Wealth* than his free-marketer Gordon Gekko wannabes often recognize.[59] Greed is a still vice, even if it has public benefits. Smith's famous argument that we should expect our neighbor's self-interest to provide our dinner, rather than their benevolence, may sound like an appeal to selfishness. But Smith is not say-

55. James J. Sheehan, *German History, 1770–1866* (Oxford: Clarendon, 1989), 79.

56. Adam Smith, *The Wealth of Nations,* in *Great Books of the Western World* (Chicago: Encyclopedia Britannica, 1952), 39: 7.

57. Augustine has three circles: home, city, world: *Civitas dei,* xix.7.

58. Loci classici include Deut. 15, Luke 14, and James 5.

59. As is argued by Macfie, *The Individual in Society,* chap. 4.

ing that self-love should be coddled, only that it has socially beneficial effects. He is willing strategically to employ it for something greater, much as the *Theory* invokes a sense of being watched to induce sympathy for others. Smith resembles a later eighteenth-century thinker, James Madison, in his willingness to conscript the incorrigible part of human nature for greater social good. If one reads the *Wealth* via the *Theory,* as I do, then self-love is an offense that brings about good. Smith's treatment of the earthquake in China makes clear that self-love can foster bizarre moral distortions. Those who praise rational self-interest are often mild abyss-artists, puffing vice into a virtue because it yields effects they like. Here again Miltonic-Pauline roots for the theory of liberty are helpful, at least in the conviction that evil brings good to pass, but that does not mean we wish that evil would abound.

The public, thanks precisely to the sublimation it requires, is the garden of the respectable virtues. In the privacy of love something of the distance between feelings can be bridged: "We are delighted to find a person who values us as we value ourselves, and distinguishes us from the rest of mankind, with an attention not unlike that with which we distinguish ourselves" (TMS, 95). But in public we cannot count on interpretive goodwill from others, whose well of amiable virtues is likely limited, since many of them are probably strangers. Actors in public must recognize the apathy of audiences. A public actor skilled in self-command will "flatten . . . his passion to that pitch, in which spectators are capable of going along with him." The effect of such "flattening" not only mellows the expression of the passion but modifies the passion itself. The actor is "constantly led to imagine in what manner he would be affected if he was only one of the spectators of his own situation. As their sympathy makes them look at it, in some measure, with his eyes, so his sympathy makes him look at it, in some measure, with theirs, especially when in their presence and acting under their observation." "An assembly of strangers" thus best fosters "that equality of temper which is so common among men of the world" (TMS, 22–23). The discipline of the unsympathetic public teaches one to view one's own passions in the dimmer light in which they appear to others, and thus to see oneself as another, a notion resonant for later notions of free speech as a rough medicine. The self must be beside itself: for the Romantics, in ecstasy or madness; for Smith, in impartial spectatorship. As in Cornewall Lewis, quoted in the introduction, the public is the site of indifference.

Smith, in sum, wants to modulate the otherness within so as to be open to the otherness without. His view of political and moral life is in many ways a tragic one: feelings are locked inside our breasts and only the utmost exertion can awake a sensitivity to the plight of others. Unlike Hume, he does not imagine the immediate communication of feelings. Pain is inevitable, but it is not a possible basis for mutual obligation or community; all we have is rational extrapolations and judgments, aided by the impartial spectator, a general teacher of self-abstraction. Smith lived in a world in which alcohol was the only anesthetic, and vaccinations and health insurance were nonexistent. Many pleasures accumulated at the top of the class ladder in Smith's day, giving their possessors gout, but pain ran up and down the entire gamut. A lively sense for the harshness of life in all its forms—so long a given in moral philosophy—has since faded for reasons that J. S. Mill was one of the first to analyze.

MILL AND THE HISTORICAL RECESSION OF PAIN

Mill's *On Liberty* (1859) has acquired worldwide eminence as the classic argument for free expression. It found a particularly receptive readership in twentieth-century America, where it served as a philosophical explanation of the First Amendment and of the cultural policy of liberal democracy more generally. Posthumously Mill became an American founding father of sorts. During his life he was a public intellectual, philosophical radical, utilitarian, member of Parliament, Romantic manqué, socialist, feminist, imperial administrator, comparative historian of Greece, Rome, and France, and codifier of research methods in social science; and his multifaceted influence still stamps Anglo-American political institutions and their many imitators, as we will see in this chapter and the following two chapters.

The backdrop for understanding Mill's arguments for free expression is his historical analysis of modern society. Mill had already worked out his story about modernity by the 1830s, and it is standard not only in his work, but in nineteenth-century social thought more generally. Even Karl Marx borrowed much of this story, with a critical twist, from Mill and from the French social thinkers and historians on which they both relied, such as Comte, Constant, Guizot, and Tocqueville. Today we associate the story of an epochal shift in social organization with late-nineteenth-century thinkers who founded the field of sociology on precisely this tale. In Germany Ferdinand Tönnies wrote of the shift from *Gemeinschaft* to *Gesellschaft* (community to society); in France Émile Durkheim described the shift from "mechanical to organic" solidarity; and in England the jurist Henry Maine wrote of a similar transition from "status" to "contract." But Mill's essay "Civilization" (1836) has all these elements in place a generation or two earlier. Civilization for Mill first means large numbers of people co-operating at a distance: "It is only civilized beings who can combine." Specifically modern civilization means the diffusion of property and intelligence from the few to the many and the rise of public opinion as a force in politics and society. Thus Mill links the rise of the bourgeoisie, the printing press, popular education, and democracy. The "government of public opinion" means popular rule in government; in society public opinion dispels both great virtues and great vices. Life becomes more reasonable and more boring; kindly virtues wax and heroic ones wane.[60] Mill considers the loss of vitality and strength the worst thing about modern life. His support of liberty is part of his lifelong aim not only to emend intellects but to regenerate animal spirits. Mill is no Rousseau. On the whole he finds civilization a good thing; but, like Tocqueville, he is clearheaded about the losses it has brought.

At the core of Mill's ambivalences about civilization is the historical recession of pain.[61] A footnote to *On Liberty* states an optimism that the twentieth century would wreck: "The era of pains and penalties . . . has passed away."[62] Mill's world is already kinder and gentler than that of Locke or Smith. Mill wrote in an age when enlightened opinion considered the elimination of torture a realistic prospect.[63] Suffering of all kinds was becoming shoved off the stage: "the spectacle, and even the very idea, of pain, is kept more and more out of the sight of those classes who enjoy in their fullness the benefits of civilization." Delicacy and refinement remained class privileges. "All those necessary portions of the business of society which oblige any person to be the immediate agent or ocular witness of the infliction of pain, are delegated by common consent to peculiar and narrow classes: to the judge, the soldier, the surgeon, the butcher, and the executioner." (Such peculiar and narrow classes, especially judges and surgeons, reappear in following chapters.) The division of labor in the management of pain meant a sliding scale of sensitivity, not an absolute decrease of suffering. Pain became the exception instead of the norm. Mill noted the modern sense that earlier generations were brutal and lacking in feeling, when everyone was "necessarily habituated . . . to the spectacle of harshness, rudeness, and violence." Face-to-face violent conflict was a daily potential,

60. J. S. Mill, "Civilization" (1836), in *Collected Works of John Stuart Mill,* ed. J. M. Robson (Toronto: University of Toronto Press, 1977), 18:122, 127, 132, 131.

61. Mill's analysis is very similar to that of another analyst deeply influenced by postrevolutionary French social thought, the great sociologist Norbert Elias.

62. John Stuart Mill, *On Liberty* (1859) (New York: Norton, 1975), 17. In the rest of this chapter, quotations are cited parenthetically in the text using the abbreviation OL.

63. Edward Peters, *Torture* (New York: Blackwell, 1985), chap. 3.

and gentlemen would not leave home without their swords. Our ancestors, however, were not necessarily more vicious than we; they simply "thought less of the infliction of pain, because they thought less of pain altogether." We ought not to regard those who committed callous acts "as cruel as we must become before we could do the like." People inured to suffering worried less about making others, or themselves, suffer. As life grows more comfortable, pain becomes more noticeable. Paradoxically, the more remote suffering is, the more salient it becomes: "most kinds of pain and annoyance appear much more unendurable to those who have little experience of them, than to those who have much."[64]

Mill is profoundly ambivalent about the recession of pain and its attendant "moral effeminacy."[65] Mill, a nineteenth-century male feminist (together with Friedrich Engels, Henrik Ibsen, and Karl Pearson, among others), was not above a lament for lost virility, though he also notes the positive civilizing role of women, a key theme of his *The Subjection of Women* (1869). He expresses no nostalgia for lost aristocratic grandeur (as Tocqueville sometimes does), nor is he a simple booster of modern liberty; he tallies gains and losses. Thus, regarding education: "I rejoice in the decline of the old brutal and tyrannical system of teaching, which, however, did succeed in enforcing habits of application; but the new, as it seems to me, is training up a race of men who will be incapable of doing anything which is disagreeable to them. I do not, then, believe that fear, as an element in education, can be dispensed with."[66] These words apply to more than education: the decline of terror makes people tenderer, for good and ill. Fear is necessary for learning; but does that mean we should cultivate fear so that learning may abound? In this, as in so much else, Mill follows Tocqueville's analysis of democracy's tendency to slide into a soft, friendly despotism rather than the "whips and scourges" of the old regime (OL, 71). The great risk Mill found in his age was enervation: "the danger which threatens human nature [now] is not the excess, but the deficiency, of personal impulses and preferences" (OL, 57–58).

At the center of Mill's analysis of modern "moral effeminacy" was Christianity. His assault on what he cattily terms "Christian morality (so called)" is nearly as sharp as Nietzsche's later: "Its ideal is negative rather than positive; passive rather than active; Innocence rather than Nobleness; Absti-

64. Mill, "Civilization," 18:130.

65. Mill, "Civilization," 18:131. This term could suggest the abandonment of public duty for personal pleasure: John Brewer, *The Pleasures of the Imagination* (Chicago: University of Chicago Press, 1997), 80.

66. John Stuart Mill, *Autobiography* (New York: Columbia University Press, 1960), 37.

nence from Evil, rather than energetic Pursuit of Good. . . . In its horror of sensuality, it made an idol of asceticism, which has been gradually compromised away to one of legality" (OL, 47–48). Like Nietzsche, he admires Jesus, but not the modern (or medieval) drift of Christian life and institutions. Mill much prefers "pagan self-assertion" to the self-denial of (Calvinistic) Christianity (OL, 59). He finds the threat of hell and lure of heaven appealing to the most selfish part of humans, the desire to find pleasure and avoid pain; pagan moral systems at least require a higher duty than utility. (Here Mill characteristically criticizes a notion of utilitarianism that only knows pleasure and pain.) Even Muslims, he notes in a bit of comparative exposé, possess a positive doctrine of obligation to the public, which Christianity utterly lacks (OL, 48). Like Hegel slamming "the beautiful soul" or Nietzsche pinning the ascetic, Mill thinks holiness is not the best model of how to be a human. Though saints are preferable to scoundrels, that choice does not exhaust the options: "It may be better to be a John Knox than an Alcibiades, but it is better to be Pericles than either" (OL, 59). There is no doubt which Mill prefers in a choice between Europe's "noble antecedents and its professed Christianity" (OL, 68). Mill, like his fellow critics of bourgeois mediocrity Marx, Kierkegaard, Thoreau, and Nietzsche, was an assiduous student of the ancient Greeks and Romans. "Familiarity with the monuments of antiquity, and especially those of Greece," he wrote, teaches us "to appreciate and admire intrinsic greatness."[67]

Admiration for intrinsic greatness was something he thought his age lacked. Writing in the 1850s, Mill sounds like a critic of what came to be called mass society a century later. "Formerly, different ranks, different neighbourhoods, different trades and professions, lived in what might be called different worlds; at present to a great degree in the same. Comparatively speaking, they now read the same things, listen to the same things, see the same things, go to the same places, have their hopes and fears directed to the same objects, have the same rights and liberties, and the same means of asserting them" (OL, 68). He is not complaining about Hollywood and television, but bemoaning newspapers and keeping up with the Joneses. In sum Mill has no nostalgia for bygone days of bloodlust, but his radical political program, shared with his father James Mill and spiritual grandfather Jeremy Bentham, is the softening of manners, the elimination of torture, the banishment of executions from public gawkery, popular education and discussion, the secret ballot (which Mill later regretted), and sundry other useful reforms, all of which make public life more dull and even. He laments his

---

67. Mill, "Civilization," 18:145.

achievements. As Habermas notes, Mill is a liberal critic of liberalism.[68] Instead of the glorious thresher of truth and error so beloved of the eighteenth-century *philosophes,* Mill defines the public as "that miscellaneous collection of a few wise and many foolish individuals" (OL, 21). This is rather a diminuendo.

Mill's analysis of the modern public sphere is hardly the happy endorsement that some readers (especially those who read only *On Liberty*'s widely anthologized chap. 2) seem to find. The rise of civilization meant a shift from state to society, from hard to soft power, from gallows and guns to propriety and public opinion as the chief threat to liberty. Much was gained in this large transformation, especially the space for individuality, eccentricity, and progress. But with it came the risk of a subtler corruption of public life than the old despotisms of crown and church could ever manage. The danger for him was not torture or jail, but the relentless magnetism of other people's opinions. "Protection, therefore, against the tyranny of the magistrate is not enough: there needs protection against the tyranny of the prevailing opinion and feeling: against the tendency of society to . . . prevent the formation, of any individuality not in harmony with its ways." (OL, 6). The "ascendancy of public opinion in the State" is "a more powerful agency" of leveling manners and morals than anything else (OL, 69). In the mid-nineteenth century the suppression of innovative ideas was not simply a matter of censorship by a scheming state, but also a matter of a suffocating social conformity that kept them from being born.

The communicative conditions in modern civilization, according to Mill, militated against the discovery of truth and favored puffery and manipulation instead. Perhaps as a public intellectual whose fame came from writing and editing in the periodical press, Mill had an insider's sense for the realities of what we later learned to call mass communication. Consider his analysis of public relations. In a face-to-face community where everyone knows each other, it is easy for people and products to gain the reputation they deserve. Continued patronage rests on high quality goods and services. In civilization, in contrast, where "the individual becomes so lost in the crowd," everything depends on image-making. (Here again he tells a *Gemeinschaft* to *Gesellschaft* story.) By giving goods and services "a gloss, a saleable look," the big city entrepreneur can make a profit without a single return customer. Signs start to drift apart from their referents. The quackery and puffery of both commerce and intellectual life are

68. Jürgen Habermas, *Structural Transformation of the Public Sphere* (1962) (Cambridge: MIT Press, 1989), sec. 15.

the inevitable fruits of immense competition; of a state of society where any voice, not pitched in an exaggerated key, is lost in the hubbub. Success, in so crowded a field, depends not upon what a person is, but what he seems: mere marketable qualities become the object instead of substantial ones, and a man's labour and capital are expended less in doing anything, than in persuading other people that he has done it. . . . For the first time, arts for attracting public attention form a necessary part of the qualifications even of the deserving: and skill in these arts goes farther than any other quality in ensuring success.[69]

John Stuart Mill sounds like C. Wright Mills in his critique of people who have substituted seeming for being, of public worlds corrupted by the inauthenticities of advertising, though there are also echoes of Rousseau and of the Platonic critique of the Sophists.[70]

Mill's solution for the modern malaise differs from the solutions offered by his contemporaries, such as class struggle (Marx), publicly ironic but privately authentic Christianity (Kierkegaard), natural extravagance (Thoreau), and self-disciplined *virtú* (Nietzsche). Mill calls for the revitalization of public argument. He shares the call for strenuousness with the others, but wants energy expressed in reforming the political and social center, not in overturning, defying, transcending, or mocking it. He wants people schooled in the arts of self-suspension rather than in cosmic creation and destruction. (Nietzsche, who owned Mill's *Subjection of Women*—in Sigmund Freud's translation—complained of Mill's "insulting clarity.") Mill's nostrum for mid-nineteenth-century England is relentlessly agonistic. Verbal combat, performed civilly and openly, would awaken the body politic. Habits must be broken, souls must be constantly on edge to combat the ever-present danger of lassitude. Mill wants to counter the twin problems of stupor and (more rarely) frenzy that rush in when overt oppression is lifted. Provoking objects need play everywhere. Voices of venom and Cloud Cuckooland alike need airing. "'Lord, enlighten thou our enemies,' should be the prayer of every true Reformer. . . . [We] are in danger from their folly, not from their wisdom; their weakness is what fills us with apprehension, not their strength."[71] Risking the discomfort of clashing doctrines is a civic duty. "The mental and moral, like the muscular powers, are improved only by being used" (OL, 55). We argue or we atrophy. For Mill the public sphere was a school, just as for Dewey later the school was a public sphere. Like

69. Mill, "Civilization," 18:132–33.

70. See, for instance, C. Wright Mills, *The Power Elite* (New York: Oxford University Press, 1956), chap. 13.

71. J. S. Mill, "Coleridge" (1840), in *Collected Works,* 10:163.

William James, who dedicated his lectures on pragmatism to Mill's memory, Mill calls for "a moral equivalent to war": something capable of producing the same "spiritual harvest" (James) of courage and fortitude without the blood, waste, and mayhem. Mill often gives discussion an explicitly martial spirit. "Both teachers and learners go to sleep at their post, as soon as there is no enemy in the field" (OL, 41). The passion for sport propels questioning and counterquestioning. Enlightened discussion, with both self and other, is a kind of cold war, a constant preemptive girding of the loins. The historical tie of belligerent passions and intellectual life is ubiquitous in Mill. Wide-ranging, two-sided, and open-ended contestation, modeled on Socrates's interrogations or medieval *disputatio,* he thought, would stir the faculties of a sleepy public and give truth a better chance of prevailing (though he did not like *disputatio*'s habit of borrowing premises from authority rather than observation).

A better chance: Mill believes in truth without guarantees. Compared with his father, James, who seems to have believed that universal literacy, suffrage, and freedom of discussion would produce an alert citizenry as automatically as a conclusion flows from a premise, Mill was much more guarded. The automatic victory of truth over error is nothing more than a "pleasant falsehood" (OL, 29): "It is a piece of idle sentimentality that truth, merely as truth, has any inherent power denied to error of prevailing against the dungeon and the stake" (OL, 30). If Milton took truth as an undefeated wrestler, never vanquished in a match against falsehood, Mill's sporting metaphor might be a batting average. He has a statistical sense of truth's emergence: "in proportion to the degree of intellectual power and love of truth which we succeed in creating [by education] is the certainty that (whatever may happen in any one particular instance) in the aggregate of interests true opinions will be the result."[72] Like the historian Henry Thomas Buckle, a disciple, Mill had a statistical sense of the aggregate emergence of truth and progress. His confidence in the productivity of conflict in public argument and institutions went together with his progressive philosophy of history. Mill compared public debate to the separation of powers, endorsing "the importance, in the present imperfect state of mental and social science, of antagonist modes of thought: which, it will one day be felt, are as necessary to one another in speculation, as mutually checking powers are in a political constitution."[73]

72. Mill, "Civilization," 18:144.

73. Mill, "Coleridge," 10:122. On the creativity of conflict as a central liberal principle, see Holmes, *Passions and Constraint.*

STOIC EAR, ROMANTIC VOICE

Various intellectual strains mix in *On Liberty.* Here I want to focus specifically on the tension between the Stoic notion of the listening citizen and the Romantic notion of the speaking citizen. Consider first Mill's attitude toward Marcus Aurelius. For Mill the Stoic philosopher and Roman emperor, whose writings he proclaimed "the highest ethical product of the ancient mind" (OL, 26), is an example of how even the wisest individuals are inevitably prone to historical blindness. Marcus Aurelius, whom Mill considers a Christian *sans le savoir* in his fundamental ethical principles and his tenderness of heart (which Mill notes managed to survive his Stoic education), persecuted Christians. If someone so wise can make a world-historical mistake of this magnitude, then what is the fallibility *a fortiori* of the mass? And when Mill defines the morality of public discussion, he turns to another fixed star of Stoic ethics in the western tradition: Cicero, "the greatest orator, save one, of antiquity."[74] "He who knows only his side of the case, knows little of that." Mill may be invoking the Ciceronian motto *Audi alteram partem* (Hear the other side). One must not only hear the other side, but speak for it as well. If one cannot argue the enemy's case, one has no ground for preferring one's own position: "The rational position for [someone who cannot argue thus] would be suspension of judgment" (OL, 36). Conviction must pass through the needle's eye of counterargumentation. The highest ethical good in public debate, says Mill, is the ability to give the adversary's argument full due without mockery or invective. Seeing clearly rather than seeing red is the true test of public character (OL, 51). Righteous citizens must withstand the buffetings of contrary opinions without losing their cool. Like Smith, Kant, and the Romantics (e.g., Shelley), Mill takes imagination as the political and moral faculty by which we enter into concourse with our fellows. "This is the power by which one human being enters into the mind and circumstances of another."[75]

Mill exemplifies the doctrine we might call "homeopathic machismo" — the faith that imbibing the poison strengthens rather than wrecks the constitution. As Marlow put it in Joseph Conrad's *Heart of Darkness,* the task is to inhale the stench of dead hippo meat without being contaminated.[76] Nietzsche's dictum "Whatever does not kill me makes me stronger" is an-

---

74. Demosthenes, one assumes, was Mill's greatest orator of antiquity.
75. J. S. Mill, "Bentham" (1838), in *Collected Works,* 10:92.
76. Joseph Conrad, *Three Short Novels* (New York: Bantam, 1960), 59.

other good example of mithridatic bravura in modern thought.[77] Failed abstinence begets fallacious cognitions: "even the most cultivated portion of our species have not yet learned to abstain from drawing conclusions which the evidence does not warrant."[78] The strong citizen, for Mill and his disciples, can descend to the underworld where abortionists, anarchists, atheists, Buddhists, censors, Christians, conservatives, Druids, feminists, liberals, radicals, socialists, Tories, vegetarians, Whigs, and other sundry characters argue, only to reemerge neither dazed nor confused but freshly committed to reason and freedom. Though appearances may "seduce" the mind from "the observance of true principles of induction," the liberal citizen must be steeled in advance to fend off the siren call of easy conclusions.[79] Like Horkheimer and Adorno's Odysseus, tied to the mast so he can hear the seductive song of the sirens without wrecking the ship, Mill's prescriptions for citizenship seem an epitome of bourgeois self-discipline.[80] Mill's stoicism and respect for antique duty are clear. His picture of the civic self—serving public duty even against private revulsion—resonates for twentieth-century norms of impassive citizenship and professionalism. Mill of course did not invent such a picture of the self, nor is he the sole channel of transmission; he is simply an influential representative of a vision of self-discipline that has prevailed throughout the history of moral theory, in Europe and, with a parallel development, in the Confucian cultures of China, Korea, and Japan as well. Mill's catalog of virtues includes bravery, inquiry, and a stiff upper lip; vices include fear, silence, quiescence, torpor, and habit. Public argument increases the intellectual stature of all who take part in it; enlivens intellectual and scientific inquiry, which is the engine of all progress; and makes citizens "to a certain extent, participants in the government, and sharers in the instruction and mental exercise derivable from it."[81] Mill explicitly connects self-denial in one's opinions to moral virtues and political ideals. Refusing that "fierce stiffness" with which Locke thought almost all of us hold our opinions is the beginning of wisdom and of a healthy civil society.

Mill defines the listening self in Stoic terms. We should subject our dear-

77. Friedrich Nietzsche, *Twilight of the Idols*, in *The Portable Nietzsche*, ed. Walter Kaufmann (New York: Penguin, 1982), 513.

78. J. S. Mill, *A System of Logic*, V.i.1, in *Collected Works*, 8: 736.

79. Mill, *A System of Logic*, V.i.1, 8: 736.

80. Horkheimer and Adorno, *Dialektik der Aufklärung*, 3: 49–54; see also their "Exkurs I" in the same work.

81. Mill, *Considerations on Representative Government*, 43: 363.

est beliefs to the rigors of open discussion. Like Hegel and the anatomists, Mill extols the heroism of facing "the negative" head-on. Truly wise men or women should rejoice in having their opinions questioned, countered, or even torn to pieces in public debate. We should voluntarily expose our fondest faith to the irritant of doubt. We should be at war against our own beliefs. "So essential is this discipline to a real understanding of moral and human subjects, that if opponents of all important truths do not exist, it is indispensable to imagine them, and supply them with the strongest arguments which the most skilful devil's advocate can conjure up" (OL, 37). Rational souls shadowbox with phantoms. We should stretch our minds into the strange shapes of opposing arguments (a gift Mill praised his wife Harriet Taylor for possessing).[82] Thus Christians should be able to argue like atheists; Marxists like capitalists; Jews like Nazis or the KKK. Freedom of expression inevitably leads to controversy, which, by airing alternatives, leads to general intellectual improvement. A belief, once discussed, can no longer remain a "mere" belief; it is raised from prejudice to reason and alters its place in the human soul. Discussion, like the philosopher's stone, changes our opinions from base into nobler stuff. The listening subject, in sum, is supposed to be an intellectual shape-shifter, able to inhabit any other position, one whose opinions have been refined into reasons and arguments. Audition, ever since the Athenian *ekklēsia*, has been the primordial civic act. Mill would never grasp Kierkegaard's saying: "purity of heart is to will one thing." For Mill it is always better to take one's meat with knowledge. Those who listen must be ready for assaults on everything they hold dear. Listeners fast in the wilderness of opinions, denying themselves the fleshpots of cognitive certainty. The likelihood that our convictions might not endure in their original form is of course part of the program, given Mill's confidence in the corrigibility of knowledge. Everything has to be run through the mill.

On the other hand, the speaker needs to be fanatically convinced and confident enough to keep the public drama high and the flow of ideas fresh. As Mill wrote of Bentham, whose philosophy structured his remarkable education and youth until his breakdown: "For our own part, we have a large tolerance for one-eyed men, provided their one eye is a penetrating one: if they saw more, they probably would not see so keenly, nor so eagerly pursue

82. *On Liberty* was dedicated to the memory of Harriet Taylor Mill, who died in 1858. Evidence suggests the themes and arguments of the book were worked out in a long oral incubation between the two Mills; see Jo Ellen Jacobs, *The Voice of Harriet Taylor Mill* (Bloomington: Indiana University Press, 2002), 245–51. But John Stuart wrote it. Authors are always approximations anyway.

one course of inquiry."[83] Strong views may be both repulsive and sincere: "the *odium theologicum,* in a sincere bigot, is one of the most unequivocal cases of moral feeling" (OL, 9). Doctrines must be proclaimed by their most forceful and convinced advocates. "Nor is it enough that he should hear the arguments of adversaries from his own teachers, presented as they state them, and accompanied by what they offer as refutations. That is not the way to do justice to the arguments, or bring them into real contact with his own mind. He must be able to hear them from persons who actually believe them; who defend them in earnest, and do their very utmost for them." Mill does not trust delegation or representation in public controversy. Commentary by neutral parties dilutes. Arguments and animal spirits are wed in some way. "Real contact" vanishes in the ventriloquism of mediation. Without hearing from their actual adherents, people will miss arguments "in their most plausible and persuasive form" (OL, 36). The convinced speaker is somehow vital to the persuasion process. Positions are colored by the voice of the believer. Like the classical rhetoricians, Mill makes the persuasive appeal of character (*ēthos*) as important a part of plausibility as logical form (*logos*).

The conviction of one's own rightness is thus both the engine and the enemy of the public sphere. Mill attacks cognitive confidence as a source of error; but he needs it as well. Without some people having a singled-minded conviction of their own rightness, Mill's agonistic public would grind to a halt. And do the arguers ever become hearers? Don't they also have an obligation to hear the arguments of others who passionately believe otherwise? And if they do, then don't they risk turning from passionate believers to judicious teachers? Won't the general tendency of reflective listening be to create a society of rational weighers? Mill certainly hopes so—though he is not holding his breath. He admits that free thought and discussion may sooner foster sectarianism than tolerance. The actors on the public stage are there for show, in part. "But it is not on the impassioned partisan, it is on the calmer and more disinterested bystander, that this collision of opinions works its salutary effects" (OL, 50). Like Paul on sin, Mill is sure that fanatical conviction will take care of itself, and that we must preach reason for the sake of the unseen audience. Mill dislikes spleen and bile as much as anyone, but he also finds a place for them. Like Smith, Madison, and Kant, Mill puts the morally problematic features of human nature

83. Mill, "Bentham," 10: 94. On Mill's negotiations between the intellectual and political antipodes of Bentham and Coleridge, see Raymond Williams, *Culture and Society* (New York: Columbia University Press, 1983), pt. 1, chap. 3.

to use in a counterpoised whole. Nasty bodily humors fuel debate so that the rest may learn to sift cerebrally through them. Though Mill clearly does not like "invective, sarcasm, . . . want of candour, or malignity, bigotry, or intolerance of feeling" (OL, 51–52), he treats them in the spirit of the biblical phrase: offenses must come, but woe be unto him through whom they come. Mill likes dogmatism no more than Paul likes sin, but dogmatism, like sin, is needed to make the grace of redemption manifest. Unlike some more recent liberals, Mill knows when to shudder.

Mill needs outlaws to keep the disciplinary machine running. He represents what Nietzsche called Socratism, the belief that life should be subordinated to rational interrogation (the concept is of course more a polemical glance at modern thought than a description of the historical Socrates).[84] The possibility that public debate is not a regime of intellectual stimulation but rather a threat to the wellsprings of conviction does not occur to Mill. He does not anticipate the neurotic wavering before choices—option paralysis—that would become a staple of ethical thinkers and jokers later. "The steady habit of correcting and completing his own opinion by collating it with those of others," he says, "so far from causing doubt and hesitation in carrying it into practice, is the only stable foundation for a just reliance on it." Only he who has examined an issue from all sides "has a right to think his judgment better than that of any other person, or any multitude, who have not gone through a similar process" (OL, 21). Assurance comes through the method of fixing belief, as C. S. Peirce would say. But carried conscientiously into practice, the weighing of every opinion would drive us wild. Possibility, in Kierkegaard's language, would infect every conviction. We could never keep the infinite at bay under Mill's counterquestioning discipline. How do we know when to stop worrying? How are we to break the infinite wavering of Kierkegaard's stroller debating the ethics of going on a walk in Deer Park, carrying on a dispute with an imaginary devil's advocate, himself? Kafka and Samuel Beckett stand at the end of the road of Millian hyperreflexivity; Hamlet stands at its beginning. Mill's rational self-suspension is beautiful and useful, but it is not the only way to live. Self-consciousness and self-division are not always a good thing.

Mill's Romanticism and his Stoicism mix uneasily. Mill wants citizens to be both half selves and whole selves. The Stoic readily concedes that public life deforms subjectivity. Only that part of the self relevant to the office (if there be such at all) need show up. But the Romantic longs for wholeness:

84. Friedrich Nietzsche, *Die Geburt der Tragödie aus dem Geiste der Musik* (1872) (Augsburg: Goldmann Klassiker, 1984), secs. 12, 13, 18, 23.

self-division is pathology. *Homo duplex* is the foe of all Romantics, as it is of Hegel, Marx, Dewey, and other thinkers who yearn to cast off a life of sundered private and public faces. Mill's Romanticism is evident in chapter 3 of *On Liberty,* with its contrast of a tree and a machine as models of human flourishing. But he does not see a trade-off of Stoic and Romantic themes. Self-denial and self-expression are twin virtues: "The same strong susceptibilities which make the personal impulses vivid and powerful, are also the source from whence are generated the most passionate love of virtue, and the sternest self-control." Strength is the key to both modes of selfhood, "much as if one should complain of the Niagara river for not flowing smoothly between its banks like a Dutch canal" (OL, 57, 61). Both promoted spontaneity and individuality amid the growing conformity he saw in Victoria's England. The best side of Mill is his advocacy of strength; the worst part is the subtle ways that he tricks strength into performing for the public good. Mill pretends such intellectual aerobatics is simple reasonableness, but it is also a campaign against subjects fanatically stuck in their own points of view. His regime of sympathetic listening, if prosecuted fully, could create a society of tepid reasoners unable to stretch their minds to some great idea without the revenge of a second-guess attacking from the wings. His vision of the public both needs and rules out a diverse bestiary of human types: madmen, saints, fools, and prophets, bigots, terrorists, and fanatics, Isaiah and Antigone, Mother Teresa and Lenin, Paul and Nietzsche, Abraham and Bartleby, bin Laden and the Dalai Lama.

Citizens are supposed to listen with ice and speak from fire. Our ears are supposed to be catholic, capable of accommodating many doctrines, but our voices are supposed to be firmly convinced in what we passionately believe to be true. How these two extremes should blend in the civic body without melting into a lukewarm mess is the question. Mill does not call for bigots, jerks, and cranks, but teaches citizens to be Socratic deliberators, able to weigh any argument in pounds and kilos alike. Yet since bigots, jerks, and cranks will inevitably arise, he wants to employ them for the educational benefit of the public. Such a flagrant contradiction should be treated less as a flaw than as a key to Mill's thinking.[85] The lack of liberal generosity is not really Mill's fault: the impossibility of full disclosure in the project of liberty goes back at least to Paul. Liberals praise the devil or his advocates for the catalytic work they do in the salvation of the world either underhandedly or with the hope that truth will take care of itself. Liberalism's key

85. Hannah Arendt, *The Human Condition* (Chicago: University of Chicago Press, 1958), 104–5.

principle is self-exile. Freedom must court the dark side. It has no positive principles except parasitism on the vitality of alien doctrine. To say, simply, that liberalism is about openness and freedom is to risk succumbing to the vacuum of emptiness or formalism. The best theorists of liberalism always manage to identify some other principle at its heart: tragedy (Berlin), self-realization (Dewey), fair play (Holmes). Mill himself sought to replenish it with the poetic imagination he learned from Coleridge and others. Liberalism is always, like the imagination, transcending itself, going out after curfew to socialize with the enemy. Its modus operandi is intellectual fraternization. Maybe the crossing over is espionage, a training exercise, or just a good time—no one can ever say. Liberalism that is only liberal is not liberal at all. It always needs to be losing itself in the other, imbibing the other's potions, scouting the regions of sin, passing through the bower of bliss. It relies on the codependence of bigots and the reasonable. To simply defend reason is not enough to keep reason alive; one must also enact reason's dive to the depths. Liberalism is a dispossessed spirit looking for a home to inhabit. Sometimes swine may have to do. With the Skokie case, as we see in the next chapter, it made do with the hospitality of Beelzebub.

PUBLICITY AND PAIN

Mill believed in the sublimation of pain, both in the psyche and in society. Civilized people needed an occasional educational encounter with a hot poker to develop fortitude and break the crust of cognitive comfort. He had enough confidence in the long-term recession of barbarity to think that hurt could play a medicinal role. He is quite frank about the internalization of pain as a policy of liberal citizenship. In this he advances a theme developed by Bentham. For Bentham, public opinion would serve as a social sanction, a penalty and check against antisocial behavior. Like Kant, Bentham believed publicity was the center of political morality, but he had more ambitious schemes for its implementation. Bentham called for a system of large-scale inspection, a society bathed in the light of mutual gazing, as insurance for good action. In moments of extreme enthusiasm, he wrote as if the abolition of secrecy would cure social ills altogether. The famous bit in his doctrine of publicity was his proposed plan for a penitentiary (or hospital, school, or barracks) called the Panopticon. In this architectural equivalent for the political principle of publicity, a guard hidden in a central tower could peer into each cell of a concentric prison. "By blinds and other contrivances, the keeper concealed from the observation of the prisoners, unless where he thinks fit to show himself: hence, on their part, the sentiment of an invisible omnipresence.—The whole circuit reviewable with little, or, if necessary, without any change of place."[86]

The Panopticon is a great metaphor, but Bentham's chief practical means of publicity was to be the newspaper press. Jokes about television as a "state periscope" aside, it is hard to appreciate how radical were the views of Bentham and his associate James Mill, father of John Stuart. The press, as an invisible omnipresence, was to function as a social superego, a moral regulator, a check on all irrational action, not only for public officials, but for all members of the social body.[87] The press was to society what the panoptical prison was to its inmates: an immediate and constant means of surveillance that kept people well behaved. Its job was not just the provision of information, but the disciplining and coordination of the social body. Since all acts were or were felt to be potentially under the watchful gaze of the press, morality would follow naturally. The "sanction" of public opinion would make a society of transparent hearts, right wills, and benevolent acts. James Mill thought that the press would solve an ancient moral riddle, Momus's complaint "that a window had not been placed in the breast of every man, by which, not only his actions alone, but his thoughts, might have been known." The press would conquer the self's isolation. "The prospect of the immediate and public exposure of all acts of this description, would be a most effectual expedient to prevent their being committed. . . . The magnanimity of that Roman has been highly applauded, who not only placed his residence in such a situation that his fellow-citizens might see as much as possible of his actions, but declared a wish that he could open to all eyes his breast as well as his house."[88] For Bentham and Mill père, publicity filled the vacuum of moral education vacated by religion, and the vacuum of political control vacated by the old regime of dungeons and tortures.

John Stuart Mill rebelled against the social control aspect of his radical heritage; On Liberty is a relentless critique of societal surveillance, the paralyzing paranoia of always being watched by the public eye. But he kept the model of the civic soul as imbibing poison in small doses. This makes On Liberty an implicit participant in a central late-twentieth-century debate about the place of pain in the public sphere: Habermas v. Foucault. Public-

86. A Bentham Reader, ed. M. P. Mack (New York: Pegasus, 1969), 194.

87. Robert Denoon Cumming, Human Nature and History: A Study of the Development of Liberal Thought (Chicago: University of Chicago Press, 1969), 257–60; Dilip P. Gaonkar and Robert J. McArthy, "Panopticism and Publicity: Bentham's Quest for Transparency," Public Culture 6 (1994): 547–75.

88. James Mill, "Liberty of the Press" (1821), in Political Writings, ed. Terence Ball (Cambridge: Cambridge University Press, 1992), 106ff.

ity for Habermas in his important *Structural Transformation of the Public Sphere* (1962) is the fundamental principle of the modern constitutional state. Whereas feudal governance involved secret assemblies by the rulers, and pomp and circumstance for the ruled, the democratic state is supposed to make its deliberations visible to the public and legitimate through reason, so that the rulers and the ruled are one. The public face of feudal power had been processions, public executions, and the court's spectacular, personality-laden fanfare, crowned by the king's body. The constitutional state, in contrast, reveals itself to the public's gaze through organs of sober publicity (Hansards, the Congressional Record, public notices, public trials, and particularly but not only the newspaper press), which are supposed to nourish the public sphere and make intelligent discussion possible. Publicity—the principle of public access to governmental decisions and of general *glasnost* within social intercourse—is the legitimating idea of modern democracy and signifies, according to Habermas, a shift in the nature of political power: in place of the fiat of the king's arbitrary power comes the reason of the public's opinions. The remaining danger, as Habermas notes, is that the public sphere may be "refeudalized" by the market and the state— the organs of publicity that are supposed to dispense enlightenment may revert to being the stage managers of spectacles that keep citizens in awe instead of in discussion.[89] Habermas tells a version of the same tale as Mill: the rise of the modern public sphere (*Öffentlichkeit*) signifies a transformation in the nature of political power, from violence to argument, with the danger of a new creepy kind of control sneaking back in.

Foucault's portrait of panopticism in *Discipline and Punish* (1975) inverts what Habermas calls publicity. Like Habermas—and Tocqueville for that matter—Foucault features the canceling of the king's body and the rise of more ethereal kinds of sanction in his narrative of modernity. "Royal power," he argues, showed itself via flamboyant public torture of the criminal's body; modern ("carceral" or disciplinary) power, in contrast, rests on the (self-)surveillance of the citizen's soul. The aim of royal power was to make one body (the king's) visible to all; the aim of modern power is to make all bodies visible to one, as in Bentham's Panopticon, which serves Foucault as an allegory of the gaze of the disciplines, a mode of punishment whose medium is vision instead of the lash. The inmates of the Panopticon,

---

89. Habermas, *Structural Transformation*. Commentary is abundant; see Arthur Strum, "A Bibliography of the Concept Öffentlichkeit," *New German Critique* 61 (1994): 155–202. Of central importance is the volume edited by Craig Calhoun, *Habermas and the Public Sphere*. My own contribution to the genre of Habermas hermeneutics is "Distrust of Representation: Habermas on the Public Sphere," in *Media, Culture and Society* 14.3 (1993): 441–71.

never knowing whether they are in fact being watched at any given moment, internalize the gaze and become wardens over their own behavior. Every citizen becomes a prisonmaster, and every soul a panoptic gallery. For Foucault citizens who think they are participating in public are only engaging in a new kind of subtle discipline of themselves and of the social body. Visibility, in Foucault's famous line, is a trap. Foucault's panopticism is what Habermas might call the nightmare of "systematically distorted communication": the inmate of the Panopticon, says Foucault, is "the object of information, never a subject in communication."[90] Foucault relies on a norm of violated intersubjectivity as a grounds of critique as much as Habermas.[91] Both Foucault and Habermas learned from Hegel to hate asymmetries of recognition, and Foucault, late in life, saw in Habermas a somewhat kindred student of the truth games that people play pair-wise.[92]

Discipline and Punish directly assaults the underpinnings of the liberal soul and public sphere in both argument and performance. Foucault pulls off a brilliant philosophical joke by attacking Bentham, Mr. Enlightenment, the fount of philosophical radicalism, a humanitarian made an honorary citizen of France during the revolution. Foucault did not pick a reactionary (e.g., Joseph Marie de Maistre) or a conservative (e.g., Edmund Burke) to attack. He went to the very heart of modern humanitarian radicalism to show that it too is contaminated with the will to power that it claims to have banished. Too often readers of *Discipline and Punish* not clued in to the joke take Bentham as an obscure eighteenth-century reactionary instead of a defender of the rights of women, homosexuals, and animals whose practical politics in many ways resemble Foucault's.[93] For Bentham the very measure of the good was the minimization of pain (and of course the maximization of pleasure); he sits at the heart of the modern reevaluation of suffering. Foucault plies the method of selective perversity: instead of attacking the bad, he attacks the bad that lurks within the good. In all our supposed liberties there prowls a jail. The penitentiary is not an institution at the margins of society; it beats in the breast of every citizen. (Such civic self-mortification is precisely what recent feminist and race theorists object to in the lib-

90. Michel Foucault, *Discipline and Punish: The Birth of the Prison* (1975), trans. Alan Sheridan (New York: Vintage, 1979), 200.

91. Peter Dews, *Autonomy and Solidarity: Interviews with Jürgen Habermas* (London: Verso, 1986), 31–32.

92. See *Critique and Power: Recasting the Foucault/Habermas Debate,* ed. Michael Kelly (Cambridge: MIT Press, 1994).

93. Lea Campos Boralevi, *Bentham and the Oppressed* (New York: de Gruyter, 1984). Bentham is the philosophical inspiration for Peter Singer's *Animal Liberation,* the Bible for the animal rights movement.

eral public.) Thanks to Foucault's bracing exaggerations, especially in the bitter conclusion to *Discipline and Punish*, which takes anything sweet or light in the past two centuries as a twisted form of cruelty, it is easy to see Bentham's proposal for a new kind of architecture as the high point of iniquity in modern times. The Panopticon is Foucault's metaphor for liberal society in general. Foucault, circa 1975, found no saving discipline in self-suspension; his later studies of ancient moral thought would take him into stranger and more serene latitudes. His critique is salutary in reminding liberals of the historic centrality of sanction and self-discipline in their political vision. In literature and in life, Foucault pushed the envelope of experience, and he knew, in ways we need not wax prurient about, the indispensability of pain both to pleasure and to the varieties of embodied experience.

Liberal friends of liberty and reason ought not to act so shocked at the revelation of discipline in their political program. Of course self-repression is part of the picture. The softer sort of liberal is easily nauseated by seeming celebrations of mutilation from naughty souls like Foucault, who know just what buttons to push, but thinkers nourished by liberalism's roots in Stoic wisdom know suffering is inevitable in any human excellence, and perhaps even in any moment of human history. (The harder sort of civil libertarian, such as Holmes, however, can cultivate a kind of naughty provocation quite similar to Foucault's.) *Discipline and Punish* wants to draw a line of complicity from the prison to the public sphere, from the panoptic gaze to the moral sentiments. In this it is an update of Nietzsche's *Genealogy of Morals*, which finds in Kant's categorical imperative the scent of cruelty and celebrates punishment as festive.[94] Of course there are lines of complicity. Foucault knows them better than most recent fume-sniffing liberals. Besides, in many respects, Foucault is a neo-Stoic.[95] Tonally, his lucid coolness, even serenity, suggests this lineage, as does his fascination with the calm endurance of violence. Above all, his contrarian tactic of attacking the core of his own beliefs shows his affinity to the liberals.

What are we supposed to make of the long courting of pain by liberal thinkers? What to do with Locke's all-bread breakfasts, Smith's roasting savages, and Mill's cool-headedness in the face of rancor? Do we condemn the whole lot as corrupt, as *Discipline and Punish* tends to do in its grimmest moments? Do we try to peel away any lingering trace of bodily presence and

94. Friedrich Nietzsche, *Genealogie der Moral*, sec. 6.

95. As Richard Rorty, not intending it as a compliment, briefly notes in "Habermas and Lyotard on Postmodernity," in *Habermas and Modernity*, ed. Richard Bernstein (Cambridge: Polity Press, 1985), 172.

pain from liberal policies and strive for the final unveiling of the full rational program? A politics without any bodies in it would not be very interesting, and life without pain would be an odd sort of void. As long as we live in the condition that Hannah Arendt called "plurality"—among other people whose experiences and preferences will always differ radically from our own—self-expression will always be encroached upon by others, in rough and gentle ways. No audience, says Adam Smith, is a perfect fit to any speaker. Concords, not unisons, are all one can hope for. Even within love (or the self) lurk insurmountable barriers that even angels can hardly hurdle. Some preparation for the rough fact that the world will remain all but forever indifferent to one's fondest private hopes is always in order. Smith and Mill invite citizens to make a basic commitment to hear first, then speak, to put the other before the self. Rather than simple self-evacuation, their lesson is hearing the other. The highs and lows of delirious effacement, the self-evacuation of hearing things foreign to one's own experience: this attitude is strangely sustained within the liberal tradition. An ethics of care lurks quietly within at least some of its moments, an almost mystic receptivity to the world outside the self. The point of public sublimation is not private punishment but the opening of the self to the strangeness beyond it.

Nothing separates Locke, Smith, and Mill more from current sensibilities than their treatment of pain. The idea, current in cultural studies, that public participation should be a pleasurable adventure of self-realization fits a world administered by doctors, helping professionals, talk show hosts, and bureaucrats whose livelihoods feed off the dream that pain is wicked and can be eliminated. Pain is an inevitable part of the human estate. "Beauty is harsh," said the Greeks. We cannot expunge pain without paying a severe price. The rarer it becomes, the more acute a role it plays. Pain is deeply connected with the sense of being alive and the possibility of pleasure. The most private and incommunicable thing we know, pain also opens the self in some inexplicable way to others, moving our bowels, in the King James phrase, with compassion.[96] Pain is an evil, but, like sin, a productive one. One should probably not say such things aloud. The point is not to celebrate or eternalize suffering, or chow down in Smithian self-satisfaction, just to ponder the tragic necessity of some kind of self-discipline for a public life of hearing others in a diverse social universe. As Cicero said, no one can be courageous who judges pain the greatest evil, as no one can be temperate who judges pleasure the greatest good.[97]

96. John Durham Peters, "Bowels of Mercy," *BYU Studies* 38.4 (1999): 27–41.
97. Cicero, *De Officiis*, I.ii, para. 5.

CHAPTER FOUR

Homeopathic Machismo in Free Speech Theory

Mithridates, he died old.
—A. E. Housman, "Terence, This Is Stupid Stuff"

THE TRAUMATOPHILIC FIRST AMENDMENT

In twentieth-century American history, the First Amendment took on an unprecedented symbolic and legal significance. The key United States Supreme Court cases that decisively redefined its legal meaning occurred only in the wake of World War I, with the overturning of the crime of seditious libel (speech that harms the state). Though the interpretation of cases and principles varies widely among judges, scholars, and citizens, most have come to agree over the past several decades on the principle of legal agnosticism about cultural worth. Private people may have their opinions about what is good and bad and about what should be let out in open circulation and what should not, but judges, as public officials, have no business restricting or evaluating any form of expression, no matter how repulsive, degenerate, or stupid, except in the most extreme cases, and even then the law must be stated with the utmost precision so as not to hamper potentially beneficial speech.

The coupling of free expression and an emotionally or evaluatively inhibited psyche owes something to John Stuart Mill's *On Liberty*, which argued at length the historical folly of premature judgment; he noted as a prime example that even the wise Marcus Aurelius had thought the Christians nothing more than a troublesome sect. The censor is guilty of the hubris of assuming infallibility. Mill's point was to spur social dynamism and intellectual progress by taming the human impulse to be oversure of one's own rightness. Openness of thought and discussion went together with a moral withholding of criticism or even disgust. An absolutist stance on free expression (that absolutely anything goes) is rarer than the endorsement of moral self-restraint in the realm of thought about free expression. It was not until the opinions and writings of Hugo Black and William O. Douglas in the 1950s that justices urged the absolute toleration of deviant expression, and it was not until *Brandenburg v. Ohio* (1969) that the First Amendment was officially interpreted as allowing the expression of dangerous ideas (but not actions). Though strict absolutism is still a minority opinion, it has a grip on the public imagination, due perhaps to the prominent position its adherents hold in education and allied cultural industries, especially journalism and libraries. People whose livings and lives depend on the propagation of information and opinion in speech and text naturally believe that theirs is holy work.

More than absolutism, the real grip on the public and legal imagination is held by the idea that we are righteous in proportion to our refusal to judge. In the last three or four decades, the Supreme Court has stood agnostic on, that is, refused to criminalize, such things as wearing clothing adorned with vulgarities, flag-burning, vicious personal attacks on public figures, sophomoric musical parodies, and even cross-burning. The Court is not saying, for instance, that Larry Flynt's attack on Jerry Falwell might possibly one day be held as one of the great unheralded intellectual achievements of our times. It is enacting something more basic: an attitude of abstention from judgment about political, social, and moral values. This attitude, often announced with a self-congratulatory grimace, is not unique to judges with liberal political positions. As we will see below, even Justice Antonin Scalia, whom no one could possibly mistake for a liberal, acts out the attitude of self-division that has been developed in liberal thought writ large. What interests me in this chapter is not the idea that courts should generally keep their hands off culture, which I think self-evident, but its attitudinal accompaniment: the sometimes contorted ways that free speech theorists persuade themselves that moral blindness or flatness is an ethical stance, even the best ethical stance, for judges and citizens. The chapter thus follows up on the potential nihilism in Mill's legacy and parallels the next chapter's look at moral abstemiousness among social scientists.

Locating the precise sources for the wider cultural meaning of the First Amendment is difficult. One reason is its curious historical plasticity as a cultural document. The First Amendment has many lives. One of these is the idea that its revival under Holmes and Brandeis places it in a lineage with the classics of British liberalism, a proposition that was probably invented by the free expression scholar and Harvard law professor Zechariah Chafee. (This book both follows and reconsiders this lineage.) In a 1925 *New Republic* article, he wrote that "the dissenting opinions of Justices Holmes and Brandeis" offer "a group of arguments for toleration that may fitly stand besides the *Areopagitica* and Mill's *Liberty*."[1] Brandeis's concurring opinion in *Whitney v. California* (1927) would stoke Chafee's fire further. He was a scholarly midwife for Holmes and Brandeis and a mythmaker in the historiography of free expression. He solidified the influential view that nineteenth-century American legal thought was a First Amendment wasteland until the explosion of interest after World War I, a view that recent scholarship is revising.[2] If the Constitution is what the judges say it is, in the famous phrase, then there are many First Amendments in different periods. (My First Amendment here focuses on speech and the press at the expense of other rights guaranteed in it—religion, assembly, and petition.)

Another difficulty in pinning down ideas about free expression is the fragmentary nature of discourse about free speech. The part often outweighs the whole. *Buckley, Associated Press, Abrams,* and *Schenck* are cases known better for single sentences—in legal as well as popular circles—than for the pages of sometimes gnarled argument they offer. The most famous statements about free expression are as often one-liners as extended treatises. "Let truth and falsehood grapple" (Milton); "The truth would certainly do well enough if she were once left to shift for herself" (Locke); "[Let critics of the republic] stand undisturbed as monuments of the safety with which error of opinion may be tolerated where reason is left free to combat it" (Jefferson); "If all mankind minus one were of one opinion, and only one person were of the contrary opinion, mankind would be no more justified in silencing that one person, then he, if he had the power, would be justified in silencing mankind" (J. S. Mill); "Sunlight is the best disinfectant" (Brandeis); "The best test of truth is the power of the thought to get itself accepted in the competition of the market" (Holmes); "Debate on public

---

1. "The Gitlow Case" (1925), in Zechariah Chafee, Jr., *The Inquiring Mind* (New York: Harcourt, Brace, 1928), 107. Chafee is the key figure in the civil libertarian reading of the First Amendment, according to Mark A. Graber, *Transforming Free Speech: The Ambiguous Legacy of Civil Libertarianism* (Berkeley: University of California Press, 1991). Chafee hailed *Schenck* in "Freedom of Speech in War Time," *Harvard Law Review* 32.8 (June 1919): 932–73, and probably helped spur Holmes to further innovations.

2. David M. Rabban, *Free Speech in Its Forgotten Years* (Cambridge: Cambridge University Press, 1997); Graber, *Transforming Free Speech.*

issues should be uninhibited, robust, and wide-open" (Brennan). Much scholarly and public talk about free expression consists of the varying redeployment of these and similar gems. The common law, owing to its reasoning from precedent rather than abstract principle, has a proverbial quality. indeed, as with many forms of knowledge, its chief findings are often stated in minimal syntactic nuggets.[3] The cognitive economies of dealing with yards of linear shelf space of legal print matter may also foster quotation consciousness. What my late colleague Michael McGee took as a general condition of postmodern culture—that readers are in the position of authors, actively constructing texts out of the swirl of cultural fragments on offer—has perhaps always been the practice of judges in the Anglo-American tradition.[4]

In this chapter I will focus especially on intellectuals' accounts of free expression and on important Supreme Court decisions. The U.S. Supreme Court is, after all, one of the world's most prolific and influential producers of communication theory. Especially but not only in its interpretations of the First Amendment, the Court has ruminated on the gamut of communicative problems facing a democratic polity, in the process offering smart and sometimes curious commentary usable for more general purposes. Its discourse on free expression is an open book about mass communication in the modern world. Admittedly, the Court produces theory of a peculiar sort. It works not by consensus, but by the issuing of divergent opinions. It is a famously uncollegial body of nine independent thinkers (the title of Max Lerner's book, *Nine Scorpions in a Bottle,* comes to mind). Interpreting law plays by different rules than philosophical argument or political discussion. Judges are constrained by the facts of the case, precedent, persuasive exigencies, and their colleagues. Extended theoretical treatments about free expression usually come from scholars or judges writing in the luxury of private thought, rather than in decisions. (Brandeis's concurrence in *Whitney* is the exception that proves the rule, and even that is only a paragraph.) The circumstances of many cases reveal the antics our species is capable of, as well as the lengths to which the aggrieved will go in search of justice. The reader of Supreme Court cases who is not snowed by the solemn language will find a feast of edification about the human circus, rather like that offered by ancient Greek comedies and tragedies. The simple operational fact that the most profound and general law is made and tested by the most ab-

3. Steven Shapin, "Proverbial Economies," *Social Studies in Science* 31 (2001): 731–70.

4. Michael Calvin McGee, "Text, Context, and the Fragmentation of Contemporary Culture," *Western Journal of Communication* 54 (1990): 274–89.

surd and peculiar situations may be one source of the notion, so important for Mill-reading justices, that extremity is essential medicine for democracy. Reading court decisions as communication theory may seem as strange as reading Paul's epistles that way, but there is ample justification. Throughout I will focus especially, to use an ugly but useful medical term, on the traumatophilic streak in First Amendment jurisprudence, the cultivation of pain and civic hardness by a variety of thinkers, from Holmes onward. Mill's homeopathic machismo—the notion that a tincture of poison will lift us to heights of tolerance and civic-mindedness—continues in visions of the ascetic First Amendment.

HOLMES AND HARDNESS

Oliver Wendell Holmes, Jr. is perhaps still the most famous exponent of the idea that the First Amendment's purpose is to teach us to appreciate ideas that we hate. Yet Holmes is a rather odd hero for civil libertarians: he had a lukewarm appreciation for public debate and saw social policy questions as differences of taste ultimately resolvable only by war.[5] After all, his famous opinions in *Abrams* and *Schenck* both allow for the restriction of dangerous talk. As Edmund Wilson says, there is a "certain element of comedy" in Holmes as a hero for the Left, especially in his laissez-faire economics. Thanks to Felix Frankfurter, Harold Laski, Max Lerner, Morris Cohen, and other much younger correspondents who knew him in his old age as an intellectually adventuresome mentor of untried people and ideas, an image of Holmes as arch-liberal, the "Great Dissenter," solidified by the second third of the twentieth century.[6] His thinking had a strong streak of nihilism, even a certain brutal authoritarianism. His consistent defense of the right of all parties to compete—a right he considered neither God-given nor self-evident but by the grace of the state—however silly he might have thought their views (as he certainly did of socialists), is a politically amphibious principle, able alike to fly through liberal air and crawl through conservative mud. Holmes is, in most respects, a latter-day Stoic. "He cannot disown, if he will not boast, his descent from the Stoic, who had no Elysium," wrote Judge Learned Hand of his hero.[7] Edmund Wilson echoes: "Justice Holmes

5. See Graber's critique of "the Holmes myth" in *Transforming Free Speech*, 106–12.

6. See David A. Hollinger, "The 'Tough-Minded' Justice Holmes, Jewish Intellectuals, and the Making of an American Icon," in *The Legacy of Oliver Wendell Holmes, Jr.*, ed. R. W. Gordon (Stanford, Calif.: Stanford University Press, 1992), 216–28.

7. Learned Hand, "Mr. Justice Holmes" (1930), in *The Spirit of Liberty: Papers and Addresses of Learned Hand*, ed. Irving Dilliard, 3rd ed. (Chicago: University of Chicago Press, 1960), 61.

was perhaps the last Roman."[8] *Romanitas* is not the only feature he shared with Pontius Pilate.

In a famous line, which became a battle cry for progressives, Holmes suggested that the key principle of the Constitution is "not free thought for those who agree with us but freedom for the thought of those we hate."[9] The principle that a dose of hate can enhance the robustness of the entire system he stated in his famous dissent in *Lochner* (1905): "[The Constitution] is made for people of fundamentally differing views, and the accident of our finding certain opinions natural and familiar or novel and even shocking ought not to conclude our judgment upon the question whether statutes embodying them conflict with the Constitution of the United States."[10] Personal preference has no relevance for constitutional interpretation. Holmes's judges and their citizen disciples are, like Odysseus tied to the mast, passive before the doctrines they (love to) hate. Holmes relished demonstrating indifference to his own preferences. "It has given me great pleasure to sustain the Constitutionality of laws that I believe to be as bad as possible," he wrote his cousin, "because I thereby helped to mark the difference between what I would forbid and what the Constitution permits."[11] Holmes believed in what we might call the Judge's Two Bodies.[12] The judge's personal soul keeps his private opinions, but he must sacrifice them to the greater glory of the whole. The judge must decide, however distasteful he may find it. Holmes, like Shaftesbury and Adam Smith, calls for self-division. His stance is magnificently perverse in a strangely cheery way.

The stance of self-discipline is also apparent in Holmes's path-breaking opinions on freedom of speech, the locus classicus being his dissent in *Abrams*.[13] The desire to persecute others who have different opinions, he argues, is perfectly understandable: those who have no reason to doubt their own premises naturally desire to obliterate their opponents. Given the natural urge to persecute, we raise ourselves beyond nature by restraining that will. A more chastened perspective loosens our attachment to narrow conceptions:

---

8. Edmund Wilson, *Patriotic Gore* ([1962]; New York: Norton, 1994), 795.

9. *U. S. v. Schwimmer* 279 U.S. 644 (1929), 644–65, Holmes dissenting. For one example, see "The Speech We Hate," *Progressive* 56 (Aug. 1992), in Sheila Suess Kennedy, *Free Expression in America: A Documentary History* (Westport, Conn.: Greenwood Press, 1999), 319–22.

10. *Lochner v. New York,* 198 U.S. 45 (1905), 76.

11. Oliver Wendell Holmes, Jr. to John T. Morse, 28 Nov. 1926, quoted in Louis Menand, *The Metaphysical Club* (New York: Farrar, Straus, Giroux, 2001), 67.

12. I allude to Ernst Kantorowicz, *The King's Two Bodies* (Princeton, N.J.: Princeton University Press, 1957).

13. *Abrams vs. United States,* 250 U.S. 616 (1919), 630.

But when men have realized that time has upset many fighting faiths, they may come to believe even more than they believe the very foundations of their own conduct that the ultimate good desired is better reached by free trade in ideas— that the best test of truth is the power of the thought to get itself accepted in the competition of the market, and that truth is the only ground upon which their wishes safely can be carried out. That at any rate is the theory of our Constitution. It is an experiment, as all life is an experiment. Every year if not every day we have to wager our salvation upon some prophecy based upon imperfect knowledge. While that experiment is part of our system I think that we should be eternally vigilant against attempts to check the expression of opinions that we loathe and believe to be fraught with death, unless they so imminently threaten immediate interference with the lawful and pressing purposes of the law that an immediate check is required to save the country.

These famous words, deeply prized by many civil libertarians, have a harsh edge not always grasped. Holmes celebrates the psychological hesitancy that historical relativity provides. (In his belief that self-consciousness inspires rather than corrupts, he shares an article of faith with the liberal tradition.) Once we discover the transience or even absurdity of dead causes, we will relinquish egotistic surety for the collective winnowing of ideas in the market. Our faith in the power of open competition to discover truth should be deeper than the foundations of our own conduct. Note the cunning "while" that begins the last sentence: even the Constitution is a fighting faith. Like Peirce, with whom he traded ideas in the 1870s, and Dewey, whose writings he admired (but not enough to forgo a few barbs), Holmes equated truth with a collective method of inquiry.[14] But whereas for Peirce truth emerged in a community of inquiry whose governing norm was collaboration or even love, and Dewey conceived of democracy as a collective mode of inquiry, Holmes characteristically placed truth in a realm, the market, whose ruling norm was competition. (If this is the theory of the Constitution, it is not one that the Founders would have recognized without boning up on their Mill, Spencer, and pragmatism.[15]) Holmes had no substantive conception of truth—he liked to provoke his friends by saying that truth was "the majority vote of the nation that could lick all the oth-

14. Even though Holmes pronounced Dewey's *Experience and Nature* (1925), which treated Holmes favorably, "incredibly ill written," he thought it showed "a feeling of intimacy with the universe that I found unequaled. So methought God would have spoken had He been inarticulate but deeply desirous to tell you how it was." Quoted in Menand, *Metaphysical Club*, 437.

15. On Holmes's reading of Mill, see Richard Polenberg, *Fighting Faiths: The Abrams Case, the Supreme Court, and Free Speech* (New York: Viking, 1987), 217–18.

ers."[16] Like Pontius Pilate, he enjoyed asking, "what is truth?" without staying for an answer. Holmes thought the "competition of the market" was dangerous and brutal and could eat people alive; that is one reason he liked it.

The whiff of decay and death presides over the whole *Abrams* passage—fighting, wagering, transience. Judges, like citizens, should be consecrated figures who can touch things fraught with death without being harmed—and if they bear scars, that only adds to their luster.[17] As evolutionary processes are governed by chance, so ethical processes are governed by gambling. What better describes the Constitution to Holmes's mind than a "prophecy based upon imperfect knowledge" upon which we wager our salvation? Holmes was clearly no absolutist defender of speech. Time, place, and manner may legitimately restrict free expression. In *Schenck*, decided earlier in the same year as *Abrams* (1919), he wrote the majority opinion supporting the conviction of Schenck for printing a pamphlet that advocated resistance to the draft in World War I. (The pamphlet was itself a gambit in constitutional interpretation, arguing from the Thirteenth Amendment that conscription was a form of enslavement.) Writing two of the best-known phrases in free speech jurisprudence, Holmes argued: "The most stringent protection of free speech would not protect a man in falsely shouting fire in a theatre and causing a panic. It does not even protect a man from an injunction against uttering words that may have all the effect of force. . . . The question in every case is whether the words used are used in such circumstances and are of such a nature as to create a clear and present danger that they will bring about the substantive evils that Congress has a right to prevent. It is a question of proximity and degree."[18] Even in his *Abrams* dissent, Holmes made clear that his decision rested on the specific content of the pamphlets by Abrams and others, not a general principle of protection for politically extremist discourse.

By all accounts the key turning point in Holmes's very long life was the Civil War, in which he served as an officer and was wounded in each of three separate battles. He endured the destruction of men all around him and lived to find a certain chilly glory in it. He was the son of one of the leading doctors—and authors—of his day, and thus, via war, medicine, and law,

16. Oliver Wendell Holmes, Jr., "Natural Law" (1918), in *American Literature,* ed. Cleanth Brooks et al. (New York: St. Martin's Press, 1973), 2: 1512.

17. Carolyn Marvin and David W. Ingle, *Blood Sacrifice and the Nation* (Cambridge: Cambridge University Press, 1999).

18. *Schenck v. United States,* 249 U.S. 47 (1919), 52.

was exposed to three key agents of professional soul-hardening in the nineteenth century (perhaps literature should be counted as well). Holmes as judge was not afraid to serve as an agent of necessity. He seemingly relished his Pilate role, something he may well have learned from his acquaintance and fellow legal scholar James Fitzjames Stephen.[19] "Everything," as Holmes was fond of repeating, "is founded on the death of men."[20] In *United States v. Schwimmer* (1929), a case in which a pacifist born in Hungary whose application for U.S. citizenship had been rejected on account of her refusal to consent to bear arms to defend the nation (the refusal was a rather quixotic point of principle since Schwimmer's age and gender would have prevented her from being asked to do so), Holmes wrote: "I do not share that optimism nor do I think that a philosophic view of the world would regard war as absurd."[21] Yet in his dissent he defended Schwimmer against the charge that her pacifist beliefs should deny her U.S. citizenship. The good soldier could execute orders he did not agree with. Holmes elsewhere noted "the tacit reference to the billy and the bayonet that lies in all the organization of the world."[22] As a Malthusian, decorated veteran, scientific naturalist, closet eugenicist, friend of laissez-faire economics, and consummate professional, Holmes is a prime candidate for the prize of brutal necessitarian. Even if it is futile, war may be necessary. Wasted blood is still glorious. Holmes's religious agnosticism could take a jocular form: whether God existed was the question "if the cosmos wears a beard."[23] Unlike William James, whose pragmatism made a wobbly space for religious faith—much to Holmes's bemused annoyance, who thought James a bit of a softie on this point— Holmes was glad to put a razor to the cosmos's whiskers. He strikes a heroic pose, staring the insignificance of it all in its face, admitting that meanings are conjured from strength of will, and admiring whatever doctrine he came across that had enough vitality to defy the inevitable moral entropy facing human endeavors. The consistent cheer with which he managed to maintain his rapprochement with the cosmos and his unstinting courage, longevity, and humor are among his most redeeming qualities.

19. Richard Posner, foreword to James Fitzjames Stephen, *Liberty, Equality, Fraternity* (1874) (Chicago: University of Chicago Press, 1991), 9–10. Stephen's defense of Pontius Pilate on 110–16 has a remarkably Holmesian flavor.

20. Holmes to Harold Laski, 14 Jan. 1920, quoted in Wilson, *Patriotic Gore*, 764.

21. *United States v. Schwimmer*, 279 U.S. 644 (1929), 654.

22. Holmes to Franklin Ford, 3 May 1907, in *Progressive Masks: Letters of Oliver Wendell Holmes, Jr. and Franklin Ford*, ed. David H. Burton (Newark: University of Delaware Press, 1982), 43.

23. Quoted in Wilson, *Patriotic Gore*, 793.

Holmes's philosophical defense of the benefits of bloodshed is most explicit in his 1895 Memorial Day speech, "A Soldier's Faith." This homage to pain clarifies what "fighting faiths" might mean. Wealth in the late nineteenth century, he notes, had replaced war among the passions of men: "we have learned the doctrine that evil means pain, and the revolt against pain in all its forms has grown more and more marked. From societies for the prevention of cruelty to animals up to socialism, we express in numberless ways the notion that suffering is a wrong which can be and ought to be prevented." Rather like Mill, Holmes clearly sees this sensitivity to pain as a loss, though he has no time for those who blindly adore war without knowing its horrors. "For my own part, I believe that the struggle for life is the order of the world, at which it is vain to repine." His nightmare of contented nullities, "a world cut up into five-acre lots and having no man upon it who was not well fed and well housed, without the divine folly of honor," can take its place as a strenuous version of the horrors of bored conformity evoked by Tocqueville and Mill in the nineteenth century and by Huxley and Orwell in the twentieth.[24] The thrill and terror of battle, even for causes without guarantees, save us from modern stupor. Stoicism, after all, has always been a soldier's doctrine.

J. S. Mill thought the civilizing process a one-way street: "We cannot undo what civilization has done, and again stimulate the higher classes by insecurity of property, or danger of life and limb."[25] Holmes, however, thought a little danger to life and limb a fine nostrum. He answers the problem of disappearing moral anchors with the divine folly of honor: "I do not know what is true. I do not know the meaning of the universe. But in the midst of doubt, in the collapse of creeds, there is one thing I do not doubt, that no man who lives in the same world with most of us can doubt, and that is that the faith is true and adorable which leads a soldier to throw away his life in obedience to a blindly accepted duty, in a cause of which he little understands, in a plan of campaign of which he has no notion, under tactics of which he does not see the use."[26] Here is one answer to the silent revolutions of opinion that emptied the churches in the nineteenth century: a heroic ethic. Bravery is one way to deal with the puzzle of death. Like Hegel, Holmes sees the will to stake honor over life as a great purgative that annihilates idle doubt and boredom. War is a mechanism for producing mean-

24. Oliver Wendell Holmes, Jr., "A Soldier's Faith" (1895), in *American Literature*, 2: 1508–12.

25. J. S. Mill, "Civilization" (1836), in *Collected Works of John Stuart Mill*, ed. J. M. Robson (Toronto: University of Toronto Press, 1977), 18: 147.

26. Holmes, "A Soldier's Faith," 2: 1509.

ing. "For high and dangerous action teaches us to believe as right beyond dispute things for which our doubting minds are slow to find words of proof. . . . I gaze with delight upon our polo players. If once in a while in our rough riding a neck is broken, I regard it, not as a waste, but as a price well paid for the breeding of a race fit for headship and command." Compared with "wallowing ease," danger is a school of virtues. (Another Harvard man of the next generation, Teddy Roosevelt, soon to be famous for a similar kind of "rough riding," would appoint Holmes to the Supreme Court, hoping to find a fellow trustbuster instead of a freewheeling nihilist; he was sorely disappointed.) Holmes's cult of strenuousness is one of many critiques of bourgeois flab ("effeminacy") in both the nineteenth and the twentieth century. Against the void of meaninglessness, you can make strong sense of the world while the bullets fly and "the shrieking fragments go tearing through your company." Unlike Paul, Holmes does not shudder at the spectacle of a broken neck; he seems rather to enjoy the catharsis it affords.

Holmes has a tragic sense: the dangers (and benefits) of speech cannot be extirpated: "Every idea is an incitement," he wrote in *Gitlow*. "If in the long run the beliefs expressed in proletarian dictatorship are destined to be accepted by the dominant forces of the community, the only meaning of free speech is that they should be given their chance and have their way."[27] The mere publication of a discourse is ordinarily not enough to void its First Amendment protections. Clearly, Holmes did not think that belief in a proletarian dictatorship would find acceptance in the long run; he could afford to be generous. He wanted a strong First Amendment not because he thought more speech was the cure for bad speech, but because he wanted o leave the evolutionary battlegrounds uncluttered—like a Roman official making sure the gladiators all have water and bread before they head into combat.

BRANDEIS AND NOXIOUS DOCTRINE

Holmes and Brandeis: as in Chafee's 1925 article, they have long been mentioned, like Lennon and McCartney or Abbott and Costello, in a single breath. Though they were longtime colleagues on the Court, allies in dissents such as *Abrams* and *Gitlow,* and pioneers in the libertarian interpretation of the First Amendment, hindsight clarifies important differences in their thought. Where Holmes was a Stoic nihilist, Louis Dembitz Brandeis was a Romantic progressive. Both had classical leanings: if Holmes admired

---

27. *Gitlow v. United States,* 268 U.S. 652 (1925), 673, Holmes dissenting.

the duty of a Hector, Brandeis admired the courage of a Pericles (something he shared with Mill).[28] Other contrasts are more obvious Holmes was born a Boston Brahmin; Brandeis was born in Kentucky to German-Jewish immigrants. Even so, both inherited healthy antinomian traditions. Holmes's Calvinist ancestors had taught that law is irrelevant if you are one of the elect, and his lifelong intellectual hero, Emerson, taught the severe discipline of following no law but one's own. Brandeis's mother, Frederika Dembitz, was from a family of Frankists, a Jewish sect in eighteenth-century central Europe that followed the pseudo-messianic heresies of Shabbetai Zevi (or Tsevi). Zevi, who engaged in strategically offensive speech acts such as uttering the sacred name of God, ultimately disappointed his followers by converting to Islam, but some of his followers interpreted this as one more sign of his chosenness, the ability to pass through the other side. Joseph Frank in turn, a convert to Shabbeteanism, taught his flock in Poland to embrace immorality as a spiritual path in the ever-popular heresy that Gershom Scholem called "redemption through sin."[29] Frederika Dembitz, like many early-nineteenth-century liberal Jews, was personally not hospitable to Shabbeteanism, but it is as least suggestive that Brandeis descended from people who acknowledged the power of incubating noxious doctrine.[30] His concurrence to *Whitney v. California* (1927) is probably the most famous and sustained reading of the philosophy of the Founders expressed in any legal decision:

> Those who won our independence believed that the final end of the state was to make men free to develop their faculties, and that in its government the deliberative forces should prevail over the arbitrary. They valued liberty both as an end and as a means. They believed liberty to be the secret of happiness and courage to be the secret of liberty. They believed that freedom to think as you will and to speak as you think are means indispensable to the discovery and spread of political truth; that without free speech and assembly discussion would be futile; that with them, discussion affords ordinarily adequate protection against the dissemination of noxious doctrine; that the greatest menace to freedom is an inert people; that public discussion is a political duty; and that this should be a fundamental principle of the American government.[31]

28. Cass R. Sunstein, *Democracy and the Problem of Free Speech* (New York: Free Press, 1993), 23–28. For Sunstein, Holmes is a laissez-faire neoliberal and Brandeis is a Madisonian deliberative democrat.

29. Karen Armstrong, *The Battle for God: A History of Fundamentalism* (New York: Ballantine, 2001), 30–31.

30. See Gershom Scholem, *The Messianic Idea in Judaism* (New York: Schocken, 1971), 93; and Leonard Baker, *Brandeis and Frankfurter: A Dual Biography* (New York: Harper & Row, 1984), 21–22.

31. *Whitney v. California*, 274 U.S. 357 (1927), 375.

Lovely though it is, Brandeis's edifying exposition of the Constitution has some wrinkles. Though it was certainly the belief of Brandeis's contemporary John Dewey in *The Public and Its Problems*, published in the same year as *Whitney* (1927), that the role of the state was to aid individuals and communities in their quest for self-realization, it is dubious whether the Framers thought so, or whether they even spoke with a single voice on this matter. Wilhelm von Humboldt, however, who influenced Mill and furnished both the epigraph to *On Liberty* and the chief historical tie between German Romanticism and liberalism, did believe that the encouragement of variegated individuality was the state's office, and Brandeis seems to have been raised with a good dose of German Romanticism. Some used to quip that John Rawls made Kant into one of the Founding Fathers; here Brandeis does the same for Humboldt. Brandeis's history of the First Amendment was pragmatically useful as a mandate for a new vision of open debate, and it would be a sorry state of affairs if we had to check all inspiring words for their historical accuracy; this is a case where a genealogy is constructed as a prelude to a future philosophy. In fact Brandeis's vision came in his *concurring* with the conviction of a revolutionary socialist for the simple bad tendency of her opinions. These words are at best generalities against which the decision of *Whitney* is an exception. The question motivating them was "why a State is, ordinarily, denied the power to prohibit dissemination of social, economic and political doctrine which a vast majority of its citizens believes to be false and fraught with evil consequence." The "ordinarily" alerts us to the proviso Brandeis shares with Holmes in *Schenck:* "although the rights of free speech and assembly are fundamental, they are not in their nature absolute."[32] The tricky part, of course, is deciding when a situation is extraordinary.[33]

Brandeis was no absolutist, though he was remarkably optimistic about the clarifying powers of speech. One of his famous quotes must owe its ultimate inspiration to Bentham: "Publicity is justly commended as a remedy for social and industrial diseases. Sunlight is said to be the best of disinfectants; electric light the most efficient policeman."[34] Like other progressives, Brandeis believed in rational reform, that exposing accumulated fact would arouse the civic conscience. In contrast to more pessimistic thinkers across

---

32. *Whitney v. California*, 374.

33. A very different kind of political thinker took up just this question at the same time: Carl Schmitt, *Political Theology: Four Chapters on the Concept of Sovereignty* (1922), trans. George Schwab (Cambridge: MIT Press, 1985).

34. Louis D. Brandeis, *Other People's Money: And How the Bankers Use It* (New York: Stokes, 1914), 92.

the intellectual spectrum in the 1920s who saw speech as propaganda for atavistic passions or a closed door of private language, Brandeis thought, together with the *philosophes* (among whom Bentham must be counted), that it was "the function of speech to free men from the bondage of irrational fears." Speech is the cure for ill speech: "If there be time to expose through discussion the falsehood and fallacies, to avert the evil by the processes of education, the remedy to be applied is more speech, not enforced silence."[35] *Whitney* marks a historically important shift away from the state as the chief enemy of free speech as in early modern political thought (muzzling journalists, suppressing dissidents, hushing up secret deals).[36] For Brandeis the First Amendment is the chief tool of the "omnipresent teacher," the government.[37] The main agenda of free speech cases from the 1920s onward has concerned private actors clashing among themselves, rather than the state squelching liberty. The state is called upon to umpire bickering factions. Like the judges who staff it, the state in *Times v. Sullivan* (1964) is treated as a stoic master, the general disciplinarian that prevents the majority from squashing opinions it finds despicable.

Holmes calls us to restrain ourselves when we face ideas that seem fraught with death. His answer is stern, even martial, self-discipline. His was a public sphere with no guarantees: it was a battleground in which the strong prevailed, and courts might make periodic intervention to give the weak a fighting chance. Brandeis's picture of selfhood rotates on a different axis. The danger is inertness, the delight is development. His public sphere had a *telos*, the progressive unfolding of truth. "Noxious doctrine" was part of the picture, but the sunlight of discussion would ordinarily banish its ill effects. Holmes had no truck with theodicy, but Brandeis had a sense that evil would not prevail. A fierce battle or a blossoming of truth; they had different visions of public communication, but for both Holmes and Brandeis tolerating death and noxiousness was part of the duty and education of the citizen-subject. Pain and self-suppression were part of the civic program.

SKOKIE SUBJECTIVITY

The Holmesian notion that righteous citizens steel themselves by learning to live with the thought they hate or the Brandeisian notion that noxious

---

35. *Whitney v. California*, 376, 377.

36. On the intellectual history of free speech against the state, see John Keane, *The Media and Democracy* (London: Polity Press, 1991); and Lee C. Bollinger, *The Tolerant Society* (New York: Oxford University Press, 1986).

37. *Olmstead vs. United* States 277 U.S. 438 (1928), 485.

doctrine is inevitable is central to the wider liberal cultural interpretation of free expression. A major historical context is the triumph of professionalism as a cultural ideal for the middle class in the late nineteenth and early twentieth centuries, something chapter 5 treats at greater length. A good example is the founding of the American Association of University Professors, led by John Dewey, in 1915. The AAUP advocated an asceticism in the realm of opinions quite like the attitudinal foundation Holmes was laying for free speech at the same time. Its Declaration of Principles argued that the speech of professors was entitled to legal protection when they spoke as professionals, that is, without any ultimate interest beyond the truth and the esteem of their colleagues. To be a professional was to keep opinions free of personal, political, and pecuniary interests. In one particularly ringing sentence, it stated: "To the degree that professional scholars, in the formation and promulgation of their opinions, are, or by the character of their tenure appear to be, subject to any motive other than their own scientific conscience and a desire for the respect of their fellow-experts, to that degree the university teaching profession is corrupted; its proper influence on public opinion is diminished and vitiated; and society at large fails to get from its scholars, in an unadulterated form, the peculiar and necessary service which it is the office of the professional scholar to furnish."[38] Conscience and peer review are supposed to be the sole legitimate motives for professionals. Note the truckload of liberal confidences: the intellectual's clarifying influence on public opinion; the lofty office of the professional; the possibility of speech unadulterated by interest. Free speech is guaranteed by accompanying self-control. In this the AAUP points to the subduction of ancient ethics by the tectonic plate of professionalism. The self-control that both the AAUP and Holmesian free expression call for reflects the professional practice of suspended judgment.

The turn of the twentieth century was an axial period for the rise of professional attitudes generally and ascetic views about free speech in particular. Take two examples. Voltaire's supposed saying, "I disapprove of what you say, but will defend to the death your right to say it," recurs with tiresome predictability in discussions of free expression: It was in fact coined not by Voltaire, but rather by E. Beatrice Hall in a 1906 book on Voltaire's contemporaries. Hall, publishing under the pseudonym Stephen G. Tallentyre, was a major exponent of the glories of eighteenth-century France in

---

38. Louis Joughin, *Academic Freedom and Tenure* (Madison: University of Wisconsin Press, 1967), 162. We do not know if Dewey wrote this passage but doubts prevail: the periods are too nice.

late Victorian and Edwardian England. By her account, when Helvétius's *De l'esprit* (1755) was attacked for its materialism and atheism, some copies even being torched, Voltaire was not worried. "'What a fuss about an omelette,' he had exclaimed when he heard of the burning. How abominably unjust to persecute a man for such an airy trifle as that! 'I disapprove of what you say, but I will defend to the death your right to say it,' was his attitude now."[39] Hall does not even put the phrase directly in Voltaire's mouth. It is indirect discourse, a device to represent his stance, as if it were a prefabricated slogan culled from contemporary culture, the civil repartee of British gentlemen who were willing to take up swords in the name of fair play.[40] The attitudinal chemistry that "Voltaire" endorses—mixed hatred and defense of principle—became a well-practiced element in the periodic table of twentieth-century culture. That we may entertain the enemy's discourse is, as we have seen, as old as Paul or Milton; but the peculiar righteous indignation of insisting on the other's right to free speech, even at the risk of one's own life, points to an emerging professional, self-sacrificial culture in which people can collect fetal specimens in bottles (like Dr. Rudolf Virchow discussed in the next chapter) and celebrate the shrieking metal fragments of warfare (like Holmes). There is something fatuous afoot: who would really die to guarantee someone else's right to speak poppycock? Our faux Voltaire protests too much, smugly proclaiming the defenders' virtue but not their vulnerability to learning something from the defended opinion. Though incorrect in attribution and bogus in spirit, the quote's prevalence teaches us something about the self-division of the liberal soul—supporting antiliberal causes as a matter of principle in the same way a doctor can study morbidity without being infected. Note the cool split of form (abstract support for speech rights) and substance (the concrete things said).

A story in the satirical newspaper *The Onion* headlined "ACLU Defends Nazis' Right to Burn Down ACLU Headquarters" provides a parable about what defending detestable doctrine to the death really means. Dependably armed with the "Voltaire" quote, the story has ACLU president Nadine Strossen defending a Georgia neo-Nazi group's rights to express itself by torching the ACLU headquarters—with all the staff inside. "Yes, my loving wife Linda and three wonderful children, Ben, Robby and Stephanie, will be

<hr />

39. E. Beatrice Hall [under pseud. Stephen G. Tallentyre], *The Friends of Voltaire* (London: Smith, Elder, 1906), 198–99.

40. The epigraph of Hall's book offers a more authentic source: "Il faut que les âmes pensantes se frottent l'une contre l'autre pour faire jaillir de la lumière." Voltaire to the Duke of Uzes, 4 Dec 1751.

devastated when I am killed next month," *The Onion* has another ACLU attorney say: "But I recognize that, in a very real sense, it would be a victory for Mr. Carver and his fellow hatemongers if I did not burn to death, because their terrible message of bigotry and intolerance would be all the more effective if suppressed."[41] The joke lies in taking to literal limit the (absurd) promise to die for the right of other people to "express" themselves. *The Onion* comically ignores the line strenuously policed by the ACLU, the courts, and most theorists of free expression between speech and conduct. The ACLU's public-spirited suspension of judgment here gets reduced ad absurdum.

A fin-de-siècle example of public stoicism in the face of objectionable talk is a nice *typos,* in Paul's term, of things to come. The quintessential progressive Theodore Roosevelt relates an anecdote in his *Autobiography* from his days as police commissioner in New York City in the mid-1890s. Rector Hermann Ahlwardt, a member of the German Reichstag and virulent anti-Semite, came to the United States to rabble-rouse (though he spoke no English). Many in the Jewish community wanted to stop him from delivering an address, but Roosevelt resisted. He feared that muzzling Ahlwardt might make him a martyr. "The proper thing to do," said Roosevelt, "was to make him ridiculous." To this end Roosevelt had the anti-Semite protected during his talk and his entire stay by a contingent of a sergeant and some forty policeman—all of them Jewish. "It was the most effective possible answer," noted a satisfied Roosevelt.[42] One can imagine Ahlwardt fulminating against Jews while he stands surrounded by two score of them, stoically guarding his right to fulminate, daring members of their own community to interfere with their defense of the thought they hate. This little episode, a dramatic performance of Gandhian beauty, represents a long history of nose-holding toleration. Roosevelt's memoir (written in the key decade of the 1910s) is not the only story. Ahlwardt's presence split the Jewish community, and he was not always received stoically but sometimes with rotten eggs and fists. The *New York Times* ran a story on his family, reporting that his daughter was in love with a Jewish boy. Ahlwardt's demonization also seems to have created mutually beneficial Jewish and Christian alliances in New York.[43]

One can hardly read of Roosevelt's stunt without thinking of the Nazis in

41. *The Onion,* 32.11 (15 Oct. 1997).

42. Theodore Roosevelt, *An Autobiography* (New York: Macmillan, 1914), 191–92. See also "Gathered About Town," *New York Times,* 15 Feb.1897: 10.

43. "Ancient Eggs for Ahlwardt," *New York Times,* 9 Dec.1895: 3; "Herr Ahlwardt Arrested," *New York Times,* 7 Apr. 1896: 1.

Skokie, doubtless the single most important case in the last third of the twentieth century for propagating the model of a civic dichotomy of personal disgust and public toleration. Legally, it did not result in any stirring opinions or clarifications; the Skokie case is much more significant as a cultural landmark, as a symbol of a certain attitude toward evil. Francis Joseph Collin was the leader of the National Socialist Party of America. Born in Illinois as Frank Cohn to Max Cohn, a Jew who survived three months in the concentration camp in Dachau, and Virginia Hardyman, an American Catholic, Collin sought to organize a Nazi march in 1978 in Skokie, Illinois, a north shore suburb and home to a substantial Jewish community that included a significant number of Holocaust survivors. Collin's plan was, not surprisingly, controversial, and also complicated (due to parade permits and insurance regulations, some of which had been implemented in the wake of civil rights marches). Stepping up to his aid was the ACLU.[44] As in Roosevelt's police force, the key defenders of the Nazis' right to march, but of course not of their doctrine, were Jews. Like all enablers, they could have taken their motto from Starbuck's comment about Captain Ahab in *Moby Dick:* "I think I see his impious end; but feel that I must help him to it."[45] How did this curious inversion come about?

Aryeh Neier's memoir, *Defending My Enemy* (1979), an account of how the ACLU, of which he served as national executive director from 1970 to 1978, chose to defend Collin and his tiny ragtag Nazi party and help them to secure parade permits, police protection, and insurance policies, is not only an excellent period piece, but also a thoughtful account of the strategy of public irony. Neier, born of Jewish parents in Berlin in 1937 and an escapee from the Holocaust, in contrast to most of his less fortunate extended family, was the eventual founder of Helsinki Watch. He makes a fascinating witness. He shrewdly notes, for instance, that though a strong Nazi movement is dangerous for Jews, a weak one forces solidarity with and empathy from Christians and encourages support for the state of Israel (shades of Rector Ahlwardt). The Skokie case occurred at the precise moment when the Holocaust was about to make its decisive entry onto the public stage in America and also in the key period of the rise of human rights politics.[46]

---

44. Philippa Strum, *When the Nazis Came to Skokie: Freedom for Speech We Hate* (Lawrence: University Press of Kansas, 1999), is the fullest account.

45. *Moby Dick,* chap. 38.

46. Strum, *When the Nazis Came to Skokie;* Tony Kushner, *The Holocaust and the Liberal Imagination: A Social and Cultural History* (Oxford: Blackwell, 1994), 255; Kenneth Cmiel, "The Emergence of Human Rights Politics in the United States," *Journal of American History* 86 (1999): 1231–50.

The Holocaust first became officially commemorated in U.S. national cere-
monies in 1979, and the Carter administration started to consider a national
Holocaust museum.[47] Neier asks a question that could perhaps still be
asked in 1979: "It remains to be seen . . . whether interest in the Holocaust
will be sustained. The subject is painful and people are eager to forget.
There was a wave of interest in the 1960s because of the Eichmann capture
and trial. It ebbed quickly. Will that happen again?" The future in which the
Holocaust would disappear from public view has long since closed. The for-
tunes of the Skokie case loom large still because it enacts a complex settle-
ment of attitudes: remembrance of trauma, together with a strenuous, if
paradoxical, self-image of the citizen-subject as a stoic defender of the outcast. One can have one's pain and virtue too. "Because we Jews are uniquely
vulnerable, I believe we can win only brief respite from persecution in a society in which encounters are settled by power," wrote Neier. Defending the
right of Nazis to march in Skokie was a public performance of what it
meant to be an enlightened Jew in America, following in the footsteps of
Holmes and more especially Brandeis, defending the thought you hate, and
in so doing, trying to create a society in which open arguments triumph
over brute force, in which the Habermasian alchemy of converting base
force to noble arguments can prevail.[48]

The Skokie case presents a key drama of liberal irony. The bystander
public is supposed to see the ACLU as so sublime in its principles that it can
defend even its mortal murderous enemy, a take-home message about the
self-abstraction due from every citizen. Collin's defenders altered Cicero's
audi alteram partem (hear the other side) into *aude alteram partem* (dare
the other side). Their point—underneath the layers—was to defend the
most stigmatized view possible and thus to question the process by which
some views are made illegitimate. Needless to say, not everyone got the message of such delicate displays of masochism. As often occurs with public
irony, the ACLU's stance was internally divisive. Its torpedoes-be-damned
absolutism is easy to burlesque, as we have seen; Neier reports, with generous good humor, one wag's suggested motto for the ACLU: "the First
Amendment *über alles.*" And yet the group showed remarkable courage in
the face of sharp criticism from within the Jewish and other communities,
and also took a significant financial hit (the ACLU lost about 15 percent of

47. Barbie Zelizer, *Remembering to Forget: Holocaust Memory Through the Camera's Eye* (Chicago: University of Chicago Press, 1998), 173; Kushner, *The Holocaust,* 258–59.

48. Aryeh Neier, *Defending My Enemy: American Nazis, the Skokie Case, and the Risks of Freedom* (New York: Dutton, 1979), 34, 72, 36, 5.

its membership and $500,000 in dues over Skokie). Rabbi Meir Kahane, of the Jewish Defense League, fiercely opposed the ACLU's policy. He had no time for inferno-artistry. Quoth Neier: "Rabbi Kahane is a street fighter. He does not believe in defending his enemies."[49] This inadvertent confession of class politics indicates the high rung the ACLU wants to occupy on the ladder of the civilizing process.[50] Members of the ACLU have their disgust thresholds calibrated at an exquisitely high level. There is a certain majesty in the Stoic claim to be beyond outrage and disgust. Self-sacrifice may feel sublime in practice, but look haughty and foolish to others. Here is the old fight between irony and plainness in public.

Neier's defense of the Nazis is something like what Shabbetai Zevi called a "holy sin," a violation of accepted morality in order to show the meaning of true liberty. (Perhaps Frank Collin's Nazism was just such a holy sin as well.) Besides Zevi's sexual transgressions, which were already offensive enough, he did the worst thing he could do: he renounced his Jewishness. Most of his followers saw his conversion to Islam as the last straw, a betrayal by a fallen prophet, but subtler reasoners found ways to see this as a logical culmination of his mission, one more demonstration of the antinomian ability of the faithful to overcome anything—even sin. The gesture of enabling the rights of the Nazis has a similar character.[51] What could be more insulting for a Jew than to champion the legal rights of a political party whose aim is to eradicate Jews from the planet? Neier's defense of his enemy seems all but calculated to be the most contrarian moral act possible. To appreciate the gesture as more than a simple accessory to genocide requires the same kind of reasoning capacity that understood Zevi's betrayal as a dialectical foray into wickedness for the ultimate sake of righteousness. One needs confidence in the cunning ironies of history, in a certain morality in transgression. One has to see, as Paul said, things that are not, not simply things that are.

Perhaps the most sustained theoretical meditation on the lessons of the Skokie case is Lee Bollinger's *The Tolerant Society* (1986). Free speech, he argues, has not only epistemological functions (the discovery of truth) but ethical ones (the formation of civic character). When a society must toler-

49. Neier, *Defending My Enemy*, 1, 125.

50. Norbert Elias, *Über den Prozess der Zivilisation: Soziogenetische und psychogenetische Untersuchungen* (1939). 2 vols. (Frankfurt: Suhrkamp, 1997). Translated into English as *The Civilizing Process*. 2 vols. (New York: Pantheon, 1982).

51. Another religious forerunner for the First Amendment is the Quaker meeting: anyone may say anything without censure, provided they speak from the inner light; it is up to the listeners to divine the meaning.

ate noxious doctrine such as Nazism, it becomes educated in the art of suspending the all-too-human propensity to condemn: "free speech involves a special act of carving out one area of social interaction for extraordinary self-restraint." Guaranteeing freedom for the words we abhor teaches us not to hate—not even to hate the hater. (Stoic *apatheia* before pain and Christian immobility before evil—the refusal to reciprocate—are, as we have seen, sources for this attitude.) The chief lesson of Skokie is not "making a pact with the devil to better secure one's own freedom" but rather the almost existential exercise it provides of confronting the potential Nazi within each of us. Skokie held up a mirror to people, reflecting the dark night their souls pass through in despising Nazis, thus risking becoming like the very thing they hate. Tolerating extremist speech teaches us to check the instinct to lash out, censure, and punish. Free speech is a kind of role-playing game in which we practice liberal attitudes. By permitting the circulation of astringents, the First Amendment gives citizens the opportunity to seek truth instead of revenge. It thus not only protects all speech, even genocidal swill; it has the grander task of serving as a moral beacon that lights up a society of what Bollinger calls "democratic personalities" who, through repeated exposure to the sublimities and vulgarities of speech without limit, have become like judges, that is, able to set aside personal feelings when listening to any argument.[52] Evaluative abstraction, for Bollinger, is desirable for the entire society. He is a descendant of Mill's call for cool listening.

Bollinger explicitly links the First Amendment as a social instructor in suspended judgment to the rise of a professionalized twentieth-century America. The First Amendment, for Bollinger, as for Holmes, Hand, Brandeis, and other judges, is an educator in the control of our passions. In an act of unreciprocated magnanimity, we give airtime to people who would give no airtime to us. As Bollinger summarizes elsewhere, "More than any other provision of the Bill of Rights, the First Amendment reflects vital attributes of the American character, . . . and by protecting harmful speech, it seeks to reinforce desired character traits including tolerance and self-restraint in dealing with bad behavior."[53] The First Amendment is a hatchery of attitudes that can then be released into the ocean of the general culture. His theory of tolerance reminds us again of Elias's civilizing process: increasing levels of self-restraint accompany the state's seizure of the means of

52. Bollinger, *The Tolerant Society,* 9, 127–31, 155, 239.

53. Lee Bollinger, "The First Amendment," in *The Oxford Companion to the Supreme Court of the United States,* ed. Kermit Hall (New York: Oxford University Press, 1992), 297–98.

violence. Bollinger even celebrates the decline of dueling, a classic symptom of the civilizing process.[54] Bollinger uses the moral contrarianism of the Skokie case to discover something deeper about the ethics of the First Amendment, namely, civic sublimation. The Constitution teaches us each to have a strong constitution.

Hall's "Voltaire," Roosevelt and his policemen, and Bollinger all have confidence in the spectator's ability to appreciate chumming with Nazis in the name of higher principles. Defending Nazis and other vile ones performs an attitude that, if generalized, is supposed to make Nazism impossible: sustaining the rights of your enemies. On the surface the world is upside down: the enemies of Nazis are their defenders. Onlookers are supposed to read diabolically, as William Blake taught, seeing hell in the perfections of heaven and heaven in the energy of hell. The performers have to bank on the power of unannotated spectacle to move hypothetical viewers. Teddy Roosevelt's police escorts, defending the anti-Semite's right to advocate the removal of their rights, are like set-apart officials, indifferent to inclination, Stoic in their apathy. They do not pass judgment on the anti-Semite any more than the Supreme Court passes judgment on offensive speech; muteness is their eloquence. These complicated gestures depend on the collaboration of an audience skilled in the art of ironic interpretation. Owen Fiss's exhortation, for instance, to "learn to embrace a truth that is full of irony and contradiction" states the classic liberal faith in an ironic theodicy—just as Milton's Satan tries to mess everything up, only to end up speeding the work along.[55] Skokie liberals usually work without an express reflection on their own theatricality or their potential swerve into a comic or tragic mode.[56] Their strategy is often less fruitful than explicitly theatrical nonviolent passive resistance, as I argue in chapter. 7. Those who snorkel in sulfurous waters and swim with the sharks bank on both the safe segregation of formal and substantive rationality and the public's ability to discern the reason for their daring. But not everyone will get, or want to get, the secret message cloaked in irony. Liberal and civil libertarian ironists avoid signposting their tactics. (Liberalism is the renunciation of meta-discourse.) A billboard wrecks the drama. It is all such a wonderfully twisted performance. Skokie subjectivity emerges from a public space where people do not (or cannot) say what they really believe and what they stand for.

54. Bollinger, *The Tolerant Society*, 183.

55. Owen Fiss, *The Irony of Free Speech* (Cambridge, Mass.: Harvard University Press, 1996), 83.

56. I owe the term "the Skokie school" to Henry Louis Gates, Jr., "Let Them Talk," *The New Republic*, Sept. 1993: 42.

The late-twentieth-century interpretation of the First Amendment contains a touch of what the Russian literary theorist Mikhail Bakhtin and his followers call "the carnivalesque," the raucous celebration of inversion, mockery, and transgression. Free speech is a liminal zone institutionalized in the heart of the order in which the rulers can be abused, the sacred can be violated, and everything can be stood on its head. Many social orders have authorized occasional festivals of misrule as a holiday, a "time out" from the normal run of events, but civil libertarian interpreters of free speech want a perpetual carnival. Though they rarely think about it in this way, liberal friends of free speech adhere to a politics and poetics of transgression.[57] They dwell in an *ordo inversus,* where everything may be stood on its head. As sponsors of a cultural zone in which it is permissible to take a vacation from reigning rules of order and morality, they are distant heirs to Paul's messianic hope in sabbatical suspension. (One person who clearly understood free expression as poetic and political transgression, and who was a charter member of the Jewish tradition of prophetic redemption through sin, was the comic-critic Lenny Bruce. His profane and profound monologues, like most treatments of free speech, were recursive: at once provocations of and comments on the law.) Foes of liberal irony, in contrast, typically reject intellectual indirection. They see abyss-redeemers as indistinguishable from abyss-promoters. Richard Delgado and Jean Stefancic, for instance, advocates of critical race theory, conclude their book *Must We Defend Nazis?* with a direct attack on the ironic mode: "The bigot is not a stand-in for Tom Paine. The best way to preserve lizards is not to preserve hawks. Reality is not paradoxical. Sometimes, defending Nazis is simply defending Nazis."[58] They renounce mental aerobatics: defending Nazis is not sustaining liberty but aiding and abetting advocates of genocide. They prefer not to pull their intellectual muscles recoding scenes of a *verkehrte Welt;* they dislike standing on their head. Their blunt simplicity is refreshing in its way. But it has its price: so reality is not paradoxical after all? Well, I'm glad that someone finally cleared that up.

Perhaps an even more cogent critique of the ideology of the hardy citizen buffeted by public agonies of doctrine is political rather than ethical. The policy of eternal suspension leaves constitutional protection open to advertisers, pornographers, purveyors of 900 telephone numbers, arms dealers,

---

57. Peter Stallybrass and Allon White, *The Poetics and Politics of Transgression* (London: Methuen, 1986).

58. Richard Delgado and Jean Stefancic, *Must We Defend Nazis? Hate Speech, Pornography, and the New First Amendment* (New York: New York University Press, 1997), 162.

political lobbyists, corporations that resist the Security and Exchange Commission's disclosure rules, and broadcasters who flout the Federal Communications Commission's public interest standard. In recent years, all these and more have found refuge in the First Amendment, as free expression cases have shifted from lone political marginals to powerful institutions protecting turf and profit.[59] The captains of the culture industries can justify their lack of responsibility for the tawdry stuff they promote by professing a noble faith in the self-regulating market.[60] In early modern political philosophy, the market was supposed to be a bulwark against the state; now calls for free markets of ideas have reached the absurd degree in which media executives will invoke the First Amendment as a shield against any criticism.[61] Perhaps more than the fear of hurt feelings, we should fault the celebration of free speech for enabling the corporatization of public life. But that is a story for another book.

Though I remain suspicious of the Skokie policy of redemption through sin, perhaps the greatest contemporary value of such moral contrarianism, and one that we desperately need in this political landscape, is to constantly demonstrate the ways that virtue and vice slide into their contraries. Finding something to defend in the Nazis is a public performance that aims to make us nervous about drawing the boundary between good and evil. As Milton said, in this world the wheat and the tares grow together, and no one but God can tell them apart. The moral contortions of Skokie liberals remind us that even the most clearly and justifiably vilified doctrine in the world (Nazism) can offer something to learn from, even if only from the exercise of confronting it with law instead of fists. Skokie liberals take to the limit the old liberal suspicion of moral certainty. Their seeming sympathy for evil serves as a standing rebuke to those people, many of whom occupy seats of planetary power, who think that they have become like the gods in knowing good and evil. Those who are completely certain about what evil is have no compunctions about bombing it to pieces. The prayer of all liberals might be, "And deliver us from 'evil.'" Keeping the scare quotes around evil is one of the best and worst things liberals do.

59. Sunstein, *Democracy and the Problem of Free Speech*, 2–3, but see all of chap. 1.

60. Consider the plight of the rap star Dr. Dre: "It felt funny going into the studio talking about 'this bitch' and 'this ho' and how 'I fucked this girl' with a wife at home. But then, I have to look at it like entertainment, and I have a set fan base, and there's certain things they want to hear." Quoted in Ekow Elshun, "The Rap Trap," *The Guardian Weekend,* 27 May 2000: 8. Ah, the Stoic duty to serve the public . . .

61. Newton N. Minow and Craig L. LaMay, *Abandoned in the Wasteland: Children, Television, and the First Amendment* (New York: Farrar, Straus, Giroux, 1995), offer many examples.

HARDBALL PUBLIC SPACE AND THE SUSPENDED SOUL

Supreme Court decisions since 1919 have forged an interpretation of the First Amendment based on such principles as the primacy of ideological diversity and antagonism, governmental agnosticism on what is orthodox in religion and politics, a requirement of extremely specific definitions for forms of expression that lack First Amendment protection (such as defamation, the right of privacy, and obscenity), and so on. In this section I focus on a few key cases since the 1960s that outline a model of the tough civic soul.

A landmark case that combines praise for cross fire in debate, the privileged role of the press as a relay for the electorate, and emotional aerobics for the citizenry is *Times v. Sullivan* (1964). It is one of many important legal fallouts of the civil rights movement. A 1960 advertisement in the *New York Times* denounced the violence that civil rights protestors were facing in the South. L. B. Sullivan, commissioner of public affairs in Montgomery, Alabama, was not explicitly named, but as the person responsible for the police, he felt libeled by some clearly inaccurate claims, most famously that the police "ringed" peaceful protestors on the Alabama State College campus. A county jury found that he had been libeled and awarded him $500,000 in damages, a decision upheld by the Alabama State Supreme Court. On appeal, the U.S. Supreme Court reversed the decision. By raising the standard of proof in libel to "actual malice," Justice Brennan, writing for the majority, said the Court was upholding "a profound national commitment to the principle that debate on public issues should be uninhibited, robust, and wide-open."[62] This "splendid sentence," thought Harry Kalven, who played professorial midwife to Brennan in much the same way that Chafee did for Holmes and Brandeis, was "possibly the most felicitous expression on free speech yet."[63] The aged Alexander Meiklejohn thought *Times* "an occasion for dancing in the streets."[64] (Special times, the 1960s, when even ninety-two-year-old political philosophers were hip to the latest hits: the Motown classic "Dancing in the Streets," sung by Martha Reeves and the Vandellas, swept the county the same year as *Times v. Sullivan.*) "Uninhibited, robust, and wide-open"—these words exude a healthy erotic afterglow. This is a

62. *Times v. Sullivan*, 376 U.S. 254 (1964), 270.

63. Harry Kalven, *The Negro and the First Amendment* (Chicago: University of Chicago Press, 1966), 64. See Steven H. Shiffrin, *The First Amendment, Democracy, and Romance* (Cambridge, Mass.: Harvard University Press, 1990), 49–53, for a discussion of the interchange between Harry Kalven and William Brennan.

64. Harry Kalven, "The New York Times Case: A Note on 'The Central Meaning of the First Amendment,'" *The Supreme Court Review* 1, 1964: 221 n125.

public space *en plein air,* not one in which mushrooms grow in the dark. Public figures, Justice Brennan holds, must be like judges, "men of fortitude, able to thrive in a hardy climate." If public figures are unjustly insulted and falsely accused in the rough and tumble of public debate, that is part of the game. Requiring strict factuality in all criticisms of public figures, elected or otherwise, "dampens the vigor and limits the variety of public debate."[65] In *Times* the Court bends over backward to avoid squelching civic ardor. Not only the call for strength but the fear of enervation recalls Mill.[66]

Times protects speech that might sting public figures. Falsehood turns out to be constitutionally protected. Sullivan's case turned on undisputed factual errors in the advertisement, but without being able to prove that the editors had been "reckless" in their disregard of the truth, he could claim no damages under the standard of actual malice that *Times* established. *Gertz,* a 1974 case that serves as an extended footnote to *Times,* clarifies two points: "Under the First Amendment there is no such thing as a false idea. However pernicious an opinion may seem, we depend for its correction not on the conscience of judges and juries but on the competition of other ideas." The government turns out to be agnostic not only on religion and politics, but also on facts. Second, those who seek public office voluntarily expose themselves to scrutiny, attention, and "increased risk of injury from defamatory falsehood." [67] If public figures want to be in the kitchen, they have to take the heat; they forfeit ordinary protection against criticism and scrutiny and have to practice equanimity when probed. *Times* assumed the burden of explaining the central meaning of the First Amendment, and thus is a key document in the amendment's growing self-consciousness. Central are the notions that public speech might hurt and citizens must have guts. The public, *Times* says—along with Cicero—is the regime of impersonality, a place of precious little tenderness. In public we relinquish any claims to the luxurious wholeness of personality that modern bourgeois culture has so steadily found in private life since the eighteenth century.[68] The public-figure rule is a twentieth-century restatement of Stoic virtue.

Cohen v. California (1971) is another case that explicitly figures public space as impersonal. In 1968 one Robert Paul Cohen walked through a cor-

65. *Times v. Sullivan,* 272 (Brennan is quoting from *Craig v. Harney,* 331 U.S 367, 376), 279.

66. See *Times v. Sullivan,* 272, for a prominent footnote to *On Liberty.* The Court's debt to Mill is also made explicit in *Red Lion* 395 U.S. 392 (1965) 392.

67. *Gertz v. Robert Welch, Inc.* 418 U.S. 323 (1974), 339–40, 345.

68. See Hannah Arendt, *The Human Condition* (Chicago: University of Chicago Press, 1958); and Jürgen Habermas, *Structural Transformation of the Public Sphere* (1962) (Cambridge: MIT Press, 1989).

ridor of the Los Angeles County Courthouse—"a place where women and children were present"—wearing a jacket adorned with the indelicate phrase "Fuck the Draft." He was arrested and convicted on the charge of disturbing the peace as defined in the California penal code. (Courthouse corridors are Kafkaesque spaces where puzzling encounters take place.) The court of appeal felt no need to produce evidence of corrupted youth or damaged minds: actual effects on audiences did not matter; it was enough that vulnerable eyes were present. Cohen's conviction was upheld. The logic of honor and its violation is an old one in public affairs. It does not matter what the results were, but simply that an insult was tendered. In obscenity law this logic was represented by *Regina v. Hicklin* (1868), a British case that made the test for obscenity the most susceptible member of a community, which held sway in the United States from the 1870s to the 1930s. Defamation cases tend to have a similar immunity to evidence, since plaintiffs sue more often out of violated honor than out of demonstrable harm.[69]

In reversing the California court of appeal decision, the Supreme Court in *Cohen* took positions both on vulgarity and on forms of communication. Unlike earlier Courts, this one had scruples about passing judgments on cultural quality. Taste became another item for government neutrality. In Justice John Marshall Harlan's famous line from *Cohen*, "one man's vulgarity is another's lyric." As in Locke, Jefferson, and Mill, "matters of taste and style," insofar as they have no bearing on the collective weal, should be left "largely to the individual." Since curses and poems alike are of private interpretation, the public realm can be noisy, but citizens must not, as the Dutch figure of speech has it, have "long toes" (to be easily stepped on). Because one man's vulgarity is another man's lyric, citizens must be able to hear various tunes without blushing or blanching. Abusive speech is a mark of a liberal society, not a degraded one: "That the air may at times seem filled with verbal cacophony is, in this sense not a sign of weakness but of strength." By their simple presence in a public space, people accept the risk of poisonous words; what does not kill them makes them stronger. Unexpected accostings, according to *Cohen,* are an inevitable part of free debate; we give tacit consent to surprising and shocking sensory experience by stepping into public. "The constitutional right of free expression is powerful medicine in a society as diverse and populous as ours."[70] The mark of the public is serendipitous exposure to strangers and strange opinions.

69. On studying defamation's effects empirically, see Jeremy Cohen and Timothy Gleason, *Social Research in Communication and Law* (Newbury Park, Calif.: Sage, 1990), chap. 4.

70. *Cohen v. California*, 403 U. S 15 (1971), 24, 25.

Justice Harlan's majority opinion does not interpret Cohen's jacket as a case of fighting words—as an incitement to imminent violence against people or property—because there was no personal dimension in its address. "While the four-letter word displayed by Cohen in relation to the draft is not uncommonly employed in a personally provocative fashion, in this instance it was clearly not 'directed to the person of the hearer.' . . . No individual actually or likely to be present could reasonably have regarded the words on appellant's jacket as a direct personal insult."[71] "Not directed to the person of the hearer" captures precisely the Stoic-liberal norm of public communication. To twist Paul, public words pay no respect to persons. The public person is a nobody, invulnerable to personal abuse. *Cohen* sees public talk as open dissemination. Public words are like the seeds of the foolish farmer in Plato's *Phaedrus,* who throws them every which way, regardless of where they land—they are cast to whom it may concern.[72] In public we are subject to being watched, heard, or even spoken to or accosted by indefinite others. Justice William Douglas wrote in an earlier case: "One who is in a public vehicle may not, of course, complain of the noise of the crowd and the babble of tongues. One who enters any public place sacrifices some of his privacy."[73] Cohen's jacket communicates in a weird limbo: for everyone and no one, it is addressed to anyone who has eyes to see. The hallmark of Stoic-liberal conceptions of public life is such loose coupling between word and address, a view that makes Harlan reluctant to limit expression to protect "unwilling or unsuspecting viewers."[74] In public "we are often 'captives' outside the sanctuary of the home and subject to objectionable speech."[75] As in Cicero, a public person is, in some ways, in subjection, a notion developed in a variety of wonderfully curious Supreme Court cases about the captive audience of communications.[76]

That a common Anglo-Saxon vulgarity received constitutional protection is a good example of the enabling role the Court played in the larger process of cultural informalization in the late 1960s and early 1970s. It opened space for more extravagant, risqué forms of expression, as long as

71. *Cohen v. California,* 20. As someone has noted, the statement is expressive rather than imperative; Cohen was not advocating sexual intercourse with the Selective Service.

72. Plato, *Phaedrus,* 276b.

73. *Public Utilities Commisssion v. Pollak* 343 U.S. 451 (1952), 468.

74. *Cohen v. California,* 21.

75. *Rowan v. Post Office Dept.* 397 U.S. 728 (1970), 738, cited in *Cohen v. California,* 21.

76. For some of the more curious cases in communications law, see *Saia v. New York,* 334 U.S. 558 (1948); *Kovacs v. Cooper* 336 U.S. 77 (1949); *Public Utilities Commisssion v. Pollak* 343 U.S. 451 (1952); *Rowan* (1970); and *Lehman v. City of Shaker Heights* 418 U.S. 298 (1974).

they did not impede the functioning of regnant institutions.[77] As in Paul or Kant, the Court thought the circumference of what is legal must be larger than the circumference of what is good. But vulgarity was permitted solely on the public side of the public-private divide. In 1973 a father and his teenage son while driving heard some—it is not clear how long they paused in their aural flânerie—of comedian George Carlin's speech about the seven dirty words you can never say over the air. The father complained to the FCC, which found Pacifica, the politically progressive network that owned the New York radio station, in violation of an FCC rule against indecency. On appeal the Supreme Court upheld the FCC's right to police indecent talk. Broadcasting as a form of speech was a special case because of its "unique pervasiveness." Because its communication circuit had a terminus in the home, it had to respect people's desires not to be assaulted with salty language. *Pacifica* confirmed broadcasting's less privileged First Amendment status compared with print media (something already clear in *Red Lion* [1969] and *Tornillo* [1973]). "As Mr. Justice [George] Sutherland wrote, a 'nuisance may be merely a right thing in the wrong place—like a pig in the parlor instead of the barnyard.'"[78] A good deal of the argument rests upon an earlier case, *Rowan v. Post Office* (1970), which probed the question whether citizens may compel mass mailers (here of erotic literature) to remove their addresses from their address lists. The complainants argued that such control would violate their "constitutional right to communicate," in a perversely valiant effort to define smut-mail as public dissemination. No dice: the Court unanimously held against them that "a mailer's right to communicate must stop at the mailbox of an unreceptive addressee."[79] *Pacifica* and *Rowan* are precisely symmetrical with *Cohen:* in public people must tolerate other people's vulgarities (or lyrics); in private people are sovereign over the communications they receive ("a man's home is his castle.") The public is defined as an open agora of messages, some good, some bad, some ugly. Visitors there must don Stoic armor. In the privacy of the home, people can cultivate their hothouse plants at will.

Very curious in *Pacifica* is the Court's own stance toward the contaminated object from which they saved the collective ears of young America. The Court duly supplied a complete transcript of Carlin's monologue,

77. Kenneth Cmiel, "The Politics of Civility," in *The 1960s: From Memory to History,* ed. David Farber (Chapel Hill: University of North Carolina Press, 1994), 263–90.

78. Quoted in *FCC v. Pacifica Foundation* 438 U.S. 726 (1978), 750.

79. *Rowan v. Post Office Dept.,* 735, 736–77. In *Rowan* the Court comments that one can turn the radio dial if struck with offensive speech; in *Pacifica,* it holds to an instant-harm thesis in which even one assault of foul language is thought enough to do harm.

justly confident perhaps that the *Supreme Court Reporter* was not as "uniquely pervasive" a medium as the radio. The justices thereby showed that they were men of fortitude, capable of flourishing in hardy climates (they had all been watching the porno movies in the basement of the Supreme Court building before the 1973 *Miller* standard anyway). In the classic gesture of a doctor who is unaffected by pathology, Justice John Paul Stevens even rose to the bait of supplying a learned vulgarity—one of the seven dirty words, but in Chaucer's middle English—in his final footnote, as if not wanting to be one-upped by Carlin's brilliant lexicography. "Even a prime-time recitation of Geoffrey Chaucer's *Miller's Tale* would not be likely to command the attention of many children who are both old enough to understand and young enough to be adversely affected by passages such as: 'And prively he caughte hire by the queynte.'"[80] Stevens's surreptitious erudition hosts a bit of dangerous doctrine. He uses a dirty word in a closed discourse circuit *entre nous*. What force does his Chaucer quote have? That it is okay to be bawdy, as long as what is said is unintelligible? My point is not to tease the justice, since my inclusion of his quote shows that I am equally weak at avoiding such temptations. Rather, the point is that you cannot regulate speech without abrogating to yourself the right to utter words you claim should not or cannot be uttered. Speaking about tabooed speech is a self-contradictory act that always verges on hypocrisy. Kant's maxim is healthier: there are no exceptions to the rules, not even for the rule makers. *Pacifica* is a recursive case: the speech in question was itself a commentary on the constitutional status of free speech. *Schenck* too was a recursive case, and these loops—of banning speech about free speech in the name of securing free speech—are easy to get entangled in. Lenny Bruce caught the police, and himself, in such nets. Here the liberal confidence that you can safely keep form and substance separate shows its true leakiness. Abyss-redeemers have their own reasons for being interested in the deep.

Three later cases demonstrate that the First Amendment is tolerant of things that even judges, in all their hardiness, are not. In *Hustler v. Falwell* (1988), the Reverend Jerry Falwell sued *Hustler* magazine for "emotional distress" for depicting him, in a clearly labeled parody of a Campari liquor ad, as having lost his virginity in a drunken sexual encounter with his mother in an outhouse. (I have rarely seen a lecture hall full of undergraduates more wide-eyed and riveted than the time I projected a copy of *Hustler*'s ad during a lecture on the First Amendment, erroneously having thought that the print would be too small to read. The parody is foul, vi-

80. *FCC v. Pacifica Foundation, 755.*

cious, mean, nasty, and clever.) As in *Times* and *Gertz,* hurt feelings cannot restrict expression. Outrageousness cannot be defined because of its inherent "subjectiveness" (William Rehnquist), and emotional distress is likewise not subject to quantification, so they are the price public figures pay for liberty. Even cruel and malicious calumny falls under the protection of the First Amendment. *Texas v. Johnson* (1989) concerned a man who burned an American flag in protest of Ronald Reagan's policies. "If there is a bedrock principle underlying the First Amendment," wrote Brennan for the majority, "it is that the government may not prohibit the expression of an idea simply because society finds the idea itself offensive or disagreeable."[81] Contrarian subjectivity—the state superego, the civic id—is the bedrock of the First Amendment. This case also brought out a bit of soul-searching by Justice Anthony Kennedy. "The hard fact is that sometimes we must make decisions we do not like."[82] His half-embarrassed personal confession is a classic case of the Judge's Two Bodies. Kennedy gets both to be offended and to do his strenuous judicial duty.[83]

The strangest example of the Judge's Two Bodies is a 1992 Supreme Court case that overturned a city ordinance of Saint Paul, Minnesota, under which some teenagers were convicted for the hate crime of burning a cross in front of a house owned by African-Americans. Wrote Justice Scalia: "Let there be no mistake about our belief that burning a cross in someone's front yard is reprehensible. But St. Paul has sufficient means at its disposal to prevent such behavior without adding the First Amendment to the fire."[84] Scalia wants the burners convicted as firebugs, not as racists. It is already a crime to light fires on people's lawns. While the pragmatism of restricting conduct rather than ideology and keeping the law simple is honorable, something went off the rails in this opinion. Holmes liked upholding bad law to prove that he was immune to the temptation of imposing his own opinions, but Scalia's inverted absolutism leaves, in effect, the First Amendment interpretively open enough to accommodate people who might want to burn crosses on their neighbor's lawns. Many have criticized this tribute to codependency, this protection of the virtue of the First Amendment (i.e., keeping it safe from the fire) by having it chaperoned by racist hellions.[85] Scalia is no Skokie

81. *Texas v. Johnson,* 491 U.S. 397 (1989), 414.

82. *Texas v. Johnson,* 420.

83. Another excellent statement of the Judge's Two Bodies is Frankfurter's self-recusal in *Public Utilities Commisssion v. Pollak* 343 U.S 451 (1952), 466–67.

84. *R. A. V. v. St. Paul* 505 U.S. 377 (1992), 396.

85. For example, Judith Butler, *Excitable Speech: A Politics of the Performative* (New York: Routledge, 1997), chap. 1.

liberal. And yet he invokes the stance of suspended judgment. He might better have written, "St. Paul has sufficient means at *his* disposal," since this is the Pauline shudder with a twist of the screw: "I personally find it reprehensible, but in my professional capacity I cannot do anything about it." While Scalia nobly poses, making sure we know that he abhors racism, he refuses to rule on the substantive question of whether racial insult and abuse are included in the First Amendment. (Could cross-burning be one of those undervalued forms of thought and expression whose greater wisdom tomorrow will discover? We think not.) Probably more than any other recent case, *R. A. V. v. St. Paul* has soured theorists on the principle of Stoic noncommitment as proof of liberty's strength. Bollinger, at least, has an argument for why we should not criminalize hatemongers without having to call up some abstractly chaste notion of the First Amendment.

Though judges typically profess reluctance when dealing with obscenity cases, the one area of free speech where liberal legal theorists sometimes wax enthusiastic is pornography. "This most maligned and scapegoated of cultural forms," writes the film theorist Linda Williams, "is often in desperate need of defense." [86] Stanford law professor Kathleen Sullivan endows it with political pathos: "In a world where sodomy may still be a crime, gay pornography is the samizdat of the oppressed."[87] Edward DeGrazia is perhaps the most enthusiastic defender of sexually explicit materials as sites of liberty, though Nadine Strossen, the head of the ACLU, would give him a run for his money.[88] Almost all the defenders of pornography use some variant on the Inquisition narrative, a heroic fight of freedom against violent censorship. In late-eighteenth-century France, pornography was indeed a political genre for criticizing or at least mocking the monarchy, though it was a tool for disaffected members of the court to get their digs in or kicks as well. Eighteenth-century attacks on the Spanish Inquisition showed its cruelty in graphic torture and occasionally erotically charged plots. From Newton's physics to Sade's novels, there was a widespread early modern interest in moving bodies and organs that forms the wider context for the deep history of modern porn. Pornography's defenders still bask in the remembered glow of crusades against Old Regime censorship.[89]

---

86. Linda Williams, *Hard Core: Power, Pleasure, and the "Frenzy of the Visible."* Expanded ed. (Berkeley: University of California Press, 1999), xi; Nadine Strossen, *Defending Pornography: Free Speech, Sex, and the Fight for Women's Rights* (New York: Scribner, 1995), 219–20.

87. Quoted in Strossen, *Defending Pornography,* 167.

88. Edward DeGrazia, *Girls Lean Back Everywhere: The Law of Obscenity and the Assault on Genius* (New York: Random House, 1992).

89. Edward Peters, *Inquisition* (Berkeley: University of California Press, 1988), chap. 7; Karen

But as Lynn Hunt points out, "once political pornography became democratized, it ceased being political."[90] While it is no doubt true that sex is one of the most important of all human topics, that much discourse of public value can be stigmatized as pornographic by people who dislike it, and that a preemptive restriction of any kind of speech, sexual or otherwise, is bound to backfire, it is the worst kind of folly in an age of an exploding multibillion dollar porn industry and global sex trade to simply defend "pornography" (whatever you take it to be) as a chief means of advancing human liberty without looking at its specific effects—economic, political, social, cultural, spiritual.[91] One of the more remarkable transformations in the mediascape in the past three decades has been the shift in the distribution of pornography. Once a print medium delivered to select recipients by mail or a performance or film medium in certain city districts, pornography is now an audiovisual mass medium distributed by diverse channels, from 900 telephone numbers, videos, and films to the internet, cable, and arguably broadcast television. Abstract defenses of the marketplace of ideas ring hollow when the market for porn has exploded in an unprecedented way. When Susan Sontag wrote on "the pornographic imagination" in 1967, she was almost exclusively concerned with literature.[92] No one today, no matter how highbrow, could treat pornography that way—the "death of the written word" is a key feature of contemporary pornography.[93] Liberal visions of free speech desperately need familiarity with communication contexts. You may, like Strossen, regard sex as an individual consumer choice, or you may regard it as a holy act, subject, like all sacred things, to corruption, or some other way, but a starting point for debates about pornography has to be an acknowledgment of the historically radical changes in its modes of operation.

Halttunen, "Humanitarianism and the Pornography of Pain in Anglo-American Culture," *American Historical Review*, Apr. 1995: 303–34; Margaret C. Jacob, "The Materialist World of Pornography," in *The Invention of Pornography: Obscenity and the Origins of Modernity, 1500–1800*, ed. Lynn Hunt (New York: Zone Books, 1993), 157–202.

90. Lynn Hunt, "Pornography and the French Revolution," in *The Invention of Pornography*, 315n, 305n.

91. One of many topics I hoped to treat in this book, but I ran out of space.

92. Susan Sontag, "The Pornographic Imagination" (1967), in *Styles of Radical Will* (London: Secker & Warburg, 1969), 35–73.

93. Walter Kendrick, *The Secret Museum* (Berkeley: University of California Press, 1996), 243–44.

IMPERSONALITY, OR OPENNESS TO STRANGENESS

There is no better example of people soured on absolutist defenses of free speech than critical race theorists. These scholars attack libertarian theory for its violence and self-abstraction. *Words That Wound* (1993), a compilation of key articles, contests at every turn the Stoic elements in civil libertarian arguments. Since its birth in the 1980s, critical race theory has met the fate of most academic movements: it has become institutionalized in tenure, textbooks, and experts. But it is useful for our purposes in offering a contrasting medium that, if swallowed, can reveal the Stoic innards of mainstream free speech theory. In contrast to the faith that names can never hurt, critical race theorists offer a speech-act theory in which verbal and physical trauma are essentially indistinguishable. Against the liberal sense that private space is a refuge against public intrusions, they attack the public-private divide for compounding the injuries of racism. In critique of impersonal citizenship, they argue that experience and opinion, body and consciousness, are inextricably linked—the call for split subjectivity only invalidates forms of knowledge not recognized by the mainstream. In contrast to the sense that pain is a tutor in civic virtue, they see pain as an evil. Bollinger believes that a refusal to be provoked by cruel and violent words stages a forceful show of our own immunity, staring down and by force of shame vanquishing moral turpitude in the finest tradition of passive resistance. Critical race theory sees such a refusal as only so much machismo. Its villains are "first amendment fundamentalists." In an intemperate but symptomatic turn of phrase, one scholar writes: "The first amendment arms conscious and unconscious racists—Nazis and liberals alike—with a constitutional right to be racist."[94] Here Bollinger and the Ayatollah, Ronald Dworkin and Hitler, the evil and the sincere, find themselves tendentiously assembled. Critical race theorists see liberals carrying the banner that the Nazis wanted to carry in Skokie: "Free Speech for White America."[95]

Critical race theory's reminder of the deeper and darker powers of the word is a useful corrective. Examining the unevenly distributed ability to shield oneself from the slings and arrows of public life is more useful than edifying remarks about Truth and Falsehood wrestling or ironic performances that only some people can decode. The critical race theorists' view

---

94. Mari J. Matsuda et al., *Words That Wound: Critical Race Theory, Assaultive Speech, and the First Amendment* (Boulder. Colo.: Westview, 1993), 15.

95. Bollinger, *The Tolerant Society,* 27. Yet another bit of recursiveness.

of the power of speech to shape or shatter one's being is closer to the classical sense that public actors risk shame and glory before the eyes of their
peers (though they will have none of the strenuous self-overcoming of a
Pericles or Cicero). Questions of communicative structure, consequence,
and power are often overdue in liberal discussions. Critical race theorists resist the stunt-pilotry of liberal irony and call instead for a tender recognition of particular cultural traits and pains. They are offended by the tough
pose of the professional and the blind optimism that the truth will prevail.
They see in the liberal toleration of evil a coddling of hostility. Mari Matsuda writes: "I conclude that an absolutist first amendment response to hate
speech has the effect of perpetuating racism: Tolerance of hate speech is not
tolerance borne by the community at large. Rather, it is a psychic tax im-
posed on those least able to pay."[96] The norm of civic fortitude, thirstily
drinking noxious doctrine that we might, with Mithridates, die old, gives
people grounds to dismiss real injury as over-sensitivity. "Self-sacrifice,"
they might approvingly quote Bernard Shaw, "allows us to sacrifice other
people without blushing."[97] Their position is tied to the triumph of the
therapeutic, with its idea that revisiting trauma is the pathway to self-
knowledge. Critical race theory is tender-minded rather than tough-
minded, calling for self-esteem and care, not abuse and rough tumbling.

The contention that ideas of unhampered public debate are held most
intensely by those in positions of power, incidentally, has solid empirical
backing. A fascinating comparative study of public opinion in five publics
in four countries (Americans, Muscovite Russians, Israeli Arabs, Israeli
Jews, and people in Hong Kong) reveals uneven patterns of support for free
expression and media rights. Support varies with demographic factors such
as education, gender, and income. The rich and the educated consistently
support free expression rights most vigorously, perhaps because they have
the readiest access to the means of expression and security against the ad-
verse social consequences of speaking out. Gender is the most robust pre-
dictor of support for freedom of the press: men are far more likely than
women to believe that the media should be able to publish whatever they
please. (Here is one empirical confirmation of the masculine—Stoic and
martial—origins of the central tenets of free expression theory.) Data from
a variety of countries, in sum, "suggest that people who are most secure

96. Matsuda et al., *Words That Wound*, 18. Bollinger clearly knows that speech can be "a means of inflicting injury": *The Tolerant Society*, 234.

97. George Bernard Shaw, "Maxims for Revolutionists," in *Four Plays by Bernard Shaw* (New York: Washington Square Press, 1972), 495.

within society are most likely to support expressive rights."[98] Like Stoicism, libertarian faith is a philosophy of the privileged.

Critical race theory's central issue goes back to the Pauline problem of personality: to what degree should citizens take noxious doctrine personally? The Skokie school says racist doctrine inoculates the soul, but critical race theory sees poisoning. It does not recognize mass communication— words addressed impersonally to whom it may concern.[99] Justice Harlan in *Cohen* argued that words not directed to the person of the hearer could not count as fighting words. In direct contrast to this logic, Charles Lawrence argues that minorities can suffer a personal insult from any racist message. For him the border of public and private vanishes in racist speech. An insult against one is an insult to all. Offensive discourse can be fighting words regardless of whether or not it occurs face-to-face.[100] Lawrence's discussion turns on an incident at Stanford University. Two students, one black and one white, bicker whether Beethoven had African ancestry. Afterward the white student paints a crude picture of the composer with exaggerated African features on a wall at Ujamaa House, an African-American student dorm.[101] Lawrence argues that this graffito was not an uncivil prank privy to the two bickering students, but a slur addressed to all African-Americans, so that he too fell within the range of its insult. Fair enough: bombs usually hit more than their intended target (if they even hit that). Lawrence denies a battle-hardened self immune to random public assaults. I may, in his logic, take any message that implicates some part of my person as intended for me.

Without endorsing vandalism or stupidity, there is another way to understand how such circuits of communication work. The meanness of racist (or any similarly abusive) messages lies not, I would argue, in their personal assault but rather in their *denial* of impersonality, their refusal to treat people as persons pure and simple. Racist messages suffer from misplaced concreteness, from a focus on the body's parts. Racist insults are precisely not abstract enough. As Paul showed, abstraction and impersonality

98. Julie L. Andsager, Robert O. Wyatt, and Ernest Martin, *Free Expression and Five Democratic Publics: Support for Individual and Media Rights* (Creskill, N.J.: Hampton, 2004), passim. The quote appears at p. 265.

99. On the continuing relevance of the concept of mass communication, see *Mass Communication and American Social Thought: Key Texts 1919–1968*, ed. John Durham Peters and Peter Simonson (Boulder, Colo.: Rowman & Littlefield, 2004, especially 1–2, 8–11.

100. Matsuda et al., *Words That Wound*, 8, 57.

101. Patricia Williams, *The Alchemy of Race and Rights* (Cambridge, Mass.: Harvard University Press, 1991), also discusses this incident.

can be sources of kindness, not just distance. Flawed as the liberal notion of the First Amendment sometimes is, it has some muffled inkling of this beneficial impersonality. Delgado and Stefancic deny such beneficial vagueness: "Most people today know that certain words are offensive and only calculated to wound. No other use remains for such words as 'nigger,' 'wop,' 'spic,' or 'kike.'"[102] This sentence overlooks not only such uses as humor, history, and lexicography, but also its own existence, since it has obviously just found another use for those words.[103] Delgado and Stefancic invoke a safety net for abusive speech that their theory should deny them: a context that redeems the use of such words. They end up being caught in the same performative contradiction as Justice Stevens, claiming a safe space for themselves that their policy negates for others.

Nobody knows enough to play semantic karma police. The sad blessed fact is that words are never binding. The most powerful terms—"thank you," "hello," "I love you," "goodbye"—are also the most empty and mundane. Like "here" and "now," they suffer from time-space depletion and glow under the anticipation of messianic presence. They are at once the richest and the most barren of all words. True, it is silly to insist on too much ambiguity in interpretation when abusive intent is obvious, as for instance in the cross-burning in *R. A. V. v. St. Paul.* As Randall Kennedy argues in his daringly titled book *Nigger,* terms of abuse mischievously defy our efforts at legislation.[104] The meaning of an utterance is a delicate matter that depends on context and the utterances that precede and follow. Meaning is a gamble. It comes belatedly, if at all. Holmes was at least right on that. Even hate speech cannot be specified in advance. Every act marks the chaotic plastic stuff of time. All action, said Emerson, has "infinite elasticity": evil can bless and ice can burn.[105] Though theodicies of offensiveness by well-fed liberals are annoying, they at least see freedom as an action, not a condition.[106] The open-endedness of meaning is the best argument against censorship, since we never know what an offense will bring forth. How to foster respect for indeterminacy without thereby also aiding the perpetuation of

---

102. Delgado and Stefancic, *Must We Defend Nazis?,* 9.

103. Butler makes this point of a similar sentence from Delgado in *Excitable Speech,* 100.

104. Randall Kennedy, *Nigger: The Strange Career of a Troublesome Word* (New York: Vintage, 2003).

105. Ralph Waldo Emerson, "Spiritual Laws," in *Selected Writings of Emerson,* ed. Donald McQuade (New York: Modern Library, 1981), 192.

106. See Wendy Brown, "Freedom's Silences," in *Censorship and Silencing: Practices of Cultural Regulation,* ed. Robert C. Post (Los Angeles: Getty Institute, 1998), 313–27.

abuses is the challenge. The wisdom and bitterness of liberal thought lies in its willingness to admit that offenses are inevitable.

An appreciation for semiotic openness in general need not prevent us from ruling on specific cases of insult. The "infinite elasticity" of action is a marvelous principle, and the chaos theorists tell us that a sneeze in Iowa can trigger a typhoon in the Indian Ocean. But most of the time, a sneeze is just a sneeze. For one thing, there are a lot more sneezes than typhoons. Chances are overwhelming that burning a cross on your neighbor's lawn is an act of intimidation, not a statement of political truth. The lack of complete certainty does not mean we lack probabilities. The dice of experience are much more likely to roll some ways than others. The policy of moral postponement or agnosticism about cultural worth may be good for judges, but I doubt whether it is always good for citizens. The latitudinarian Stoicism that Mill taught risks creating a society of people for whom ultimate concerns wither away into private preferences, in which questions of ultimate concern are always shelved for tomorrow. Better than a blanket defense of all speech, Holmesian valor has something to offer: daring to fight for causes whose justice has no guarantees (though we can do without the broken necks). We need not be moral and intellectual Gumbies while we wait for the returns to come in on the gore and vomit that some of our liberal colleagues want to suspend judgment on. Life is too short to think we can postpone some decisions forever. Impersonality is, as Paul knew, a good norm to live by, but it does not mean that we stop fighting for decency in the meanwhile.

Does the First Amendment require a stony heart? What kind of moral furniture best equips people to scout in the regions of sin? The twentieth-century First Amendment is a late inheritor of the bourgeois dream of self-realization and solid ego-development. The literate, public-spirited, self-reflective soul embodied not only in the theories but in the persons of Milton, Mill, and Holmes, for instance, has been the unspoken anchor for theories of citizenship. What to do with its masculine, martial, Stoic residues is a key question for free expression theory today. The task, I believe, is to find ways to sustain the openness and other-mindedness prized by the libertarian story without the moral dithering, the cult of toughness, or the unexplicated irony. Though we must think beyond literate rationality, masculine composure, and martial self-discipline as bases of current forms of democratic citizenship, I do not think we can get around the basic fact that sacrifice, in some form, has long been the rule of the public realm. Today in public we may not need to offer up sheep and calves to the gods, but we cannot avoid offering parts of ourselves to others.

The dream that citizens could be fully recognized as whole personalities in public settings is central to left-wing political romanticism generally (including critical race theory); it is a dream that finitude denies. Recognition is rare and precious; how many of us go through life without ever seeing the nose on our face? How should we recognize the diverse experiences of a multitude of strangers? In public one has no choice but to classify and generalize. Publics are partly statistical entities. No person can be fully represented in public—or in private. A genius like Proust devoted his life to self-revelation, only to discover all the fabrications and traps in that project. What should the rest of us expect? If we take limits on sympathy seriously—and Adam Smith was deeply anti-Romantic in treating sympathy as a scarce resource—publicness can only be a norm of openness, listening, or receptivity. The public is a regime of incomplete and distorted representations of *everybody*'s soul. Sacrifice marks the public realm. Public forms are necessarily open and abstract. Though they may favor certain kinds of people over others, the norms should not be abandoned, but instead be radicalized and redeemed.[107] Our damnably blessed ignorance about each other's (and our own) hearts means the impossibility of a policy of public communication that would recognize every person in his or her particularity. A politics of recognition risks an infinite regress.[108] Taking impersonality seriously as a virtue would equip, not disable, the fight against racism, sexism, and similar abuses. A sounder basis would be an ethic of receptivity, the neighborly art of listening, the musical appreciation of other people's voices. Sympathy is too airy and too selfish; we need baser, more common elements to provide the material for public communion. Sheer open giving or receiving in the bliss of regardlessness is perhaps what Paul meant by grace. It is also perhaps what Dewey and others meant by democracy.

107. In this my sympathies are fully with Habermas.
108. See my "Nomadism, Diaspora, Exile: The Stakes of Mobility Within the Western Canon," in *House, Exile, Homeland: Film, Media and the Politics of Place,* ed. Hamid Naficy (London: Routledge, 1999), 17–41.

CHAPTER FIVE

Social Science as Public Communication

Rehearse death.
—Seneca

And if, by this means, it is not in my power to arrive at the knowledge of any truth, at the very least it is in my power to suspend my judgment.
—Descartes, *Meditations*

The projects of social science and free expression were born twins. Both are chapters in the book of modern self-denial. Though such vast cultural and political projects can never be reduced to individual origins, it is convenient to point again to Mill, who was one of the first to imagine a central place for social science in the liberal polity. In book 6 of his *System of Logic* (1843), he treated all the controversies still debated in social science: the suitability of human beings for scientific investigation; the probabilistic character of generalizations about society; the difficulty of applying causal reasoning to human acts; the bewildering scope of human variation; the "backwardness" of the social sciences relative to other sciences; the tension between observational and experimental methods, as of qualitative and quantitative methods; and the fault line between facts and values. Mill ventured that the social sciences were "probably destined to be the greatest intellectual achievement of the next two or three generations of European thinkers."[1] He envisioned something law-like and predictive, not unlike what his French compatriot August Comte, coiner of the term positivism, had in

---

1. J. S. Mill, *A System of Logic* (1843), in *Collected Works of John Stuart Mill,* ed. J. M. Robson (Toronto: University of Toronto Press, 1977), 8: 952.

mind, but he also saw social science as a shaper of human character and thus as an aid to social reform. This vision found resonance among American progressives such as Dewey, as well as their sleeker social-scientific successors. Mill's notion of "moral sciences" was translated by Wilhelm Dilthey into German as "*Geisteswissenschaften*," a notion with a long and controversial career from then on as the partner and rival of the natural sciences. Once reimported back into English via the Progressives in the 1890s, German émigrés in the 1930s, and translators in the 1960s, the notion of a qualitative or critical social science became a player in debates, peaking in the 1970s, about the merits of quantitative social research. In the face-off of qualitative and quantitative methods, a key episode in the intellectual history of the late twentieth century, two wings of Mill's legacy meet and clash.

POSITIVISM AS CIVIC DISCIPLINE

Mill thought scientific study could save us from our natural cognitive biases. Like both his liberal forebears and much post–World War II American social psychology, with its repeated experimental findings of how readily people resort to mental contortions to maintain their preconceptions, Mill was convinced of the natural sophistry of human knowledge. "The natural or acquired partialities of mankind are continually throwing up philosophical theories, the sole recommendation of which consists in the premises they afford for proving cherished doctrines, or justifying favourite feelings: and when any one of these theories has been so thoroughly discredited as no longer to serve the purpose, another is always ready to take its place." In the 1840s Mill sounds like a 1950s cognitive consistency theorist. "This propensity," he continues, "when exercised in favour of any widely-spread persuasion or sentiment, is often decorated with complimentary epithets; and the contrary habit of keeping the judgment in complete subordination to evidence, is stigmatized by various hard names, as scepticism, immorality, coldness, hard-heartedness, and similar expressions."[2] Though Mill affects a rather beleaguered tone, his list of "hard names" states many of social science's preferred virtues: questioning authority, self-denial, remoteness from emotion, and respect for facts. Social scientific method teaches the cognitive-civic art of "keeping the judgment in complete subordination to evidence." Mill wants to raise up political subjects who are capable of many-sided sympathies and none too certain of their own rightness. Truth shines through the crystalline medium of a self-sacrificing intellect. The liberal

2. Mill, *A System of Logic*, 8: 738.

public is designed to foster a particular set of beliefs, or rather, a particular attitude about holding beliefs; liberalism is not an open field for all beliefs to compete in, since it sifts out beliefs that are extreme or passionate. Disciplined inquiry has been the royal road for liberals to create a self able to suspend passion, interest, and prejudice. Inquiry breeds hesitation to lash out against strange ideas or expressions. Leaky schemata and tolerance of ambiguity are prerequisites for a liberal citizenry. As Emerson counseled, reflecting an old Stoic equation, study nature: know thyself.[3]

The project of a value-free science of society advances the central projects of liberal modernity: the disciplined self, the attainment of civil discourse, and the creation of a public sphere in which reason rather than violence or mere ideology would prevail. From Locke to Mill to the shoptalk of political scientists and experimental psychologists today, cognitive and political orders intertwine. Locke's vision of science (the effort to form trustworthy knowledge from the flickering material of private experience) was also political (the effort to form a social compact from the diverse properties accumulated by individual labors). For Mill social science was a schoolmaster in forming the habits of mind necessary for citizens in a modern democracy. Inquiry not only probes nature; it schools human nature by purging us of bias and egoism. Social scientists in turn often talk as if their chastity in inference, their obedience to data, and their poverty of political-ethical values did nothing less than sustain the possibility of civil converse and rational decency in a world on the verge of spinning into irrational chaos and violence. Militant ignorance in the face of propositions that are unaccompanied by evidence is not just a pose on the part of social scientists; it is a performance of moral and political virtue. Social scientists are a beacon on a hill modeling the virtues of impartiality, openness to evidence, and immunity to private preference; their clear rules of procedure and communication are supposed to show enlightened modes of communal association. As Robert K. Merton, perhaps the greatest sociological theorist in twentieth-century America, said, "methodological canons are often technical expedients *and* moral compulsives."[4]

Robert Park, the intellectual leader of sociology at the University of Chicago in the 1920s and 1930s, once said that race relations should be studied with the same detachment with which a biologist studies the potato

3. Ralph Waldo Emerson, "The American Scholar," in *Selected Writings of Emerson*, ed. Donald McQuade (New York: Modern Library, 1981), 48.

4. Robert K. Merton, "A Note on Science and Democracy," *Journal of Legal and Political Sociology* 1, 1942: 116.

bug. By subordinating personal opinion to the discipline of evidence, the social scientist enacts norms of civic decorum. The natural sciences have proved an enticing model for social scientists, not only because of their more obvious rigor and explanatory success, but also because the natural scientist's attitude of detachment to objects such as potato bugs seemed to contrast so sharply with the subjective attachment to attitudes that prevailed socially on subjects such as race. Social scientists have often far outdone natural scientists in the fierceness with which they hold the duty of objectivity. Just as potatoes flourish in Europe, cocoa in Africa, and rabbits in Australia, so notions of "science" prevail most intensely in the social sciences. Species flourish in exile. G. Stanley Hall, a key figure in the early history of the field of psychology (he played host to Freud in 1909 at Clark University and invented the modern notion of "adolescence"), argued that true scientific investigation required "whole-souled self-abandonment."[5] The dream of a unified science building on physics retailed by Vienna Circle émigrés such as Carl Hempel was taken much more seriously in the wannabe social sciences than the natural sciences. Physicists—through the first two-thirds of the twentieth century by far the most successful and inventive of all scientists—might sometimes talk this way, but they have historically been a much more freewheeling bunch. Social scientists always had a double mission—to explain society and model political-intellectual morality. Like Skokie liberals, they have had to rely on spectators to decode their silence about morality or politics as itself a statement of a higher kind of morality or politics.

Inquiry into human gregariousness and institutions is as at least as old as moral and political philosophy, but the project of an organized science of society dates to the early nineteenth century. The professional social sciences appeared toward the end of the nineteenth century as scholarly identities and university departments—anthropology, economics, history, political science, psychology, and sociology—though they have since multiplied into a diverse array of subfields and practices.[6] My focus here is the professional culture of social science, with its stories of self-justification and norms of decorum—the kind of thing social scientists say in their official documents when they put their best explanatory foot forward. "Positivism" is one of those words that is used only by its detractors, but it is a ser-

5. Peter Novick, *That Noble Dream* (Chicago: University of Chicago Press, 1988), 23.

6. Thomas Haskell, *The Emergence of Professional Social Science* (Urbana: University of Illinois Press, 1977); Dorothy Ross, *The Origins of American Social Science* (Cambridge: Cambridge University Press, 1991).

viceable name for the dominant narrative of social science since the late nineteenth century.[7] The positivist narrative has lost some steam since its heyday in the social sciences from the 1920s to the 1960s, though its vitality depends enormously on what part of the vineyard you find yourself in; it has been dead in cultural anthropology for decades but is flourishing in economics, political science, psychology, and much of sociology. The most strident forms of the messianic vision of social science may be gone, but the peculiar and fussy habits of being bound by data, worrying about generalizability, and fencing off values from inquiry remain rituals that hold a universe of liberal political values together.

A skepticism toward any and all firm beliefs is institutionalized in the research practices of social scientists. Their renunciation of judgment, like the monk's renunciation of sex, gives them the privilege of being clean from the besetting human sin—the passionate intolerance and violence that follow from a judgment too quick on the draw. They fast in the wilderness of opinions, keeping their vows of nonengagement with the world. A 1942 textbook on social research methods takes an epigraph from William Graham Sumner: "Men educated in [the critical habit of thought] cannot be stampeded by stump orators and are never deceived by dithyrambic oratory. They are slow to believe."[8] Social scientists do penance for the inferential sins ordinary folk so abundantly commit. (Perhaps this is one reason for the common delight in counterintuitive findings.) Owing to their prodigious powers of self-restraint, social scientists would make ideal participants in Rousseau's social contract or Kant's kingdom of ends, for they would always see the general will and favor it, whatever their own personal inclinations—or they would at least realize that what everyone else thought was true was really just another illusion. As Descartes notes, we can at least suspend our judgment. Research is separate from use: "It is not the business of a chemist who invents a high explosive to be influenced in his task by considerations as to whether his product will be used to blow up cathedrals or to build tunnels through the mountains."[9] Epistemological or ethical inertness is a

7. J. S. Mill, *August Comte and Positivism* (1865) (Ann Arbor: University of Michigan Press, 1961), 2: "Indeed, though the mode of thought expressed by the terms Positive and Positivism is widely spread, the words themselves are, as usual, better known through the enemies of that mode than through its friends."

8. Graham Sumner, *Folkways*, quoted in George A. Lundberg, *Social Research: A Study in Methods of Gathering Data* (New York: Longmans, Green, 1942), vi.

9. George A. Lundberg, quoted in Robert K. Merton, "Science and the Social Order" (1938), in *On Social Structure and Science*, ed. Piotr Sztompka (Chicago: University of Chicago Press, 1996), 283, n11.

badge of honor, a bulwark against demagoguery and suggestibility. In the periodic table of intellectual life, social scientists would be the argon.

In addition to ethical norms of disinterestedness, official tales of social science have served political missions. As James Carey has pointed out, the positive social sciences have helped ground the possibility of a democratic order in the United States.[10] Large-scale social research, such as the Presidential Commission on Recent Social Trends organized by Herbert Hoover, was seen in the 1920s and 1930s as protection against the chaos of modern capitalism, in the 1940s as a tool to fight fascism, and in the 1950s as a bulwark against the prefabricated knowledge of Soviet psychology or sociology.[11] George Kennan's famous long telegram in 1946 analyzing the Soviet threat paints objective social analysis as one of the leading fruits of a free society. For the Soviet Union, "the vast fund of objective fact about human society is not, as it is with us, the measure against which outlook is constantly being tested and reformed."[12] The cold war vision of social science as the distinctive proof of democracy could reach a high level of flatulence.[13] The ever-dialectical Theodor W. Adorno, a sharp critic of positivist social science who saw it as complicit with a capitalist culture industry and even worse as a form of metaphysical resignation, even argued in 1952 that market research during the Nazi era actually could have had an enlightening function. "The much-attacked inhumanity of empirical methods is still more humane than the humanizing of the inhuman"—that is, it is better to have crude American counting than Nazi "Geist."[14] The claim to discover things as they are rather than as they are painted by power, imagination, or wish is always a potent political claim.

10. James W. Carey, *Communication as Culture: Essays on Media and Society* (Boston: Unwin Hyman, 1989), chaps. 3–4.

11. Edward A. Purcell, Jr., *The Crisis of Democratic Theory: Scientific Naturalism and the Problem of Value* (Lexington: University Press of Kentucky, 1973); Robert Staughton Lynd, *Knowledge for What? The Place of Social Science in American Culture* (New York: Grove Press, 1939); Harold Dwight Lasswell, "Why Be Quantitative?" (1949), in *Harold Lasswell on Political Sociology*, ed. Dwaine Marwick (Chicago: University of Chicago Press, 1977), 257–66.

12. George Kennan, "On the United States and the Containment of the Soviets," in *Social Theory*, ed. Charles Lemert (Boulder, Colo.: Westview, 1999), 283–86.

13. See, for instance, Daniel Lerner, "Social Science: Whence and Whither," in *The Human Meaning of the Social Sciences*, ed. Lerner (New York: Meridian, 1959).

14. T. W. Adorno, "Zur gegenwärtigen Stellung der empirischen Sozialforschung in Deutschland" (1952), in *Soziologische Schriften* (Frankfurt: Suhrkamp, 1972), 1: 482.

THE ARTS OF CHASTE DISCOURSE

The ideology of the professional social scientist, as we have seen, came to occupy and transform the ideals of civility, reasoned discussion, self-control, and public space that had been central in the liberal Enlightenment. One key site for this work of sublimation is in the colorless style of social scientific writing. The norm of moral noninvolvement has a stylistic expression; objectivity can mean both a stance of impartiality and unopinionated (adjective-free) prose. The ideals found in positivist social science ground the ideal of clear and unencumbered communication that is implicit, though under-theorized, in democratic political theory. Imperatives about style encode assumptions and aspirations about human nature and the political order. The peculiar patterns of professional speech are due at least partly to the sense that social scientists could be an island of reason in a sea of contention, an oasis of facts in a desert of opinion, a voice of reason within a cacophony of passions. Dreams of modern democracy are themselves clearly bound up with assumptions about forms and genres of communication. As Habermas argues, the ideal of a public sphere of citizens participating actively in debate about politics was sustained by literary practices of diary keeping, letter writing, newspaper reading, and cultural criticism, along with the talk that accompanied them.[15] That forms of communication embody political ideals can be seen in the sharp political inflections given to discussions today of the decline of letter writing, critical thinking, and literacy, and debates about the state of education more generally. The peculiar discursive habits of social scientists—however deserving of mockery they may be for what C. Wright Mills called "grand theory," "abstracted empiricism," or "methodological inhibitionism"—are intimately tied to the virtues of detached inquiry (as they also are, obviously, to the mystifications of insider-speak that maintain professional aloofness).[16] Qualification, tentativeness, fear of over-generalizing—all proclaim a mindset exquisitely sensitive to facts and their nuances. A hedging style performs a scrupulous evidential sensibility, an openness to otherness and detachment from the ego.

Benjamin Franklin is an apt precursor of the combination of self-suspension, public spiritedness, scientific vitality, and civil style. His success—as inventor, entrepreneur, public servant, author, scientist, statesman, *philosophe,* and lover—owed much, he suggests in his *Autobiography,* to his

15. Jürgen Habermas, *Structural Transformation of the Public Sphere* (1962) (Cambridge: MIT Press, 1989), sec. 5.

16. C. Wright Mills, *The Sociological Imagination* (New York: Oxford, 1959).

discovery of a peaceable, noncontentious mode of discourse. Like Locke, whom he read, and Addison, whose prose he emulated, Franklin believed that polite conversation should eschew certainty, given the difficulty of any sure knowledge in our fallible state. One should adopt a tone of mellow persuasiveness rather than contentious conviction. About a conversation partner holding a contrary opinion, he said: "not knowing but that he might be in the right, I let him enjoy his opinion, which I take to be generally the best way in such cases." In his youth fiery in tongue and pen, and often in trouble for contentiousness, Franklin later discovered what he called a Socratic verbal style: "I . . . dropped my abrupt contradiction and positive argumentation, and put on the humble enquirer." He did so, quite characteristically, not because of some abstract commitment to the virtues of humility or inquiry, but because it was pragmatically an excellent way of winning arguments and entangling opponents without directly incurring their wrath. Like Martin Luther King later, Franklin found in Socrates a model of the power of passivity. With age, Franklin dropped the Socratic pose, "retaining only the habit of expressing myself in terms of modest diffidence, never using when I advance anything that may possibly be disputed the words, 'certainly,' 'undoubtedly,' or any other that give the air of positiveness to an opinion." The pose of humble inquiry and the avoidance of "dogmatical expressions" served him to "great advantage" because others often thought his ideas their own. He gave this speech etiquette a rather noble lineage: in his *Autobiography,* he summarizes the virtue of humility (rather unhumbly) in the maxim "emulate Jesus and Socrates."[17]

Max Weber chose Franklin as his chief exhibit of the Protestant ethic, particularly in his dream of perfection via moral bookkeeping and his belief that time is money. In other matters such as sexuality or general uptightness, Franklin does not cut too Protestant a figure; anxiety about salvation never seems to have bothered him much, and his attitude about "venery" (sex) is quite jolly. In his list of thirteen virtues, he says of sex: "Rarely use venery but for health or offspring."[18] That sex is used (rather than a worm at the core of one's being) and that health is one ground for its expression suggest a temper less close to the worried souls Weber was interested in (for private reasons of his own) than to the swinging aristocrats among whom Franklin lived in 1780s Paris. ("Never 'use' venery," replied

17. Benjamin Franklin, *Autobiography and Other Writings* (Boston: Houghton Mifflin, 1958), 140, 14, 15. On Franklin, see the brilliant piece by James Patrick McDaniel, "Snarls of Civility: Liberal Legacies from Ben Franklin's Theater of Pain for Terror's Unruliest Children," *Communication and Critical/Cultural Studies,* forthcoming.

18. Franklin, *Autobiography,* 77

D. H. Lawrence.)[19] Rationalization is a key term for both Weber and Franklin. For Weber it is a world-historical process, both inevitable and tragic, touching institutions, music, modes of cognition; for Franklin it is a psychological universal. A famous episode in his *Autobiography* occurs when Franklin finds himself on a becalmed boat between Philadelphia and Boston. At that time he was diligently following a vegetarian diet, having been convinced that "the taking of every fish [was] a kind of unprovoked murder." As the crew hauls in great quantities of cod and begins frying them, poor Franklin recounts that they "smelled admirably well. I balanced some time between principle and inclination till I recollected that when the fish were opened, I saw smaller fish taken out of their stomachs. 'Then,' thought I, 'if you eat one another, I don't see why we mayn't eat you.' So I dined upon cod very heartily and have since continued to eat as other people, returning only now and then occasionally to a vegetable diet." The punchline: "So convenient a thing it is to be a reasonable creature, since it enables one to find or make a reason for everything one has a mind to do."[20] This is rationalization, reason as the servant of whatever ends we choose. Note the momentary wavering between principle and inclination—very Kantian this—but with a very un-Kantian resolution into appetite as aided by reason. The discovery of cognitive contortionism took place well before 1950s social psychology! The secret affinity between Franklin and Weber is their sense of the ultimate arbitrariness of ends. Like Mill's public sphere and the U. S. Supreme Court, they find virtue in postponing ultimate things and in agnosticism about values. Both have more than a little Stoicism in them.

Modern science in the English-speaking world emerged from a culture dense with norms of genteel civility and conversation.[21] "Our debates," Franklin writes of the Junto, a mutual improvement society he founded, "were to be under the direction of a president, and to be conducted in the sincere spirit of enquiry after truth, without fondness for dispute or desire of victory; and to prevent warmth, all expressions of positiveness in opinion or of direct contradiction were after some time made contraband and prohibited under small pecuniary penalties."[22] Warmth, like passions and women, were excluded from the quest for truth—and with fines to pay. In 1741 Franklin founded the American Philosophical Society, an institution whose creation is sometimes seen to mark the genesis of the American

19. D. H. Lawrence, *Studies in Classic American Literature* (Baltimore: Penguin, 1971), 24.

20. Franklin, *Autobiography*, 31–32.

21. Steven Shapin, *A Social History of Truth: Science and Civility in Seventeenth-Century England* (Chicago: University of Chicago Press, 1994).

22. Franklin, *Autobiography*, 54.

Enlightenment. He modeled it on the British Royal Society, which famously put all rhetoric, politics, and divinity outside its pale. Thomas Sprat, in his *History of the Royal Society* (1667), wrote of its founding members: "Their first purpose was no more, then onely the satisfaction of breathing a freer air, and of conversing in quiet one with another, without being ingag'd in the passions, and madness of that dismal Age. . . . Their purpose is, in short, to make faithful Records, of all the Works of Nature or Art which can come within their reach. . . . And to accomplish this, they have endeavored to separate the knowledge of Nature, from the colours of Rhetoric, the devices of Fancy, or the delightful deceit of Fables."[23]

Since the Royal Society's founding, the self-policing of speech has been seen as the path to a civil and peaceful society, an escape from religious and other strife. Franklin provides a model of the liberal public sphere. Time, not contention, is the measure of truth; participants must restrain themselves and their passions in the quest for truth; discourse must be mellow, irenic, and civil. Like Locke, Franklin turns down the heat of contention by checking egotism and certitude, refusing to give "the air of positiveness to an opinion," and cultivating a fluent, middling style of expression. It was not so much that every idea should be aired in Franklin's liberal public sphere as that each voice should conduct itself with a decorum that shunned extremes and extravagances. Franklin's nexus of style, virtue, and political order remains a ghostly presence in the talk of social scientists. His Socratic pose shows up in the delight they take in claiming not to know things that others think so obvious. Franklin's conspicuous ignorance, like that of Socrates, aims to puncture other people's certainty. His self-imposed ban on dogmatic statements echoes in the scrupulously qualified character of social scientific talk, which is often meant to serve as a standing rebuke to all theories tainted with prophecy or excessive surety. The art of circumscribing certainty can even take a statistical form: significance tests quantify our degree of doubt. In much social science writing, empirical statements are accompanied by a numerical calculation of the probability of their being wrong. The phrase "$p < .05$" proclaims not only epistemological circumspection but moral rectitude. In graduate school, one of my professors wrote next to this formula the words Constantine had seen in his vision of the flaming cross: *in hoc signo vinces* (in this sign you will conquer). The virtues that are supposed to grow from a skeptical stance toward one's own opinions from Locke to Holmes reappear in the notion of a "confidence in-

23. Thomas Sprat, *History of the Royal Society* (1667). Annotated facsimile ed. (St. Louis: Washington University, 1958), 53, 61, 62.

terval." Throw down your significance tests, positivism suggests, and you are soon bound to take up your swords.

DEMOCRACY AND NUMBERS

Statistical analysis is, in many ways, the lingua franca of the social sciences, and it represents the kind of self-effacing style Franklin perfected. Despite the obvious epistemological power of statistics—the aggregation of observations into an intelligible totality that a single human could never oversee—there is a subtler civic dimension as well. As Theodore Porter notes, "quantification is a technology of distance" that is "well suited for communication that goes beyond the boundaries of locality and community."[24] Harold Dwight Lasswell, an innovator in the use of quantitative methods in political science and communication research, argued in his 1949 essay "Why Be Quantitative?" that counting overcomes the fundamental scholarly problems of trust and communication. Clear numerical procedures for selecting evidence allow readers to evaluate or even reach the conclusions for themselves. (As one of my teachers once said, in a good social science article you should be able to skip the prose and go straight to the tables.) Numbers, for Lasswell, can attain a precision of mental access and sharing that words rarely do. Quantitative methods serve to promote "collaboration and communication" in the social relations among inquirers. Because numbers expel private interests and ambiguity, they are respected as trustworthy forms of discourse.[25] In this story about quantitative inquiry, numbers are the signifying system that bears the burden of the political dream of transparency. At least since Pythagoras thinkers have dreamed of a universal language of number: a notion revived in the Renaissance and worked out most grandiosely by Leibniz with striking relevance for our age of universal digitization, when all signification is potentially reduced to ones and zeroes. How one says "two plus two equals four" in Chinese or Swahili I have no idea, but the equation "$2 + 2 = 4$" will be instantly understood wherever Hindu-Arabic numeracy has spread—the closest thing there is to a universal ideographic language. Numbers model universality, rigor, and publicity. (Despite this narrative, everyone knows how vulnerable numbers are to all the perversions, distortions, and blessings that attend any form of sign.)

Numbers and democracy have an ancient elective affinity. Democracy is

24. Theodore Porter, *Trust in Numbers: The Pursuit of Objectivity in Science and Public Life* (Princeton, N.J.: Princeton University Press, 1995), ix.

25. Lasswell, "Why Be Quantitative?" Also see Porter, *Trust in Numbers*.

itself a quantitative method. Its key principle is the priority of quantity over quality. At least in elections, despite the many modifications possible, decisions are made by the simple tally of the vote. Counting trumps argument, justice, passion, and wisdom. There is something resolutely simple-minded in this form of intelligence. Tocqueville noted that the rule of the majority was an assault on the last bastion of human pride: each person's confidence in the trustworthiness of his or her own reason.[26] In voting the individual is effaced by the majority, an agent Tocqueville famously thought dangerous because of its tendencies to tyranny. The personal vote is always overruled by the force of the total. Once the vote is cast into the great pool, its link to the person of the voter is completely severed; the vote is now just one counter among many. Votes, like other things cast, such as arrows, dice, lots, lures, and radio signals, are out of the hands of the one who casts. Democratic culture celebrates the self-sacrifice to acknowledge the greatest number as legitimate. Voters must be willing to go through the motions. In voting, the thoughtful must live with split knowledge of the gap between private action and collective outcome. All voters know that their votes will likely have no effect on the outcome and thus take part in a ritual that may well be in vain for them personally. But the sum of such quixotic individual acts is an election. Democracy establishes justice and legitimacy through a social force, the majority, which exists only by way of math.

A democratic election is, in principle, a single voice emergent from the collective. J. S. Mill encouraged people to vote as if they were the only voter in the election. This rather megalomaniacal contrivance to encourage public-spiritedness requires people to suspend a lot of disbelief. Elections, like statistics, show that central tendencies in large aggregates are invisible at close levels of magnification. Wittgenstein's dictum that fuzziness is sometimes exactly what we need applies to elections as well as statistics, both of which, like impressionist paintings, require a blurred gaze to discern the pattern. The will of the people is visible only at very low resolutions. In U. S. presidential elections, for instance, millions of nuanced reasonings are reduced to a single bit of information, A or B. (The "hanging" and "pregnant" chads of the U.S. presidential election in Florida show the chaos that results when the level of magnification for voting is suddenly altered.) The self-delusion that each vote makes a difference becomes true when everything is summed. The totality of the turnout depends on very large numbers of individuals gambling that voting is worthwhile. "All vot-

26. Alexis de Tocqueville, *Democracy in America* (1835). 2 vols. (Garden City, N.Y.: Anchor Books, 1969), 1: 247.

ing," wrote Thoreau, "is a sort of gaming, like chequers or backgammon, with a slight moral tinge to it, a playing with right and wrong."[27] We vote not because of the hope that we will make all the difference, but because we know that if everyone gave it up, there would be no outcome at all. (In fact the view that voting is vain plays an important part in elections, since political disaffection is never randomly distributed.) Voting is a secular form of divination. Little wonder that talk of democratic decisions still has a religious tinge, as if a suprahuman voice were giving utterance. Vox populi, vox dei: the voice of the people is the voice of God. In Calvinism, for instance, the theological notion of election means being selected as one of the elect by God's inscrutable preference; the notion of a mandate has a similar cast. Notions of representation, political and otherwise, owe much to medieval theology, with its bodily delegation from father to son and son to king.[28] Elections, like oracles, manifest a will that would otherwise remain obscure. They model the principles of civic selflessness and the sublimation of private opinion.

Impersonality is a norm shared by quantitative research and democratic elections. Democracy has long made decisions by impersonal means. In ancient Athens the *klērotērio* (a mechanical device holding forty-nine black balls and one white ball, whence we get our term "to black ball") was used to select tribal heads for the council. Randomization devices have long been used for decision making and play an important role in archaic state-formation; the ritual of the coin-flip still opens football games.[29] Urns full of colored balls, still a favorite example in probability theory, originated in elections. Here we encounter two enduring democratic principles: equality (anyone and everyone is fit to serve) and impersonality (decisions about power holding are removed from private interests). Plutarch discusses an early quantitative method for the democratic election of senators in Sparta in the era of its mythical constitution-giver, Lycurgus. Judges were enclosed in a room adjacent to the assembly from which they could neither see nor be seen by the voters. They could, however, hear the noise of the crowd. The candidates, having drawn lots to determine the order of their appearance before the assembly, would silently walk before it, eliciting a cheer; the judges would rank the size of the crowd's roar without knowing how they

27. Henry David Thoreau, *Walden and Civil Disobedience* (New York: Norton, 1966), 228.

28. Ernst Kantorowicz, *The King's Two Bodies* (Princeton, N.J.: Princeton University Press, 1957).

29. Hugh W. Nibley, "The Arrow, the Hunter, and the State" (1949), in *The Ancient State* (Salt Lake City: Deseret Book Co., 1991), 1–32.

matched with candidates. The closed room, the classic site of worries about communication, has its political analogue here: the evaluation of quantity (the acoustic volume of the acclamation) is separated from the persons of the political actors.[30] Anonymity is a key moment in democratic sociability. The Spartan election judges are, like Paul's God, no respecters of persons. Quantity, blindness, election: atavistic ingredients in normal social inquiry.

In modern times elections still speak the vatic language of numbers. Edison's first patent, in 1869, was the Electrographic Vote Recorder (though it was for counting votes in Congress, not popular elections). Here are the electrification of writing and the recording of voices, ambitions not far from Edison's phonograph, invented a few years later. For public use, voting machines were first introduced in the United States in the 1890s and spread slowly. As Michael Schudson notes, "The mechanical voting machine offered a perfect embodiment of Progressive Era hopes for democracy" with its claims for privacy, anonymity, efficiency, and impartiality—though the aftermath of the 2000 presidential election in Florida revealed in excruciating detail the faults of mechanized voting.[31] Voting machines are supposed to be assist-devices for the artificial person of the body politic, as Hobbes put it, producing a collective text without any individual author. Democracy is the rule of no/body: collective authorship must in some way be mechanical. Voting is an inscription technology that amasses voices. As Friedrich Kittler remarks, "whatever democracy may be, it rests in any case on the mechanical processing of anonymous discourses."[32] Voting is a kind of data-reduction, the crunching of countless opinions and attitudes into a single summary. Democracy has always depended on intellectual devices of abbreviation. Little wonder that pollsters have been so successful in popularizing opinion surveys as an organ of democratic life.[33] The notion of a randomizing machinery that divines the people's will has an ancient lineage stretching to the *klērotērio*. There is a mystic democratic voice that is still thought to reside within quantitative methods of examining society.

Numbers are democracy's ideal language: suited for gods, machines, and collectives. Numbers refuse to acknowledge petty differences. They are remote, impartial, and inhuman. There is something both cruel and gracious about their indifference to our projects. It might be a terrible world if we

30. Plutarch, *The Lives*, in *Great Books of the Western World*, ed. Robert Maynard Hutchins (Chicago: Encyclopedia Britannica, 1952), 14: 45.

31. Michael Schudson, *The Good Citizen: A History of American Civic Life* (Cambridge, Mass.: Harvard University Press, 1998), 173–74.

32. Friedrich A. Kittler, *Draculas Vermächtnis* (Leipzig: Reclam, 1993), 29.

33. Schudson, *The Good Citizen*, 223–38.

treated each other like numbers, but it might be wonderful as well. Numbers are uniquely universal and uniquely vacuous: they do not care what they are counting. Their impersonality can be both godlike and demonic. Democracy's ethics has a similar mix of the concrete and the abstract. Democracy invites both private engagement and public decisions. The emotional code of democracy mixes attachment and detachment. Recognizing marks of difference such as race, age, and gender is democratic; so is ignoring them. A personal investment is required on the part of all of its citizens. For ancient democracy this could include the willingness to bear arms on the battlefield, a requirement diluted but certainly not destroyed in modern democracy. The act of voting cannot be delegated; at some point the citizen's bodily presence is required at a place appointed to collect voices. Even with absentee ballots, voting is strictly tied to individuals and the body-extending surrogate of the signature. Times for voting, like other forms of national collective action, are usually consecrated. (The United States is an exception in not making election day a holiday.) And yet once the returns are in, all that personal investment and preference are supposed to be suspended in favor of the majority vote. Similarly, the citation style of the American Psychological Association that dominates the social sciences reduces given names to an initial, celebrating the effacement of the individual, the democracy of the surname, one of many minute practices that encode an entire philosophy of science, "encyclopedic incrementalism," the notion of a cumulative, collective enterprise in the name of reason and progress.[34] It is reminiscent of the early motto of the British Statistical Society: *aliis exterendum,* "to be threshed out by others." This tribute to postponed reckoning with ultimate meaning could be a motto for the liberal public sphere.

Though distorted by ideological pressure, official narratives of social science dream of a pure zone of knowledge that is also a pure zone of social relations. The lingering force of the dream of objectivity is moral, not epistemological. Objectivity, ethically understood, is an ideal of receptivity; politically, it is a stance of virtuous inaction. Despite its many sins mainstream social science has invoked enduring political and human aspirations. Several waves of brilliant epistemological and ethical criticism have failed to sap it of its cultural and political power. Value-free social science has an immense stubbornness in the face of critiques that should, if the world ran like a seminar, have put it out of business long ago. Politicians,

34. Charles Bazerman, *Shaping Written Knowledge* (Madison: University of Wisconsin Press, 1988).

businesspeople, administrators, and reporters, like Milton's angels, shed a few drops of ichor when sliced through by the sword of critical theory, and instantly return to their professed faith in social research. None of the critiques of positivism have been able to generate institution-sustaining narratives or mobilize key social resources to the degree that it did. As a set of communication practices, quantification specifically claims to establish open relations among colleagues, present clear standards of evaluation, and subject opinions to facts. It imagines a community of enlightened, altruistic people that bow before the best data. Despite the severity of quantitative social scientists, they are often among the biggest utopians around.

OBJECTIVITY AND SELF-MORTIFICATION

Asceticism always accompanied *theōria*, but one high point was the midtwentieth century. The tough guy vision of the social scientist's vocation perhaps peaked with John B. Watson's behaviorism in the 1920s and 1930s and the renunciation of fuzzy concepts like consciousness in favor of an unsentimental monitoring of what people observably do. Watsonian behaviorism was part of the hard-boiled culture of the middle decades of the twentieth century, found in film, literature, and politics, the masochistic social scientist taking his place next to the hard-boiled journalist, soldier, cowboy, and detective.[35] These guys knew the morgue-keeper on a first-name basis and took their whiskey and pain without flinching. In their controlled passivity they tapped into a long moral and political lineage dating at least to Roman times. Their courage and even humility are stirring and almost pardon their sin of hardness. Midcentury tough guys, consummate professionals all, usually ended up being degraded by their prowess, since it made tenderness a liability: Raymond Chandler's Philip Marlowe, John LeCarré's George Smiley, Francis Ford Coppolla's Harry Caul in his film *The Conversation* (1974), various cowboys played by John Wayne and James Stewart, who both can bring an exquisitely subtle inward torment to their otherwise very different masculinities. Smiley is systematically abused by the two things he loves most, the Circus and his wife Ann. Marlowe, always paying his own bills, refusing to be in anyone's debt, taking shots to the head and heart like a prize fighter, brilliantly divining motives and interpreting events, is a walking paragon of agnostic rationality. Asked who he works for, he replies: "I never know. Often, when I do know, I don't know how. I just fumble around and make a nuisance of myself. Often I'm pretty inade-

35. Thanks to Ken Cmiel for this point.

quate."[36] Marlowe is less pretentious than the best and the brightest of postwar social scientists but he is at least proud to announce that he does not know.

Vietnam was one death knell for the social scientific dream of objectivity in the United States, and Graham Greene's *The Quiet American* (1955) remains one of the best analyses of that developing debacle, specifically what happens when objectivity and idealism try to deal with a world out of control. Fowler, a down-and-out British reporter stationed in Vietnam, affects the hard-bitten pose of the objective journalist: "'You can rule me out,' I said. 'I'm not involved. Not involved,' I repeated. It had been an article of my creed. The human condition being what it was, let them fight, let them love, let them murder, I would not be involved. My fellow journalists called themselves correspondents; I preferred the title of reporter. I wrote what I saw. I took no action—even an opinion is a kind of action."[37] Like Marlowe, Fowler is morally more complex than contemporary social scientists such as Daniel Lerner and Walt Rostow; Marlowe and Fowler at least knew they could not save the world. Yet the wider resonance of Fowler's protestation of noninvolvement is clear. He is called "Monsieur Fowlair" by the French-speaking Vietnamese, and indeed, he spends his life breathing foul air—including the opium he smokes. The narrative arc of the novel refutes Fowler's claim to noninvolvement as he gets sucked into the cauldron of killing in Vietnam—again like Rostow. But Fowler's cynicism at least prepared him to cope with the quagmire.

Perhaps a dying breed, this masculine type takes special inspiration from doctors, especially pathologists, who find in morbidity lessons of the living form, not cause for disgust. They snorkel in seas of formaldehyde, admiring the submarine produce. Their brutal integrity and Spartan dispassion shield them from the fauna of the deep. They might admire a particularly beautiful cancer; a ballistics expert I once saw on TV called the 1995 Oklahoma City bombing "a Rembrandt" of an explosion. There are connoisseurs even of calamity. Being steeled against everything else, the hardboiled epistemologists are libertarians in the realm of expression: nothing should be banned, because nothing can hurt. Again, social scientists are just one branch of this family tree, but they have a distinct place. In a society of "stiff and fierce opinion," as Locke put it, the social scientist is a kind of *homo sacer* above and beyond the norms. Social scientists sometimes boast that they test theory "the hard way"; they submit themselves to the trial and

36. Raymond Chandler, *Playback* (New York: Ballantine, 1958), 164.
37. Graham Greene, *The Quiet American* (London: Heinemann, 1973), 22.

torture of evidence; they forgo the sybaritic luxury of easy speech, the eloquent rapidity of conclusion of the journalist, humanist, believer, or theorist. Their hearts are ice in a world of heat. Like professionals in general, social scientists achieve, to speak with Kierkegaard, a teleological suspension
of the ethical. They put common feelings and attachments on hold in their
work; they are ready to kill for a higher cause. Their shoptalk favors macho
images of distance and detachment: evidence is a trial of hypotheses, one
must murder one's flawed brainchildren, results shoot down hypotheses,
and data are preferably "hard." Torture, infanticide, warfare, and ordeals
mark social scientists as the class whose suffering saves the rest.

Hardheartedness applies above all to scientists' attachments to their own
work. They rejoice in the perdition of their dear ones: "Good scientists get a
perverse thrill out of proving themselves wrong."[38] Karl Pearson put the
duty of the scientific inquirer well: "the single-eyed devotion to truth, even
though its acquirement may destroy a previously cherished conviction."[39]
George Lundberg concurs: "Herein lies one of the most important tests of
the true scientist: has he the power coldly to set aside his preconceived subjective notion of the outcome of an experiment or investigation when the
carefully checked objective data lead to other conclusions?"[40] A scientist
should not seek immortal fame but hope to be swallowed up in the onward
march. Mourning for departed theories must be brief. Charles Sanders
Peirce nicely stated the imperative to abandon attachments: "But the scientific spirit requires a man to be at all times ready to dump his whole cartload
of beliefs, the moment experience is against them. The desire to learn for-
bids him to be cocksure that he knows already. Besides positive science can
only rest on experience; and experience can never result in absolute certainty, exactitude, necessity, or universality."[41] Similarly, in a 1919 speech,
"Science as Vocation," Max Weber, one of the foremost examples of a Stoic
ethic in our times and probably the most important architect of social science in the twentieth century, suggested that a scientist's greatest honor is
to have his or her work outdated. "In science, each of us knows that what
he has accomplished will be antiquated in ten, twenty, fifty years. That is
the fate to which science is subjected; it is the very *meaning* of scientific

38. Michael Slater, "Augustine's Cup: Locating Science in a Post-postmodern World." Manuscript, Colorado State University, 2002.

39. Karl Pearson, *The Ethic of Freethought: A Selection of Essays and Lectures* (London:
T. Fisher Unwin, 1888), 19.

40. Lundberg, *Social Research*, 49.

41. Charles Sanders Peirce, "The Scientific Attitude and Fallibilism," *Philosophical Writings of
Peirce*, ed. Justus Buchler (New York: Dover, 1955), 46–47.

work. . . . Every scientific 'fulfillment' raises new 'questions'; it *asks* to be surpassed and outdated. Whoever wishes to serve science has to resign himself to this fact."[42] Scientists who have learned their Protestant lessons of asceticism and self-denial rejoice in the inevitable irrelevance of what they have passionately toiled over. Like Oliver Wendell Holmes, Jr.'s soldiers, they die for causes whose ends they will never see. Resignation to fact—one could hardly state the Stoical ideal of science better.

Though the hardboiled stance peaked in the twentieth century, it has clear predecessors in the mystically brutal self-suppression of nineteenth-century positivism. The German species was perhaps the most virulent, since it got a double dose—scientism and classicism—in the natural and human sciences. The self-effacement of modern fact and the Olympian impassivity of the ancients cross-fertilized, no less in a classical philologist such as Ulrich von Wilamowitz-Moellendorf than in a natural science genius such as Hermann von Helmholtz. Freud inherits both strains. Nietzsche rejects the scientism but keeps the classicism. His dissidence from the culture of *Wissenschaft* is easily misunderstood: Nietzsche admires the harsh vitality, the brusque autonomy of fact, but for moral rather than epistemological reasons. Hard facts are a fate we should love, not an epistemological gauntlet we should endure. For him objectivity meant the power to stare the negative in the face, to look at history as it has unfolded and to have the strength to say: So I would have wished it.

After the founding of the University of Berlin in 1809, the world's first research university, one of Germany's chief exports was attitudinal, a contempt for the merely human realm compared with godlike *theōria*—something it is hard not to look back on without a shudder. William James, who knew German research in the overlapping areas of psychology, physiology, and physics as well as anyone in the English-speaking world, was an acute observer of the frigid temperature at which German *Wissenschaft* could operate. The great Helmholtz, for instance, was the first to measure the speed of nervous propagation, and James describes the larger significance of this discovery: "The phrase 'quick as thought' had from time immemorial signified all that was wonderful and elusive of determination in the line of speed; and the way in which Science laid her doomful hand upon this mystery reminded people of the day when Franklin first 'eripuit coelo fulmen' [pulled fire from heaven], foreshadowing the reign of a newer and colder race of gods." German *Psychophysik* (psychophysics) aimed to measure the capaci-

42. "Science as a Vocation" (1919), in *From Max Weber*, ed. Hans Gerth and C. Wright Mills (New York: Oxford University Press, 1946), 138.

ties of the human sensory organs (including memory) as mechanical processes.[43] James describes it at his witty best: "This method taxes patience to
the utmost, and could hardly have arisen in a country whose natives could
be bored. Such Germans as Weber, Fechner, Vierordt, and Wundt obviously
cannot." Then came an even more ferocious generation: "The simple and
open method of attack having done what it can, the method of patience,
starving out, and harassing to death is tried; the Mind must submit to a regular *siege*. . . . There is little of the grand style about these new prism, pen-
dulum, and chronograph-philosophers. They mean business, not chivalry."
They favor "spying and scraping," "deadly tenacity, and almost diabolical
cunning."[44] The psychologist is subject to horrendous spells of *acedia* and
ends up in a sort of trench warfare, putting the soul under siege. Somehow
under the protective shield of science, "harassing to death" and diabolical
cunning become virtues. Yet it is too ready a cliché to call nineteenth-
century German science ruthless and militaristic. Anyone who has read
Helmholtz or Wilamowitz knows the joy they took in knowing at a time
when major discoveries seemed plentiful as huckleberries.

In late-Victorian England and the United States, there were several paths
for scientific tough-mindedness, notably including social Darwinism (Herbert Spencer), legal Pilatism (Oliver Wendell Holmes, Jr.), and medical deduction (Sherlock Holmes). To believe in mind, common sense, or consciousness was to be dangerously sentimental. James Clerk Maxwell, who
brilliantly applied social statistics to the dynamics of gases, gives us a whim-
sical view of impersonality: "But I carefully abstain from asking the molecules which enter where they started from. I only count them and register
their mean velocities, avoiding all personal enquiries which would only get
me into trouble."[45] A charming British discretion about private matters explains the sublime impersonality of molecules. Though an epistemologist
of the first rank, Maxwell, as a believing Christian, is perhaps not the best
representative of scientific self-mortification. That award would have to go

43. Compare Friedrich A. Kittler, *Aufschreibesysteme: 1800, 1900* (Munich: Fink, 1995), 259–
88. I have touched on Helmholtz in "Helmholtz und Edison. Zur Endlichkeit der Stimme,"
trans. Antje Pfannkuchen, in *Zwischen Rauschen und Offenbarung. Zur kulturellen und Medien-
geschichte der Stimme*, ed. Friedrich A. Kittler, Thomas Macho, and Sigrid Weigel (Berlin: Aka-
demie Verlag, 2002), 291–312.

44. William James, *The Principles of Psychology* (1890). 2 vols. (New York: Dover, 1950), 1: 85–
86, 192–93. Emphasis in the original.

45. *Maxwell on Heat and Statistical Mechanics: On 'Avoiding All Personal Enquiries' of Molecules*, ed. Elizabeth Garber, Stephen G. Brush, and C. W. F. Everitt (London: Associated University Presses, 1995), 422.

to Darwin's cousin Francis Galton, inventor of eugenics, statistician, and general polymath. His tough-mindedness included a statistical debunking of the efficacy of prayer, though that foray is sadly humorless compared with the jaunty blasphemies of a Holmes or the witty railings of a Nietzsche.[46] Galton's posturing is choice: "those who are not accustomed to original inquiry entertain a hatred and horror of statistics. They cannot endure the idea of submitting their sacred impressions to cold-blooded verification. But it is the triumph of scientific men to rise superior to such superstitions, to devise tests by which the value of beliefs may be ascertained, and to feel sufficiently masters of themselves to discard contemptuously whatever may be found untrue."[47] Cold-bloodedness and contempt are raised to the level of principle. Here Miltonic cocooning of the negative goes off the rails.

Perhaps the most interesting figure in late Victorian reflections on science is Galton's disciple Karl Pearson. Pearson did much to establish quantification as a political and scientific value in the late nineteenth century. He coined the term "standard deviation" in 1893 and invented techniques of correlational analysis, a fact memorialized in Pearson's "r" (a measure of the linear relationship between two variables) that statistics students still learn today. With the discovery of correlation and regression in the 1880s, statistical analysis moved into the young social sciences, and Pearson was a key figure in this importation.[48] A man of many interests, Pearson was fascinated by the history of German literature, especially the passion play; a socialist, who changed the spelling of his name from Carl to Karl in tribute to the greatest socialist of all; an odd sort of feminist; and a student of comparative mysticism. Pearson saw scientific method as a kind of spiritual discipline, a modern equivalent to mysticism. According to him, the "scientific man has above all to aim at self-elimination in his judgments." Statistical study was the royal road to the extinction of the ego, but it also had direct civic relevance: a "judgment free from personal bias . . . ought to be one of the training grounds for citizenship."[49] Pearson went beyond the well-worn point that quantification is both a moral and a political value. Invoking Buddhism, he suggested that scientific self-elimination was a spiritual practice involving our escape from enslavement to the phenomenal world.

46. Francis Galton, "Statistical Inquiries into the Efficacy of Prayer," *The Fortnightly Review* 12.68 (Aug. 1872): 125–35.

47. Francis Galton, "Generic Images," in *Proceedings of the Royal Institution*, 25 Apr. 1879. Reprint in British Library (pamphlet), 10.

48. Stephen M. Stigler, *Statistics on the Table: The History of Statistical Concepts and Methods* (Cambridge, Mass.: Harvard University Press, 1999).

49. Karl Pearson, *The Grammar of Science* (London: Walter Scott, 1892), 7.

He thought that science and mysticism alike shared the aim of the "relief of spiritual misery."[50] Sheer mystic disinterestedness reveals being. This stance ignores the petty clamorings of both the ego and the madding crowd. Few statisticians since have dared to state the moral mission of statistics so baldly. Who would have thought that research methods would be the narrow portal through which Taoist and Buddhist passivity and noninterference would come to permeate western culture as a positive moral ideal?

Pearson knew something of self-sacrifice in the name of science. He reports that he "personally" studied "540 dolichocephalic German skulls found in the Row-Graves of the fifth to ninth centuries": this cocktail of gravedigging, biometrics, and the German middle ages is very Pearsonian.[51] In his 1894 essay "Scientific Aspects of Monte Carlo Roulette," he recounts: "25,000 tosses of a shilling occupied a good portion of my vacation, and, being conducted frequently in the open air, gave me, I have little doubt, a bad reputation in the neighborhood I was staying." The scientist's ways are not those of the rest of us. A former pupil helpfully provided Pearson with data from 8,200 penny-flip trials and 9,000 tickets drawn from a bag, and another 23,000 drawings of counters, colored and numbered.[52] What an emancipation from the curse of toil was the advent of the computer! C. S. Peirce spent much of his professional employment as a "computer," that is, someone who performed mathematical calculations for weeks and months on end with nothing more than pencil, paper, and slide rule, and this job, like another job of discourse-processing whose name combines a person and a machine, "typewriter," would become largely the province of women well into the mid-twentieth century. The nineteenth-century call for diligence and self-sacrifice in science had practical weight. The drudgery of accumulating large numbers of reliable observations (e.g., in astronomy) could expose one to insufferable stretches of dullness: immunity to ennui was a chief requisite for the calling of scientist.[53] Late-nineteenth-century scientists rummaged around in graves, besieged the soul, and bored themselves silly with coin flips. No wonder science won a reputation for violence to the soul.

50. See his 1883 lecture, "The Ethic of Renunciation," in *The Ethic of Freethought*, 78–114. The following work appeared as this book was going to press: Theodore Porter, *Karl Pearson: The Scientific Life in a Statistical Age* (Princeton, N.J.: Princeton University Press, 2004).

51. Karl Pearson, "The Chances of Death," in *The Chances of Death and Other Studies in Evolution*. 2 vols. (London: Edward Arnold, 1897), 1: 19.

52. Karl Pearson, "Scientific Aspects of Monte Carlo Roulette," in *The Chances of Death*, 1: 44.

53. Simon Schaffer, "Astronomers Mark Time: Discipline and the Personal Equation," *Science in Context* 2, 1988: 115–45.

MEDICAL COMPOSURE

Late-nineteenth-century medicine was one summit of coolness in the face of morbidity. Doctors earnestly took to heart Emerson's advice: "It behooves the wise man to look with a bold eye into those rarer dangers which sometimes invade men, and to familiarize himself with disgusting forms of disease, with sounds of execration, and the vision of violent death."[54] The practice of medicine offered a moral model of professional composure that later spread into many other professions. Here we consider three late-nineteenth-century figures, two historical, one fictional, as models of cool.

The first is Rudolf Virchow. As the great consolidator of the field of pathology, Virchow was one of the most influential scientists of his era. He was also a liberal member of the Reichstag, a classicist and archaeologist (a friend of Heinrich Schliemann, the excavator of Troy and Mycenae), and a comparative anthropologist and zoologist with a huge collection of skulls and other odd specimens. An archetype of the modern doctor, Virchow used his position at the University of Berlin from 1856 onward to shape modern medical research generally. He is remembered for his work in histology and his pioneering use of the microscope, though his approach to pathology using large tissue specimens was ultimately surpassed by that of his younger French contemporary, Claude Bernard, who advocated the use of small samples and indicators.[55] Virchow started performing autopsies in 1844 and continued to supervise hundreds of them annually at the Charité hospital complex in Berlin through the rest of his long life; he is a chief inventor of modern autopsy technique. In his book on the subject, he shows a certain dogmatic insistence on methodology that is too easy to stereotype as "German"—for example, a proper autopsy should take no more than three hours and should follow a strict protocol that guarantees a thorough assessment—as well as a remarkable coolness to mayhem. Take his discussion of knife technique. Beginners use the knife too tentatively, holding it like a pen and making many small cuts when they should learn to use their shoulders and their entire arm. While visiting a slaughterhouse Virchow discovered that he should use a wider and even longer knife for initial incisions (which also keeps the examining doctors from pricking themselves so often). Butchers, he notes, were the first explorers of dissection techniques, and he whimsically endorses the favored knife stroke of the medieval Holy Roman emperor Frederick Barbarossa. He calls for an almost military deci-

54. Ralph Waldo Emerson, "Heroism," in *Selected Writings*, 237.
55. Russell C. Maulitz, "The Pathological Tradition," in *Companion Encyclopedia to the History of Medicine*, ed. W. F. Bynum and Roy Porter (London: Routledge, 1993), especially 181–85.

siveness: a smooth wrong incision is better than a correct uneven one. "I am a fanatical admirer of a large incision," he says in an uncharacteristically enthusiastic moment.[56] We should not be surprised that those who cut open the bodies of the dead can take a certain relish in it. The professional class has always involved butchery, back to the priests in diverse cultures who performed animal sacrifices.

The public outlet for Virchow's labors was a pathology museum he founded to be a forum for medical education and research. Virchow's collection, which once held 23,000 specimens, many of them personally handlabeled by him, lives on today in the form of the Berliner Medizin-Historisches Museum. Some 300 of the specimens that once adorned his office remain among the thousand or so on display, having survived World War II and the Berlin Wall. This hall of specimens is the main attraction: an appalling, diverse, grotesque collection of balloon-like skulls, twisted spines, gangrenous feet. As a viewer it is hard to know whether to weep, vomit, or stare. There is no professional insulation against stuff this strong. Let me put it this way: Virchow's pathological museum beats the raunchiest production of the id by a mile. It presents Lacan's *corps morcelé* according to scientific principles. Virchow's bottled fetuses, a centerpiece of his collection, look blankly back at us from their briny wombs: they are our kind, but suffer the curious abuse of being suspended from decay for the sake of an unsentimental education in the morphological variety of the human tabernacle. His sepulchral bottles hold some of the strangest things that await the resurrection. What sort of irreverence is it to gaze at what once a mother carried for nine months and gave birth to? What flickering love for fish and fowl once rocked her breast and still hovers about the jars? The museum as an institution, like the institution of medicine itself, tries to preserve us from the smell of our own fishy interest in the disfigured bodies. The museum's very existence presupposes a particular tuning of the soul, an advanced stage in the civilizing process. In the heart of the visitor comes "an indescribable feud," as Keats said of another museum, "a most dizzy pain."[57] One swings between wonder at the lavish excess of births, outrage at the public desecration of the dead, compassion for one's pickled kin, amazement at one's own blank tolerance, and a moistly libidinous glee at being alive. Virchow's statement at the public dedication of the museum in 1899 is

56. Rudolf Virchow, *Post-Mortem Examinations* (1875), trans. T. P. Smith (Metuchen, N.J.: Scarecrow Reprints, 1973), 35–46.

57. John Keats, "On Seeing the Elgin Marbles," ll. 10–11.

a central text in the art of abyss-redemption: "the dead material should be nothing more for us than the illustration of the living."[58] He seems to warn against gratuitous fascination, but more important, he is confident that when we face pathological deformity, we will find eyes to see living form. He trusts our powers of sublimation. The doctor facing the specimen impassively is the defining model of objectivity.

Sherlock Holmes, unlike his creator Arthur Conan Doyle, was not a doctor, but he clearly embodies one aspect of the medical rationality of the late nineteenth century. When he is first introduced to Watson and to the reading public in "A Study in Scarlet" (1887), the introducer says: "Holmes is a little too scientific for my tastes—it approaches to cold-bloodedness." His "passion for definite and exact knowledge" is then exemplified: in a recent experiment he beat cadavers in dissecting rooms with a stick in order to study the possibility of bruising after death. When Watson first meets Holmes, Holmes is jubilant at having discovered a chemical reagent for detecting minute traces of blood, and to demonstrate, he jabs his finger while announcing, "Let us have some fresh blood": Sherlock Holmes, brother to Dracula. But then Holmes notes that he must carefully bandage the pricked finger, since "I dabble with poisons a good deal," and Watson observes that his fingers are covered with small bandages (evidently he pokes himself a lot).[59] Here we have one vision of late-nineteenth-century medicine: kinky commerce with corpses in the name of science, bloodletting without flinching, and an intimacy with poisons—ever since Mithridates the chief way of proving steeliness against physical or other assaults. Yet it is all done with a certain British offhanded lightness: Holmes dabbles.

Holmes is something new in the annals of the literary detective. Edgar Allan Poe's Auguste Dupin, the first in a long lineage, belongs to a Romantic world in the 1840s, Holmes to a positivist one in the 1880s. Dupin reasons from parts to wholes, seeks identity with the other's mind (even if criminal), and loves the idiosyncratic. These mark the Romantic turn of his interpretive method, just as do his fascinations—the night, old obscure books, the variegated splendor of Paris as a city. Dupin has a soul, however bizarre. He reads cities, faces, clues, newspapers the same way the theologian Friedrich Schleiermacher and the philosopher Wilhelm Dilthey read

58. ". . . denn das todte Material soll für uns nichts weiter sein, als die Illustration des Lebenden. Immer ist es das Ziel, das Lebende zu erkennen und beurtheilen." Quoted from text on display, Medizin-Historisches Museum, Berlin.

59. Sir Arthur Conan Doyle, "A Study in Scarlet" (1887), in *The Complete Sherlock Holmes* (Garden City, N.Y.: Doubleday, 1930), 1: 17–18.

texts: empathetically.[60] Holmes is an altogether harsher sort. His probabilities are abstract and statistical; he uses a "curious analytic reasoning
from effects to causes," rather than Dupin's reading of chains of signifiers.
Holmes's coldness extends to his masculine identity: "love is an emotional
thing, and whatever is emotional is opposed to that true cold reason which
I place above all things. I should never marry myself, lest I bias my judgment." Women, like feeling, inhabit the realm of bias. Holmes is as keen an
observer as Dupin is, but his is a medical, physiological look, closer to Bernard or Virchow than Schleiermacher: "You know my method. It is founded
on the observation of trifles."[61] It is not altogether clear that Holmes possesses a soul. He has a brooding side that could sustain a Romantic reading;
he shoots cocaine and is a melancholic immobilized by acedia or calmed by
violin playing when the clarifying stimulus of work is not upon him. But
he lacks a personal center. "If I claim full justice for my art, it is because it
is an impersonal thing—a thing beyond itself. Crime is common. Logic is
rare."[62] Deduction has neither soul nor body. Holmes regards himself as a
vessel chosen to solve crimes, not to follow his bliss. He is acquainted with
the night, but he does not redeem it to a sparkling daylight. He spends his
life with crime not because of a wish to save the world, but because it is what
he does. He has a certain joshing levity about his self-incineration. In this
Holmes is one progenitor of the hard-boiled heroes, detectives, cowboys,
spies, and social scientists who intimately know the cancer of war, crime, or
deviance without being able to endow their work with any larger rationale
or even personal satisfaction. Like his namesake across the Atlantic, Oliver
Wendell, Sherlock Holmes celebrates Stoic chilliness.

Our gallery of late-nineteenth-century hardness would be incomplete
without another doctor who, like Holmes, based his inquiry on the reading
of trifles, and like Virchow (and under his influence), spent years in a histo-
logical lab studying cellular pathology. Sigmund Freud can be read in more
than one way: as a cold-blooded anatomist of hell, as its spellbound tourist,
as a bold Satanic poet rising up against the forces of light, and still others.
Freud's Miltonic sources are clear. *Flectere si nequeo superos, Acheronta
movebo,* a line from Virgil, is the epigraph to his proudest book, *The Interpretation of Dreams:* "If I cannot weave the heavens, I will shake hell." The

60. See Edgar Allan Poe, "The Murders in the Rue Morgue" (1841), in *Complete Stories and
Poems of Edgar Allan* Poe (Garden City, N.Y.: Doubleday, 1966), 2–26

61. As brilliantly treated in Carlo Ginzburg, "Clues: Roots of an Evidential Paradigm," in
Myths, Emblems, Clues, trans. John and Anne C. Tedeschi (London: Hutchinson Radius, 1990),
96–125, 200–214.

62. *The Complete Sherlock Holmes,* 1: 90, 157, 214, 317.

discovery of the unconscious involves the formula of Satanic gleeful resentment. He provides another statement of the art of abyss-redemption: "Indeed, even the museum of human excrement could be given an interpretation to rejoice my heart."[63] Freud could look at anything without losing heart and took great pride in this. At the end of his life at least, he had no positive answer to give, since all such answers merely consist of further illusions. In a friendly reading, his answer is like Nietzsche's: the implied command to be strong, to have immense fortitudes on tap, to sup with the gods and race with their adrenalin on the good days, and do your level best not to be too big a schmuck on the others. Freud said fate would do a better job of saving neurotics from their misery, but the power to bend fate is not ours. So we move what we can: not heaven or hell, but our willingness to take responsibility for our pasts. His Stoic passivity is clear in his contention that the analyst must bear the negative transference bravely and refuse to exploit the positive transference, that is, the analyst had to know how to not take the patient's accusations or attractions personally. Freud had enough continuity with the ancients not to think the way out of hell was easy.

If one mark of the modern liberal is to not shrink before the productions of hell, Freud belongs to this select bunch. More than Virchow or Holmes, Freud is a liberal archetype in his tell-all-ism, his faith in the fruits of analysis and the "liberation" of the hidden, and his fondness for parading in public with the creatures he has met while scuba-diving. Freud practices liberal irony. His refusal to take a moral stance implies a certain kind of higher morality—like that of either of the Holmeses, the morality of renouncing the hankering for a higher morality. The idea that life has a purpose, he argues in *Civilization and Its Discontents* (1929), is a quintessentially religious idea. He criticizes the notion that the universe was made especially for our satisfaction as a kind of presumptuousness. For Freud it is not only civilization that creates misery; nature itself does so. (Ancient Stoics sought to harmonize with nature; modern Stoics wean themselves of the idea that nature cares for them; both seek to undercut the ego.) "One feels inclined to say that the intention that man should be 'happy' is not included in the plan of 'Creation.'"[64] Of course to say so presupposes a fairly privileged grasp of Creation (or "Creation"). Freud refuses to ask the purpose of life, leaving those of us interested in that question dangling. The fortitude to live with-

63. Sigmund Freud, *The Interpretation of Dreams*, in *The Standard Edition of the Complete Works of Sigmund Freud*, ed. James Strachey et al. 24 vols. (London: Hogarth Press, 1953–74), 5: 469.

64. Sigmund Freud, *Civilization and Its Discontents*, trans. Joan Riviere (New York: Norton, 1930), 25.

out an answer is, of course, his answer. His rhetorical stance is that of an anatomist who sees the dirty truth but refuses to prettify it for the demands of lesser men who long for comfort and reassurance. Impassivity before pathology is his model. Sharing with the American and British Holmeses a scorn for tenderness, he takes comfort as a proof of weakness, of not having the stomach for science: "Thus I have not the courage to rise up before my fellow-men as a prophet, and I bow to their reproach that I can offer them no consolation: for at bottom that is what they are all demanding—the wildest revolutionaries no less passionately than the most virtuous believers."[65] What prophet admits to being a prophet? They all deny it; reluctance is part of the job description. His image is archetypal. Comfort-seeking hordes reproach the solitary voice in the wilderness for refusing to cater to their demands. Thus Moses scolds the children of Israel fed up with an exclusive diet of manna: cannot you see the higher law, something better than fish, pickles, and watermelons? Freud portrays himself precisely as that which he refuses. He enacts the classic gesture of prophetic critique by denying it.[66] (Poor Freud: he gave his readers the tools they ever use against him, as I just did.) He is a prophet whose message is that there can be no prophets.

WAYS TO REHEARSE DEATH

Virchow, Holmes, and Freud are *typoi* or *figurae* who embody one particular attitude about how to cope with morbidity. They descend from the Aristotelian confidence that exposure to painful sights can have a medicinal value.[67] They are sources for the notion that scholars and citizens alike deserve to be professionally tough-minded, and that the suspension of tender feelings is a good thing. But all three also reveal chinks in the Stoic armor. Any effort to revive Stoic elements as a basis of public life will have to deal with the bottled fetuses, bruised cadavers, and excremental museums that its advocates propose as material for raising the soul to transcendence. Toughness traditionally involves scoffing at death, and Virchow, Holmes, and Freud deal daily in their various ways with death. The moral claim of social science as a set of disciplined methods of knowing ultimately lies in its

65. Freud, *Civilization*, 111.

66. Freud's complex relationship to the great lawgiver is well known. In his 1914 essay on the Moses of Michelangelo, *Standard Edition*, 13: 213, Freud places himself among the horde who wish to be delivered back to their idols and illusions. See Jean-Joseph Goux, *Les iconoclastes* (Paris: Seuil, 1978).

67. On Aristotle and catharsis, see chap. 6.

lessons about death. (Obviously there is a huge moral gulf between rehearsing your own death and rehearsing that of your neighbor.) Such existential or morbid topics rarely show up on the explicit agenda, but they are part of the deep meaning of social research—including of statistical method.

Statistics at first were observations about regular patterns among births, marriages, crimes, and deaths. Statistics, as the name implies, had to do with numerical indexes of the state. Statistical knowledge reveals patterns in populations, not data about individuals. In the eighteenth century, the era that saw the earliest discoveries of aggregate regularities, Kant was one of the first to consider the philosophical significance of statistics. The ability to see the human race *"non singulorum, sed universorum"* (not as individuals, but as a species) put us, he thought, in the god's-eye view of a spectator of the drama of world history. The philosopher can discern a design in the drama that is hidden from the actors.[68] History involves dramatic irony, the spectators knowing more about fate than the characters do. The statistical leitmotif in Kant is particularly clear in his 1785 essay, "Idea for a Universal History with Cosmopolitan Intent." The annual statistics of large nations reveal regularities in the patterns of marriages, births, and deaths. Though these mark the most critical and personal events in anyone's life taken singly, they aggregate into patterns, just as the weather, though erratic from day to day, keeps the rivers flowing and the plants nourished. The "confused and fortuitous" actions of people add up, if taken "on a large scale," to an order imperceptible to individuals. "Individual men and even entire nations little imagine that, while they are pursuing their own ends, each in his own way and often in opposition to others, they are unwittingly guided in their advance along a course intended by nature."[69] (Kant's Stoic vision of nature is more classical than Freud's.) In our private choices we unwittingly promote something else. Kant's name for the large-scale view of statistical order in history is providence. He offers a version of the symphony usually thought to be conducted by Adam Smith's invisible hand: order emergent from the cumulative blind interests of individuals.

The great events of an individual life are, seen statistically, error variance. What better way to teach the puniness of the ego! Death as a horizon or end point of each of our lives is doubtless a significant definer of our being and experience, but *sub specie aeternitatis* there are only statistics. For me that

68. Immanuel Kant, "The Contest of the Faculties" (1798), in *Kant's Political Writings*, ed. Hans Reiss (Cambridge: Cambridge University Press, 1970), 184. My take on Kant is derivative of Hannah Arendt, *Lectures on Kant's Political Philosophy*, ed. Ronald Beiner (Chicago: University of Chicago Press, 1982).

69. Immanuel Kant, "Idea for a Universal History" (1785), in *Kant's Political Writings*, 41.

traffic accident may change my life forever; for the insurance company it was an actuarial risk. Statistics ignore individual fates. *War and Peace* gives a different view of Napoleon's campaign in Russia than Minard's famous graphic of the same, which represents the disastrous attrition of the French army over both time and space with an ingenious image and accompanying numbers.[70] Novels focus on individual life-and-death stories; Minard's graphic impassively portrays six hundred thousand deaths. Emerson noted "the terrible tabulation of the French statists" (statisticians), which "brings every piece of whim and humour to be reducible also to exact numerical ratios."[71] Why are statistics "terrible"? Why did Galton mock people horrified at statistics? Statistical thinking chastens possessiveness, the ego's attachments, in an almost Augustinian way: taming the temptation to love the wrong things. It has a soupçon of callousness and is actively designed to desentimentalize, to banish the pathetic fallacy that nature mirrors mind or psyche mimics physics. Its moral force lies in the claim to see life cold, without reference to the mortal-size units in which experience is normally parceled out. In acknowledging only aggregate patterns, knowledge of which requires evidence and not experience, social scientists look on with Olympian abstraction. Statistics confirm the finitude of our epistemological apparatus and the faultiness of our senses. "There are heights of the soul from which even tragedy ceases to look tragic."[72]

It is not only figures such as Kant, Emerson, Tolstoy, and Pearson who find something chilly and sublime about statistics. That statistical reasoning takes us beyond the bias of the subjective point of view is central to the very influential social psychology of the late Amos Tversky and the Nobel laureate Daniel Kahneman, who show how rarely people interpret events objectively. We experience life as meaningful, however erroneously. With a dourness worthy of a Thucydides, Tversky and Kahneman observe that "the human condition is such, that by chance alone, one is most often rewarded for punishing others and most often punished for rewarding them."[73] Regression toward the mean predicts that superb performances tend to be fol-

70. Etienne-Jules Marey, *La méthode graphique dans les sciences experimentales et principalement en physiologie et en médecine* (Paris: Masson, 1878), 72; compare Edward R. Tufte, *The Visual Display of Quantitative Information* (Cheshire, Conn.: Graphics Press, 1983).

71. Ralph Waldo Emerson, "Swedenborg, or The Mystic" (1850), in *Representative Men: Seven Lectures,* ed. Andrew Delblanco (Cambridge, Mass.: Harvard University Press, 1996), 62. Presumably Emerson was referring to Quetelet who, though often mistaken for a Frenchman, was, like Hercule Poirot, actually a Belgian.

72. Friedrich Nietzsche, *Beyond Good and Evil* (1886), trans. Walter Kaufmann (New York, Vintage, 1984), secs.30, 42.

73. Amos Tversky and Daniel Kahneman, "Judgment Under Uncertainty: Heuristics and Bi-

lowed by more mediocre ones, just as lousy performances tend to be followed by better ones. But people tend not to recognize this tendency of
events to cluster around the center. Good performances invite praise, but
the odds are that the next round will be worse. The difference between each
performance might have nothing to do with our praise or blame, just the
tendency of events to bounce. Few people recognize the autonomy of events
from their own willings and doings. If we confuse cause (regression) and effect (our acts), we are caught in the irrational mess of ordinary cognition,
praising and blaming the wrong things. Like the ancient tragedians, Tversky and Kahneman anatomize the human failure to recognize workings
outside our control; like the Stoics, they advance a recipe for soul purifica-
tion; like the modern friends of method, they find in statistics and social science a model of the discipline that helps us fight our hubris.

Tversky and Kahneman valorize statistical social science, properly conceived, as the normative model of cognition. Everyday thinking for them,
no less than for Hobbes and Locke, turns on infatuation with our opinions.
The quotidian cognitive mistakes Tversky and Kahneman study—illusory
correlation, sampling error, overconfidence—are also classic errors in data
analysis. Ordinary cognition for them is like sloppy social science. Humans
consistently (and mistakenly) believe that there is justice in the world and
strenuously search for order. Blessed are they, however, who remember that
meaningfulness lies only in the aggregate. The tendency on the part of both
citizens and scientists to be overconfident in insufficient samples even
provokes a little joke: "Fortunately such a conviction is not a sufficient condition for a journal publication, although it may do for a book."[74] Cognitive
virtues, specifically of self-sacrifice in the realm of opinion, Tversky and
Kahneman tie to the literary genre par excellence of the quantitative social
scientist—the peer-reviewed article, a genre whose task it is to remove the
potential sources of bias and to impose a collective check (via the replication
of results) on knowledge claims. Kahneman and Tversky's norm of good
cognition turns out to be social science, renouncing opinions that lack evidence, under the constant check of peers, and with a rational orientation to
the universe that acknowledges the relative insignificance of the individual.

Statistics laugh at death. They offer the ultimate in Stoic distance. From
their height no tragedy looks tragic any more, as in Stalin's chilly dictum,

ases," in *Judgment Under Uncertainty: Heuristics and Biases*, ed Daniel Kahneman, Paul Slovic,
and Amos Tversky (Cambridge: Cambridge University Press, 1982), 9, 11.

74. Amos Tversky and Daniel Kahneman, "Belief in the Law of Small Numbers," in *Judgment
Under Uncertainty*, 24, 25

"one death is a tragedy, a million deaths is a statistic." Pearson and his older contemporary Peirce both knew the importance of death to statistical thinking. In his 1897 essay, "The Chances of Death," Pearson compared the medieval dance of death with the modern sense. Reviewing several fifteenth- and sixteenth-century paintings, he notes: "The shadow of death, more strongly even than blood or nation, maketh mankind kin; it arouses sympathy and understanding, which surmount all the barriers of caste and nation. The old Dances of Death supplied what fails so much in our modern life—an artistic representation appealing to all classes of at least one experience common to the whole of humanity." He even tried, with only partial success, to get an artist to depict his conception: a thousand people crossing the bridge of life while death stochastically picks them off, taking about a hundred years to finish off the whole cohort. "Our conception of chance is one of law and order in large numbers; it is not that idea of chaotic incidence which vexed the mediaeval mind. . . . Artistically, we no longer think of Death as striking chaotically; we regard his aim as perfectly regular in the mass, if unpredictable in the individual instance."[75] Like Maxwell's gases, Pearson's death makes no personal inquiries. The most intimate acts in life—birth, marriage, crime, voting, death—can all be predicted en masse. Human experience (which is always confined to individuals) and data (en masse) are at odds. Statistics brings out the two sides of personhood, the unique and the abstract.

Peirce in turn saw the gap between individual experience and statistical pattern as a sampling problem. Dramatic turns in our personal histories may be, statistically speaking, random perturbations. Viewed *sub specie statisticarum*, life's turning points may be cosmic commotion. Life experiences are, in a sense, artifacts of insufficient sampling. If we were truly logical creatures, Peirce claimed, we would not be seduced by the illusions of selfhood; via statistical revelation of the social whole, we would see that others have as much claim to goods and recognition as we do. Seeing our insistently private needs in the light of the community would diminish their pull (an optimism he shared with Kant and Smith).[76] Statistical discipline teaches us to place the other before the self. As Mary Douglas quipped in a book review some years back, Peirce offers us faith, hope, and probability.[77] Probabilistic indifference to the individual schools us in ego-deflation. And

75. Pearson, "The Chances of Death," 8, 15, 39.

76. Charles Sanders Peirce, "The Doctrine of Chances," in *Chance, Love, and Logic*, ed. Morris R. Cohen (Lincoln: University of Nebraska Press, 1998), 73–75.

77. Mary Douglas, "Faith, Hope, and Probability," *Times Literary Supplement*, 13.10 (23 May 1991): 6–8.

yet experience comes only in individual-sized, lifetime-long chunks. The tendency to be more sanguine than experience would give us reason to be is not a cognitive defect, but a result of the finite units of measurement allotted to mortals. Because we are finite our experience of fortune is guaranteed not to be as disastrous as an eternal experience of chance would prove to be: "death makes the number of our risks, of our inferences, finite, and so makes their mean result uncertain." Finitude bars us from ever getting an adequate sample of reality—a fact that has both scientific and political import. "If man were immortal he could be perfectly sure of seeing the day when everything in which he trusted should betray his trust, and, in short, of coming eventually to hopeless misery. He would break down, at last, as every good fortune, as every dynasty, as every civilization does. In place of this we have death."[78] Peirce's brilliant counterintuitive insight is that death is the ground of our hope. If we lived forever, we would be certain of being ruined; sooner or later we would inevitably hit that patch of bad luck that would wreck everything. Our inevitably small sample sizes may limit us from ever seeing the whole; but they also liberate us from the inevitability of catastrophe. Streaks of good or bad luck allow us enough pattern to make some narrative sense of our lives precisely because the sampling frame is finite. The meaningfulness of life stems from its restriction to nonrandom scales of experience. Our brief life spans guarantee us a favorably skewed apprehension of the universe's meaningfulness.

Like his friend and supporter William James, Peirce is both tender-minded and tough-minded. For Peirce our need for self-transcendence calls for statistics; our limits call for stories. Finite experience yields a limited harvest of reality, and statistics challenges the egocentric predicament. Because of our small sample sizes, all knowledge is necessarily probabilistic, an experimental grip on an ever-evolving world. Like his fellow pragmatists Dewey and Mead, Peirce considered scientific method an almost complete code of ethics—intersubjectivity, publicity, open-endedness, and self-discipline. Getting the method of inquiry right for him was not simply a question of accurate knowledge but a matter of ordering the relationships among inquirers. Methods are social practices, means of forming good communities, not just tools for poking at reality; ultimately, they are the laws by which the universe grows. Peirce transcends the old fight between qualitative narrative and quantitative rigor in the social sciences. There is no reason to be absolutist about either aggregated data or novelistic narrative as research methods. The tension between qualitative and quantitative

78. Peirce, "The Doctrine of Chances," 72.

methods reflects the contradiction between the impersonal and personal faces of democracy, the moral need to both respect and transcend our finitude. Scholars who defend storytelling as prima facie a more sensitive and humane mode of analysis than counting see in numbers only cruelty and none of their austere beauty. And yet any sober survey of storytelling in both everyday talk and the arts would reveal that most stories are formulaic. Stories can and should fudge details—not telling all is a virtue. Stories compress characters and events, and statistics reveal patterns we would have missed otherwise. Their key difference lies at another level: in the approach to death. Stories teach us to mourn, and statistics teach us to see impersonal order. (Such intuitions abound among social scientists who have never heard of Peirce or know Pearson only for his "r.") Stories teach the ethic of caring, statistics the ethic of not caring. Statistical thinking is a methodological Buddhism. In this, the empirical social sciences are one of the varieties of modern moral suspension. They have contributed to the making of a soul that is calm before morbidity, tolerant with difference, and flustered by views whose sources lie deeper than doubt.[79]

79. This chapter is dedicated to the memory of two teachers of mine, Merrill Carlsmith and Steve Chaffee.

CHAPTER SIX

"Watch, Therefore": Suffering and the Informed Citizen

Watch, therefore, for you know neither the day nor the hour.
—Matthew 25:13

In some terrible way, modern media and modern warfare are bound up with each other. Both are means of multiplying, distorting, and dispersing bodies, of turning people into ghosts. Guns shoot and make people dead; the camera shoots and makes people immortal. Milton and Mill once had great confidence in partaking freely of every tree of knowledge, but what are we to do in an era in which exposure and information are much less likely to lead to a happy ending of intellectual or moral redemption? To be informed about the wider world today means to be acquainted, among other things, with the endless variety of ways in which the human body can die. The maxim gun, modern surgical techniques, trench warfare, psychoanalysis, modernist literature, photojournalism, the Holocaust, Hiroshima, Hollywood, the porn industry, satellites, cable TV, free speech law, computer games, the internet, and genocide are some of the things that have conspired to make depictions of the body in pieces part of the background noise of everyday life in the modern world.

To be sure, violence is nothing new. The vengeance-fest in book 22 of Homer's *Odyssey* set a high standard for glorious mayhem, as did the biblical book of *Judges*. The Hindu goddess Kali with her necklace of bloody skulls beats almost anything found in the movies. The Roman circus probably practiced every imaginable variant of butchery on human or animal bodies, and the Aztec temples, according to the conquistadores, were caked with layers of coagulated blood up to several feet thick. There is a threshold in gruesomeness and revulsion that was probably already attained historically with stones and clubs, and institutionalized in the butcher's, soldier's, priest's, and doctor's arts. Death is death, and it has always been unspeakably interesting.

It is extremely difficult to get a historical fix on the intensity of representations of violence and suffering, in part because the culture industries feed on a rhetoric of progressively broken taboos and hence tend to distort measures of comparative standards. It is not only outraged critics who like to think of frontiers never before transgressed. Shock always seems terribly new. Responsibility to the pain of others, in turn, is very old in the ethical traditions of humanity. And yet at least one thing does seem new today: constantly updated global news of suffering in word, sound, and image. How to square the new informatics of suffering with the old ethics of engagement? What is our responsibility to distant and local suffering? When, if ever, is it just to shut our eyes to the misery of the world? How do we cope with the almost spastic spotlight of global attention to disaster provided by the news media—floods in Bangladesh today, earthquakes in Iran yesterday, slaughter in the Congo tomorrow? Is failure to know always a failure of responsibility? Are ethical filters ever justified? If we may never legitimately shut our eyes, we risk being blackmailed into withholding judgment on the tawdry stuff served up by the culture industries (including the news business). The suspended judgment praised by judges and social scientists is a wonderful guide for treating other people's art and words, but it does not help us decide how to parcel out our own brief seconds on earth, where action and choice are always urgent.

The norm of the informed citizen may once have meant the duty of citizens to arm themselves with facts and reasons that prepared them to take intelligent part in political life.[1] But the Holocaust and related atrocities have forever changed the meaning of the term. The question of what citizens know is no longer only a question of information-budgets but also one of complicity in crime. A tour of the Nazi death camps by German civilians in 1945 occasioned the century's most famous denial, *wir haben es nicht gewusst*, we didn't know, a claim that has continued to signal the potential evil of a citizenry who actively or passively chooses not to know. The question of what the Germans knew is not simply whether they read the papers but the extent of their willing collaboration with the extermination of their

---

1. Perhaps the classic theorist of the civic duty of information is Walter Lippmann. See, for example, *Liberty and the News* (New York: Harcourt, Brace & Howe, 1920); and *Public Opinion* (New York: Macmillan, 1922).

neighbors. The norm of information is inevitably tied to participation: in the act of knowing people become witnesses and thereby in some way responsible for the things they know. It is also tied to exposure. Yet to keep up with the news is to risk moral and emotional callousness, since the range and extent of misery we know about will always outstrip the misery we can relieve, let alone feel bad about or pay attention to. Most of us ignore news on a daily basis of people near and far who could somehow benefit from our aid. A few seconds of exposure can theoretically obligate us to hours, days, months, or years of action. But a single television news broadcast contains many such stories. How do we reconcile such grand awareness with such puny action? In the news tragedy and banality nestle side by side as if collaged by some perverse god with a cruel sense of humor.[2] Curiously, most outrage about depictions of violence has to do with imaginary mayhem in comics, film, television, and computer games rather than with violence against actual people. Civil libertarians typically argue that knowledge is worth the sacrifice of tenderness, and that exposure to sickening scenes and sounds is the side effect of living responsibly in the world. Liberals make exposure to blood and guts an integral part of the crusade for global justice; for them, to flip the off-switch is a cop-out or retreat. In this view serenity is cowardice.

Exposure to suffering is an excellent test case for the notion, so central to the liberal project, that consorting with the dark can be ethically inspiring. Historically there are three main justifications for the civic act of looking upon suffering: catharsis, compassion, and courage.

CATHARSIS

Aristotle's *Poetics* stands at the beginning of a long debate about how to understand the human fascination for scenes of pain. Whatever "catharsis" precisely means, Aristotle provides an influential account of the beneficial effects of viewing staged sorrow. The ethical problem of tragedy is why people enjoy seeing things that would terrify or disgust them in real life: "we enjoy beholding the most accurate images of things which are themselves grievous to see, such as the shapes of dishonorable beasts and corpses." Since sights arouse pain, the puzzle of tragedy is the strange pleasure spectators take in things abhorrent to the eye or heart. Our attraction to the repellent, says Aristotle, stems from our inbuilt gift for mimesis and our ca-

---

2. One classic example is the ending of John Cheever, "The Enormous Radio," in *The Enormous Radio and Other Stories* (New York: Funk & Wagnalls, 1953).

pacity to recognize the universal truths that it is poetry's distinct office to provide. History, in contrast, delivers only particulars. Mimesis transfigures what normally incites disgust or terror. As Medea kills her children or Oedipus blinds himself we can find justice within carnage. Mayhem somehow reveals truth. Pain is the distinctive feature of tragedy. Comedy, in contrast, is marked by laughter, and "the laughable comprises any fault or mark of shame which involves no pain or destruction."[3] In tragedy pain is not supposed to excite spectators' identification with the victim, but to take spectators to a more barren place where representation clarifies what is possible in life. Terror (*phobos*) and pity (*eleos*) are homeopathic juices, medicinal in small doses, that stir the soul to reflection and clear it of passions. In contrast to the idea that exposure stimulates action, Aristotle's spectator is not moved to violence; the purgation is subtler and serves the public weal. Thus Aristotle answers Plato's attack in the *Republic* against art as an anti-civic distraction. Drama is useful to the polis, giving citizens a chance to vent, a psychic safety valve for public health. "Poets," as William Fyfe quips in his introduction to Aristotle's *Poetics*, "must be recalled from exile to serve as medical officers."[4]

Though no Aristotelian, David Hume was a subtle analyst of the play of the passions in tragedy, as always. He noted the odd fact that spectators of tragedy "are pleased in proportion as they are afflicted" and concluded that their delight stems from a subterranean negation of the reality of the play. "A certain idea of falsehood" lurking at the bottom of our experience sustains the combination of passions characteristic of tragedy. "It is certain, that the same object of distress, which pleases in a tragedy, were it really set before us, would give the most unfeigned uneasiness." The dramatic theater, like the operating theater, is a special zone in which we neutralize the ethical demands of pain and modulate its intensities for the sake of experiment or cure. Real distress calls for our aid, not our imagination. Fiction, in contrast, somehow releases us from the duty of commiseration. The acute pleasure of theatrical tragedy depends on the inner reminder that it is all artifice, that the suffering we see—though plausible and surely felt by someone in history somewhere and perhaps even by some contemporary now on some part of the globe—is a representation. Awareness of artifice comforts our tender nerves. "The agreeable sentiment of affection here acquires force from senti-

3. Aristotle, *Poetics* (Cambridge, Mass.: Harvard University Press, 1995), ed. Stephen Halliwell, 1488b9–12, 1449a33–35.

4. William Hamilton Fyfe, introduction to Aristotle, *Poetics* (New York: Putnam, 1927), xvii.

ments of uneasiness."[5] Hume offers an oppositional economics of the passions: you need musk to sniff sweetness. Reality is morally compulsive; it lacks the blessing of negation. Yet the feeling of unreality in a play must stay subterranean because it would otherwise ruin the pleasurable suspension. The effect depends on the threat of reality that stems from our postponed skepticism. Fact is not as emotionally complex as fiction. For Hume, seeing a tragedy was not morally dangerous (as Rousseau, for instance, thought). But it was not an exercise in callousness or brute fascination, either; it was an exercise rather in the strange balance of our passions. Hume's analysis gives us a picture of the liberal soul, able to hold two feelings at once. Psychoanalysis, later, would bulldoze such delicate analyses as mental gymnastics designed to shield ourselves from the simple fact that we enjoy cruelty. Like Paul, however, Hume sees in double-mindedness more than a simple lie: it is the condition for complete moral and emotional judgments.

As we saw with Milton, the Renaissance gave a new visibility to the inner organs and retreated from the long-standing compunction about prying into the body's secrets.[6] Vesalius's 1543 anatomical atlas, *De humani corporis fabricā,* whose engravings of classically posed corpses expose their muscles and organs underneath flayed skin, is a landmark in the history of anatomical illustration. Renaissance humanists like Hamlet found edification in skulls, skeletons, and graveyards. A favorite genre was the "vanitas," an arrangement of worldly objects that proclaimed *sic transit gloria mundi.* The Amsterdam collector Frederic Ruysch, for instance, made a *vanitas* statue of fetal skeletons, kidney stones, and a hardened vas deferens.[7] William Harvey, in his preparatory studies for *De Motu Cordis et Sanguinis* (1628) on the two-way circulation of the blood, performed autopsies on both his father and his sister in a remarkable bit of sangfroid. The tradition of the pathological museum, which arranged human bodies and other wonders of nature into pedagogical spectacles, goes back to the Leiden Theatrum Anatomicum, founded in 1594.[8] The particular interest of Netherlanders in

5. David Hume, "Of Tragedy," in *Essays: Moral, Political, and Literary.* Rev. ed. (Indianapolis: Liberty Fund, 1987), 216–25.

6. For example, Augustine, *The City of God* (Cambridge: Cambridge University Press, 1998), 1163 (22.24).

7. Lorraine Daston and Katharine Park, *Wonders and the Order of Nature, 1150–1750* (New York: Zone Books, 1998), chap. 2.

8. Tim Huisman, *Een theater voor de anatomie: Het Leidse theatrum anatomicum, 1594–1821* (Leiden: Museum Boerhaave, 2002). See also Lawrence Weschler, *Mr. Wilson's Cabinet of Wonder* (New York: Pantheon, 1995), 84–89.

dissection (Vesalius was the Latin name for Wessels, a Fleming) is taken up famously in Rembrandt's painting *The Anatomy Lesson of Dr. Tulp* (1632). Nowhere is the age-old quandary of what to do with your eyes when you come near a corpse better illustrated: as the doctor wields his knife, five of the student observers seem to studiously avoid looking at the body on the table, while the other two stare, transfixed, at the bloody goings-on.[9]

From Aristotle to Rembrandt to Virchow to Francis Moore (a key innovator in twentieth-century surgery), medicine teaches a strategic callousness. As William Hunter, one of the first great British anatomists, explained in his lectures at the Royal Academy of Art in London, "Anatomy is the Basis of Surgery, it informs the Head, guides the hand, and familiarizes the Heart to a kind of necessary Inhumanity."[10] In his "Course of Anatomical and Chirurgical Lectures," he reviewed methods of dealing with cadavers: "Macerating, Boiling, Injecting, Corroding, etc."[11] Hunter and his brother John were the most influential anatomists in eighteenth-century Britain. John had a collection of anatomical specimens, human and animal, healthy and pathological, which he formed as a museum of some 13,000 items; many are still on view in the Hunterian Museum in the Royal College of Surgeons, London, one of the more important examples of the late-eighteenth-century emergence of the morbid anatomy museum, the respectable twin to the wax museum. Both institutions have a common origin in anatomical display. Mme Tussaud's father was one of many eighteenth-century medical doctors who excelled in the art of anatomical modeling to compensate for a scarcity of cadavers for dissection. She claims she learned her art by producing death masks from the plentiful heads made available by the French revolution, an untrustworthy claim meant to provide a lofty lineage for her palace of macabre effigies. Her museum's chamber of horrors has the guillotine as its historical *a priori*. Writing a history of the display of the body-in-pieces surpasses my resources, but objectivity, understood as the imperative to hold disgust for the sake of education, clearly derives in part from the contemplation of corpses. What death is to statistics, pathology is to medicine: a device for teaching us self-abstraction. How curious that the depiction of the highest cognitive achievements in the Eu-

9. For the cultural and art-historical context of Dutch dissection, see Norbert Middelkoop, *De Anatomische Les van Dr. Deijman* (Amsterdam: Amsterdams Historisch Museum, 1994); on this painting, see p. 6.

10. Quoted in Ruth Richardson, *Death, Dissection, and the Destitute* (London: Penguin, 1988), 30–31.

11. Quoted from manuscript on display, March 2000, Science Museum, London.

ropean tradition often refers to sundered and putrefying bodies that we are supposed to behold with a transcendent philosophical eye.[12]

The conquering Allies in 1945 forced German civilians to view the corpses in the camps and in photographs, as if the act of looking alone would administer some kind of chastisement—a policy ordered by Eisenhower himself. Journalists facing the task of reporting the death camps took tropes from the objectivity of the professions, especially medicine, to explain their jobs to themselves and their publics. A Reuters journalist who toured the camps in April 1945 after their liberation by the Allies cautioned that his testimony "would offend public morality if given in any other form than a medical report."[13] During a 1945 broadcast Edward R. Murrow said, "If I have offended you by this rather mild account of Buchenwald, I am not in the least sorry."[14] He saw himself in the tradition of providing a necessary offense. George Rodger, a British photographer who shot images of Belsen, said: "the world must know the pits of such depravity to ensure that they are never descended to again."[15] Something of this confidence shows up more recently in the comment of Martin Bell, a former BBC war correspondent, that graphic war imagery needs to be shown so that citizens can be "battle-softened": "people have to be left with *some* sense of what happened, if only through the inclusion of pictures sufficiently powerful at least to hint at the horror of those excluded. . . . We [journalists] should flinch less. We should sometimes be willing to shock and to disturb."[16] The project of exposing the citizenry to trauma—whether as punishment (for the occupying Allies in Germany), as witness and memorial (for Holocaust activists), or as civic instruction (for reporters)—rests upon the confidence that exposure to violence brings health rather than disease. Whether we will greet such exposure with activism, cynicism, or pleasure is a hard question.

12. G. W. Hegel, for example, treats philosophical achievement as an anatomy lesson in *Phänomenologie des Geistes* (Hamburg: Meiner, 1952), paras. 32–33.

13. Quoted in Barbie Zelizer, *Remembering to Forget: Holocaust Memory Through the Camera's Eye* (Chicago: University of Chicago Press, 1998), 84.

14. Quoted in Tony Kushner, *The Holocaust and the Liberal Imagination: A Social and Cultural History* (Oxford: Blackwell, 1994), 214.

15. Quoted in Zelizer, *Remembering to Forget*, 211.

16. Martin Bell, "The Journalism of Attachment," in *Media Ethics*, ed. Matthew Kieran (London: Routledge, 1998), 20, 21. Emphasis in the original. See also Susan Sontag, *Regarding the Pain of Others* (New York: Farrar, Straus, Giroux, 2003).

COMPASSION

A second, and less confident, answer about the human delight in corpses and strange beasts has been most strongly developed in the Christian tradition, though it has deeper roots in Jewish and Greek thought. The notion that suffering can be redeemed through a moral meta-narrative is rooted in Christianity's martyr complex and specifically its ultimate martyrdom, the crucifixion. That scenes of suffering should arouse compassion for the victim or outrage at the perpetrator is central to the history of western art from Cimabue to Francis Bacon to Mel Gibson's film *The Passion of the Christ* (2004). Pain, in this view, must bear a moral witness, not present an aesthetic spectacle (although it always veers close to it). This is also a political-moral claim. Depictions of the crucifixion are not supposed to tickle the palate but are meant to turn the soul and excite devotion. Its constellation—sight of trauma, moral response from beholder—is alive and well in today's politics of pity, however secularized.[17]

Christian devotion can be remarkably gory, exulting in blood every bit as much as Sherlock Holmes. One key source is the medieval culture of personal identification with the sufferings of Christ, which is connected with the fresh interest in the theological meaning of Christ's suffering by thinkers such as Anselm and Abelard, and in Abelard's persecutor, Bernard of Clairvaux, "the most respected and influential churchman of the twelfth century."[18] "For what," asked Bernard, "can be so effective a cure for the wounded conscience and so purifying to keenness of mind as steady meditation on the wounds of Christ?"[19] In late medieval devotional art, literature, and spiritual practice (if these can even be separated in that period), the contemplation of Christ's wounds was supposed to serve as a homeopathic cure for the heart's wounds. Especially in the German tradition, Christ's wounds and splattered blood are emphasized—a gory sensibility that reaches an apex in a seventeenth-century German printmaker's nearly pornographic close-up images of Christ's wounds and the bloody nails and spear that inflicted them.[20] Here the sublime and the accursed nestle to-

17. Lilie Chouliaraki's forthcoming work on global proximity is of interest in this connection.

18. Edward Peters, *Inquisition* (Berkeley: University of California Press, 1988), 42.

19. Sermon 62 on the Song of Songs, in *Bernard of Clairvaux: Selected Writings*, trans. G. R. Evans (New York: Paulist Press, 1987), 250–51.

20. *Seeing Salvation: Images of Christ in Art*, ed. Neil MacGregor (New Haven, Conn.: Yale University Press, 2000).

gether, the triumphant spirit and the uncanny cadaver: what Durkheim called the pure and impure faces of the sacred.[21]

Medieval devotion invents many of the images of public mourning and trauma still with us. Vietnam war photography, for instance, drew upon representations of suffering from the Judeo-Christian tradition such as the Pietà (mother with dead or wounded child), the Exodus (the people of God fleeing Pharaoh's armies), and the Passion (the innocent victim moving all humanity with his or her pain).[22] Yet the Pietà—the depiction of Mary with the wounded body of Christ after its removal from the cross—is a pure invention of the fourteenth century; it has no basis in the text of any of the four Gospels. (The word pity, derived ultimately from the Latin *pietas,* or "piety," emerges from this context.). The notion that contemplating the Savior's blood and body awakes compassion and purifies the mind is one wellspring of the notion that viewing trauma can be edifying. J. S. Bach wrote a hymn adoring a sacred wounded head and closed his *Saint Matthew Passion* with a graveside lullaby to the torn limbs of Christ. In this, he was in the mainstream of German Christianity, with its ability to find transcendent meaning in gruesomeness. Much of the history of Christian devotion is shocking to tastes formed in the wake of nineteenth-century sentimentalism. As Julia Kristeva remarks, "One of the insights of Christianity, and not the least one, is to have gathered in a single move perversion and beauty."[23]

A deposit of the mixture of beauty and perversion persists in the modern secular iconography of distant pain. Central to reformist culture since the late eighteenth century is the vivid, sometimes prurient depiction of other people suffering.[24] Philanthropic mobilization of care for distant wretchedness exploded in nineteenth-century Europe and America, especially in efforts to abolish slavery and form Christian missionary societies. Slaves, women, "heathen," and animals all became remote objects of pity. Karl Marx, Friedrich Engels, Charles Dickens, Harriet Beecher Stowe, and Victor Hugo depicted the downtrodden near and far. The greatest Dutch novel of the nineteenth century, *Max Havelaar,* denounced colonial policy in the

21. Émile Durkheim, *Les formes élémentaires de la vie religieuse* (1912) (Paris: Presses universitaires de France, 1985), 584–92.

22. Kari Andén-Papadopoulos, *Kameran i krig. Den fotografiska iscensättningen av Vietnamkriget i svensk press* (Stockholm: Brutus Östlings Bokförlag Symposion, 2000), chap. 12.

23. Julia Kristeva, *Powers of Horror,* trans. Leon Roudiez (New York: Columbia University Press, 1982), 125.

24. Karen Halttunen, "Humanitarianism and the Pornography of Pain in Anglo-American Culture," *American Historical Review,* April 1995: 303–34.

East Indies. American social reformers such as Jacob Riis, Lewis Hine, Dorothea Lange, and Walker Evans drew on a venerable iconography of suffering in their journalism and photography. Philanthropists believe in redemptive looking at pain. In confronting a scene of suffering, one is supposed to speak out, bear witness, or ask, What is to be done? Much of the emotional palette and rhetorical armory of progressive politics amounts to a peculiar attitude of looking at images in which delectation, terror, and moral arousal intertwine in curious ways. Humanitarian care and spectacular sorrowful images go together. These are historical structures of feeling that shape our world of images and responses to them.

If modern reformers, like medieval worshippers, believe in the moral benefits of viewed mayhem, some Christian thinkers are nervous about dwelling on the gory details too long, thinking that pain ought not to be interesting for its own sake, but to testify of a higher truth. Augustine had much to say about the ethics of looking—and listening—to the forbidden. Rather than the medical confidence that seeing violence can serve higher ends, he worries about its capacity to incite cruel acts or attitudes. The eye seems the main window for distraction: Curiosity involves a kind of "*concupiscentia oculorum,*" the lust of the eyes.[25] In this Augustine shares with the elite philosophical traditions of Greece and India a suspicion of the sensory swirl. Yet he does not condemn our passion to know and to see, which is moved by our enormous drive to love; the problem is our constant falling in love with the wrong things. Augustine even reports becoming diverted from his devotions by the spectacle of a spider catching flies—rather like someone flipping channels on cable TV. Augustine solidified "the opposition between wholesome wonder and morbid curiosity," an opposition that resounded up to Erasmus, Montaigne, and Pascal and still plays in the background of the twentieth-century critique of the distractions of the mass media.[26] Wholesome wonder acknowledges the greatness of God's creation; morbid curiosity descends into nooks and crannies. The difference for Augustine, as for Milton, lies in the heart of the looker. He doubts the Stoic professional assurance that one may inspect corpses and miracles (*mirabilia*) for pure purposes, scientific or otherwise. He is always attuned to the devious interests that rush in to fill any brief depression of our hearts. For Job the problem of evil was, Why has this happened to me? For Augustine it was, Why am I made this way?

25. Augustine, *Confessions,* book 10, sec. 35.

26. Daston and Park, *Wonders and the Order of Nature,* 306 (also see 122–24 passim); Leo Lowenthal, *Literature and Mass Culture* (New Brunswick, N.J.: Transaction, 1984).

In the *Confessions* Augustine gives two extended examples relevant for the ethics of exposure: the gladiatorial games and the theater. A favorite student named Alypius contracted a passion for the games: "the whirlpool of Carthaginian habits (amongst whom those idle spectacles are hotly followed) had drawn him into the madness of the Circus." Augustine was saddened to see Alypius's virtue sapped and his promise wasted. During a lecture Augustine used a metaphor from the gladiatorial contests, "seasoned with a biting mockery of those whom that madness had enthralled." Alypius, sitting in the audience, took the point as specifically intended for him.[27] Alypius, upon hearing "that speech, burst out of that pit so deep, wherein he was willfully plunged, and was blinded with its wretched pastimes; and he shook his mind with a strong self-command; whereupon the filths of the Circensian pastimes flew off from him, nor came he again thither." Leaving Carthage to study law in Rome, Alypius for a while resisted the temptation of the bigger-and-better games in Rome, until one day some frat-boy fellow students tried to drag him to the circus. He cried out, "Though you hale my body to that place, and there set me, can you force me also to turn my mind or my eyes to those shows? I shall then be absent while present, and so shall overcome both you and them." This boast whetted the appetite of his friends even more, and they carted him off like a reformed drunk to a drinking party. They took their seats, and though the whole stadium was aflame, Alypius, "closing the passages of his eyes, forbade his mind to range abroad after such evils." Unfortunately he forgot to stop his ears. Hearing a shout, Alypius opened his eyes, expecting—perhaps with a cool medical gaze—to look with superior disdain and detachment. But, with something like the inevitability of orgasm, "so soon as he saw that blood, he therewith drunk down savageness; nor turned away, but fixed his eye, drinking in phrenzy, unawares, and was delighted with that guilty fight, and intoxicated with the bloody pastime." He shouted and cheered with the rest, reveling in blood-drunkenness. But there is a happy ending. Alypius would later give up the games for good, and his experience "was already being laid up in his memory to be a medicine hereafter."[28] That memory of sin can be curative describes the modus operandi of the *Confessions* and also shows the difficulty of cleanly separating compassion from catharsis as motives for tolerating violence. The genre of confessions, which teases the reader's prurient

27. We might call this a "for-someone-as-anyone structure." See Paddy Scannell, "For Anyone-as-Someone Structures," *Media, Culture and Society* 22 (2000): 5–24.

28. Augustine, *Confessions*, in *Great Books of the Western World*, ed. Robert Maynard Hutchins (Chicago: Encyclopedia Britannica, 1952), 18: 38–39. (The translation by Pusey is stilted but I rather like it here.)

interests with the ever-postponed promise of juicy revelations, is a variant of Paul's flirtation with daring doctrine. Here again the Christian tradition incubates attitudes of suspended judgment about evil, allowing exposure to trauma for educational purposes. Augustine is ever wary of taking pleasure in the pain of others.

Though it is doubtful that Augustine read Aristotle's *Poetics*, his critique of the theater in chapter 3 of the *Confessions* reads like a direct counterpoint. The theater was one of the habits he says he fell into during his stay in Carthage's "cauldron of lusts." He asks the old question, "Why is it that men enjoy feeling sad at the sight of tragedy and suffering on the stage, although they would be most unhappy if they had to endure the same fate themselves?" Augustine notes the same emotional twist—enjoyment in sorrow—as Hume, but with a deeper pathos, since Augustine takes it as a comment on the perversity of the human heart. The audience is supposed to feel sorrow with the victim, not offer aid, and the better the drama, the more intense the pleasure taken in sorrow. The stage channels our naturally friendly feelings toward our fellow beings into the sewage of lust, a notion, we must remember, that is not exclusively sexual for Augustine. The theater is no escape valve to blow off steam, as it is for Aristotle, but a vehicle for stirring up emotions; spectators are voluntarily "diverted from their true course and deprived of their original heavenly calm." We lust to identify with represented others. Does the theater's frenzy of sympathy mean, Augustine asks, that "we should arm ourselves against compassion?" Augustine hedges on a question to which Emerson, Nietzsche, Arendt, and Foucault in their various ways all answer yes. "There are times when we must welcome sorrow on behalf of others. But for the sake of our souls we must beware of uncleanness." As much as Nietzsche, Augustine thinks pity can be a corruption, both of inner calm and of the opportunity to render genuine succor. False pity brings pleasure to the one who pities and offers little help to the object of pity. Its paradigm is the theater. True pity, he says, causes the pitier pain, not pleasure, and arouses action or aid of some sort. Its paradigm is care.[29]

For Augustine the question in exposure always lies in the receiver's heart. The problem with the theater for him is not that it exposes spectators to vulgar materials but rather that it perverts the moral faculty of care into a source of remote pleasure. Augustine grasps the truth—useful for considering the cascades of images of suffering that the news and mail bring daily—that feelings of sympathy and care are just as subject to manipula-

29. Augustine, *Confessions*, trans. R. S. Pine-Coffin (New York: Penguin, 1961), 55–57.

tion as appetitive and selfish ones. (The very idea that care and sympathy might be something other than appetitive or selfish is perhaps only conceivable in a framework like Augustine's that takes love in the sense of *caritas* seriously.) The classic analysis of media manipulation has centered on desire: the culture industries offer up dream worlds in which all our wishes will be fulfilled. Few have remarked the equal extent to which our capacity for compassion can be toyed with. Our guts can be spun as much as our gonads, heart, or head. Watching or reading the news can be an exercise in Pavlovian compassion. A little hardness—though Augustine is nervous about this expedient—prevents the dagger from hurting afresh every time. Our good parts are as prone to being taken advantage of as our base parts, maybe even more so. Outrage and empathy are chief means of audience manipulation.

Augustine gives reasons both for confident exposure to trauma and for its avoidance. Despite his warnings, he ultimately counsels against hardening. Discussing news of war, he writes: "Let every one, then, who thinks with pain on all these great evils, so horrible, so ruthless, acknowledge that this is misery. And if any one either endures or thinks of them without mental pain, this is a more miserable plight still, for he thinks himself happy because he has lost human feeling." In contrast to the Stoic virtue of implacability, Augustine worries if news of disaster does not evoke a genuine emotional response. A life of care is one of sorrow. "He who will have none of this sadness must, if possible, have no friendly intercourse." To be a sociable creature is to remain vulnerable to the buffetings of grief: "the more friends we have, and the more widely they are scattered, the more numerous are our fears that some portion of the vast masses of the disasters of life may light upon them."[30] Though pity can be manipulated, Augustine would never allow that we can honorably tune out the world's crime and hurt from our consciousness. As long as we have friends, we will be agitated by actualities. (Since the time of Voltaire and Adam Smith, the question has been compassion for distant strangers, not friends.) Looking on sorrow is never a safe adventure in catharsis, but a dangerous excursion into upset and hurt. To be blasé is already to have lost. Augustine recognizes no neutral zones of mere entertainment. Everything seen or heard is tinged with moral and spiritual implication. Augustine authorizes both the abyss-redeemer who ponders lust for lessons about our deep appetite for God and the abyss-avoider who skips inferno and purgatory and goes straight to paradise.

30. Augustine, *De civitate dei*, xix:7–8 (515).

COURAGE

A third answer to the ethics of viewing suffering greets pain as a worthy antagonist, not as medicine to be taken or neighborly woe to be nursed. Pain becomes an occasion for the show of creative strength, an athletic or aesthetic expression of stamina or dedication, of the courage to defy the temptation of pity. The stance has multiple sources. Homeric battle, Dionysian frenzy, Maccabean martyrdom, Stoic tranquility, and Christian asceticism all embrace pain in a variety of ways. Indeed, as historians of pain, including J. S. Mill and Michel Foucault, have noted, it was not until the rise of humanitarian sensibility in the eighteenth century that pain was widely stigmatized as an evil. If there is a platitude of modern life, it is that suffering is both bad and avoidable. People did not always think this way. Achilles was never afraid of physical trauma. Saint Sebastian greeted his tortures with a spirit of exultation (if we believe the paintings).

Friedrich Nietzsche, lover of Greek harshness, admirer of Emerson, and analyst of the sometimes malicious lusts of *Schadenfreude*, is one good choice for a theorist of the athleticism of pain. For Nietzsche neither an Aristotle nor an Augustine takes suffering seriously enough. Both ultimately refuse to come to terms with its brute facticity, making it into something else—medicine for the soul or a spiritual lesson to be recollected in tranquility. "We should reconsider cruelty and open our eyes. We should at long last learn impatience lest such immodest fat errors keep on strutting about virtuously and saucily, as have been fostered about tragedy, for example, by philosophers both ancient and modern. Almost everything we call 'higher culture' is based on the spiritualization of cruelty, on its becoming more profound; this is my proposition. That 'savage animal' has not really been killed off; it lives, flourishes and has only become—divine."[31] In one stroke Nietzsche dispatches Aristotelian and Christian-humanist views of pain. Aristotle's idea that Greek tragedy sublimates bloodlust creates an alibi for the sources of tragedy's "painful voluptuousness," just as Christian "compassion for the other" conceals the delight in both damming the wellsprings of instinct within and lording it over others without. "Pity is the praxis of nihilism."[32] As Nietzsche sees it, we enjoy watching tragedy not because it purges our emotions or teaches us compassion but because we are fascinated by cruelty. Nietzsche at least has the advantage of frankness.

31. Friedrich Nietzsche, *Beyond Good and Evil*, trans. Walter Kaufmann (New York: Vintage, 1966), 158 (sec.229). I have slightly modified Kaufmann's translation.

32. Friedrich Nietzsche, *Der Antichrist*, sec. 7.

People who claim sublimation, as both Aristotle and Augustine do, are always vulnerable to arguments that unmask what they have sublimated.

Nietzsche performs a sleek ironic switch: the problem is not so much cruelty itself as the horror of cruelty.[33] The outrage against cruelty is itself an icy, spiritualized version of cruelty. The whole of European culture, Christian and humanist "morality" alike, is for him a spiritual regime whose viciousness has a subtlety and dominion undreamt of by those more superficial (and hence better) connoisseurs of cruelty, the ancient Greeks. He rejects catharsis as a trick and reminds us that Christian-humanist moral arousal feeds on a constant tickling of the taboo against taking aesthetic pleasure in the agonies of others, the kind of thing eternally associated (thanks to Tacitus and Hollywood) with the Roman games and Nero's persecutions. For Nietzsche the very urge to pity becomes the site of domination. The urge to contain pain within a redeeming narrative is a first act of wickedness. Though Nietzsche's philosophy has often been misread in the English-speaking world (e.g., by Bertrand Russell) as aristocratic swagger, proud to wear the scars of youthful duels on its cheeks, his aim is not to celebrate pain, but to reveal the tyrannies of compulsory compassion, the blackmail of empathy, the layer of interpretive worry that keeps us from confronting human feeling in its elemental states. No less than the Sermon on the Mount, he hates the corruptions of second thoughts. Nietzsche could endorse Jesus's view that self-consciousness corrupts authentic action. He thinks catharsis and compassion give us too much time to think and not enough embodied shivering before stimuli that cannot be turned away. Pity is the guilty luxury of the fearful.

According to the virtuosi, we should admire the defiant courage of depictions of human misery that lack apparent compassion. The paintings of the late Francis Bacon (d. 1992), for instance, present violence in a deadpan way that rigorously refuses to evoke terror or pity, identification or sorrow. Bacon explicitly neglected the call to conscience found, for instance, in Picasso's *Guernica* or the photographs of a Dorothea Lange or a Walker Evans. Bacon studiously avoided compassion campaigns. Like Foucault, he had no desire to stir woeful pity for bodily mutilation. (Foucault's enduring emotional reaction to the story of Pierre Rivière, who murdered his mother, sister, and brother, was an appreciation of its "stupefying beauty."[34]) If Bacon's point was, "Oh man and woman, know that thou art meat," this is a moral

33. For his analysis of modern pain, see, for example, *Genealogie der Moral*, 2nd essay, sec. 7.

34. *Moi, Pierre Rivière, ayant égorgé ma mère, ma soeur, et mon frère: un cas de parricide au XIX siècle*, ed. Michel Foucault (Paris: Gallimard, 1973), 11.

truth of the first order. What kind of sense can we make of an artist so obviously obsessed with the Holocaust and the medical and military violation of the human body (he collected corpses during the blitz and was fascinated by X-rays and surgical illustration) who refuses to acknowledge the larger context? His art tries to remain unusable for either cathartic release or humane identification. His moral abstemiousness can be read as a refusal, a heroic struggle against closure.[35] He might seem a connoisseur of splattered flesh, but critics rarely leave him in the abyss. Gilles Deleuze says Bacon teaches us pity for meat. Do his paintings indict our carnivorous diet and war-filled ways? Is Bacon like the psychoanalyst who takes in a patient's stream of free associations without comment in the hope of not interrupting the healing? Bacon's paintings perform and publicize a style of looking at the human body, its "necessary inhumanity," as William Hunter called it, that was once held mostly to anatomical theaters. Yet after all this work to show Bacon's socially redeeming value, I still find his paintings deeply disturbing. The abyss is always with us.

Consider another pity-defying visual artist. The critical reception of Diane Arbus's photographs is a litmus test for liberal outrage since so much of her work consists of portraits of grotesques—midgets, nudists, the retarded, the disabled. Is she mocking people who cannot know they are being mocked? Susan Sontag opines: "The authority of Arbus's photographs derives from the contrast between their lacerating subject matter and their calm, matter-of-fact attentiveness."[36] Sontag is certainly right about the uncanny deadpan quality of Arbus's pictures, but what exactly about the subject matter is "lacerating"? Sontag misplaces the site of laceration, which is not the subject matter, but the guilty viewer who cannot reciprocate the gaze of the subject. There is nothing lacerating about human beings: these people are our kin. We all have probably had a photograph taken some time or other that managed to turn us into a freak. Arbus knows that the camera is a freak machine. The notion that her subjects are innocent victims put before knowing viewers who will be titillated by their freakishness is less satisfying than crediting her subjects for having no shame about how they are put together. They face the camera knowingly, not as zoo specimens conned into posing for distant audiences. What is lacerating is the viewer's wrestle between the desire to stare and the desire to circumvent the claim to recog-

35. Robert Newman, "(Re)Imaging the Postmodern Grotesque," in *The Image in Dispute*, ed. Dudley Andrew (Austin: University of Texas Press, 1997), 205–22.

36. Susan Sontag, *On Photography* (New York: Farrar, Straus, Giroux, 1977), 35. I have benefited from the work of Christopher Smit on Arbus, in "Photography and the Disabled Body," Ph.D. dissertation in progress, University of Iowa.

nition by a human face. (In Arbus-interpretation, I am obviously closer to the make-the-viewer-reflect school than the exploitative-photographer school.) Arbus is an artful voyeur. No less than Virchow, she is a chronicler of the range of shapes that our species can assume. Her camera does not exactly deprive freaks of their dignity; it deprives us of the pretension that such people have none. If this is laceration, we deserve it. That is Nietzsche's point: let us stop lying to ourselves about why we look.

One more anti-pity performer, less famous. Beggars in modern Greece, like the music and food, are one of the clearest ways that that land, despite its growing wealth and eagerness to belong to western Europe, is tied to the Middle East. Beggars present themselves not as morally privileged vessels chosen for our compassion, but as pragmatic seekers after money, admittedly often with horrendously clamorous needs, crying out like the lepers in the New Testament. Beggars in Greece typically portray themselves as people to whom life has dealt a hard blow who are doing the same thing we would do in the same circumstances.[37] I once saw a beggar close to Omonoia Square, the Piccadilly Circus of Athens—a gypsy kid, probably around twenty, on his back on a carpet as if break dancing, showing off his two variously hewn thigh stumps that had irregular scars and lumpy endings like hams. I did not sense any interiority, shame, or pride in his state. He wanted people to look, be grossed out, and empty their pockets. And I thought about it and decided I would do the same thing if I were in his place. I would do it aggressively; in fact I would want everyone to see my stumps and give me money. There was a certain dignity in the pity-free matter-of-factness of his gesture, compared with the praying beggar I once saw by the Louvre on his knees, looking so pathetic in his saintliness. Nothing about this gypsy kid would pass as saintly; yet his playing on a fascinated disgust for mutilation seemed more honorable than the Parisian beggar trying to conjure a sublime compassion for holy ones.[38] Both were after money, but only one admitted it. The amputee meets us in our grossness and petty fascinations; the penitent tempts us to batten on the nobility of giving, as if we were fording a vast spiritual gulf to condescend or rather ascend to the communion of saints. There is no space for sincerity and self-consciousness in the amputee's stunts. We are all beggars: the Greek amputee knows this, the French pietà does not. Maybe gut-wrenching shock is

37. An adequate sociology of begging in Greece would have to start with gender, age, ethnicity, and the historic bonds of affinity and antipathy for various groups (e.g., Serbs vs. Albanians). Thanks to Dalila Honorato.

38. For sustained mockery of histrionic French pity, see Milan Kundera, *Immortality,* trans. Peter Kussi (New York: Grove Weidenfeld, 1991).

as good a motive for care as sublime pity since it removes scruples, compunctions, and halos.

Interpreting the virtuosi of suffering is tricky. Their moral work is done performatively, implicitly, contrastively. Nietzsche, Foucault, Bacon, Arbus, and friends deploy word and image in a culture in which compulsory pity for suffering is the norm. They do not—probably—like mutilation, but they refuse to announce this, lest their aim of suspending all moral recuperation be blunted. (They want the "probably" to remain ever open.) They may or may not be making critical commentary on social justice; to read them that way may domesticate their wildness, but democracy is always in the middle. Deconstruction is the strategy of selective perversity, and its practitioners sometimes complain about the ruin of their moral stunt pilotry by interpreters interested in social applications. Connoisseurs of the abyss, like performance artists, depend on the strategy of metacommunication. Arbus does not directly say to her viewers, You should be ashamed at the self-congratulatory way you have been taught to look at other people. But her eloquent muteness may say that more forcefully than if she had said it explicitly. Bacon's hovering between delight in sadomasochism and critique of violence can likewise be read as a criticism of a society that sunders legitimate and illegitimate mixtures of bodies. Abstention from speech can be strong speech. Civil libertarians defending the rights of neo-Nazis offer a similar performance of public irony (the courage of a passivity that trusts in the presence of a witness). Passivity speaks with gestures and renounces—like Bollinger's good citizen—the temptation to retaliate or reply to an ill-informed or ill-willed interlocutor. Understood as a tightrope walk over the abyss instead of a celebration of it, the withholding of moral commentary can be a beautiful gesture. Yet its irony can be so stratospherically refined that public-spirited translators must remain on call for the confused *demos*.

PITY AND ITS CRITICS

A rich mix of attitudes can shape our response to scenes of pain. We can find psychological relief or intellectual illumination in contemplating the painful extremities of human life, be aroused to sympathy and called to action of some sort, or vigorously vaunt in the thrilling terror. We can also close our eyes and dwell on other things. At worst, the first seems irresponsible, the second hypocritical, the third inhumane, the fourth weak. This set of options recalls chapter 2: catharsis is abyss-redemption, compassion is abyss-exposure, courage is abyss-artistry, and closing your eyes is abyss-avoidance. None always trumps the others, and each has something to say to such questions as, In what ways are citizens to be informed? At what price? When is ignoring the world legitimate? Is a moral holiday always an abdication? When may we celebrate a sabbath from conscience and action?

Samantha Power's gripping book on U.S. policy (mainly of inaction) toward genocide in the twentieth century—in Armenia, Nazi Germany, Cambodia, Iraq, and Bosnia—paints the American public as alarmingly similar to the German civilians and their feeble *wir haben es nicht gewusst.* "Time and again," she writes, "decent men and women chose to look away. We have all been bystanders to genocide." She documents both the abundance of knowledge in the daily press to those who had eyes to see and the repeatedly missed opportunities for diplomatic or military intervention that, though they might not have stopped the slaughter completely, certainly could have saved many lives. It is a rare elected official who is willing to risk political capital on countries most of his or her constituents cannot spell or find on a map (one of the best and worst things about democracy is its acute focus on local interests). Still rarer is a William Proxmire, the former senator from Wisconsin, who with quixotic persistence delivered 3,211 speeches in the Senate chamber over a nineteen-year period in favor of an international treaty against genocide. Power's book raises many questions and certainly ought to do much to prick our pachyderm conscience. Her implied philosophy of responsibility for suffering at a distance might be boiled down into a series of propositions: distance is no excuse for ignorance; too much faith in human decency and due process keeps us unprepared to cope with the brutal realities of genocide; to speak of tragedy is both to eternalize provisional conflicts and to exonerate oneself from the duty of action, however flawed or limited it might be; and people who could know, but do not bother, are implicated to some degree in the crime they could have helped prevent. She does grant different degrees of responsibility: many did not know but could have known (the public), a smaller group knew but found reasons to do nothing (most public officials), and a few both knew and campaigned tirelessly for something to be done, such as Proxmire and Raphael Lemkin, the coiner of the term genocide, crusader for its international prohibition, and dispenser of guilt trips in at least six languages.[39]

In Power's picture, blood-guilt sticks to all but a few. A clear conscience is only possible for those who are deeply aware of the worst horrors of the

39. Samantha Power, *"A Problem from Hell": America and the Age of Genocide* (New York: Basic, 2002), especially vxi–xvii, 61, 71, 166.

past century. We gain relief from the demands of other people's pain not in contemplation, tender feelings, or raucous gusto, but in agitation to raise consciousness. Decent men and women who look away are morally complicit in remote and ramified ways with mass murder. Her views are of a piece with the invitation to watch Daniel Pearl's beheading (*The New Republic* is her publisher). Her model of the civic soul has a touch of the Stoic in the idea that a head full of slaughter ought not to harm our character, but her call to urgent immediate action is anything but Stoic.

A similar call is heard in the novelist-activist Ariel Dorfman's 2001 commencement address: "At this moment that I speak, a bomb is tearing apart someone's father . . . a woman is being raped . . . another woman's throat is being slit because she has dishonored her family by getting pregnant. . . . The heart of a young man with AIDS has stopped beating. . . . Someone is bribing an official so that a stream can be polluted, so drugs can poison a street, so guns can cross a frontier, so justice can be undone."[40] His survey of what he calls "the infinite pain of the world" aims to jolt us out of complacency and mobilize us as fighters of injustice. Exposure to trauma he finds essential for participation. Dorfman stands in a long line of righteous revolutionaries dating to Robespierre and Saint Just whose giant pitying hearts yearn for social justice in "heroic frenzies of commiseration."[41] The Jacobins exalted pity all the way to the guillotine: "Par pitié, par amour pour l'humanité, soyez inhumains!"[42] Yet something indecent lurks in Dorfman's panorama of pain, his prophetic privilege on the watchtower, his perfect victims abstracted from the human nexus that got them into trouble in the first place. Dorfman gives us bad guys—terrorists, rapists, patriarchs, gun- and drugrunners—without any redeeming features. And the spectacle of the Other's violence, as Sartre noted, serves to justify one's own, since violence is usually considered only a response and never an original (unprovoked) act.[43] Listening to people like Dorfman is enough to make you want to pick up a gun and go do something.

Debates about what to do about distant sorrow have raged since the 1750s and 1760s, when the matter became a preoccupation for thinkers such as Edmund Burke, Adam Smith, Voltaire, and Immanuel Kant. The sudden interest was not a coincidence. Cases of spectacular trauma gave the moral

---

40. Quoted in *USA Today*, 1 June 2001: 17A.

41. Clifford Orwin, "Compassion," *American Scholar*, Summer 1980: 312.

42. On the violence of pity in the French Revolution, see Hannah Arendt, *On Revolution* (New York: Viking, 1963), chap. 2. The quote appears at p. 85.

43. Jean-Paul Sartre, *Critique of Dialectical Reason* (1960), trans. Alan Sheridan-Smith (London: NLB, 1982), 1: 133.

problem of watching others in pain an immediate historical urgency, especially the Lisbon earthquake of 1755 and the public execution by quartering
of the French regicide Robert Francis Damiens in 1757, a scene that seems to
have obsessed contemporary Englishmen in particular. (In beginning *Discipline and Punish* with Damiens's execution, Michel Foucault shrewdly revived an old topos.) Burke seems both refreshingly honest and potentially
brutal: "I am convinced we have a degree of delight, and that no small one,
in the real misfortunes and pains of others." Terror, Burke says, is "the common stock of every thing that is sublime." (The origin of the sublime for
Burke lies in violence, and that of the beautiful in sex.) For Burke delight in
terror is almost built into human nature: "terror is a passion which always
produces delight when it does not press too close." The sublime, he says, is
"the strongest emotion which the mind is capable of feeling" and consists in
whatever excites ideas of pain or danger. [44] Burke's psychology and aesthetics of suffering do more to account for why people watch horrific movies
than more ginger accounts of human nature. In an age sated with images
of the dying, the moral meaning of pleasure in sublime representations is
tangled.

   Smith, as we saw in chapter 3, is likewise remarkably frank about insensibility to distant suffering with his hypothetical earthquake that destroys
China. As if thinking directly of Dorfman, he complains of "those whining
and melancholy moralists" who "regard as impious the natural joy of prosperity" and invite instead sorrow for the world's infinite agony. According
to them, says Smith, we should "think of the many wretches that are at every
moment labouring under all sorts of calamities, in the langour of poverty,
in the agony of disease, in the horrors of death, under the insults and op-
pressions of their enemies. Commiseration for those miseries which we
never saw, which we never heard of, but which we may be assured are at all
times infesting such numbers of our fellow-creatures, ought, they think, to
damp the pleasures of the fortunate, and to render a certain melancholy dejection habitual to all men." Smith rejects such "artificial commiseration"
because the sufferers "are placed altogether out of the sphere of our activity." He even imagines a global survey of relative contentment: "Take the
whole earth at an average, for one man who suffers pain or misery, you will
find twenty in prosperity or joy, or at least in tolerable circumstances. No
reason, surely, can be assigned why we should rather weep with the one than

44. Edmund Burke, *A Philosophical Enquiry into the Origin of Our Ideas of the Sublime and
the Beautiful*, ed. James T. Boulton (Notre Dame, Ind.: Notre Dame University Press, 1968), 64,
39, 45, 46, 57.

rejoice with the twenty."[45] Smith is an early critic of liberal guilt and not simply a capitalist with a cold conscience.[46]

Another text published in the same year as *The Theory of Moral Sentiments* (1759) gave a different answer—Voltaire's *Candide.*[47] In Candide's picaresque travels across Europe and Latin America, he keeps bumping into things undreamt of in his philosophy, rather like Forrest Gump, clueless to his collusion with the miraculous events that keep happening to him. The novella features fields of corpses. Torture, rape, disemboweling, horrendous battles, and public executions of the Foucauldian sort occur throughout in a kind of black humor that Monte Python surely learned from but that is missing, by definition, from most latter-day reformers. The perception that the world is a slaughterhouse is not unique to the twentieth century, and Voltaire believes that knowledge of the suffering of distant strangers can impose moral and political obligations. *Candide* is one source for modern consumerist guilt, the sense that the pleasures of the rich are paid for by the misery of the poor, that sugar, for instance, is tainted with the blood of slaves. *Candide* is not afraid to expose its readers to conscience-arousing trauma. Like many other social reformers, Voltaire traffics in graphic and sometimes kinky depictions of distant suffering.[48] Whatever his flippancy about ultimate solutions in *Candide,* Voltaire clearly despises the blithe explaining away of agony.

Voltaire and Smith both faced the morally grotesque disproportions of pity. Smith compared the relative trauma of a lost pinkie to the destruction of China, and Voltaire wickedly paints Candide's joy that a shipwreck killing a hundred people somehow managed to spare one of his beloved llamas. In each case a minor private pain or pleasure scandalously overshadows a major public one. In 1764 Kant took up the twistedness of our imaginative identifications. He similarly argued that pity, however praiseworthy it might at first seem, should not be honored as a virtue. (Like Aristotle, he thought pity a theatrical effect.) "A suffering child, an unfortunate and pretty woman, will fill our hearts with this sweet melancholy, while at the same time we will coolly receive the news of a great battle in which, it is easy to consider, a more considerable portion of the human race must undeserv-

45. Adam Smith, *The Theory of Moral Sentiments,* ed. D. D. Rafael and A. L. Macfie (Oxford: Clarendon Press, 1976), 139–40.

46. Julie Ellison, *Cato's Tears and the Making of Anglo-American Emotion* (Chicago: University of Chicago Press, 1999), 10–12.

47. One could add a third work to make a 1759 trio: Samuel Johnson's *Rasselas,* another attack on cosmic optimism.

48. See Halttunen, "Humanitarianism."

ingly succumb to cruel calamities." Pity has no sense of proportion. A single face can monopolize the news while faceless thousands perish in hunger. In the same way, Kant continues, many a prince has turned away from the sight of an unfortunate person and yet given ill-founded orders to wage war that will cause the death of many. How can such delicacy and callousness inhabit the same breast? "There is here certainly no proportion in the outcome."[49] Pity involves the pathological distortion of caring for a loveable individual and slighting the deaths of nameless masses. Where is the face that represents the statistical sorrows of the world?

Where eighteenth-century critics of pity worried about the neglect of the vague many in favor of the vivid singleton, nineteenth-century critics of philanthropy worried about an emotional inflation in which care for distant sorrow justified a neglect of local ills. *Middlemarch* (1871–72) cites the definition of a philanthropist as "a man whose charity increases directly as the square of the distance" (but this is not George Eliot's view).[50] Fyodor Dostoevsky's *Brothers Karamazov* (1880) notes the advantages of distance for affecting a love for humanity. "The idea of loving one's neighbor," says Ivan, "is possible only as an abstraction: it may be conceivable to love one's fellow man at a distance, but it is almost never possible to love him at close quarters."[51] Søren Kierkegaard was ever alert to the comic potential in projects that profess goodness: "Social endeavors and associated beautiful sympathy become more and more widespread. In Leipzig, a committee formed out of sympathy for the sad fate of old horses has decided to eat them."[52] For a century and a half, critics of distant caring have seen sympathy as a form of self-deception that allows one to eat other creatures in good conscience. Pity is the totalitarianism of the righteous. "If I knew for a certainty that a man was coming to my house with the conscious design of doing me good," said Thoreau, "I should run for my life. . . . [In] this case I would rather suffer evil the natural way."[53]

Thoreau's mentor Emerson, one of philanthropy's most arctic critics, likewise denounced emotional athleticism on behalf of others. "We sink as

49. Immanuel Kant, *Beobachtungen über das Gefühl des Schönen und Erhabenen, Werke in Sechs Bände* (1764), ed. Wilhelm Weischedel (Wiesbaden: Insel, 1960), 1: 835–36.

50. George Eliot, *Middlemarch* (1871–72) (London: Penguin, 1994), 383.

51. Fyodor Dostoyevsky, *The Brothers Karamazov* (1880), trans. Andrew R. MacAndrew (New York: Bantam, 1970), 285.

52. Søren Kierkegaard, *Either/Or: Part I* (1843) (Princeton, N.J.: Princeton University Press, 1987), 33.

53. Henry David Thoreau, *Walden and Civil Disobedience* (1854) (New York: Norton, 1966), 50.

easily as we rise, through sympathy."[54] He thought the "love afar" of the abolitionists went together with "spite at home."[55] Emerson despised moral compulsion of any sort and found it lurking especially in the pretense of largesse. It is humiliating to have to receive. "It is not the office of man to receive gifts. How dare you give them? We wish to be self-sustained. We do not quite forgive a giver." The receiver of a gift *must* be grateful. You never have fewer options than when accepting a gift. (That grace gives no choice but gratitude is one of Paul's hardest teachings to swallow.) "It is a great happiness to get off without injury and heart-burning from one who has had the ill-luck to be served by you."[56] Givers might consider apologizing for the imposition—Diogenes once refused a dinner invitation because the host failed to show sufficient gratitude on the previous occasion![57] Emerson's diabolical reading of gifts does not mean he dislikes receiving; he warns against fantasias of one's own goodness that brutalize others. The righteous should be prepared for the resentment their goodness can provoke (something central to the strategy of passive resistance). Emerson, like Nietzsche later, found the price of pity too high. People in complete command of the good can be insufferable.[58]

Pity is the onlooker's luxury. As Adam Smith noted, sympathy rarely means matching the other's feelings. We shudder in thinking of a dead person not because the corpse feels bad but because we would feel bad if we, being alive, were dead. Sympathy is an interpretation of how we would feel in the other's place, not a replication of the other's feelings. Sympathy is extrapolated subjectivity. Outrage for the abuse of others is often a projection of our own feelings rather than theirs. Pity has a large ego. People full of pity can be more interested in reassuring their own anxiety than in alleviating pain. The pity of the onlooker is often more intense than the sorrow of the supposed victim. The injured have other things to worry about than their pain. Mourning is for the bereaved, not the dead. Pity is to pain as representation is to life: the staged version is often more moving than the real thing. It is often easier to cry at movie weddings than at real ones, at story deaths than at funerals, which never manage to come at the right time. Distance furnishes clarity and catharsis. Up close there is no relief from the sentence

54. Ralph Waldo Emerson, "Society and Solitude," in *Selected Writings of Emerson*, ed. Donald McQuade (New York: Modern Library, 1981), 816.

55. Ralph Waldo Emerson, "Self-Reliance," in *Selected Writings*, 132–33.

56. Ralph Waldo Emerson, "Gifts," in *Selected Writings*, 387–88.

57. Diogenes Laertius, *Lives of the Philosophers* (Loeb ed.), 34.

58. See James Fitzjames Stephen, "Philanthropy" and "Doing Good" (1859), in *Liberty, Equality, and Fraternity and Three Brief Essays* (Chicago: University of Chicago Press, 1991).

of daily life—all those contingencies that blur the contours of the plot and its climaxes. William James, who witnessed the San Francisco earthquake of 1906 while teaching at Stanford University, discovered this truth for himself. In a letter to his brother Henry, he wrote: "In battle, sieges, and other great calamities, the pathos and agony is in general solely felt by those at a distance, and although physical pain is suffered most by its immediate victims, those *at the scene of the action* have no *sentimental* suffering whatever."[59] At the scene of the action people need water, jokes, news, blankets, a change of clothes. Catastrophe, like everything else, is amazingly mundane. "What opium is instilled into all disaster," said Emerson.[60] Life does not stop being dispensed one second after another at a battlefield, crime scene, or prison camp.

Thoreau had it right: "If you should ever be betrayed into one of these philanthropies, do not let your left hand know what your right hand does, for it is not worth knowing. Rescue the drowning and tie your shoestrings."[61] He does not say not to serve, only not to gloat. Arming yourself against pity is a risky pact with hardness that can protect you from the tyranny of compulsory sympathy, the daily bloodletting of or by the news. News produces liberal guilt. Its global survey of knowledge outstrips the orbit of possible action. A heart swollen with grief for "the infinite pain of the world" does not do much to help one's neighbors. The hubris of "saving the world" occurs to those watching from a great distance. Is the pain of the world really infinite? If pains could be summed, cumulatively, no human cup could hold them. Imagine even the pain of ten thousand hang-nails concentrated. Yet pain, in some deep sense, is private, even to ourselves.[62] As Edgar Allan Poe said, "The true wretchedness, indeed—the ultimate woe—is particular, not diffuse. That the ghastly extremes are endured by man the unit, and never by man the mass—for this let us thank a merciful God!"[63] Even the maximum threshold of pain at the limit of death, torture, and bodily destruction comes in body-tight containers: only a god could drink more than a single mortal's share of suffering. The world's pain is statistical. "Suffering is not increased by numbers," said Graham Greene; "one

59. William James to Henry James, 9 May 1906, quoted in Linda Simon, *Genuine Reality: A Life of William James* (New York: Harcourt Brace, 1998), 342. Emphasis in the original.

60. Ralph Waldo Emerson, "Experience," in *Selected Writings*, 327.

61. Thoreau, *Walden and Civil Disobedience*, 53.

62. "Pain has an element of blank." Emily Dickinson, quoted in *The American Tradition in Literature*. 3rd ed. (New York: Norton, 1967), 1022

63. Edgar Allan Poe, "The Premature Burial," in *Poetry and Tales* (New York: Library of America, 1984), 666.

body can contain all the suffering the world can feel."[64] Hurting, like dying, everyone does alone. Outside of medication, there is precious little we can do to relieve pain beyond minor gestures of care: a cup of water, a towel, fresh bedding, a kind word, friendly face, or flower. How, then, are we supposed to solve the suffering of the world? The closer we get to real pain, the more helpless we are to do anything to help. Care is weak. The great theatrical delights of pity mislead us about what kind of relief is possible.

NEWS AND THE EVERLASTING NOW

Criticizing the politics or postures of pity is not the same as giving up on social justice. This is one lesson the nineteenth-century critics of philanthropy teach. Thoreau—a Yankee Diogenes who drank deep from the cheerful wells of cynicism—both renounced the spiritual compulsions of the news and helped invent a new kind of moral politics at a distance, whose implications I explore in the next chapter. Why read the times, he asked, when you can read the eternities? It would be better to read what was never old. "And I am sure that I never read any memorable news in a newspaper. If we read of one man robbed, or murdered, or killed by accident, or one house burned, or one vessel wrecked, or one steamboat blown up, or one cow run over on the Western Railroad, or one mad dog killed, or one lot of grasshoppers in the winter,—we need never read of another. One is enough. If you are acquainted with the principle, what do you care for a myriad instances and applications?"[65] Thoreau, recognizing that journalism is parasitic on news about damage to life and limb, suggests that the stories could all be written twelve months in advance or twelve years after the fact; the last worthwhile news from England, he says, was the revolution of 1649. Reacting to the penny press of the 1830s and 1840s, whose rising circulation was paired with a fresh appetite for sexual and violent scandal, Thoreau is not just a drop-out from responsibility, but an archetype of the modern engaged conscience. His essay *Civil Disobedience* (1849) announces a new kind of political action by linking the almost absurdly minor personal act of refusing to pay a poll tax to a criticism of distant exploitation (the military adventures of the United States in Mexico). Thoreau was not opposed to distant care (he traveled the globe while at Walden Pond, as he said, and was a passionate abolitionist), but he did resist being wind-

64. Graham Greene, *The Quiet American* (London: William Heinemann and the Bodley Head, 1973), 205. Thus Greene neatly captures the theology of the atonement.

65. Thoreau, *Walden and Civil Disobedience*, 63.

whipped by scandalized people interested in keeping the wounds open. Opting out from the clamor and scandal of sensation is not necessarily incompatible with standing for justice. The daily news industry is not always the best way to find out what is going on in the world. The question Thoreau did not answer was how one decides when it is time to tune out and time to protest? Everyone knows that we humans cannot know or do everything, but deciding how and when to act is always fraught with trouble.

Thoreau joked that news could be written in advance, but what news teaches is precisely our failure to foretell the future. Kierkegaard, who had his own troubles with the popular press, quipped that if we treated news as if it happened fifty years ago, we would sound its true importance. He is right about triviality but misses what he normally sees so lucidly: the present moment as the point of decision. We cannot treat today as if it were yesterday. News, as the name suggests, is about how things stand in the world now, about the surprises and disruptions to the world as we knew it yesterday. News matters because of the special character of the present. The demands of yesterday are often, blessedly and horribly, of a completely different order than today. The present moment is one of the most combustible substances we know. "It was" can be both pathetic and joyous words. News informs us of deadlines, time frames within which our action must take place or prove fruitless. There is no need to keep fighting after the armistice is signed. That the light was green a few seconds ago does not protect you from a crash. This sliver of time between past and future is our single chance to act. We have to pay attention because the present is different from what was and what will be. God may live in an Everlasting Now, the *nunc stans* of medieval theology, but so do we. Everything that happens happens in a "now." The past is solid, the future is gas, but the present is liquid. Fortuna, goddess of history and gamblers, reveals her face only in the present. In the past she appears under the guise of necessity, in the future under the guise of probability.

The present is both rich and poor. It is charged with meaning (as our only field of action) and just as fast deprived of it (as the most brittle thing we know). In Hegel's well-known analysis, "here and now" at first seems the richest and most certain kind of reality, buzzing with presence and meaning. But "now" turns out to be poor and abstract, subject to radical evacuations of content and meaning as it is orphaned by the passage of time. What is now so certifiably night is tomorrow undeniably day. The "now" is ultimately empty and abstract, as unstable as the English weather.[66] The past,

---

66. Hegel, *Phänomenologie des Geistes*, paras. 90–110.

in some sense, is safe, but the present is catastrophic.[67] A swerve of the steering wheel or a pull of the trigger can change everything. Possible futures (and pasts) come into being or vanish with every event. In a second the penalty kick is made or missed, a life conceived or taken. Time past and time future are contained in time present. The present is full of alarm. Paul wrote of *ho nun kairos,* the time of the now, but in modern Greek, *kairos* means "weather." The present is both universal and contingent. News is less valuable as information than as a guide to action. (Who cares about yesterday's weather?) To stay current may be useless for the philosopher, as Thoreau said, who understands that we are mortal and trauma is our lot; but for the caring person there is no escaping some duty to know what others are suffering or even what fellow citizen-strangers are talking about. Care involves "instances and applications." Obligation is to particulars, and particulars are unstable. Pain, like the here and now, is the most fragile of appearances, but that does not lift our obligation to it. In love the particular is higher than the universal. News speaks of mortal lives rather than of philosophical universals. This is not just another disaster, says the report: this is the airplane in North Carolina that crashed into a house, just missing a school. This is not just another crime: someone you might know has hit his brother-in-law with a baseball bat. News tells of individual deaths, not actuarial tables. As long as we have friends in this world, Augustine said, we will hear news with interest and anxiety. For the sake of tranquility and *apatheia,* we should avoid the news; for the sake of care and *agapē,* we should attend to it. Neither Stoic apathy nor Christian compassion quite seems proportional. Whatever we do is never enough. The now will never leave us in peace. Whether we pay attention to the news or ignore it, we will regret it either way.

"Now" is *critical* in the medical, judicial, and philosophical senses all at once. We may weep for the slaughter of the innocents two thousand or sixty years ago, but we owe them nothing secular besides remembrance and historical respect. "Live" pain is different. Obligation to the living is distinct from obligation to the dead. The dead require something from us, but their care can never be as urgent as for the living. The dead can wait; the messy diaper cannot. The patient in critical care does not need oxygen in two hours, but now. The now is exigent. Its explosiveness helps explain the enormous cachet of "live" events in broadcasting, as it does the appeal of gambling (which is a playing with possible futures). It also explains the difference between the relief of fiction and the ethical duty of fact. Fiction may lead to

---

67. We cannot exclude a philosophy of history that would allow new happenings in the past.

catharsis, but delight in real pain is sadism. The metaphysical distinction between fact and fiction is subtle, but the contrast is ethical before it is epistemological. Facts have an anchor in the body's pain. Facts require witnesses; fictions only need narrators. Facts impose obligations that fictions do not. Perhaps the disbelief that always seems to greet the first reports of atrocity—seen in the delayed reactions worldwide to the Turks' slaughter of the Armenians in 1915, the Nazis' slaughter of the Jews, and the Khmer Rouge's slaughter of all and anyone in the 1970s—is an indirect way to postpone action.[68] Calling something fiction lifts the burden of responsibility.

The notion of news cannot help recalling Paul's *euaggelion,* good news, a message that once you hear it does not leave you in peace but compels you to action in every moment; but unlike Paul's theology, the news media have no mechanism to save you from the impossible burden they impose. News of distant suffering is ethically recalcitrant. Its factual nature disqualifies us from the relief of catharsis. Distance and multiplicity complicate our desire to aid. Being stops short of consciousness. The world is full of terrible things. Take your pick from the headlines: land mines, AIDS, poverty, ignorance, clitoridectomies, al-Qaeda, capitalism, kiddie porn, anti-Semitism, acid rain, torture, mink farms, floods, forest fires, vaccine-resistant viruses, hog waste, SARS, kidnapped children, jackknifed trains, genetically modified foods, war profiteering, U.N. sanctions, looted antiquities, famine, or the diminishing rain forest, ozone layer, and ice caps. Any such list is inadequate, and even a thousand items would be egregious in its incompleteness. Anyone can prick your conscience by showing what you have left out. There is no decent way to sort through the multiple claims on our time or philanthropy.[69] Spinoza found determinism a doctrine conducive to peace of mind since it relieves us from the stress of choice.

How are we to decide what causes to support or which people to aid? Augustine's answer is to let fate decide: "since you cannot do good to all, you are to pay special regard to those who, by the accidents of time, or place, or circumstance, are brought into closer connection with you." You love the one you're with. Augustine sees love as an indivisible object (like a coat or a book) instead of something like time, attention, or money. If you have two equally deserving friends and one gift, how do you decide who gets it? By a coin-flip. "Just so among men: since you cannot consult for the good of them all, you must take the matter as decided for you by a kind of lot, ac-

68. Power, *A Problem from Hell.*

69. Mary Midgley, "The Problem of Humbug," in *Media Ethics,* ed. Matthew Kieran (London: Routledge, 1998), 37–48, especially 45–46.

cording as each man happens for the time being to be more closely connected with you."[70] *Agapē*, supposed to cover everyone alike, alights randomly. We drop the hubris of deciding where to intervene and accept the fate of being neighbors with people we did not choose in the lottery of love. The best response to this view is that charity is a capitulation to the abusive standing relations of power. If fortuitous love of one's neighbor is the only way to cancel injustice, say Horkheimer and Adorno, compassion (*Mitleid*) is an accomplice in the universal alienation it tries to relieve.[71] Calls for big structural change can be merciless; love of one's neighbor can be clueless. Renouncing pity can foster ethical tranquility, and denouncing injustice can foster political change. Samantha Power reminding us that the world is on fire is not a deficient model of how to engage with evil. Neither is the Buddha serene in meditation (who also knew the world was burning).

A happy merger of Marxist social critique and Christian love might be the ticket—indeed, with some imagination one might find something like that in Paul of Tarsus—but there is no easy answer other than keeping one's eyes open, at least when one is not asleep. As bystanders to genocide, to litter, to daily chatter, and to everything that happens within the range of our presence, we are all witnesses. Being a witness is a restless, thankless fate. A witness can suddenly find his or her life changed. Ovid was banished to the Black Sea for seeing something in the emperor's court he wasn't supposed to. In Graham Greene's *Brighton Rock,* a gangster marries the only witness to a murder he committed in order to make her testimony, as a wife, inadmissible (but of course, as usual in Greene, a sort of redemption occurs via the corruption). Witnesses never know in advance what is a gem and what is dross. The present may be the point of decision, but it is always underinformed about what will come later. We do not know what tidbits of today's myriads of sensations will prove decisive for some future event, the butterfly that triggered the hurricane. Bearing witness has the structure of repentance: retroactively caring about what we once neglected, revisiting an earlier time in which we were not fully awake. All we can do is regard the present as if it were the forerunner of a great future or say to the past, so I would have wished it. Citizenship is a vigil, watching over the dying and dead, waiting for the marriage feast or newborn child.

States of emergency are both rare and common. That several dozen people will die today on American roads is a statistical fact whose odds and

70. Augustine, *On Christian Doctrine,* in *Great Books of the* Western *World,* 18: 632.

71. Max Horkheimer and Theodor W. Adorno, *Dialektik der Aufklärung: Philosophische Fragmente* (1944), in Adorno, *Gesammelte Schriften* (Frankfurt: Suhrkamp, 1981), 3: 123.

costs can be predicted within well-defined ranges of probability. For the victims, family, and witnesses, these accidents are life-changing (life-ending) events. For the three hundred million or so Americans unaffected, these deaths are at best a season-like regularity. The ratio of the unaffected to the affected approaches 100,000 or 1,000,000 to 1. A certain blasé brutality is the price we pay for large, highly connected societies. Almost everyone shrugs at highway fatalities. "This discrepancy," Michael Warner notes, "in how seriously we take different organizations of injury is a source of never-ending frustration for airline executives."[72] A hundred people killed in a plane crash one day is a headline; forty thousand people killed in car accidents per year is an actuarial risk. The world is on fire if we look at the accidents, but if we look at the average road, things are chugging along in their boring, predictable ways. Common sense says life is pretty stable and emergencies are rare. But to act as if we are immune to emergencies is to be unprepared for the inevitable hour when one will come (we all, at least, are guaranteed to die). Common sense says that civilized societies do not build gas ovens for their citizens: common sense thus risks missing (and did miss) the Holocaust. The world is mostly normal but never always normal.

States of emergency are chronic (if we take the world as a whole) and acute (if we take the spot where they occur). You can save a life if you are on the scene within minutes of an accident. So you learn CPR, just in case. How do we decide when we are in a state of emergency? For Carl Schmitt the power to determine this was the mark of sovereignty. But those who believe in a politics and ethics of conscience cannot cede such judgment to the state or any other sovereign. To say we are always in an emergency, as Samantha Power claims, does injustice to our finitude; to say we never are, as Adam Smith suggests, does injustice to our responsibility. Yet emergencies call forth heroism, and thus monopolize the moral imagination: they are morally satisfying since they demonstrate so concretely our importance and the results of our intervention. Medical students may prefer to specialize in surgery, but on the whole, far greater benefits come to public health from preventive medicine and mundane practices such as wearing seatbelts, not smoking, and exercising. We prepare for emergencies, but in the meanwhile the world is saved statistically. Here again the curious moral force of statistics appears, the cohabitation of the mean and the exceptional. In facing the world's pain, perhaps we should renounce the wish to be morally great, accept an ethical division of labor, and work through states, nongovernmental organizations, and service agencies. Faces of children in

72. Michael Warner, *Publics and Counterpublics* (New York: Zone Books, 2002), 177.

pain are perhaps useful only for fundraising. We may give because we take pity on the brown baby's face, but our dollar diffuses into budgets and bureaucracy. Pity is a persuasive technique rather than an ethical virtue. In *Middlemarch*, a book that asks whether saintliness is possible in the modern world, George Eliot had it right: "the growing good of the world is partly dependent on unhistoric acts."[73] If such acts are weak against thugs with tanks and tyrants with five-year plans, so be it. There is a power in powerlessness. Catharsis is for the theater, compassion is for the neighbor, and defiance of pity is for the world's propaganda machines. Rescue the drowning and tie your shoestrings.

73. Eliot, *Middlemarch*, 838.

"Meekness as a Dangerous Activity":
Witnessing as Participation

For power is brought to completion in weakness.
—Paul of Tarsus, 2 Corinthians 12:9

The middle of the nineteenth century saw the emergence of the leading options that have roughly defined the political history of the modern world: the
Seneca Falls Convention (1848), the birthplace of the women's movement;
The Communist Manifesto (1849) by Marx and Engels; *Civil Disobedience*
(1849) by Thoreau; and *On Liberty* (1859 by Mill. (The fundamentalist alternatives that precisely *oppose* the modern world did not arise until the early
twentieth century.) Marx wanted revolution; Mill wanted reform, as did the
Seneca Falls Convention; Thoreau wanted resistance. Class, gender, and race
are all here. Marx fought mainstream institutions; Mill and first-wave feminism worked within them; Thoreau plied a politics of conscience and shame
outside of all institutions. (Thoreau belonged to no associations, said Emerson, because none of them could bear the satire of his presence.) Marxism,
feminism, and liberalism have gotten the most airtime in recent political theory, but the transcendental politics of passivity has the good fortune of inspiring some of the most successful political leaders over the past century, notably Gandhi, Martin Luther King, Václav Havel, and Aung San Suu Kyi. They
all understood the body as an agency of participation. They all drew on the
Cynical tradition's fundamental insight that putting oneself, as a speaker of
truth, in a position of peril is a way to mobilize the public conscience. Civil
disobedience, nonviolent resistance, and exaggerated civility are all underex-
plored resources in the theory and practice of democratic communication.
And they all make the best sense of liberty's long flirtation with pain and evil.

Liberalism and Marxism both exalt activity as the highest human excellence. Civil disobedience, in contrast, knows the power of passivity, the ways that the sheer objecthood of human bodies can embarrass the levers of power into motion. Though it is often mistakenly equated with liberalism, transcendentalist politics has a realism liberalism lacks about the material and spiritual conditions of communication and is free of the sometimes merciless absolutism that can infect both Marxism and liberalism (in different ways). Nonviolent resistance does not violate the personhood of the foe; it tries to draw forth the human side of the oppressors by shaming them. It is an expressly theatrical politics that counts on bystanding witnesses to bear testimony, trusting even the vilest imperialist, racist, or thug to be ashamed, though its wisest practitioners knew enough not to hold their breath for too long. It is a politics of claiming justice through human thingliness. It discovers universality without abstraction, democratic participation without rationalist browbeating, and the recognition of suffering without pathos or pity. Though Gandhi, King, Havel, and Aung San Suu Kyi followed different routes to power, in each case the ultimate outcome turned on the willingness of a state apparatus to relent. Gandhi in India and King in the American South both led mass movements that not only elicited widespread support on moral grounds, but more crucially, gained sympathy in high places. Havel, in contrast, was part of an underground network in Czechoslovakia whose ultimate success depended on the withdrawal of the Soviets under glasnost. Aung San Suu Kyi draws moral capital from the spectacle of the courage of a sole woman, combined with massive rallies in Burma.

Mass movements, samizdat, and solo spectacle, respectively, vary in openness and audience size, but all are equally weak against tanks and machine guns. But is too easy simply to call nonviolent resistance utopian, and largely wrong: it has a spectacular record of political success, as well as a relative immunity to moral corruption. The policy has not required the sacrifice of ethical integrity or the awful notion of historical necessity. The nonviolent resisters all used the light of publicity to preserve their lives and causes against government reprisals (though not, in the case of Gandhi and King, against assassins). The Nobel Peace Prize, international journalism, and human rights organizations have clearly helped to preserve Suu Kyi's life. Thoreau's children are perhaps the most creative heirs of the discovery that the public realm puts the body and its pain on display. The practice of civil disobedience involves a defiance that needs the public glare. Visibility is a trap—sometimes for one's foes. One can hide from the light; one can also hide in the light. Passive resistance turns on exposure of body rather than purity of heart. It passively, circumspectly, slyly courts aggressive responses before witnesses. How provoking it can be to have nothing justifiable to be provoked about, to find oneself sputtering with rage while the object sits there sweetly. Aggressiveness is instantly exposed as illegitimate. Passivity in protest is a strategic use of the double bind: it exploits the obnoxiousness of righteousness, the unbearableness of genuine humility.

WITNESSING WITH THE BODY

As I argued in chapter 6, the informed citizen accepts all the burdens of witnessing. But the concept is multiple: one can witness with the eyes, the voice, or the body. The concept of witnessing calls forth all the body's communicative resources. The three sources of law, theology, and atrocity endow "witnessing" with its extraordinary moral and cultural force, since each ties the act of witnessing, in some deep way, to life and death. In law the idea of the witness as a privileged source of information, sometimes extracted under torture, for judicial decisions is ancient. In theology the notion of witness, especially as martyr, developed in early Christianity and rabbinical Judaism, though it is embraced in other religious traditions as well.[1] The most recent sense dates from World War II: the witness as a survivor of hell, prototypically but not exclusively the Holocaust, who lives on to tell the world about the untellable. The procedures of the court, the pain of the martyr, and the cry of the survivor raise basic questions about what it means to watch, to narrate, or to be present at or re-present an event. Witnessing raises questions of truth and experience, presence and absence, death and pain, seeing and saying, and the trustworthiness of perception—in short, fundamental questions of communication. Witnessing is an amazingly subtle array of practices of securing truth from our sensitivity to pain and our inevitable death. It reorients our conception of what citizens can do. In witnessing, information and participation are one.

The practice of witnessing has both a passive and an active face—seeing and saying. Witnessing can be a sensory experience—the witnessing of an event with one's own eyes and ears. But witnessing is also the speech-act of stating one's experience for the benefit of an audience that was not present at the event and yet must make some kind of decision about it. Witnesses serve as surrogate sense organs for the absent. If what we have witnessed is

---

1. For the argument that martyrdom was crucial for both traditions, see Daniel Boyarin, *Dying for God: Martyrdom and the Making of Christianity and Judaism* (Stanford, Calif.: Stanford University Press, 1999).

crucial for a judgment, we may be summoned to a formal institutional setting: a court of law, a church, a television studio. A witness is a medium, a means by which experience is supplied to others who lack access to the original. In passive witnessing an accidental audience observes events; in active witnessing a speaker, as a privileged possessor of knowledge, produces it in a forensic setting in which the bond between speech and truth is strictly policed. What one has seen authorizes what one can say: an active witness must have first been a passive one. Similarly, every active witness needs a passive witness to bear record of the record borne. This contrast is similar to the one between a signer and a countersigner: the signer attests that the statement is true, whereas the countersigner attests that the signatures are true.[2]

The noun "witness" suggests all three points of the basic communication triangle of speaker, speech, and listener: the agent who bears witness; the utterance itself; and the audience who witnesses. We could, for instance, say, the witness (speech-act) of the witness (person) was witnessed (by an audience). A witness can also be the performance itself (e.g., the Holocaust survivor's witness against fascism or oblivion). In African-American churches, "Can I get a witness?" invites audience affirmation and participation as a public gesture of faith. A witness can also mean an inward conviction of religious truth, which in turn may motivate the activity of "witnessing" (evangelizing). In law, literature, history, and journalism, a witness is a source possessing privileged (raw, authentic) access to facts. In historiography the witness of the dead has special testimonial privilege. In sum, a witness can be an actor (one who bears witness), an act (the making of a special sort of statement), the semiotic residue of that act (the statement as text), the inward experience that authorizes the statement (the witnessing of an event), or the cultural performance (witnessing).

At the heart of witnessing lies a veracity gap. Witnessing presupposes a discrepancy in what different people know and thus is an intensification of the problem of communication more generally. The difficult juncture between experience and word, the journey from experience (the seen) into words (the said) is precarious. No transfusion of consciousness ever takes place. Words can be exchanged, but experiences cannot. Testimony is the discourse of another whose universe of experience diverges from one's own. Like somebody else's pain, testimony always has a twilight status between certainty and doubt. A parent may bear witness to a child that a stove

2. Robin Wagner-Pacifici, "Witness to Surrender," chapter 2 in *The Art of Surrender: Decomposing Sovereignty at Conflicts End* (Chicago: University of Chicago Press, forthcoming).

is hot, but getting burned may be more persuasive. Witnessing is a discourse with a hole in it that awaits filling.

Though awareness of the poor epistemological quality of witnessing is ancient, twentieth-century social science has explored it in detail. Eyewitness testimony, for instance, has been subject to intense social-psychological study, propelled by the recognition that witnesses commonly misidentify faces, with potentially devastating consequences for justice.[3] Fabrication seems inherent in the loose coupling between sentences and sensation; witnesses, like all media, are a fallible transmission and storage medium for sensory experience. The law has a long history of excluding "unreliable" witnesses such as non-Christians, convicts, spouses, children, the insane, slaves, and colonized peoples. The historic treatment of women as incompetent witnesses has had disastrous results for sexual justice. As in social research, the law has an acute awareness of the ways that modes of interrogation (e.g. leading questions) can invent, rather than elicit, testimony. Witnessing, an act of communication meant to establish the truth, often reveals the fragility of the forms that carry truth.

A variety of solutions has been offered to cope with the fallibility of witnessing since antiquity (the ninth Mosaic commandment makes false witnessing a central crime—not the same thing as simple lying). One can vouch for veracity by an oath promising to trade death or pain for truth, a practice that persists in the childish oath, "cross my heart and hope to die." One may appeal to ultimate authority: "God is my witness." Aristotle noted that witnesses in a court of law testify at risk of punishment if they do not tell the truth; he considers dead witnesses more trustworthy than living ones—since they cannot be bribed.[4] To witness as if you were as dumb and indifferent as the dead is an old ideal, since you would be free from interest, interpretation, care, and spin. (A signature is a testimony—"in witness hereof"—and like all forms of witnessing, it is subject to forgery.) The requirement of swearing on the Bible before testifying in court is yet another device to enforce truth-telling, presumably by raising the specter of eternal consequences.

Passivity or even dumbness is another source of believable witnessing. Mechanical witnesses can be preferable to smart ones.[5] Montaigne's essay on cannibals, the founding text of cultural relativism, starts out with a med-

---

3. See, for instance, *Adult Eyewitness Testimony: Current Trends and Developments*, ed. David Frank Ross, J. Don Read, and Michael P. Toglia (Cambridge: Cambridge University Press, 1994).

4. Aristotle, *Rhetoric*, 1376a.

5. Louis Georges Schwartz, *Mechanical Witness*, forthcoming.

itation on the trustworthiness of travel narratives, particularly about reports from the New World. He praises his own source, a somewhat dull chap who had lived there for ten or twelve years. "This man I had was a simple, crude fellow; a character fit to bear true witness; for clever people observe more things and more curiously, but they interpret them; and to lend weight and conviction to their interpretation, they cannot help altering history a little. They never show you things as they are, but bend and disguise them according to the way they have seen them; and to give credence to their judgment and attract you to it, they are prone to add something to their matter, to stretch it out and amplify it. We need a man either very honest, or so simple that he has not the stuff to build up false inventions and give them plausibility; and wedded to no theory."[6] In the same way, medieval copyists who thought about the biblical text were often more dangerous to the integrity of its transmission than those who copied dumbly, since conscientious copyists would sometimes harmonize, reconcile apparent gaps in the text, or inadvertently editorialize.[7] The conscious mind may not know what is the most valuable evidence. In the same way, a witness in a trial may not offer an "opinion," but may only describe "the facts." There can be an old odd valuing of stupidity and blankness in some kinds of witnessing (e.g., in nonexpert testimony). Since a dumb witness does not know what is at stake, there is no motive to lend comfort to one party or the other. The dumb witness is objective, an observer numb to human concerns. The mechanization of the witness got a new lease on life in the second half of the nineteenth century.[8] As James Lastra notes of cultural worries about photography, especially in the wake of the Kodak's easy operation, "the camera made it possible, perhaps for the first time in history, to make a legible image entirely by accident." Already with the daguerreotype, many commentators noted the camera's ability to compose pictures without any guidance from a superintending will. The camera raised for art the problem Darwin suggested for nature: the problem of order without a designer.[9] It caught hitherto unnoticed detail, as did the phonograph, thus fitting those media into a longer lineage of dumb witnesses.

6. *The Complete Essays of Montaigne*, trans. Donald M. Frame (Stanford, Calif.: Stanford University Press, 1958), 151–52.

7. Bruce M. Metzger, *The Text of the New Testament.* 2nd ed.(New York: Oxford University Press, 1968), 195–96.

8. Peter Galison and Lorraine Daston, "The Image of Objectivity," *Representations* 40 (1992): 81–128.

9. James Lastra, *Sound Technology and the American Cinema: Perception, Representation, Modernity* (New York: Columbia University Press, 2000).

Of all the historic solutions to the unreliability of witnesses, torture is one of the most persistent, from the ancient Greeks to modern intelligence-gathering. As Page duBois argues, the ancient Greek word for torture, *basanos,* originally meant a touchstone against which you could rub golden artifacts to test if they were genuine; if they were, a bit would rub off and leave a mark. From there, *basanos* came to mean any test of truth or authenticity (e.g., of friendship or fidelity) and eventually moved specifically into torture, which served as an instrument of proof in ancient Athens. (Its modern Greek heir, *vasano,* means not only torment, but also steady boyfriend or girlfriend, which says something about the Greek view of romance.) Torture demarcated slaves (who respected only bodily pain) from citizens (who spoke the *logos* in freedom). Since slaves supposedly lied compulsively, torture exposed the truth by extinguishing the power to invent. (Here again we see snobbery about who is a truthful witness.) Slaves were ruled by necessity (*anangkē*). Though a slave could not appear in court, testimony obtained under torture was admissible as evidence. Yet there were doubts about the notion that pain produced truth. Aristotle thought testimony obtained under torture "inartistic," but this is not a ringing indictment, since he thought all testimony inartistic.[10] He was, as usual, right.

The renewed prestige of the confession as a legal proof in thirteenth-century Europe and beyond reintroduced judicial torture. It was understood not as a kind of punishment, but, cruel as it may sound, as a kind of data-gathering; that innocent people might suffer and even die under interrogation was considered a regrettable by-product of legal investigation.[11] Judicial torture was an attempt to ensure the validity of the confession, a rather nasty way of coping with the veracity gap. In our grisly age torture is both a method of punishment and a means of extracting intelligence, a fact signaled in the French term *la question,* which means both torture and interrogation, and the English phrase "to put to the question." The polygraph test treats the physiological indicators of the body as a haven of truth immune to conscious fabrication. Deathbed confessions possess special status, since the incentive to deceive is thought minimal (though some people are infinitely wily). As a late-eighteenth-century judge wrote, "they are declarations made in extremity, when the party is at the point of death, and when every hope of this world is gone; when every motive to falsehood has

---

10. Page duBois, *Torture and Truth* (New York: Routledge, 1991); Aristotle, *Rhetoric,* 1377a.

11. John H. Langbein, *Torture and the Law of Proof: Europe and England in the Ancien Régime* (Chicago: University of Chicago Press, 1977); Edward Peters, *Torture* (New York: Blackwell, 1985), chap. 2.

been silenced, and the mind is induced by the most powerful considerations to speak the truth."[12] Death or pain impels the mind to forgo the temptation to embellish. Edgar Allan Poe introduced his story "Ms. Found in a Bottle" with an epigraph by Philippe Quinault: "Qui n'a plus qu'un moment à vivre / N'a plus rien à dissimuler."[13] Elaine Scarry argues that pain can anchor—and defy—the play of words. Words, which have an endless capacity to make worlds, are bound by pain to the brute reality of sensation and are thus hindered from their most fantastical possibilities. For Scarry both torture and war connect "the hurt body" to "unanchored verbal statements."[14] Suffering checks the word's power to deceive. It reduces "the motive to fabricate" to zero. Just so, the survivor's witness, offered as a cold duty rather than self-promotion, fits in the tradition of establishing authenticity via compulsion.

The Enlightenment, roughly speaking, sought to put testimony on a rational footing—rather than the old basis of suffering. Locke was central to the new role of witnessing in modern science, and the problem of how the apparently private stuff of sensation has input into the public world of intelligible words is central to empiricist philosophy.[15] Modern science's demand for observations from many eyes and ears led to a reevaluation of the low repute of testimony, something first achieved in seventeenth-century England among gentleman scientists, whose shared status and norms of civility established a social basis for mutual trust.[16] As Peter Lipton quips, gentlemen prefer gentlemen.[17] Without trust in other's testimony, science as we know it would be impossible. Scientific instrumentation was another means to bypass the subjectivity, fallibility, and bias of sensation. The microscope and telescope, as mere recorders, were credible in their indifference to human interests. Instruments, like the forensics of the trial, the pains of the martyr, and the memoirs of the survivor, are attempts to overpower the melancholy fact that direct sensory experience—from the taste of pineapple to the pangs of childbirth—vanishes when put into words and remains inaccessible to others except inasmuch as they claim to share simi-

12. 1789 case, cited in Sir Rupert Cross, *Evidence.* 4th ed. (London: Buttersworth, 1974), 472.

13. "He who has no more than a moment to live has nothing left to hide."

14. Elaine Scarry, *The Body in Pain* (New York: Oxford University Press, 1985), 139.

15. See his *Essay Concerning Human Understanding* (1690) (Oxford: Oxford University Press, 1975), book 4, especially chaps. 14–16.

16. Steven Shapin, *A Social History of Truth: Civility and Science in Seventeenth-Century England* (Chicago: University of Chicago Press, 1994).

17. Peter Lipton, "The Epistemology of Testimony," *History and Philosophy of Science* 29.1 (1998).

lar experiences directly. Our nerve endings encircle sensation into privately personal ontologies. The potential for solipsism always lurked in empiricism. Much of what we know as sociability consists of efforts to make incommunicable goods—sensation, grief, pleasure, pain, joy—common by rhetoric, celebration, eating and drinking, making love, singing, mourning.

Etymologically, the bodily basis of testimony is clear. The English "testimony" stems from the Latin *testamentum*, "covenant" (*testis* plus *mentum*). *Testis*, which means both "witness" and "testicle," itself stems from *tertius*, meaning "third" (party); as will be recalled, it is also the name of the assistant who took Paul's dictation in the letter to the Romans. In ancient Greek the word for witness is also the word for testicle: *parastatēs*, which literally means "bystander." In German *Zeugnis* means "testimony," and *zeugen* means "to testify" as well as "to procreate." The explanation of this pervasive and odd system of metaphors is obscure—and I have found no evidence for the scholarly urban legend that in ancient times a judge slipped a hand under the witness's toga to clasp his testicles as a warning of the pain that might result from bearing false witness—but one may conjecture that the testicles, as physical bystanders to the act of procreation, were thought witnesses of paternity or virility in Indo-European culture.[18] That knowing firsthand should be associated with the testicles suggests the ancient virility of this act. This curious web of metaphors attests to some deep assumptions about the bodily side of witnessing. So does the term autopsy. Now generally used to describe the coroner's inspection of a corpse so as to ascertain the cause of death, it once meant first-person eyewitness testimony (from the Greek *auto*, "self, "and *opsis*," sight"). The body serves as collateral for the loan of our credence. The whole aim to ensure truthfulness, from torture to martyrdom to courtroom procedure, only testifies to the strange lack at its core. Witness is borne under sanction—whether of pain, death, jail, or dishonor. One testifies quite literally *sub poena*—under threat of punishment. Witnesses can find themselves compelled to appear bodily in court. It does not take a Foucault to see that today witnessing is policed at its boundaries by an apparatus of pain.

Martyrdom is another attempt to bridge the gap between inner conviction and outer persuasion. As Paul Ricoeur notes, in Greek a *martus* is a witness, and bearing witness somehow shifted from stating a belief to dying a violent death. "Testimony is both a manifestation and a crisis of appear-

18. Neither the OED, the LSJ, nor Richard Broxton Onians, *The Origins of European Thought About the Body, the Mind, the Soul, the World, Time, and Fate* (Cambridge: Cambridge University Press, 1954), explicates this. Thanks to Prof. E. B. Holtsmark for advice on this point.

ances." The martyr is willing to trade life for truth, but even that is not necessarily fully persuasive. "A strange hermeneutic spiral is set in motion; the circle of Manifestation and of Suffering. The martyr proves nothing, we say, but a truth which is not strong enough to lead a man to sacrifice lacks proof."[19] Here are the outer limits of persuasion, of *pistis*. We can do pathetically little to stop the infinite regress. Pain is the ultimate index. It points mutely to something beyond it. In martyrdom bodily privacy (the suffering and death) and public act (the spectacle of martyrdom) come close but do not touch for sure. The martyr's death demonstrates the limit-case of persuasion, the vanishing point at which proof stops and credence begins. Saint Stephen or Saint Sebastian, or their secular equivalents, the many political martyrs whose legacies are so powerful today, may impress bystanders with their composure under the most gruesome abuses, but their deaths alone will not convince anyone: one needs internal grounds for believing. To bear witness is to put one's body on the line. Within every witness, perhaps, stands a martyr, the will to corroborate words with something beyond them, pain and death being the last resorts.

Witnessing can involve peril to life or liberty. Witnesses of a crime or conspiracy can suddenly find themselves threatened. The FBI runs the evocatively named witness protection program, which provides personal security and sometimes new identities for people willing to turn state witness. That simply seeing can set your fate is a suggestive way to get beyond the idea of mere spectatorship. In recent years scholars have argued for the agency of media audiences and have demonstrated just how "active" audiences may be in construing their own meanings or devising their own practices. But witnessing reminds us of a sober fact: agency does not only mean the freeing of audiences from constraining ideologies; it also means their capture within webs of responsibility or complicity. Being informed can be a profoundly life-transforming event. Witnessing, as Robin Wagner-Pacifici notes, recognizes no contrast between action and observation.[20] Witnessing is a mode of communication intimately tied to the mortality of both the one who bears witness and the one who witnesses. In the words of Jorge Luis Borges: "Deeds which populate the dimensions of space and which reach their end when someone dies may cause us wonderment, but one thing, or an infinite number of things, dies in every final agony. . . . In time there was a day that extinguished the last eyes to see Christ; the battle

19. Paul Ricoeur, "The Hermeneutics of Testimony," in *Essays in Biblical Interpretation*, ed. Lewis S. Mudge (London: SPCK, 1981).

20. Wagner-Pacifici, "Witness to Surrender," 2.

of Junín and the love of Helen died with a man."[21] The knowledge that dwells among mortals rather than other repositories—this is the stuff of witnessing.

WITNESSING FROM CAPTIVITY

Witnessing uses words to approximate presence; body-witnessing uses presence to approximate words. One takes place in court, the other on the streets or wherever the strategy and tactics of nonviolent resistance arise. Civil disobedience is a method to bridge the veracity gap in witnessing. Prison is a key site for artists of passive resistance. Thoreau stated the basic principle: "Under a government which imprisons any unjustly, the true place for a just man is also a prison."[22] Prison is the house of witness. Doing time can produce moral authority. Paul, like many early Christians, proudly went to jail and thought his captivity a moving scene: "my bonds in Christ," he wrote to the Philippians, "are publicly visible [*phanerous*] in all the pretorium and in all other places" (Phil. 1:13). Jail with dignity is a performance of moral authority. Penal conviction overlaps with spiritual conviction. In the United States the first native literary genre was the captivity narrative, and it persists, in a transmuted way, in the African-American tradition, from Frederick Douglass and Sojourner Truth through Malcolm X and Martin Luther King, all of whom rose from slavery or prison, or both. (Oprah Winfrey tells a latter-day version of the story: emergence from abuse.) The African-American captivity narrative self-consciously follows Exodus's tale of the children of Israel escaping from bondage in Egypt. Those who have languished in captivity stand as witnesses against inhumanity and gain political and moral stature: Dietrich Bonhoeffer, Jacobo Timerman, Varlam Shalamov, Aleksandr Solzhenitsyn, Nelson Mandela, Václav Havel, Kim Dae-Jung, Aung San Suu Kyi, to name a few. Prison literature has proved as influential in the twentieth century as slave narratives were in the nineteenth.[23]

The chief voice of witnessing out of captivity today probably comes from the Holocaust. Writers such as Primo Levi, Anne Frank, Paul Celan, Victor Klemperer, and Elie Wiesel—the Papa of all Holocaust survivors—

21. Jorge Luis Borges, "The Witness," in *Labyrinths: Selected Stories and Other Writings*, ed. Donald A. Yates and James E. Irby (New York: New Directions, 1964), 243.

22. Henry David Thoreau, *Walden and Civil Disobedience* (New York: Norton, 1966), 233.

23. See Gerard A. Hauser, "Prisoners of Conscience and the Counterpublic Sphere of Prison Writing," in *Counterpublics and the State*, ed. Robert Asen and Daniel C. Brouwer (Albany: SUNY Press, 2001), 35–58.

have gained enormous cultural authority as witnesses of atrocity. Witnessing has accrued a moral cachet, as an act that always belongs to the unjustly abused (the Nazi who wrote up memoirs as a "witness" would violate some implicit cultural grammar). Not surprisingly, there has been something of a scramble to ride the prestige of the victim-witness. A book on the making of the movie *Schindler's List* is pretentiously called *Witness*, confusing the film and what the film was about. Wiesel has made a great career reflecting on the privilege and loneliness of the survivor. One's responsibility to bear witness, he argues, cannot be delegated; testimony is the unique property of the survivor. The witness can neither remain silent nor describe the event. Wiesel's paradoxical task is to proclaim experiences that cannot be shared and to immortalize events that are uniquely tied to the mortal bodies of those who went through them. The militancy in the survivor's voice owes to the battle against oblivion and indifference, just as the martyr likewise uses the spectacle of his or her body in pain to convict the conscience of the observer. Already having cheated death, the survivor seeks to save his or her experiences for (or sometimes from) others who can never have them. Few can corner a monopoly on righteousness like the survivor. King, at least, was clear that he meant to be a moral bully, and his targets were racists, not guilty liberals ready to pay nice speaker's fees. Nothing quite exploits like the good. A gentle cynicism equips us better to cope with the abuse of the morally sanctioned.

The moral privilege of the captive and martyr goes back to Socrates and Jesus, and they stand for two modes of witnessing from prison. Both require composure on the part of the convict, who must be polite, gracious, and charming, and treat the captors with dignity, as people doing a dirty job they did not choose. Jesus saw the soldiers who crucified him as tools, knowing not what they were doing, so he forgave them as good professionals. Socrates in his cell was joking and witty, making fun of his disciples' efforts to spirit him away, trying his hand at setting Aesop's fables to poetry, and showing an utter lack of sympathy for his wife Xanthippe's desire to mourn (in Plato's rather chilly account).[24] He embodied the ideal of making light of death, enjoying his last hours without moping. Socrates had rehearsed death, inspiring the Stoics later. The emotional register of Jesus's death was different: "I thirst" (John 19:28). The hemlock was a drowsy transition, but the crucifixion was a prolonged agony. These two modes of witnessing from captivity, levitas and gravitas, buoyancy and pathos, remain

24. Plato, *Phaedo*, 60a–b.

the two chief options.[25] Neither Socrates nor Jesus lacked any dignity; both were beside themselves.

Just so, the civility of civil disobedience secures its moral authority. Self-sacrificial passivity goes best with a certain mildness of self-presentation or even mirth. John Rawls makes the smart comment: "To be completely open and nonviolent is to give bond of one's sincerity, for it is not easy to convince another that one's acts are conscientious, or even to be sure of this before oneself."[26] Lee Bollinger agrees: "The injury voluntarily sustained helps to establish, both to oneself and to others, the depth of one's feelings and the purity of one's motives."[27] The veracity gap looms even in the microscopic distances of the self. Putting yourself in danger is an all but foolproof way to establish good faith. It is maddening to opponents for the same reason, since they lose moral legitimacy by enacting their power. Sincerity is not an inner state of pure intention but the attitude of living up to promises.[28] If passive resistance is a way to prove truthfulness to the self, it is also a way to neutralize public cynicism. Any engaged cause awakes suspicions of bias. Self-sacrifice quells a doubting audience.[29] Suffering abuse without retaliation, even with cheerfulness, shields the victim from critical inspection about unrighteous motives. It was thus easier for figures such as Havel and Solzhenitsyn to keep an unblemished moral profile in jail. Out of prison, their faults (such as managerial incompetence or grumpiness) became clear. Taken as a spectacle (not as an experience), prison suspends time and vices. Prisoners are immune from themselves, at least to their spectators.

There is a moral alchemy in the performance of voluntarily endured affliction. Passive resistance involves the choice to convert oneself into an eloquent thing vulnerable to fists and clubs. As in the martyr or the victim, pain seems to suspend the motive to fabricate. Voluntary jeopardy implies sincerity. Refusing to fight back makes clear to bystanders who the aggressor is. As soon as one is drawn into a tit-for-tat exchange one loses the moral advantage (it takes two to tango). Nonresponsiveness enacts freedom from the ego, the eloquence of muteness. (The scientist's muteness before statistics is a similar attitude.) Refusing to respond prevents the victim from be-

25. Thanks to Charles Taylor for suggesting this contrast.

26. John Rawls, *A Theory of Justice* (Cambridge, Mass.: Harvard University Press, 1971), 367.

27. Lee C. Bollinger, *The Tolerant Society* (New York: Oxford University Press, 1986), 122–23.

28. J. L. Austin, *How to Do Things with Words* (Oxford: Clarendon Press, 1962), 10.

29. Robert K. Merton, with Marjorie Fiske and Alberta Curtis, *Mass Persuasion* (New York: Harper, 1946).

coming a victimizer (people long abused can become as vile as the ogres that persecuted them, once they get the chance for revenge). Passive resistance means bridling one's righteous indignation: the burning desire to see justice done is cousin to the desire for revenge. Stoic discipline of the self goes with a Cynical goading of the other. To employ the tactic of passively resistant body-witnessing is to forge a moral monopoly that will embarrass anyone on the wrong side. Shaming people is powerful medicine for recruiting adherents and forcing change. There is nothing quite as vexing as a cheerful person who is completely justified. Billy Budd's moral perfection and innocence drove Claggart wild in Herman Melville's story.[30] Passive resistance is certainly open to abuse, but bullying can have its uses, like everything else. Every abuse has a use; every use has an abuse. Paul and Milton knew this.

PERSONS AS OBJECTS

Body-witnessing from prison or captivity unlocks the moral resources of the fact that human beings are also things. In some profoundly nondemeaning way we are things to each other and ourselves. We can be ethically and politically engaged by simply being in the Sabbath of action. "We, however, who enjoy and use other things are things ourselves," said Augustine.[31] Yet to say we are things can seem like a capitulation to the murder factories. Crimes against humanity remove all the social relations that would normally rescue people and give them identity as persons—as fathers and mothers, men and women, friends and neighbors.[32] But the reduction to our lowest common denominator occurs not only in the death camps. It is a radical act of ethics to treat each person we meet as a person, nothing more and nothing less. Democratic citizenship is based precisely on such beneficial abstraction. No matter what throne you sit upon, you still sit on your own behind, said Montaigne. Such a reduction, as it were, of every person into a being with a bottom cuts radically against social practice, where hierarchy and status of every sort reign. Like Quakers calling everyone "thou" and "thee"—a daring act of leveling in seventeenth-century England—radical social action may lie no farther than simply treating other people as people. To do so requires a willingness to suspend fame, rank,

30. Herman Melville, *Billy Budd and Other Stories* (New York: Penguin, 1986).

31. Augustine, "On Christian Doctrine," in *Great Books of the Western World*, ed. Robert Maynard Hutchins (Chicago: Encyclopedia Britannica, 1952), 18: 269.

32. Michael Ignatieff, *The Warrior's Honor* (New York: Henry Holt, 1997), 19–21.

beauty, history, accomplishments—indeed, everything that is specifically personal about them. Individuality does not fully matter for personhood. One needs no acquaintance with another person to honor that person's humanity; a face or liver is enough (not all people have faces). True, Pauline blindness does not alter social hierarchies, but it also does not reproduce them. It renders them momentarily irrelevant, putting them into a state of sabbatical cessation. This is the messianic option dwelling in any moment of social interaction.

Resistance to the notion that people are objects comes from multiple sources. One is the Marxist critique of reification, or *Verdinglichung* (lit., "thingification"). For Georg Lukács, its chief theorist, reification extends the capitalist logic in which things are loved and people are used: "properties and abilities are no longer bound to the organic unity of the person, but rather appear as 'things,' which man possesses and disposes of [*veräussert*] just like the various objects of the external world."[33] For Lukács, to see people as things is to capitulate to a historical situation that he finds revolting. Martin Buber, whose *I and Thou* appeared in the same year as Lukács's *History and Class Consciousness* (1923), believed in an ultimately Kantian sort of way that subjects should be treated as subjects, and objects as objects.[34] Despite the obvious differences of the two thinkers, both believe that modernity means the growth of the dominion of the "it," and that the critical task is to break through the crusts of thinghood (via revolution for Lukács, via a renewed ethical appreciation for the thou-ness of the world for Buber). I-thou relations reveal a wholeness, Buber claims, that I-it relations never can. Finally, feminists have pointed out that "empathy with the inorganic" is not a neutral option.[35] It might be one thing for a secure white male body to claim solidarity with things, but other sorts of bodies may find the intellectual and moral ideal of metaphysical personhood a necessary insurance policy, especially when women and people of color were long treated as property. The antiporn faction in feminist thought argues that pornography objectifies women and thus reproduces patriarchal domination in image, sound, and word. There is a certain kind of looking, Catherine MacKinnon argues, that vaporizes women into mobile targets of egotistic delectation.[36] As long as capitalists exploit, institutions treat people as

33. Georg Lukács, *Geschichte und Klassenbewusstsein* (1923) (Neuwied: Luchterhand, 1970), 194.

34. Martin Buber, *Ich und Du* (Leipzig: Insel Verlag, 1923).

35. Christine Buci-Glucksmann, *La raison baroque: De Baudelaire à Benjamin* (Paris: Galilée, 1984).

36. Catherine MacKinnon, "Feminism, Marxism, and the State," *Signs* 8 (1983).

things, and sex is tied to violence, Lukács, Buber, and MacKinnon would argue, some critique of objectification remains a key political resource.

I have no problem with the moral-political impulse of creating conditions of respect for our fellow creatures, but the outrage may be misplaced. There can be something blessed about things. The critics of human thingliness underestimate the degree to which subjects are objects and objects are subjects. People in comas or in need of intensive nursing, unborn children or infants, are all obviously objects. The asymmetrical grace of caring in such settings is no moral shipwreck. People are not only numinous objects when they are dead or incapacitated, possessing the full horror of corpses; they are always that way. As the anthropologists teach us, people are sacred objects. All kinds of prohibitions about touch and contact reign in interaction, and there is a hushed distance in the presence of a stranger, or even a loved one, as acute as before any shrine—even in cultures that foster more intimate personal spaces than the northern European and Anglo-American. We all walk around carrying an invisible sanctum walling off our persons from others. A headline in a French gossip magazine announces that the actress Cathérine Deneuve is afraid of being loved for her physique and not for her "qualities." It must be hard to be one of the most beautiful women in the world, never knowing if someone cares about you or just wants you as a trophy. She implicitly equates the soul with qualities and the body with something else. But what if someone truly loved Deneuve for who she is: aren't her beauty, her face, hair, and body part of who she is? Isn't her physique also a quality? As if one who loved her for her qualities could not love her for her beauty as well.[37] The man or woman without quantities would be worse off than one without qualities.

As persons we possess qualities and quantities we did nothing to deserve. We are not, said Paul, our own. Let us not demean the language of possession with reference to persons. Our size and shape and health and face are all in some way both alien to us and exactly us. Those qualities and quantities are not luggage we can check. Birth is the most arbitrary gift in the universe. Anglo-Americans and northern Europeans sometimes wear their bodies around like ill-fitting clothes. To see each other as unique, irreplaceable, and sacred *things* is not just objectification. It is the beginning of humanity. Tragedy, in the technical sense of a story in which no graceful exit is possible, stems at least in part from the nature of personhood, from the fact that our bodies are gifts we receive whose limits, though movable, are ulti-

37. Giorgio Agamben, *Le temps qui reste: Un commentaire de l'Epitre aux Romains* (Paris: Éditions Payot et Rivages, 2000), 201.

mately out of our control. Our thingliness is at odds with our wishes, as some of our wishes are at odds with other wishes. Thinking will not add a cubit to our stature. Need and want are often strangers who board with us, entertaining and irritating us variously. We are as surprised by their force or laziness as anyone else. Lucky the woman Theodore Roethke knew: "Her several parts could keep a pure repose."[38] The soul is whole but the body has parts.

In a world where oppression reigns, it may be sound advice to love subjects and use objects. Buber and company are right that confusing subjects and objects can be dangerous. They provide valuable criteria for criticizing many aspects of commercial society. People are not simply objects—but any vision of the human estate that forgets our objecthood is a wasteland. A world without objects would be a sensible emptiness. Is there ever a relation with an other—or a self—without an element of itness? Are partial relationships necessarily corrupt? Democracy is precisely a web of relationships-at-a-distance among relative or total strangers. Buber views the I-it link as degenerate, when I-it precisely defines a public constellation, one open to witnesses. Every thou is also an it and every it is potentially a thou. Uncanniness (I as it) and animism (it as I) are not only pathologies. The openly gracious realm of things, so accepting and oblivious of us, has lessons of which the wise Buber has not supposed.[39]

Only angels love people as ends—perhaps because they cannot touch them. You can only recognize a subject, said Hegel. Alexandre Kojève and his French disciples, Lacan chief among them, amend: you can only desire a subject. You can, however, hold an object. These ratios make sex enormously complicated, especially if one seeks intersubjective recognition, a juncture of two Buberian thous. The term sex object is a frequent lament. Some sex acts do bring acute sorts of sexual objectification. But acute crimes should not obscure chronic truths. Interobjectivity can be as profound as intersubjectivity. The discipline of the object is inescapable in our mutual dealings. Friendship, said Emerson, "must plant itself on the ground, before it vaults over the moon. I wish it to be a little of a citizen, before it is quite a cherub. We chide the citizen because he makes love a commodity. It is an exchange of gifts, of useful loans; it is good neighborhood; it watches with the sick; it holds the pall at the funeral; and quite loses sight of the delicacies and nobil-

38. Theodore Roethke, "I Knew a Woman," in *Literature: An Introduction to Fiction, Poetry, and Drama,* ed. X. J. Kennedy (Boston: Little, Brown, 1976), 553, l. 19.

39. Jorge Luis Borges, "Las cosas," in *In Praise of Darkness: A Bilingual Edition* (New York: E. P. Dutton, 1974), 56.

ities of the relation."[40] Friends are comfortable in making use of each other. "Love makes good usage," said Paul (khrēsteuetai hē agapē; 1 Cor. 13:4). A bit of "commodity," as Emerson used the term, is inevitably part of friendship, love, and sex. Lovers are citizens before they are cherubs.

Let us not erect impossible metaphysical scaffoldings to achieve what solidarity, in all its weakness, can provide. Killers and bad doctors reduce people to warmish albuminoid matter; but discovering that the thing by the side of the road is not a corpse but a person is the start of compassion, according to the parable of the Good Samaritan. The bad doctor treats humans indifferently as experimental specimens; the good doctor knows that we are things, and because of that, is able to minister to our needs as things—and hence as people. Anyone fortunate enough to have ever been treated by a good doctor will know exactly what I mean. Recognizing human thingliness has curiously double implications: it can reduce or lead to an embrace full of *misericordia*. That we humans are meat is a moral lesson of the first order. The archaic Greeks "thought that this thing that will die, which unless it is properly buried will be eaten by dogs and birds, is exactly the thing one is."[41] Perhaps we should treat subjects as objects (caring for their bodies) and objects as subjects (hearing their speech). "Sweet young thing" is a term of objectification, but "poor thing" one of compassion. Either can have a wicked or happy edge. We subjects are dispersed across the field of the objects we labor with and love. Persons are tied up with properties. We can only beg for mercy that our qualities will not be reduced to the most instantaneous, least time-filled ones. What could be a better bulwark against murder, as the philosopher Emmanuel Levinas argues, than the singular irreplaceability of that thing, another's face?[42] In passive resistance the face in its unique fragility confronts power—and wins, sometimes.

Admitting ourselves into the kingdom of thinghood would open up wider ranges of solidarity. Let the androids and the dead join in, the elephants and the stones, the trees and the swelling silicate species that communicates in impulses our senses will never perceive and at speeds our brains will never reach.[43] It is not our supposedly most exalted portions,

---

40. Ralph Waldo Emerson, "Friendship," in *Selected Writings of Emerson,* ed. Donald McQuade (New York: Modern Library, 1981), 214.

41. Bernard Williams, *Shame and Necessity* (Berkeley: University of California Press, 1993), 24.

42. Regard for the other's face is one of the leading themes of Levinas's philosophy. See, for instance, "Ethics as First Philosophy," in *The Levinas Reader,* ed. Seán Hand (Oxford: Blackwell, 1989), 82–84.

43. George Dyson, *Darwin Among the Machines: The Evolution of Global Intelligence* (Cambridge, Mass.: Perseus Books, 1997).

our rationality, as Descartes thought, that distinguishes humans from—or as—creatures. We are most human in the thing that allies us with other animals: our vertebrae and viscera, our abilities for compassion—*compassibilitas*—the possibility and impossibility of communicating with our fellow creatures. We need know only one thing to recognize another, that this other is in some way a person. Plutarch found love superior to justice: "We see that kindness or humanity has a larger field than bare justice to exercise itself in; law and justice we cannot, in the nature of things, employ on others than men; but we may extend our goodness and charity even to irrational creatures."[44] Love encompasses protoplasm and may contact organic and inorganic matter at every level.

MARTIN LUTHER KING'S PRINCIPLED PASSIVITY

The theory and tactics of Martin Luther King, Jr. offer a case study in monopolistic moral appeals and the power of passivity and of drama. His political theory and practice have diverse sources: the biblical prophets; Jesus and Socrates; the Cynical tradition from Diogenes to Thoreau; Tolstoy and Gandhi; 1950s alienation sociology; liberal theology and its critics (Niebuhr); and the black church. King's liberation theology, despite its absorption by official ideology, strikes me as one of the best options for coping with abuse in this world. He taught people how to bear witness with their presence, thus underlining that democracy has to do with where your body is. King disliked the label passive resistance, since he found nothing passive about action that puts people in peril; he preferred the more virile "direct action." By "passive," I mean a performance of immobility, nonresponsiveness in the face of abuse, voluntarily putting oneself at risk for the sake of political or moral criticism. Passive resistance shares with civil disobedience conscious submission to the pain that follows a violation.

King knew from Thoreau how prison can produce an untainted witness, though he probably learned it as much from Socrates and Jesus. "I would rather stay in jail the rest of my days," King quoted the Puritan writer John Bunyan, "than make a butchery of my conscience."[45] We might restate it: I would rather stay in jail than make a butchery of my moral legitimacy. Give me justice or give me captivity. Being released would undermine the performance: Socrates refused Crito's pleadings and offer of escape, Jesus rebuked

44. Plutarch, *Lives,* in *Great Books of the Western World,* 14: 279.

45. David J. Garrow, *Bearing the Cross: Martin Luther King, Jr. and the Southern Christian Leadership Conference* (London: Jonathan Cape, 1988), 246.

Peter's attempt to save him by the sword, and Thoreau was annoyed when someone paid his poll tax. King used jail as a synecdoche for the fate of black people in the American South generally, and much of his moral authority doubtless derived from the legacy of slavery as captivity. A prisoner of conscience can suck dry any claim to legitimacy by the jailing regime in the same way that a beggar can embarrass a passerby. The behavior of the prisoner must be irreproachable: "the means we use must be as pure as the ends we seek" said King.[46] Over-eagerness to escape a prison sentence betrays an unseemly interest in the merely personal.

In his first phone call to his wife Coretta Scott King from Birmingham City Jail in April 1963, King inquired about local and national press coverage of the protest. Some of his colleagues were surprised to find a man of the cloth so concerned with publicity, as he consistently was, as if he should have had a more stoic or honorable indifference to audiences. But he was quite conscious of his authorship of media spectacles. The violent suppression of peaceful protests, and even more, the national news coverage thereof, were crucial to the success of the civil rights movement. Images of Eugene "Bull" Connor's fire hoses ripping the clothing off the backs of peaceful protestors still circulate in collective memory and were reported to have made President John F. Kennedy "sick" (and also inspired a Warhol silkscreen).[47] The Southern Christian Leadership Conference found an ideal enemy in Connor. A demagogue who sought to bolster his somewhat flimsy political support by playing to white supremacist sentiment, thereby risking the backing of moderate whites, Connor made a superb villain. A scenario of dramatic contrast, a spectacle of unambiguous right and wrong, could hardly have been scripted better: willing victims abused by the worst of the Old South. The dry style of journalistic objectivity in the words and cameras of the reporters matched the passivity of the protestors. The active witness (in peril) of the protesters depended on the passive witness (in safety) of the press. The best part of "objectivity" is not the braggadocio impartiality of the positivist scientist but the humble registration of facts and events as if told by an idiot: the protestors protest not with words but with their persons. "We would present our very bodies," said King, "as a means of laying our case before the conscience of the local and national commu-

46. Martin Luther King, "Letter from Birmingham City Jail" (1963), in *A Testament of Hope: The Essential Writings of Martin Luther King, Jr.*, ed. James Melvin Washington (San Francisco: Harper & Row, 1986), 301. King took much from Marx about exploitation, but he could never forgive his willingness to let the end justify the means.

47. The year 1963 was a watershed in photojournalistic shock, from the self-immolation of the South Vietnamese Buddhist monk to the assassination of John F. Kennedy.

nity."[48] Compare Havel: "[The dissident] does not seek power. He has no desire for office and does not woo voters. He does not attempt to charm the public, he offers nothing and promises nothing. He can offer, if anything, only his own skin—and he offers it solely because he has no other way of affirming the truth he stands for."[49] Or Thoreau: "Let your life be a counter friction to stop the machine."[50]

King was highly aware of the long Jewish and Christian tradition of moral stuntsmanship. Ezekiel is the mother of all stunt artists, the ancestor of such body rhetoricians as the Earth Firsters.[51] He put on public minidramas in abjection and inhumanity for the instruction and warning of all Israel, including tying himself up and refusing to speak, going naked and lying on his side in public, mixing human excrement with bread dough and then eating it, shaving his head and beard into thirds, and not weeping at his wife's death. Paul tells the Corinthians that they are "made a spectacle unto the world, and to angels, and to men. We are fools for Christ's sake" (1 Cor. 4:9–10). The cross itself is supposed to be a moral spectacle. A long line of flamboyant martyrs and ascetics stretches from Jesus to King: you do not spend your life sitting on a pole, even in a desert, if you do not want some kind of attention. Everything was a scene for Saint Francis, says Erich Auerbach, including squawking like a chicken and dressing up like a beggar to crash his own party.[52] King had plenty of warrant in biblical literature for acts that attract, spellbind, and shame audiences, or openly court public sanction (such as Daniel praying in defiance of Darius's decree—with his window wide open).

King also had warrant in Gandhi, the proximate inspiration of his political method, who made sure reporters were within witnessing distance whenever he staged an exercise in passive resistance. Gandhi was a master of grand gestures that caught the attention of his foes and sympathizers worldwide: spinning and wearing cotton dhoti cloth, distilling salt from the sea, launching hunger strikes. Drama is a resource, not the dead end, of progressive politics.[53] "The purpose of . . . direct action," wrote King, "is to cre-

48. King, "Letter from Birmingham City Jail," 291.

49. Václav Havel, "Anatomy of a Reticence," in *Open Letters: Selected Writings, 1965–1990*, ed. Paul Wilson (New York: Knopf, 1992), 320.

50. Thoreau, *Walden and Civil Disobedience*, 231.

51. See Kevin Michael DeLuca, *Image Politics: The New Rhetoric of Environmental Activism* (New York: Guilford, 1999).

52. Erich Auerbach, *Mimesis* (Garden City, N.Y.: Doubleday, 1957), 162.

53. See James Patrick McDaniel, "Liberal Irony: A Program for Rhetoric," *Philosophy and Rhetoric* 35 (2002): 297–327.

ate a situation so crisis-packed that it will inevitably open the door to nego-
tiation. . . . We who engage in nonviolent direct action are not the creators
of tension. We merely bring to the surface the hidden tension that is already
alive. We bring it out into the open where it can be seen and dealt with." Direct action is a strategic outing that brings the repressed to consciousness, a
psychoanalysis or anamnesis on a social scale. "Society needs nonviolent
gadflies": King was not afraid to apply a moral vice to people just as relentless as the Socratic *elenchos* ("interrogation")—thus his apparent oxy-
moron of "nonviolent coercion." [54] King in fact compared direct action to
Socratic cross-examination. Direct action was publication, transforming
something already there to visibility. In this, King had basically a Kantian
approach to morality. Whatever cannot withstand the glare of publicity is
ipso facto wrong. Kant could have written this statement of King's: "An unjust law is a code that a majority inflicts on a minority that is not binding on
itself." [55]

King had confidence in publicity. Like Kant and Mill, and perhaps stem-
ming from his early study of liberal theology (before his encounter with
Niebuhr's darker doctrine), King thought that the truth would win out:
"right defeated is stronger than evil triumphant." [56] Getting the hatred out
in the open would transform it into something else. He had no fear in tarrying with the negative. Confronting disease meant not infection but conva-
lescence: "Only through this kind of exposure will the cancer ever be
cured." [57] Indeed, in classic pathological fashion he thought the benefit of
airing morbidity justified the potential revulsion: "Like a boil that can never
be cured as long as it is covered up but must be opened with all its pus-flow-
ing ugliness to the natural medicines of air and light, injustice must likewise
be exposed, with all of the tension its exposing creates, to the light of human
conscience and the air of national opinion before it can be cured." [58] King
invokes both the impassive exposé of medical morbidity and the self-
resolving quality of public ventilation like one schooled in the Stoic arts of
courage.

To critics who disliked his offensive dramas, King provided a lucid analysis of the available means of persuasion: "Lacking sufficient access to televi-

54. All the preceding King quotations are from Garrow, *Bearing the Cross*, 245–51.

55. King, "Letter from Birmingham City Jail," 294. On Kant's criterion of publicity as the political equivalent to moral universality, see Jürgen Habermas, *The Structural Transformation of
the Public Sphere* (1962) (Cambridge: MIT Press, 1989), sec.13.

56. King, "Letter from Birmingham City Jail," 300.

57. Martin Luther King, Jr., *Chaos or Community?* (London: Hodder & Stoughton, 1967), 91.

58. King, "Letter from Birmingham City Jail," 295.

sion, publications and broad forums, Negroes have had to write their most persuasive essays with the blunt pen of marching ranks. The many white political leaders and well-meaning friends who ask Negro leadership to leave the streets may not realize that they are asking us effectively to silence ourselves. . . . Nonviolent direct action will continue to be a significant source of power until it is made irrelevant by the presence of justice."[59] Being "polite" would mean not speaking at all. The streets were the medium of communication available to African-Americans—"the poor man's printing press." In the words of Ralph Ellison's Dr. Bledsoe: "These white folks have newspapers, magazines, radios, spokesmen to get their ideas across. If they want to tell the world a lie, they can tell it so well that it becomes the truth."[60] Publicity stunts are the refuge of those without access to establishment media; terrorism is the extreme form. King's violence affected only innocent and willing victims, the protestors themselves. His colleague E. D. Nixon rebuked nervous black ministers who hesitated to participate in the Montgomery bus boycott out of fear "that the newspaper men will be here and your pictures might come out in the newspapers. Somebody has got to get hurt in this thing."[61] Though he likely did not mean the metaphysical necessity of sacrifice, Nixon caught the harsh calculus of publicity: spilt blood mobilizes attention. This resembles the Pauline analysis of sin: No, it is not good to break the law, but sometime, somewhere, the law must be broken so that grace may abound. Somebody has got to get hurt in this thing. Offenses must come but woe to him through whom the offense comes!

Besides creating publicity, in either the Kantian or the public relations sense, the aim of civil disobedience is to provoke a response. It is goading at its purest, not with malice, but with a sly generosity and even glee: two of King's favorite words were "prod" and "sensitize." King's practice has roots in the philosophical tradition of Cynicism, which, as Michel Foucault has shown so lucidly, is a key source of the critical tradition of speaking truth to power. Passive resistance is practical Cynicism. Diogenes's *parrhēsia* in telling Alexander to step out of the sunlight won Alexander's admiration even though he was often on the verge of killing Diogenes for his impertinence. Foucault's account of the Cynical practice of "parrhēsia," a Greek word that literally means "all-speaking," but can also mean "public speech," "free speech," "frankness," or "courage," notes three main aspects: "(1) critical preaching; (2) scandalous behavior; and (3) what I shall call the 'pro-

59. King, *Chaos or Community*, 139.
60. Ralph Ellison, *Invisible Man* (New York: Random House, 1980), 143.
61. Garrow, *Bearing the Cross*, 23.

vocative dialogue.'" All three are relevant to King's practice: the preaching is obvious, many people thought everything he did was scandalous, and direct action is precisely a provocative dialogue. The Cynical dialogue is distinct from the Socratic in that its chief target is the pride, rather than the ignorance, of the interlocutor. Diogenes had neither political nor military power, but his praxis consisted in exposing himself to both in the name of truth. There is no provocative dialogue if the provocateur does not risk harm or even death. If Diogenes's encounter with Alexander is taken as the prototype, the provocative dialogue enrages, then engages, the other in a wave of taunts and lessons, forcing the opponent to internalize the struggle for truth and justice. The weakness of the interlocutor is supposed to call forth mercy and reflection rather than violence.[62] (The ACLU found in the National Socialist Party of America a Cynical dialogue of provocation.)

King also built on the Christian analysis of the dynamics of offense-taking and -giving (e.g., Matt. 5:23–24). Since the offender will take offense if confronted about the offense, the recipient of the first offense has the responsibility to clear things up. Offenders rarely recognize themselves as a source of abuse; nothing is more offensive than being told one is offensive. The Sermon on the Mount teaches passivity—turning the other cheek instead of responding—as protection against a vicious cycle of further offense-taking. One plays along in a way that refuses to play along. Jesus's teachings are full of such calculated inversions. The logic is clear, for example, in Peter's query about how often we should forgive people who offend us: seven times? Jesus answers, "seventy times seven" (Matt. 18:22). He does not directly contradict Peter; he takes Peter's logic to an absurd extreme, multiplying it unmanageably (distortions of scale are frequent in Jesus's rhetoric). He does not say, counting is not the way to think about forgiveness, stop keeping score! He enters into the flawed logic and takes it to the limit, in a multiplicatio ad absurdum. Performative negation is a favored mode of ironists. To a dull interlocutor, Jesus's reply could seem to agree with Peter's assumptions. Jesus plays along, leaving the receipt of the critique up to the sensitivity of the listener. Similarly, the Sermon on the Mount suggests doubling onerous tasks that we are compelled to do: if a man requisitions your coat, give him your shirt as well; if a soldier makes you carry his shield one mile, carry it one more as well (Matt. 5:40–41). Such aggressive passivity can drive you mad if you can detect it, and it is not surprising that some commentators have noticed analogies between Jesus's teachings and those of the

---

62. Michel Foucault, *Fearless Speech* (1983), ed. Joseph Pearson (New York: Semiotexte, 2001), 7, 119, 126–33 passim.

Cynics. Both are capable of sly humor and subversion that are easy to miss. Critique is not always in your face; it can also be behind your back. Jesus was an original practitioner of morally motivated absurdist dramas.

Civil rights protestors knew how to play a game with their opponents, entering into engagements in which they would not engage. They anticipated countermoves in dialogue and neutralized them. Activists need "double-consciousness": readiness to see themselves from the others' point of view as offenders and to take abuse for it. "One who breaks an unjust law must do it *openly, lovingly* . . . and with a willingness to accept the penalty."[63] Direct action practices stoic treatment of the self as an other. King insisted on drilling and preparing protestors to forsake retaliation and be ready for prison if need be. "Self-purification" was the first of King's four steps in nonviolent direct action; lest this sound cluelessly impractical to some, his lieutenants would often collect hundreds of knives from participants in the name of self-purification prior to protests. King led a disciplined movement. It takes a weird kind of will to be pleasant to your abusers. As Harry Kalven noted, the civil rights movement "has the muscle tone of revolution. Yet thus far it has been executed with an astonishing sense of tact and legality."[64]

Almost too much tact and legality. Civil disobedience is supposed to be, well, civil. Emerson already clarified the modus operandi in 1841: "let him take both reputation and life in his hand, and with perfect urbanity dare the gibbet and the mob by the absolute truth of his speech and the rectitude of his behavior."[65] Recent thinkers have criticized decorum for being conservative, stuffy, and exclusionary—masculine, middle class, and white, to put a point on it. The radical critics of civility today believe that being nice is an excuse for the existing order, and that codes of civility are infested with rules of privilege and deference. King's analysis was subtler. He agreed with the notion that civility can be conservative, but he did not abandon civility; he exaggerated it. He spoke of black youth who "cheerfully became jailbirds and troublemakers."[66] The conviction of the other's conscience comes from a civility taken to its extreme. With a mockery so infinitesimal that no one

63. King, "Letter from Birmingham City Jail," 294. Emphasis in original. Note the Pauline pair of openness and love.

64. Harry Kalven, *The Negro and the First Amendment* (Chicago: University of Chicago Press, 1966), 124.

65. Ralph Waldo Emerson, "Heroism," in *Selected Writings,* 236.

66. Martin Luther King, Jr., *The Trumpet of Conscience* (London: Hodder & Stoughton, 1967), 57. Note that King's preferred word "direct" often serves as a counter to alienation or distance.

could ever detect it for sure, four young men in Greensboro, North Carolina, in 1960 kept asking for "a cup of coffee, please" at the whites-only lunch counter in Woolworth's. This practice of hypercorrectness echoes the advice of the dying grandfather in Ellison's *Invisible Man:* "Live with your head in the lion's mouth. I want you to overcome 'em with yeses, undermine 'em with grins, agree 'em to death and destruction, let 'em swoller you till they vomit or bust wide open." He spoke "meekness as a dangerous activity."[67] King, like Emerson, had no interest in a civility that only colludes with other people's pet pictures of themselves.[68] The Greensboro four verged on absurdist theater with their incessant, maddening repetitions to people who were not listening to them. Their dialogues, no less than those of contemporary playwrights such as Samuel Beckett, seemed to go in circles. When the medium is exaggerated to the point of distortion—as civil rights protestors do with civility or Foucault does with his gory descriptions—the audience is forced to guess whether the point is obeisance, mockery, hypercorrectness, or something else. The Greensboro tactic of bodily presence is certainly a critique, in the sense that it is directed against abusive power, but it does not take the direct form of speech or deliberation. Habermas believes the public sphere should be governed by critical-rational debate, but King and friends offer another, less cerebral option: critical-nonrational debate. Critique, perhaps hard for a post-Kantian to see, can be found in drama as well as thought, performance as well as discourse, the ironic interstices between actor and audience as well as the logic of deliberation.

TRANSCENDENTAL BUFFOONERY

Václav Havel, absurdist playwright and later president of the Czech Republic (two roles, as he was the first to note, that shared more than one might expect), worked in the same tradition as King, a lineage neither liberal nor Marxist, though it is easy to mistake some elements of his transcendentalism for both.[69] His 1978 essay "The Power of the Powerless" says the powerful can be made powerless, and the powerless powerful.[70] Living in the truth is enough to effect this prophetic inversion. "Demanding that the laws

67. Ellison, *Invisible Man,* 16.
68. Compare Emerson, "Friendship," 207–8.
69. We know that while Havel was in prison, he saw a TV documentary on Martin Luther King: John Keane, *Václav Havel: A Tragedy in Six Acts* (London: Bloomsbury, 1999), 295.
70. Keane, *Václav Havel,* 271. Keane places Havel's thinking in the context of Jan Masaryk's interest in "small-scale initiatives," *drobná práce,* 275–76. Compare Václav Havel, "The Power of the Powerless," in *Open Letters,* 172ff.

be upheld is thus an act of living within the truth that threatens the whole mendacious structure at its point of maximum mendacity."[71] This is the old tactic in labor resistance of "work to rule": doing only what has been explicitly authorized by management. It is also the comic-robotic behavior of buffoons who stick to orders, like Jaroslav Hasek's good soldier Švejk, bumbling in his obedience (and a central figure in Czech literature and culture). For Havel obeying the law is not a collaboration or sell-out but the parody and refutation of a corrupt world. Force is vulnerable to farce. Preemptive tomfoolery can paralyze the opposition. Playing dumb can reveal the stupidity of those who presume to know best. In liberal irony you need an informed audience of bystanders to discern the self-canceling behavior of the powerful. Unlike liberal irony, Havel has an unerring sense for how a bit of Dada—the Frank Zappa variety—can secure the dignity of the protestor.[72] "It seems that in our Central European context," Havel notes, "what is most earnest has a way of blending uneasily with what is most comic." Cut off from real power, as well as the dangerously slippery zone of utopia, "the dissident can be himself and even make fun of himself without danger of becoming ridiculous to everyone."[73] Like Thoreau and King, Havel knows the riches of cynicism, the lightness and liberty it gives to the self, and the goading of power it affords. Cynicism is a way to maintain dignity under oppression—or boredom.

To critics who reject nonviolent resistance as weak or impractical, King says that it needs to be organized, disciplined, and massive—on a national, and ultimately international scale as well.[74] His aim, especially in his largely suppressed political evolution after the "I Have a Dream" speech in 1963, was the end of exploitation of all kinds, not just racism. The saving garnish of cynicism prevents direct action from being tractionlessly utopian. Passive resistance is an intensely practical politics, immediately available to everyone, a truly universal option, since we all have bodies we can put on the line. It prods the repressive apparatus to cope with the human face. It courts the snake to show its venom publicly. It is surely weak against thugs with guns, or bureaucrats with poison gas or napalm, but then we are in the

71. Havel, "The Power of the Powerless," 190.

72. The Reagan-appointed ambassador to Czechoslovakia, Shirley Temple Black, once arrived at the Prague airport at the same time as Frank Zappa and precipitated a national crisis there when she was caught on television saying she didn't know who he was. What sort of ambassador, the Czechs must have wondered, could be so ignorant of the treasures of her own culture? For this choice tidbit, see Keane, *Václav Havel*, 387.

73. Havel, "Anatomy of a Reticence," 309, 320, 321.

74. King, *The Trumpet of Conscience*, 70ff.

realm of war, not politics. Yet even the Nazi case confirms—tragically—the political potential of resistance by living in truth: the killing machine rested on the collaboration of much of the German citizenry (the precise quantity is still a matter of fierce debate). A withdrawal of consent from the murder of neighbors by nationwide protests and strikes in Germany—if only!— would have forced the Nazis into the open much sooner, and the Allies would never have been able to say they too did not know. Nonreactive measures can force the truth into the open by refusing the compromises of the private realm. Goading clarifies motives. The Cynical dialogue of provocation is not a failed politics. Its weakness is its strength. Power, as Paul said, is brought to completion in weakness.

Passive resistance has a curious attitudinal mixture of self-control and provocation. As a supposed African proverb has it: When the visiting chieftain comes, bow deeply and fart silently. Farting loudly would not be, after all, an act of *civil* disobedience, and doing so could place the farter's life or at least honor at risk. But to fart silently preserves public order while keeping the soul of the farter dancing—an underestimated political value! Some messages leave no discernible effects and yet play an important role in the welfare of the world. The question in civil disobedience, as Thoreau said about his poll tax, is not the effects of my dollar, but the effects of my allegiance. Some may say that this stance is so radical as to be inconsequential, that it is too preoccupied with the soul and not enough with social conditions and consequences. Yet what Friedrich Schlegel called "transcendental buffoonery" is a premier political capacity.[75] The oppressor may not even catch the taunt in the too-scrupulous reverence of his obedient subjects. As many noticed and parodied, Margaret Thatcher's curtsy to Queen Elizabeth II always seemed suspiciously deep, overdone to the possible point of insincerity, but never verifiable. Such cheekiness involves moral stuntsmanship with the self as well as the other. (The odd presence of Margaret Thatcher in this discussion shows that sometimes even people in power cannot resist the tactics of powerlessness.) Transcendental buffoonery is a sign that the self-other relationship is properly adjusted. King and Havel put themselves cheerfully in peril. *Levitas* and joking are ethical matters. Democracy needs both Stoic listening and Dadaist rowdiness, community-minded neighborliness and irrepressible resistance. In the beginning, says Arendt, was the crime.[76] Adam and Eve were the first to break the law for a higher cause.

75. Friedrich Schlegel, "Die Heimat der Ironie," in *Romantik I,* ed. Hans-Jürgen Schmitt (Stuttgart: Reclam, 1986), 102.

76. Hannah Arendt, *On Revolution* (New York: Viking Press, 1963), 11.

Their lesson is the productivity of disobedience. Understanding the tactic of redemption-minded provocation would make more sense of why liberals might want to defend the rights of pornographers or neo-Nazis.

Democracy needs civil disobedience as a constant comment on its moral inadequacy. Not the least service transcendental buffoonery performs is to remind us that democracy, even at its healthiest, can never exhaust or fully satisfy our moral aspirations. John Dewey has perhaps done the most to paint democracy as a high ethical, even aesthetic ideal. The glowing community he paints, beautiful as it is, does not respect the need for transcendence, whether from above or below. For Dewey, we should be satisfied with democracy's secular promise of the *jouissance* of rubbing elbows with one's fellows. Dewey never felt the grace of cynicism, only its bite. Cynicism is a protest against the world as it is. Saying no to the cosmos as a totality is nihilism, but it is also imagination. Dewey's energy against the darkness is admirable; his failure to measure its dominion is fatal. Graham Greene's quip about a character whose idealism knew no limits applies somehow to Dewey: he "was in his element now with the whole universe to improve."[77] Dewey did not know frivolity or folly, cackling at the moon, what Malinowski called the coefficient of weirdness. Dewey is a good choice, like Habermas, as a chief theorist of communication and democracy, but even better are those who laugh with the anarchy and still roll up their sleeves to get to work: Emerson, Thoreau, James, Arendt, King, Havel. Democracy requires Confucian virtues during the weekdays but Taoist ones on the weekend. Democracy is no small thing in the scale of human goods and a great achievement whenever it is tried, but it is at best a horizon of brotherhood and sisterhood, a moral principle of solidarity. Many of its fans recognize only half of Kant's great formula "asocial sociability." Civil disobedience takes care of the asocial side of the equation. Henry David Thoreau put the right attitude with a precision worthy of being chiseled into Vermont granite: "I am as desirous of being a good neighbor as I am of being a bad subject."[78]

Thoreau, Arendt, Havel all knew how to laugh. Their faith in small-scale initiatives and quixotic acts of communication went together with a tasty vinaigrette cynicism. Cynicism has come to mean the snickering attitude that follows from disappointed attempts at enlightenment. I want to rehabilitate the older philosophical sense: Cynicism not as the bitterness of fail-

---

77. Graham Greene, *The Quiet American* (1955) (London: William Heinemann & the Bodley Head, 1973), 10.

78. Thoreau, *Walden and Civil Disobedience*, 239.

ure, but as the cheery starting point of recognizing our shared folly.[79] One of Arendt's greatest gifts as a political thinker is her nose for what she calls "sheer absurdity," the bizarre contraptions people make in their efforts to justify themselves.[80] She dares to laugh where others wax solemn in compulsory reverence. She culls this ludicrously delicious morsel, for instance, from strategies proposed by Nixon's best and brightest for fighting the war in Vietnam: (1) issue pamphlets; (2) pour contaminants into the engines of French buses; (3) offer English lessons for "mistresses of important personages"; and (4) "hire a team of Vietnamese astrologers."[81] The crescendo from standard to desperate tactics is part of the humor—as if "personages" in all their awkward pomp would have mistresses anyway!

Arendt reports that she laughed often and hard while reading the transcripts of the trial of Adolf Eichmann, the logistics manager for the Nazis' "final solution." She had the courage to analyze the trial without pieties or prejudices, defying the pressure of compulsory loyalty to Israel. And yet she reverenced the dead with the sheer honest truthfulness of her analysis of "the enigma of a mass murderer who never killed." Eichmann abhorred cruelty on the personal level but was willing to countenance terrible things at a distance. He showed outrage not when he was accused of killing hundreds of thousands but when a witness accused him of having beaten a Jewish boy to death. Eichmann was not a cruel or malicious person, as Arendt documents at length, but rather something of a dullard. His was not the steely stance of medical passivity before morbidity. He had a tender stomach and was horrified on the rare occasions when he saw the disposal of corpses. He even rejected Nabokov's *Lolita* when it was offered to him for his reading pleasure in jail: he found the book "unwholesome." Having once slapped a Jew bothered his conscience more than having sent innumerable Jews to their deaths. He had never personally entertained any bad feelings toward Jews and even apparently had a Jewish mistress for a period.[82] Eichmann presents the problem of straining at a gnat and swallowing a camel, in the vivid biblical phrase. He was moral in some small things but without a compass in the large. He remained a person to the end, one of us, dogged by petty preferences and guilts, too small to grasp the magnitude of his mon-

---

79. Peter Sloterdijk, *Critique of Cynical Reason* (Minneapolis: University of Minnesota Press, 1987), contrasts *zynicism* (failed enlightenment) and *kynicism* (cheekiness). Erasmus is a wellspring of the latter.

80. Hannah Arendt, *Crises of the Republic* (New York: Harcourt, Brace, Jovanovich, 1972), 40.

81. Arendt, *Crises of the Republic*, 21–22.

82. Hannah Arendt, *Eichmann in Jerusalem: A Report on the Banality of Evil* (1964)(New York: Penguin, 1992), 109, 87–89, 49, 47, 30.

strousness; he was completely out of scale with the deeds he authored. Common morality—being decent in one's choice of literature, not having unkind thoughts toward people—is blank before the enormity of mass murder.

Though Arendt's book on Eichmann was maximally controversial, she was not laughing at the Holocaust; she was sizing up the human circus. She understood the trial as a spectacle choreographed by the state of Israel for political reasons, justice being secondary. She was an equal-opportunity analyst: hardly anyone comes off well, yet even Eichmann, the banal mass murderer, goes to the gallows "with great dignity." And she did not deny the possibility—though rare and intermittent—of genuine saintliness, courage, or righteousness. Eichmann is "even funny."[83] The funniness of evil is an equally interesting, if less famous, point as the banality of evil. Arendt took responsibility for every line she wrote, taking flak even from the great Gershom Scholem, who lamented her human-philosophical point of view when he thought an ethnic-religious one more politically urgent, a clearly Jewish, pro-Israel one. Arendt replied that it was precisely her Jewishness that informed her imaginative sympathies. Arendt had the courage to make judgments without the blackmail of other people's righteousness.

Such thinkers as Thoreau, Arendt, Foucault, and Havel laugh at the preposterous devices people conjure. They are not surprised by every new flare-up of the sickness unto death. What some grow sweaty over, they treat with what Emerson called "immortal hilarity."[84] Not from a lack of seriousness—few know the meaning of seriousness as well—but from an acquaintance with folly. Laughter grows from recognition, from a rigorous respect for the rough edges of facts. It knows the gap between profession and being. The Pentagon boys did not see the joke when they suggested teaching English to the mistresses of personages; they probably gloated about their own cleverness and naughtiness. To laugh at the world can be a disillusioned dismissal, but it can also be an apt response to its ways. There is a cynicism of engagement as well as disengagement. Cynicism wards off the dangerous side effects of our ideals—disillusionment chief among them. "I wish sometimes you had a few bad motives, you might understand a little more about human beings. And that applies to your country too, Pyle," says Graham Greene's hard-bitten reporter Fowler.[85] Cynicism can be a cleansing irritant, not just a wrecker of the true faith: it affords relief from pomp or

83. Arendt, *Eichmann in Jerusalem*, 252, 288.
84. Ralph Waldo Emerson, "Love," in *Selected Writings*, 195.
85. Greene, *The Quiet American*, 148.

sobriety. Healthy cynicism is a remedy for the sick version. The first fruits of self-knowledge are cynicism. "Yes," said Socrates to the traveling physiognomist who saw in his pug-nosed face a man full of lusts and demons and iniquities, "you know me."[86] The believer is a cynic about all the false faiths abroad. King was a practical cynic when he noted the arrogant ways people can hold high ideals. His practice was to subject the accusers afresh—including himself—to the abuses they were protesting. When professed sincerity is not enough, we put our bodies on the line.

The transcendental cynicism I favor is not one of resignation; it is one of absurd hope (if that is not a redundancy). Arendt can find the posturing of the wicked amusing and painful all at once, but like Thoreau and Havel, she believes in the enormous resonance of small acts. She denies, for instance, that nonviolent resistance against the Nazis would have been futile. Even the most totalitarian regime cannot hide every testimony. She dismisses the claim of many Germans that resistance to the Nazis would have done nothing more than secure them a quick anonymous death. No death goes unwitnessed. "It is true that totalitarian domination tried to establish those holes of oblivion into which all deeds, good and evil, would disappear," just as the Nazis tried to cover up evidence of their deeds (one reason for the ovens). But "all efforts to let their opponents 'disappear into silent anonymity' were in vain. The holes of oblivion do not exist. Nothing human is that perfect, and there are simply too many people in the world to make oblivion possible. One man will always be left alive to tell the story."[87] Nothing human, she thinks, lacks a witness—a remarkably sanguine view. Like Thoreau and Havel, she believes that one person can make a universal difference—a very different logic of communication than we are used to in an age of advertising. Arendt is not claiming that the millions who died in the Holocaust were somehow sending a message; their blood cries from the ground against anyone who thinks that nonviolent resistance can cost anything less than everything. She casts her vote for memory over oblivion, even in polities that murder the bearers of memory. Havel has a similar hope. As soon as someone breaks the rules to expose the truth, the whole system wavers: "It is utterly unimportant how large a space this alternative occupies: its power does not consist in its physical attributes but in the light it casts on those pillars of the system and on its unstable foundation."[88] Havel's apparent indifference to numbers is reminiscent of Thoreau's con-

86. Nietzsche, "Das Problem Sokrates," in *Götzendämmerung*, sec.3.
87. Arendt, *Eichmann in Jerusalem*, 232–33.
88. Havel, "The Power of the Powerless," 147.

viction that "any man more right than his neighbors, constitutes a majority of one already."[89]

Thoreau, Arendt, King, and Havel all seem to hold a near-mystical vision of truth radiating in public without amplifiers, microphones, or auditors. As Havel notes, "every meaningful cultural act—wherever it takes place—is unquestionably good in and of itself, simply because it exists and because it offers something to someone." What if there is no audience? (The tree falls in the forest for the thousandth time.) Of course Havel thought it was better for art to have a large audience, just as he invited western friends to help spread the word. "Being happy if five thousand rather than five people can read a good text or see a good painting is, I think, a wholly legitimate understanding of the meaning of culture."[90] Yet the yeast of truth flourishes in small spaces. Truth is a "bacteriological weapon" that "makes its influence felt in the obscure arena of being itself." Havel's faith that a spotlight on the system will expose its corruption builds, with King, on the Kantian notion of publicity as banisher of evil. Injustice flees before the light. Revolution in the sense of overthrowing a state apparatus, however necessary it sometimes is, is not radical enough, since it fails to get at the root of the problem. We carry responsibility everywhere, he says, and cannot escape to a monastery or to an ashram, for neither of those options is universally available. "Christianity is an example of the opposite way out: it is a point of departure for me here and now—but only because anyone, anywhere, at any time, may avail themselves of it."[91] Havel, finding in the *nun kairos,* the time of the now, a portal into the universal, is one of Paul's descendants. His picture of public space and communication is quite different from the liberal one of the free marketplace. It is not simply that ideas jostle there for preeminence but that being has the possibility of being exposed.

DEMOCRACY AND IMPERFECTION

Few topics so seem to invite the best of us to wax earnest as democracy. Discussions of democracy are often sincere, dull, and infected with nostalgia. A certain wistfulness about the ignorance, apathy, or callousness of the people at large regularly wells up among liberal and communitarian (but not realist) commentators. Yet we sell democracy short by our ponderousness. The rule of the people is hardly a solemn concept—it should take its place

89. Thoreau, *Walden and Civil Disobedience,* 232.
90. Václav Havel, "Six Asides About Culture," in *Open Letters,* 284.
91. Havel, "The Power of the Powerless," 149, 153, 180, 184, 196.

among the most wonderful and preposterous ideas ever floated. A modicum of basic goofiness should garnish democratic theory. Anyone who believes in popular rule must have some taste for the outlandish. This is not to mock the hopes deposited in the people, but to sustain them in a democratic way. Vulgar tastes seldom run to high seriousness. Democracy is demotic. A touch of lightness, an appreciation for anarchic and festive potentials, is healthy for democratic theory. Must we deceive ourselves to be democrats? We should not have to posit mental faculties of rationality and selflessness none of us possess to believe democracy to be viable. Democracy is as much about folly and naughtiness as it is about wisdom and obedience. Tone and attitude are underrated resources in democratic theory. Democracy, as the Greeks said, is *es meson*, in the middle. Democracy is for tricksters, figures who can mediate multiple demands. The sincerest democrats often miss the music (sincerity is perhaps precisely the problem). Cynicism, understood as the cheerful wisdom that has made its peace with imperfection, has democratic value, not just demerit. It allows us to treat our neighbors with a decent respect. Cynicism, like vinegar, is better taken in splashes than gulps; it can save a salad, but you do not want to chug it straight from the bottle. Diogenes of Sinope, the wellspring of Cynical philosophy and practice, may have been crude, but he was the only person to win Alexander the Great's admiration by having the courage to tell him off. How his frankness must have shone in a crowd of toadies! What better attitude for democracy than the willingness to tell power to stop blocking the light?

Really existing democracy—the only kind there is—is always fatally flawed. The flaws are what make democracy admirable; they are not things to be squinted away into a blurry wish. Democracy is a form of government and way of life whose peculiar strength lies in its ability to cope with the inevitable failure of our best-laid plans. Democracy is the clearest refutation of all ideals and utopias. It wrecks every romantic ship. Its history is a catalog of error and grace, stupidity and fumbling genius. At its best democracy reminds us not of the great wisdom of the people, but of our great folly, and teaches us to check ourselves. It teaches us not that distance can be scaled, but that local life is hard and in need of our labor. And it suggests that the effort to knock down all barriers to participation is an infinitely receding horizon, for the causes of exclusion are sown in the nature of interaction and personality. A heroic pursuit of the horizon is perhaps a less apt democratic attitude than solidarity with the struggles of our neighbors. Democracy needs not our faith but our tenderness, being a form of life that insists on its own, and our own, incompleteness at every turn. It is the principle of imperfection in politics, something we should embrace, not be embarrassed by. As Adam Michnik says, democracy "is eternal imperfection, a mixture of sinfulness, saintliness, and monkey business."[92]

This book has treated a basic idea in twentieth-century thinking about communication and democracy: that the civic garden can dare to cultivate the flowers of evil. Two related ideas are likewise so basic that they rarely receive even the courtesy of an analysis or critique: citizens are supposed to be informed about public affairs and citizens are supposed to take part in self-government. Taken together, these three pillars lay out the central problems facing democracy today: Exposure (to diverse ideological climates), information (about the wider world), and participation (in the forums of collective life). They imply norms of character, knowledge, and action, as well as preferred conditions of communication and exchange. Liberty, for Mill and his followers, is supposed to guarantee the flourishing of all three: free public spaces provide a clash of views (exposure), which educates the public (information) and moves it to engagement and involvement (participation). These assumptions rarely transcend the status of platitudes in recent discussion, despite a deep intellectual heritage. Information, participation, and exposure correspond loosely to modern psychology's division of human faculties into cognition (knowing), behavior (doing), and attitude (feeling), and can even be read as a version of Kant's three fundamental questions: What can I know? What should I do? What may I hope for?

When explored in depth, the triad turns out to be stranger and more interesting than most of us had thought. Information raises problems of witnessing and responsibility; participation raises questions of what kind of material or symbolic creature public space is in a digital age and what resources can fund (in any sense) civic engagement; and exposure, as we have seen, often implies a dubious optimism about reason and progress and a stance toward evil that can verge on a taste for morbidity. These pillars are anything but safe or dull, despite the best efforts of our journalists, judges, politicians, and civics teachers to make them so. Considered seriously, they lead to labyrinthine questions of suffering, cynicism, and the ultimate meaning of the world or our own action in it. To be informed in our times is to be exposed to the full range of human harm—war, famine, crime, poverty, mayhem, death. When we read a newspaper, listen to the radio, watch television, attend the cinema, or surf the internet we participate, in

92. Adam Michnik, "Postface: Gray Is Beautiful," *Letters from Freedom: Post–Cold War Realities and Perspectives* (Berkeley: University of California Press, 1998), 326.

some way, in the wider world, but what is the civic meaning of unreciprocated or unnoticed acts of textual involvement? Is there a politics of muteness, of unreciprocated acts of communication? If citizens are free, are they
also free to tune out? Are small acts and gestures of the *logos*—giving talks,
making donations, writing letters, joining clubs, organizing protests—the
best we can hope for from democratic participation? What does it mean to
make a difference? Participation is a conundrum of great theoretical and institutional complexity that deserves a book of its own. Despite edifying talk
of the *vox populi*, there are no institutions that allow an obstacle-free communication of the citizenry with itself, though some once saw that promise
in the newspaper and some today find it in the internet. The American Fed-
eralists were foes of political presence, expressly breaking up assembly as a
desirable mode or site of political action, yet participation remains norma-
tively central. In the United States the notion that every citizen has the
power to speak the word, and that deprivation of the opportunity to participate is death, owes much to the Protestant idea that even the foolish and
unlettered may be wrought upon by the Holy Ghost to speak words of wisdom. In the act of speaking, a redeeming transformation is supposed to
come over the civic voice. Hegel stated the problem of participation with his
usual lucidity: "In our modern states, the citizens have only a restricted
share in the public business of the state, yet it is necessary to provide the ethical person [*Menschen*] with public activity beyond their private ends."[93] In
modernity, universal democratic participation is pragmatically impossible
but ethically necessary.

Each pillar is internally contradictory. Information calls for both abstracted distance (detachment) and engaged proximity (care). Participation wants citizens to make their voices heard and take action, but it is hard
to find forums with sufficient resonance in hypercomplex societies. And exposure calls for self-disciplined listening while also needing the yeast of un-
ruly speech. People who are full of information are not necessarily inspired
to action; people who desire to make a difference can waver between grand
quixotic gestures and feelings of alienation or futility; and exposure risks
moral callousness. (And if exposure is such a good model for the civic soul,
how do we handle children and the perennial problems of sex and violence?) The three norms are also in mutual tension. Exposure would like us
to be as detached as the gods in facing noxious doctrine, while participation
would have us be as passionate as lovers in our concern for the common

93. G. W. F. Hegel, *Grundlinien der Philosophie des Rechts* (1821) (Frankfurt: Suhrkamp, 1970),
sec. 255.

good. Information wants our antennas ever tuned to the news of the world. Participation wants us to get involved in local communities. Exposure loves the clash of incompatible doctrines in spaces where there is no such thing as a false idea, while defenders of information often call for ideology-free facts. Is information supposed to encompass the world's violations fully? If so, how do we maintain the confidence and self-efficacy that participation wants in the face of the demoralization that information can bring? Should citizens cultivate an ethic of detachment or an ethic of engagement? The result leaves the good citizen both caring and calloused, engaged and remote, stubborn and teachable, militant in argument and tender to the plight or right of others. No wonder romantics, the religiously devout, and others who long for wholeness distrust liberals and their call for a divided heart.

One is typically supposed to approach the end of books with answers rather than questions, but these norms, with all their ironies, strengths, and contradictions, seem the fundamental problems that twenty-first-century democrats will have to deal with. This chapter has forwarded a tradition of political-ethical thought and action often mistakenly classed as a simple branch of liberal thought, the transcendental politics of passivity imagined and practiced by Thoreau, Tolstoy, Gandhi, Martin Luther King, and Václav Havel, among many others. This tradition is the most robust strain of thinking about liberty in deeply democratic conditions for a world where critical rationality, cultural relativism, and antimodern fundamentalism are duking it out. It teaches us that participation lies within the reach of anyone who has a body and reminds us of the infinite responsibility we all assume when we dare to know or speak about the world.

Responsibility to Things That Are Not

Thus the foundation of evil is necessary while its actualization is but contingent. In other words, it is necessary that evil be possible, but contingent that it be actual.
—Leibniz, *Theodicy*

THE SUSTAINABILITY OF FREE EXPRESSION

Twentieth-century free expression theory praises the capacity to behold morbidity without flinching. It shares modern thought's deep confidence that pathology can bear intellectual or moral fruit, a commitment found in souls as diverse as Hegel, Emerson, Virchow, Baudelaire, Dostoyevky, Nietzsche, and Freud. The First Amendment is not usually associated with such figures, typically preferring the more modest company of English-speaking judges and jurists, but much of its twentieth-century meaning rides the same waves that gave us modern literature, science, medicine, and art in all their "uninhibited, robust, and wide-open" glory. The high modern confidence in free expression rests implicitly on ways of containing evil and offense. Mill invoked the modern division of labor when he noted that the eyewitnessing of pain was increasingly restricted to "peculiar and narrow classes" such as butchers and surgeons. Jurists like Holmes and philosophers like Dewey sought to educate people to appreciate the thought they hate, invoking soldierly, professional, or scientific virtues as models of civic comportment. Defenders of the rights of Nazis to march in Skokie provided a performance art whose provocative contraries sought to teach the rest of us to cope with evil—not by direct confrontation but by treating it with a legal care so scrupulous that it verged on parody. Symbolic transgressors banked on a knowing audience to grasp the ultimate meaning of their inversions. The three preconditions of societal segregation, psychic self-abstraction, and confidence in the triumph of sense, in other words, all provided a context in which to discern the social, literary, artistic, or scientific value of public exposure—good, bad, or ugly. A few toxins in the cultural diet would not kill us; they would make us stronger. Mill praised the "salutary shock" of ideas that "explode like bombshells."[1]

Confidence in free expression has weakened in Anglo-American culture today. An absolutist stance that courts rather than skirts offense has become a boutique position held by some lawyers, journalists, and librarians, among others, rather than an establishment ideology. Perhaps fuller support will return but the softening has its real reasons. What do we have to show for nearly a century of sustained legal theorizing and decisions about free expression? We have the protection of Nazis, of flag-burning, of "obscenity" and four-letter words, and, more recently, corporate rights, among other things. For all the fuss, the results might seem pretty meager (unless one reads with an eye to ironic redemption, as most true believers in free expression do, sometimes quite persuasively arguing that such small guarantees keep society intellectually vibrant and politically flexible). The shaken faith that liberty can take anything since evil can be redeemed is in many respects a casualty of the social and cultural changes sometimes called postmodernism. Like many, I have reservations about this term—for one thing, it is out of date, as one might have predicted of a term that claimed to have surpassed modernity. (Modernity chews up anything claiming to be new.) But it does usefully point out some of the problems of sustainability that free expression theory faces today.

First, the program of civic self-discipline and sublimation derived from Greco-Roman norms and practiced by English-speaking gentlemen from Locke to Smith to Mill to Holmes is largely in wreckage. It perhaps deserves to be, and few of us have much interest in reconstructing a world ruled solely by white gentlemen.[2] Commitment to the moral and civic benefits of Greek and Latin literature no longer dominates elite education, as it did before the twentieth century. The ideal of the self-transcending citizen has been exposed, with eminent justice, as having clear ties to social privilege. The psychic act of sublimation, taking a whiff of civet to make the perfume sweeter, has indirect ties to class, race, and gender inequalities. In the eigh-

---

1. John Stuart Mill, *On Liberty* (1859) (New York: Norton, 1975), 45.

2. Though it might be preferable to being ruled by white jerks, the norm as of this writing.

teenth century the bourgeois ideal of *Bildung* (self-realization, education) began to supplement the Ciceronian ethic of ego-transcendence. According to bourgeois humanism, whose spirit was democratic rather than aristocratic, Romantic rather than classic, the soul was ruled as much by art and imagination as by abstraction and duty. The cultivation of an aesthetic sensibility, especially through literature, was supposed to equip citizens to live an integrated life of experience. In Adam Smith and Mill, as we saw, Romantic strains (sympathy and eccentricity, respectively) mix with classic ones (self-command and public obligation), and free expression theory's love of energy, excess, and extremity points to Romantic elements. Ancient Stoic and bourgeois humanist ideals agree, however, on the importance of an integrated, self-transcending ego. The former finds such transcendence in *theōria* and *praxis* (contemplation and public service), and the latter in imagination and art. Though not quite an endangered species like Roman humanism, *Bildung* is also in trouble. The stereotype of the Nazi *Kommandant* who savors Schiller and Beethoven at night and runs the ovens by day, the pressures on universities to moderate generalist liberal arts ambitions, and the waning of reading and writing as the monopoly medium for civic rationality have all done their bit to weaken the ideology of the aesthetic as the main recipe for ethics and education.[3] Free expression theory presupposes an integrated and literate psychic platform: what are its prospects today?

Second, postmodernism heralds the breaking of old dams of social and cultural segregation. The older idea that class refinement guarantees a proper frame for risqué materials—for example, the Victorian "secret museum" that restricted ancient erotica to the purview of an elite of male "scholars"[4]—has been shattered not only by attacks on the psychology of restraint, but also by the blurring of cultural levels and the rising public importance of audiovisual media. The boundary between elite and popular taste, though never completely secure, has become increasingly fuzzy since the late twentieth century—in television, music, film, literature, education. The unprecedented abundance and circulation of signs, so celebrated by postmodern theorists, changes in some way the meaning and power of expression—free or not. The long revolution from print to audiovisual media lowers barriers, especially literacy, to cultural access. The theory of free expression was born twins with the printing press. Though theorists such as

---

3. Thanks to David Depew's analysis of the ideology of the aesthetic.

4. See Walter Kendrick, *The Secret Museum: Pornography in Modern Culture* (New York: Viking, 1987).

Milton saw the press as an agency of cultural dissemination, print clearly contains and segregates culture as well. Literate adults were always the assumed audience for free expression—Mill excluded children and "barbarians" from public life without batting an eye.[5] Images and sounds circulate in different paths from books. Dirt, said Mary Douglas, is matter out of place.[6] Electronic media, especially those operating in a capitalist context, are extraordinarily leaky and prone to cause ritual pollution and offense. Shock is an effect, in part, of cultural spillage or soilage. (If the liberal-stoic program had its way, of course, no one could ever be shocked). An ironic by-product of global flows of media is that offense and misunderstanding are likely to increase rather than decrease. That much of such offense is taken on behalf of others (e.g., children again) does not make it any less important socially.[7] Yet the promiscuous circulation of signs can also mean the exhaustion of shock, the reign of the blasé. The post-Holocaust generation of photographers, activists, and memorialists, for instance, believed in exposing people to images of atrocity in order to inoculate them. Today the saturation of screens and pages worldwide with pictures of the dead has failed to prevent further atrocities. The Holocaust has become, at least in part, a string of images and tropes that can be played out for various agendas.[8] Free expression theory long presupposed literate adults dealing with cultural materials contained on the page. What is it to do with volatile pictures and sounds that are deemed either too shocking or not shocking enough?

Third, the credo that anything is permitted because everything in the end advances the public good looks dubious, and the theodicy that pain always bears fruit seems indecent. The nineteenth century and much of the twentieth was drunk on progress. "The wounds of the spirit heal without leaving scars," wrote Hegel. [9] Emerson agreed: "the march of civilization is a train of felonies, yet, general ends are somehow answered."[10] The nine-

5. Mill, *On Liberty*, 11.

6. Mary Douglas, *Purity and Danger: An Analysis of Concepts of Pollution and Taboo* (New York: Praeger, 1966).

7. On the dynamic of the third-person effect, see, for instance, Albert C. Gunther and J. Douglas Storey, "The Influence of Presumed Influence," *Journal of Communication* 53 (2003): 199–215.

8. Barbie Zelizer, *Remembering to Forget: Holocaust Memory in the Camera's Eye* (Chicago: University of Chicago Press, 1998).

9. G. W. F. Hegel, *Phänomenologie des Geistes* (1807) (Hamburg: Meiner, 1952), para. 669.

10. Ralph Waldo Emerson, *Representative Men: Seven Lectures*, ed. Andrew Delbanco (Cambridge, Mass.: Harvard University Press, 1996), 104.

teenth century was, with some notable exceptions, a long, relatively peaceful interlude in the history of the world, so confidence in progress had some basis. A bloody century and a half later, Sartre echoed Hegel: "Violence, like the spear of Achilles, can heal the wounds which it has made."[11] I am not sure what pharmaceutical indulgence prompted that effusion from his pen but to say this in the later twentieth century seems the height of callousness and delusion. Perhaps to treat violence as curative is always crazy: as Dostoyevsky's Ivan Karamazov said, undercutting the nineteenth-century trust in sacrificial redemption, it would not be worth torturing a child to save the whole universe. It is hard to find any redemptive meaning in the hundred million people murdered in the twentieth century. Even an effort at explanation violates the dead. (This is part of the objection to the term holocaust, with its connotation of redemptive sacrifice.) As Arendt noted, the view that history heals all wounds belongs to the winners, not the losers.[12] Or Nietzsche: "But to find in history the realization of the good and the just, that is blasphemy against the good and the just."[13] A challenge facing free expression theory today is the collapse of a progressive philosophy of history. Few of us believe that human history is assured a happy ending or that exposure to "disgusting forms of disease, sounds of execration, and the vision of violent death" (Emerson) will make us wise. How is free expression theory, especially the idea that offense, Paul's *skandalon*, brings forth grace, to thrive in a world that is more jumpy about evil than it used to be? Strategic acts of transgression can seem a celebration rather than critique of violence. Is there a theory of free expression for a world suffering from post-traumatic stress?

These three challenges to free expression theory return us to the threefold clash of intellectual and moral options that opened this book. Modern scientific rationality requires a self capable of impartiality and abstraction. Postmodern cultural relativism stems from the overwhelming blurring of genres and the viral spread of images. And moral absolutism or "fundamentalism" is sick and tired of a patient or solicitous approach to wickedness and crime. The fate of free expression in theory and practice depends on precisely the larger intellectual maelstrom. I cannot pretend to resolve this tension—and in any case tensions like that are not solved in books—but it is the force field in which we should think about free expression today.

11. Jean-Paul Sartre, preface to Frantz Fanon, *Les damnés de la terre* (Paris: Maspero, 1961), 26. "La violence, comme la lance d'Achille, peut cicatriser les blessures qu'elle a faites."

12. Hannah Arendt, *Lectures on Kant's Political Philosophy,* ed. Ronald Beiner (Chicago: University of Chicago Press, 1982), 5.

13. Friedrich Nietzsche, "Notes (1873)," in *The Portable Nietzsche*, ed. Walter Kaufmann (New York: Penguin, 1982), 39.

THE WAGES OF STOICISM

In the *Nicomachean Ethics* (1.7) Aristotle defines happiness as an activity (*energeia, praxis*). The western world has pretty much followed him since in exalting activity as a human good. That non-doing could be a good and repetition could be profound, that circles can be spirals, and soft forces stronger than hard ones, were notions largely left to the Indians, Tibetans, Chinese, Koreans, and Japanese. To be sure, Aristotle's notion of *theōria*, and contemplative traditions within Judaism, Christianity, and Islam have recognized the virtues of, as Pascal said, staying in one's room. This book swims upstream to the virtues of passivity. Stoic passivity is profoundly ambiguous. Taken sympathetically, it is an ethic of receptivity, listening, respect for the material, for plants, animals, and minerals—and for the person. Taken as it appears to be, it is a sponsor of mayhem and coldness. Stoics, unlike Christians, allow suicide. The duty of passivity in the face of death is almost an archetypal pose. Abraham Lincoln, the Stoic-Romantic, presiding over the ridiculously wasteful Civil War, believing, as he put it in his second inaugural address, that God gave "to both North and South this terrible war, as the woe due to those by whom the offense came," is perhaps the greatest modern representative, but Marcus Aurelius fits as well. Or Churchill, giving his all to save the democracies so that they could get back to the follies that almost destroyed them. Robert E. Lee, personally in favor of the Union, eventually became the leader of the Confederate army out of loyalty to his native state of Virginia—even though he was first asked by Lincoln to lead the Union army. The great literary examples include Lear, Achilles, and the *Bhagavad Gita*'s Arjuna, who is counseled by the god Krishna to set aside his compunctions about killing and throw himself into the battle even though he will mow down his kinsmen. Such men survey the vast fields of corpses they have survived, created, or dissected, fighting the enemy without and fear or revulsion within, not convinced of the righteousness of their cause, but blindly carrying through because, well, because it is the thing to do. Anything, even death, can become normal after a while.

There can be an immortal hilarity in survival, the sheer ridiculous joy that you have looked into death's face and lived to tell the tale. A desolate tranquility lies on the other side of the catastrophe, Lear holding Cordelia, Oedipus at Colonos, Achilles and Priam taking pity on each other, every last drop of grief already having been shed. Tragedy teaches the eerie calm that follows when all feeling is spent, the surprising blessing of being alive. "Catharsis" may have a precise medical meaning of purgation—the salty cold sweaty sheer relief that follows after the worst nausea is like the calm you feel when Fortinbras marches onto the stage at the end of *Hamlet.* The origins of this self-transcending elation in warfare persist in the self-abstracting soul forwarded by Mill's *Liberty,* the twentieth-century First Amendment, and social science's vision of statistical analysis. The moral harvest of war is one of the most terribly ambiguous things around. Adolf Eichmann said during his trial: "I sensed a Pontius Pilate kind of feeling, for I felt free of all guilt." Eichmann had read Kant and adopted a version of his philosophy in which making exceptions was the worst crime and obedience against inclination was the mark of a just act. (Eichmann's Kant is the precise inverse of Arendt's: rote duty versus imaginative judgment.) Arendt mentions other cases of inner absolution by way of self-division among Nazis. One Dr. Otto Bradfisch, leader of an *Einsatzgruppe* that oversaw the killing of fifteen thousand people, told a German court that he had always been "inwardly opposed" to what he did. A *Gauleiter* named Arthur Greiser tried the same trick in a Polish court. Only his "official soul" had committed the crimes, while his "private soul" had not consented. So only his official soul, with its body, was hanged in 1946. Arendt describes such psychological contortions: "So that instead of saying: What horrible things I did to people!, the murderers would be able to say: What horrible things I had to watch in the pursuance of my duties, how heavily the task weighed upon my shoulders!"[14] Eichmann is of course no fair representative of Stoicism, but he does show one possibility in the elation provided by self-division: shameless killing.

Is there "a teleological suspension of the ethical," as Kierkegaard asked? Can we suspend moral law in the name of a higher end? The whole theory of free expression, from Paul to Milton to Mill to Holmes, banks on just this possibility. We are supposed to entertain the thought that we passionately believe may wreck everything. Kierkegaard's case in point was Abraham, commanded by God to sacrifice his son Isaac: should religious duty override the law against killing? Kierkegaard had the courage to make murder the centerpiece for pondering teleological suspension. Central to the whole tradition of free expression is the stance of ethical suspension. Aristotle saw spectators of tragedy achieving a teleological suspension of the ethical, as Virchow did in his autopsy technique. Mayhem and corpses were there to enlighten and educate, not fascinate and disgust. Such moral differentiation is the premise of modern professionalism. Milton argued for liberty to

14. Hannah Arendt, *Eichmann in Jerusalem: A Report on the Banality of Evil* (New York: Penguin, 1994), 114, 215, 127, 106.

scout in the regions of sin and wrote great swelling words for the inhabitants of hell. Justice Holmes enjoyed making laws that went counter to his beliefs. The ACLU put every political-ethical disgust on hold when it decided to fight for the rights of the National Socialist Party of America, a group whose ideology rests on murder. The ethics and aesthetics of rancidness, aptly sublimated, provide the heady air in which suspended souls breathe. Free expression theory cannot deny, in its modern libertarian form, the traces of killing.

In this book I have emphasized themes that are usually not treated directly in popular and learned debates about free expression: evil, hell, suffering, offense, and death. They are, however, central to its moral and political meaning. They have a way of haunting debates and sooner or later always appear on the agenda. Since life is short, the now is insistent, and the stakes are great, liberals and civil libertarians cannot begrudge anyone who has no patience to wait and see whether ideas "fraught with death," as Holmes put it, will bear happy fruit. Liberals and civil libertarians rest their practice on the astonishing discovery that any act of speech, with enough interpretive work and the right framing, can yield some "socially redeeming value." They—quite wonderfully—insist on due process for debate and restraint of the urge to punish ideas deemed dangerous. But they also sponsor a moral inversion in which the cutting open of bodies or the exploration of incest or genocide can become one's daily bread. Paul rejoiced in the suspension of the law, but the place beyond good and evil can be desolate. Defenders of absolute openness might ponder the price we pay for the scope of our minds. How hard must our hearts become? Liberals have no time for tenderness, no regard for faith or folly. If life and death are at stake, who can blame people firm enough to close their eyes? Sometimes simple outrage is a more humane response than rational consideration. The condescending term fundamentalist does not do justice to the impulse to say no to the madness of the world. Must we watch the video of Daniel Pearl being beheaded? Is *Hustler* publisher Larry Flynt a great hero, as Milos Forman's film suggests? Please.

Stoicism usefully teaches an attitude of courage and self-transcendence, but it can be so abstract that crude common sense, the gut-level feeling of solidarity with one's fellows, vanishes. In my view we cannot take our Stoicism straight. A hospitable public philosophy might take tragedy from the Greeks, prophetic social criticism from the Jews, *caritas* from the Christians, cheekiness from the Cynics, cosmopolitanism from the Stoics, imagination from the Scots, and transcendence from the Romantics. Adam Smith's call to sympathize with others, especially to have sympathy with their lack of sympathy for us, is an excellent recipe for public decorum. He blended the chief ethical maxims from Stoicism (treat the self as an other) and Christianity (treat the other as a self). Stoicism can only be voluntary; the true stoic is invisible to others (unless his leg gets blown off and he vents not a moan). As soon as it is preached to others, Stoicism is oppression. It is a philosophy for emperors and generals. "We know that even the Stoics do not really despise pleasure; they only decry it in public in the hope of having it all the more to themselves."[15] I would defend sentimentality against machismo, cynicism against perfection, and stoicism against therapeutic ideas about the self. We need self-mastery in reason, savviness in culture, and mercy for the beliefs of other people. Friends and family deserve the benefit of our sentimental sympathy. Our institutions deserve the respect of our tough-minded cynicism. The pains arising from self and world call for stoicism from within—and within only. Cynicism in the life world is bad, but healthy in the realm of system; sentimentality about the system is bad, but healthy in the life world. But there is a danger in any too-clean contrast between the ethical and the political. We can be cynical about our own best intentions and tender-minded about beliefs that other people passionately hold. The formula might be: stoicism for the self, cynicism for institutions, and sentimentality for others.

Again we meet the triumvirate of reason, cultural pluralism, and moral certainty. One of the world-historical tasks of the twenty-first century is to forge some sort of reconciliation between critical liberty and orthodox faith under postmodern conditions. The issue is not simply something like "the west vs. Islam" or "rationality vs. fundamentalism." Communities of faith have diverse impulses, and liberals can be orthodox; the sacred and openness are destined to remain—blessedly, miserably—at odds. Such reconciliation requires widened and deepened social justice sooner than an intellectual synthesis. But as an intellectual resource for this task, there is nothing better than the prophetic tradition represented by figures such as Paul and Milton, Thoreau and King, Arendt and Havel, a tradition this book has attempted to reconstruct. Such figures are sometimes mistaken as conservatives by those who note their deep moral and spiritual feeling and their call to turn back to core values; they are sometimes mistaken as liberals because of their passion for freedom. They belong instead to the radical center. Radical centrists defend liberty and fear for evil. Unlike liberals, they see the constant temptation to corruption in liberty, and unlike conservatives, they see the immense wickedness done in the name of fighting evil. They call for

---

15. Erasmus, *The Praise of Folly* (New York: Limited Editions Club, 1943), 18.

both impersonality and love. They are centrists because they favor funda-
mentals and distrust the self-certain zealotry of the Left and the Right; they
are radicals because of their cheerful readiness to disobey the law and put
anything existing in peril. They are serious in their playfulness and light-
hearted in their duties. "The great," wrote Emerson," will not condescend to
take anything seriously."[16] The radical center provides a spot in which we
can oppose both moral nihilism and capitalist abuse, shudder at both the
pornography industry and the censorship of state or church, and fight
against global military-industrial empires for reasons both material and
spiritual. The middle path is the way of enlightenment. Paul, Milton,
Thoreau, King, Arendt, and Havel found ways to act as if sin, kings, boredom, racism, mass society, and totalitarianism did not exist, and to act as if
salvation, liberty, wonder, justice, democracy, and truth did. They played
with things that are and were responsible to things that are not. There are
few better formulas for coping with the world in its glory and madness.

16. Ralph Waldo Emerson, "Heroism," in *Selected Writings of Emerson*, ed. Donald McQuade
(New York: Modern Library, 1981), 240

The United States presidential election of 2004 left onlookers with the spectacle of the world's most powerful country seemingly split between the religious Right and the secular Left. Much of the world looks on the United States with the same puzzlement with which the United States looks on radical Islamists and other anti-American groups: how can people believe and do such things? The election and its worldwide resonance showcase the intractable face-off of perspectives with which this book begins (though postmodernist relativists are getting squeezed out). Liberal arrogance and Gestalt-like differences of understanding have both been in full flower. *The Daily Mirror*, a British tabloid, put prevailing anti-Bush opinion well in a headline on 4 November 2004: "How can 59,054,087 people be so DUMB?" One vicious satire circulating widely on the internet addresses Bush voters thus: "I'm talking to you, you ignorant, slack-jawed yokels, you bible-thumping, inbred drones, you redneck, racist, chest-thumping, perennially duped grade-school grads." People say all kinds of silly things online and elsewhere, but insulting 51 percent of a nation's voters does too much damage to the commitment to democracy and claims a monopoly of intelligence for one side only. The more interesting puzzle is how so many reasonable people of character and intelligence could have voted for Bush; my personal list of such people, which I am compiling as a kind of duty and penance, keeps growing and growing.

Somehow the Right captured the moral imagination. Regular church attendance and concern for the moral direction of society were supposedly key predictors of a vote for Bush. How a swaggering former governor of a state with the highest execution rate of prisoners in American history came to represent moral values is a mystery for others to solve. But the Right paints with the brush of the sublime. It conjures apocalyptic battles between liberty and terror, between the family and its enemies. It is not beyond good and evil but smack dab in the middle of them. It has a compellingly chiaroscuro account of modern life and of its abundant failings and tackles unsolved troubles of sex—no stupid thing in itself. The Left, and even center, has good stories too, but they have largely grown stale, as this book shows. Instead of evil and its redemption, the Left offers pale toleration, strenuous self-sacrifice, hope in progress, or flirtatious pugilistics with noxious doctrine. John Kerry's candidacy rebuilt a hard-hearted liberalism, with him serving as a stoic soldier personally eager to "kill" America's enemies, but he never managed to sing the poetry of democracy in a compelling way. The bloom is off the Left's courtship of the abyss.

Yet the liberal tradition, if we include Paul of Tarsus and John Milton, did not always flee from the abyss; it sought its redemption. The tradition has equally robust stories to tell. For Paul and Milton the free and open encounter of good and evil not only provides human beings with a field of moral choice; it is also, somehow, the privileged way divine love chooses to show itself. Martin Luther King Jr., a latter-day heir to Paul and Milton, gave a deep grounding for the open debate of good and evil: "Here is the true meaning and value of compassion and nonviolence when it helps us to see the enemy's point of view, to hear his questions, to know his assessment of ourselves" ("Beyond Vietnam: A Time to Break Silence," 4 April 1967). King hit on the deepest reason for granting noxious doctrines their time in the sun: the injunction to love your enemy. Evil is best handled in his view not by pulling the trigger but by countering it with good. The prophetic tradition sees the battle of good and evil as a call to ethical action (or passivity), not an excuse for killing (or incarceration).

This book attempts to move democracy beyond the impasse of a religious but parochial Right and a secular but arrogant Left. (The Right is best when secular, the Left best when religious.) The founding thinkers of liberty such as Paul and Milton were both religiously devout and deep critics, in different ways, of their social orders. It's a good time to reclaim their noble heritage if we want to get out of the mess of red and blue states in the United States and the mess of reason and progress "versus" religion and faith everywhere. This should be the starting point for rebuilding democracy.

ACKNOWLEDGMENTS

I thank the Leverhulme Trust, which supported an eight-month stay at the Department of Media and Communications at Goldsmiths College, University of London, as well as the University of Iowa Department of Communication Studies, College of Liberal Arts, and the Obermann Center for Advanced Studies for support. A short-term fellowship from the Swedish Institute also helped, as did a grant from the Fulbright Foundation.

I am grateful to people who commented on drafts of chapters, including Menahem Blondheim, Kevin DeLuca, Clark Farmer, Cătălin Mamali, Samuel McCormick, James McDaniel, Kembrew McLeod, Claudia Moscovici, Christopher Mount, Louis Schwartz, Peter Simonson, Michael Slater, and Alvin Snider. Conversations with Kenneth Cmiel, James Curran, Per-Anders Forstorp, Carolyn Marvin, and Paddy Scannell crucially helped. People who generously shared their work include Misook Baek, Eliot Blake, Lilie Chouliaraki, Tracy Thorpe, and Robin Wagner-Pacifici. A group of ingenious and tireless research assistants have contributed much: Hugo Burgos, Young-Cheon Cho, Jung-Bong Choi, Hee-Eun Lee, Hun Yul Lee, Yong Li, Tracy Routsong, and Minkyu Sung. Many graduate students in my classes have also contributed. Audiences at Brigham Young University–Hawaii, Middle Tennessee State University (in several visits over the years), New School University, and New York University helped me to refine drafts. Doug Mitchell, editor and correspondent extraordinaire, and his team at the University of Chicago Press, were a pleasure to work with. Freelance editor Barbara Mnookin pruned many infelicities. Three readers went beyond the call of duty and enabled a radical rethinking of the book: David Depew, Dilip Parameshwar Gaonkar, and Michael Schudson.

Every work of art, said Theodor Adorno, is an uncommitted crime. This particular work is an uncleaned basement. For patience, love, and bemused tolerance, I thank Marsha Paulsen Peters and Daniel Peters.

I have ransacked bits of previously published pieces, creating a paradox in which the parts are more complete than the whole: "Witnessing," *Media, Culture and Society* 23.6 (2001): 707–24 (chap. 7); "'The Only Proper Scale of Representation': The Politics of Stories and Statistics," *Political Communication* 18 (2001): 433–49 (chap. 5); "Publicity and Pain: Self-Abstraction in Adam Smith's *Theory of Moral Sentiments*," *Public Culture* 7 (1995): 657–75 (chap. 3); and "Rhetoric's Revival, Positivism's Persistence: Social Science, Clear Communication, and the Public Space," *Sociological Theory* 8.2 (1990): 224–31 (chap. 5).

INDEX

pain, 124, 284; pain as proof, 249–59; and testicles, 106, 255

women, 202; excluded from public sphere, 24n40, 107–8, 189, 251; and free speech, 176–77; Mill on, 125; objectification of, 261–64; Paul and, 50–54; and sentiment, 117–18, 206. *See also* feminism; gender; masculinity

Wortman, Tunis, 16–17

Wright, N. T., 35n16

Yeats, William Butler, 100–101

Zelizer, Barbie, 160n47, 221n13, 287n8

Zevi, Shabbetai, 153, 161

Žižek, Slavoj, 30, 103